AQUINAS'S THEORY OF
NATURAL LAW

Aquinas's Theory of Natural Law

An Analytic Reconstruction

ANTHONY J. LISSKA

To: Ron
With deep appreciation
for our friendship and
our philosophical dialogue
over the years. Your philosophical
support for my work in Thomas Aquinas
has certainly helped my analysis
of some of the important issues in
western philosophy.

With all best wishes to you
and to Margo.

Tony
9/16/96

CLARENDON PRESS · OXFORD

1996

Oxford University Press, Walton Street, Oxford OX2 6DP
Oxford   New York
Athens   Auckland   Bangkok   Bombay
Calcutta   Cape Town   Dar es Salaam   Delhi
Florence   Hong Kong   Istanbul   Karachi
Kuala Lumpur   Madras   Madrid   Melbourne
Mexico City   Nairobi   Paris   Singapore
Taipei   Tokyo   Toronto
and associated companies in
Berlin   Ibadan

Oxford is a trade mark of Oxford University Press

Published in the United States
by Oxford University Press Inc., New York

British Library Cataloguing in Publication Data
Data available

Library of Congress Cataloging in Publication Data
Aquinas's theory of natural law: an analytic
reconstruction/Anthony J. Lisska.
Includes bibliographical references and index.
1. Natural law.   2. Thomas, Aquinas, Saint, 1225?–1274.
I. Title.
K447.T452L57 1996   340'.112—dc20   95-37006
ISBN 0-19-826359-7

1   3   5   7   9   10   8   6   4   2

Typeset by Rowland Phototypesetting Ltd.
Printed in Great Britain on acid-free paper by
Biddles Ltd., Guildford and King's Lynn

PREFACE

This book, like so many studies undertaken by philosophy professors, has been a long time in the making. It began some ten years ago when my interests in medieval philosophy, especially in Thomas Aquinas, led to an attempt at rethinking Aquinas's moral theory. Having undertaken advanced philosophical work in both classical scholasticism and analytic philosophy and being a philosopher interested in the major issues of medieval philosophy, often I used the tools of analytic philosophy to help make sense of the arguments found in medieval philosophy texts. Major projects directed towards the texts of Aquinas dealing both with perception theory and with natural law moral theory were undertaken. Long convinced that there are important philosophical chestnuts in these texts of Aquinas, I have wrestled with them in order to provide clearly articulated conceptual analyses of Aquinas's work. The goal has been to render an account of Aquinas which is understandable to philosophers well versed in what is generally known as the analytic tradition in English language philosophy.

Another point must be noted. Prior to all of this cognitive effort blending analytic philosophy with classical scholasticism, however, was the experience of a young philosophy student who read for the first time Thomas Aquinas's *Commentary on the Nicomachean Ethics*. That reading had a profound existential influence on this student — who, of course, is the author of this book — in that for once in his life, a moral theory actually made philosophical sense. This initial reading came under the watchful eye of C. I. Litzinger, OP, in whose classes we used early drafts of the texts which eventually became his monumental translation and publication of Aquinas's *Commentary*. Later this student, reading analytic philosophy, ran into the pitfalls brought against natural law theory, especially by contemporary meta-ethical discussions so dependent upon G. E. Moore's naturalistic fallacy. The issues posed so stridently by the author of the *Principia Ethica* and by his philosophical ancestor, David Hume (did the naturalistic fallacy really refute Aristotle and Aquinas so easily?)

would not go away. This confrontation of analytic meta-ethics —
through its questioning of the foundations of ethical naturalism —
with Aquinas's insightful commentary on what counts for a morally
virtuous life, prompted a long set of worries about the philosophical cogency of Aristotelian and Aquinian ethics. How might
Aquinas's moral theory be reconstructed, if such a case were
possible, in order to surmount the dominant anti-naturalism of analytic meta-ethics? These problems with ethical naturalism so
common to analytic philosophy serve as the intellectual backdrop
for this book.

The first formal attempt to elucidate a reconstruction of Aquinas's
theory of natural law came in 1981 with an invitation to deliver the
annual Aquinas Lecture at the Josephinum School of Theology.
What remains of that initial attempt at a revised meta-ethical analysis
of natural law theory in Aquinas, long since expanded, modified, and
developed, comprises Chapter 4 of this book. The key concepts
found in this chapter served as the basis for a 1995 Smithsonian
Lecture in Washington, DC.

A wonderful sabbatical in 1984 provided the opportunity to read
and study philosophy at the University of Oxford during Hilary and
Trinity terms. There I attended the lectures of John Finnis, Ronald
Dworkin, John Ackrill, Michael Woods, Dorian Scaltis, Brian
Davies, and, in particular, Herbert McCabe, who delivered thoughtful Blackfriars' Lectures on Aquinas's moral theory. During this
time, Brian Davies, the book review editor for *New Blackfriars*, asked
that I review John Finnis's *Fundamentals of Ethics*. To be introduced
seriously to Finnis's revisionist treatment of Aquinas's theory of
natural law added an important dimension to my ongoing research
into Aquinas's moral theory. About this time, I also began to reread
carefully the work of Henry Veatch on Aristotle, Aquinas, and natural law. This project now had a new wrinkle, however, brought about
through the attempt to reconcile Finnis and Veatch on the nature
and structure of natural law theory in Aquinas. Several years'
research efforts have gone into the project of sorting out the conceptual similarities and differences between Finnis and Veatch. The
conceptual differences in interpretation and analysis of Aquinas on
natural law, which Finnis and Veatch offer, are referred to often
throughout this book.

An article, assorted book reviews, and several papers read at professional meetings evolved and developed from the discussions and

studies mentioned above. 'Finnis and Veatch on Natural Law in Aristotle and Aquinas' appeared in the *American Journal of Jurisprudence*. An earlier, shorter version was read at the Pacific Division Meetings of the American Philosophical Association. The role Finnis's analysis plays in classical realist interpretations of Aquinas was first presented at a regional meeting of the American Catholic Philosophical Association. Chapter 6 is heavily dependent on these earlier works. The worries about the role God plays in Aquinas's account of natural law were first formulated in a paper read at the Central Division Meetings of the American Philosophical Association. This philosophical analysis in an expanded form is now found in Chapter 5. The analysis of Henry Veatch's 'Ontological Foundationalism', which makes up Chapter 7, first took written form in a paper read at a regional meeting of the American Catholic Philosophical Association. Several issues discussed in parts of this book appeared in various book reviews on natural law, on rights theory, on Finnis, and on Veatch which were published in *New Blackfriars*, the *Heythrop Journal*, and *Teaching Philosophy*.

The National Endowment for the Humanities Summer Institute on 'The Moral Philosophy of Aquinas', held under the tutelage of Ralph McInerny at the University of Notre Dame, was particularly useful. Conversations that summer with Ralph McInerny and David Solomon of the Institute staff, and with Alasdair MacIntyre, Joseph Boyle, John Finnis, and Alan Donagan, assisted immensely as this project was beginning to take its present focus. The published work of Professor McInerny has helped me continually refine my thinking on the nature and structure of Aquinas's account of natural law.

As a young philosopher, my first fledgling efforts at reconstructing Aquinas's philosophy in order to provide *explicationes textus* consistent with the rigours of contemporary analytic philosophy began under the guidance of Professor Robert G. Turnbull. I have relied often on his always helpful counsel and thoughtful criticism of my work. More than anyone else, Professor Turnbull guided my early efforts to use analytic philosophy as a tool to make sense of the important philosophical issues in the texts of Aquinas. At this time I began reading the analytic commentaries by Anthony Kenny and learned very much from his penetrating insights. Of course, the writings of Peter Geach were always full of enlightening suggestions on reading Aquinas.

A huge debt of appreciation goes to Professor Henry B. Veatch. During the last decade, Professor Veatch has written very many penetrating comments and offered constructive suggestions on several drafts of papers in which too often I offered 'woolly' elucidations of Aquinas on natural law. In addition, he read thoughtfully and offered important and extended insights on two earlier drafts of this book. Professor Veatch never failed to provide sage advice as I continued this project which overlaps in many ways with his own important work in Aristotelian moral philosophy. It was Professor Veatch's marvellous analysis of contemporary meta-ethics, *For an Ontology of Morals*, which first stimulated my own rethinking of Aquinas on natural law and suggested creative ways to reconsider Aquinas's meta-ethics. Ed and Abby Holtz (Ed, a good friend and Trustee-Emeritus of Denison University) kindly introduced me to Henry and Janie Veatch, friends of theirs, when both lived in Georgetown during the time Professor Veatch served as Chair of the Philosophy Department at Georgetown University.

I am extremely grateful for all the help and assistance Brian Davies, former Regent of Studies for the English Province of the Dominicans and Regent of Blackfriars at the University of Oxford, now of Fordham University, offered so graciously and so continuously during the final stages of this project. He not only read a large part of an early draft of this manuscript, but also gave his advice and encouragement which assisted immensely in the final efforts of publication.

Over the past few years, Robert McKim, David Solomon, Joseph Boyle, Ruth Caspar, Bernard Gendreau, and John Finnis have offered suggestions on various parts of my research efforts into Aquinas's natural law theory. Alasdair MacIntyre has continued to give warm encouragement for the timely completion of this study. The philosophy students in my Denison University classes and seminars on natural law theory and on jurisprudence have continually offered creative responses helpful to refine many of the arguments in this book.

Marianne Lisska deserves a special word of thanks and appreciation. A writer for a major international corporation, Marianne must have thought she was constantly on the proverbial 'busman's holiday'. None the less, with devotion and aplomb beyond any ordinary spousal responsibility, over the last five years she has carefully and thoughtfully read many drafts of this manuscript. Her valuable and always cogent suggestions have greatly improved the clarity and directness of the text. Megan and Elin Lisska both wished their father well often during the many stages of this book's completion. Cookie Shields kindly undertook the tedious task of rendering the final drafts of the manuscript into the proper computer format suitable for the publisher. My Denison colleagues, Michael Gordon, Garrett Jacobsen, and Keith Boone, graciously read the author's translation of the texts of Aquinas on natural law.

Throughout the different stages of development of this book, the staff of Oxford University Press have been very generous, most patient, and extraordinarily helpful. Hilary O'Shea, editor for classics and theology, first expressed interest in this manuscript and then directed her attention to guiding the text through the various stages necessary for acceptance. Liz Alsop, desk-editor, kindly watched over the final stages of manuscript preparation, and Sylvia Jaffrey, copy-editor, assisted immensely in rendering the text more readable and more clearly elucidated. My appreciation and gratitude is given to the Oxford University Press staff with whom I have worked for their generous assistance through the steps required for the publication of this book.

Support for the research and travel undertaken in order to write this book generously came from various sources: The Denison University Research Foundation, The Robert C. Good Faculty Fellowship Program, The Denison University Faculty Summer Development Program, and the National Endowment for the Humanities Summer Institute Program. I acknowledge my indebtedness and express my grateful appreciation to all the above funding organizations.

My thanks also go to the *American Journal of Jurisprudence* for kindly permitting me to quote from my article 'Finnis and Veatch on Natural Law in Aristotle and Aquinas', published in 1991.

This book owes so much to all the people mentioned above — and to my Denison University colleagues in philosophy, Ron Santoni, David Goldblatt, Steve Vogel, and Phil Glotzbach, each of whom spent time with a now not so young philosopher as he tried valiantly to unpack conceptually the natural law themes in the philosophy of Thomas Aquinas. Of course, none of the many philosophers who read and discussed these matters will agree with every point asserted perhaps too confidently in this book. However, the creative suggestions always assisted the ongoing development of this journey into Aquinas's natural law theory as seen through the lenses of twentieth-century analytic philosophy. My warmest wishes and sincere thanks to each and every one of you who helped so much in bringing this project to completion!

                                                        A.J.L.

Granville, Ohio
15 May 1995

CONTENTS

1

The Renewed Interest in Natural Law Theory

THIS introductory chapter serves as a narrative indicating the intellectual background necessary to understand more clearly both the renewed interest in natural law theory in general and the natural law canon proposed by Thomas Aquinas in *Summa Theologiae* in particular. This chapter also discusses the nature and scope of the present inquiry and indicates how the following chapters relate to the purpose of the book.

ELIZABETH ANSCOMBE
MODERN MORAL PHILOSOPHY

In 1958, Elizabeth Anscombe published a provocative article entitled 'Modern Moral Philosophy'[1] asking, first of all, if contemporary moral philosophy had not forgotten a principal concept, namely the development of an adequate philosophical psychology. Secondly, Anscombe suggested that the concepts of 'moral obligation' and 'moral duty', so central to meta-ethical discussions in analytic philosophy, needed rethinking. Thirdly, she argued that the differences found in English moral theory since the time of Sidgwick 'are of little importance'. Anscombe's point was that moral philosophers in mid-twentieth-century philosophy had forgotten — or neglected — the concepts of moral theory central to the Aristotelian tradition. These concepts — virtue, practical reason, acquired dispositions, etc. — so forcefully articulated in the Aristotelian tradition were, so

---

[1] G. E. M. Anscombe, 'Modern Moral Philosophy', *Philosophy*, 33/124 (Jan. 1958), 1–19.

Anscombe suggested, largely forgotten in the ethical treatises written by analytic philosophers in the English-speaking world.

In a structural sense, Anscombe's article was a harbinger of things to come regarding the development of analytic meta-ethical theory. At the time of its publication, this provocative analysis of ethical theory prominent in English-speaking countries largely went unnoticed. None the less, many of the issues Anscombe raised and discussed have determined the renewed interest in ethical theory as argued by Aristotle and Thomas Aquinas. Much recent work in ethical naturalism and 'virtue ethics' has significant conceptual similarities with Anscombe's suggestions criticizing analytic ethical theory in contemporary philosophy.

ALASDAIR MACINTYRE
THE FLIGHT FROM THE ENLIGHTENMENT

Twenty-three years after the appearance of Anscombe's article, Alasdair MacIntyre published a book destined to change the direction of ethical discussions in English-speaking philosophical circles. *After Virtue* contained a trenchant critique of the structure and development of post-Enlightenment ethical theories. All of these theories MacIntyre judged deficient. He called for a rediscovery of the 'way of Aristotle', which he suggested would breathe new life into the manner in which twentieth-century philosophers, especially those in the analytic tradition, discussed ethical issues.

Beyond calling attention to the fact that philosophers in the mid-twentieth century had neglected to write about practical reason, virtue, and dispositions, Anscombe's article and MacIntyre's book had the effect of reintroducing Aristotle into mainstream ethical discussions. In particular, an account of practical reason and the role of virtue became important topics for analysis and discussion. This brought about a general reconsideration of post-Enlightenment ethical theory, which certainly was the paradigm of moral discourse during much of the twentieth century.

While Hume and Kant, among others in the history of Western philosophy, certainly had written about practical reason in various ways, none the less it is Aristotle's *Nicomachean Ethics* where one finds probably the most articulate account of practical reason. Aristotle's analysis of practical reason proposes that this use of reason is more than merely a use of theoretical reasoning in a moral situation.

Aristotle goes to great lengths to argue that practical reason is an activity structurally different from speculative or theoretical reason. Each avenue of reason – the speculative and the practical – has its own set of first principles and its own set of objects. Always looking towards an 'end' or goal as a principle of explanation – that Aristotle's use of *telos* is fundamental to his system is not to be denied – Aristotle posits 'truth' as the end of speculative reason and 'good' as the end of practical reason. Moreover, Aristotle developed different modes of argument for speculative and practical reason – conveniently calling the process of the former the 'speculative syllogism' and the latter the 'practical syllogism'. At the level of both principles and modes of arguing, Aristotle distinguishes speculative reason from practical reason.

In the Middle Ages, Thomas Aquinas followed the insights on practical reason put forward by Aristotle in his discussions of ethical naturalism. In his commentary on the *De Trinitate* by Boethius, Aquinas writes about speculative and practical reason in the following way:

A theoretical or speculative inquiry is distinguished from a practical inquiry in that the former is directed towards discovering truth claims considered in themselves. The latter, to the contrary, is directed towards the doing of something. Thus, the purpose of speculative inquiry is truth, while the purpose of practical inquiry is action, in the area of actions in our capacity to undertake. The goal of a speculative inquiry is not about determining means to ends – i.e., actions to be undertaken.

(*Opuscula*. XVI, *De Trinitate*, 5. 1.)

Aquinas reiterates this point in the *Summa Theologiae* when he writes that 'as the speculative reason discusses the theory of things, so the practical reason debates the problems of actions' (*Summa Theologiae*, I q. 79 a 12). What is important here is that Aquinas – following Aristotle – accepts a paradigm of speculative and practical reason. Practical reason is not just speculative reason working in practical matters. The structure of the intentional activity is categorically different in speculative and practical reasoning. Speculative reason 'is aware of' or 'knows', whereas practical reason 'undertakes' or 'carries forward' what is to be done. The conclusion of the speculative syllogism is a 'piece of knowing', while the conclusion of the practical syllogism is a 'piece of doing'. This is an important point largely lost in discussions of practical reason since the time of Hume.

A more detailed account of speculative and practical reason will be discussed in Chapter 8.

One effect of Anscombe's article and MacIntyre's book was to force contemporary philosophers to face these differences between moral discourse and argument since the Enlightenment and the concepts and arguments central to Aristotelian ethics. The difference in the concept of reason as elucidated in Aristotelian ethics is a radical departure from discussions about reason since the time of Descartes. Of course, the general influence of the philosophy of the later Wittgenstein helped bring about a serious reconsideration of Cartesian epistemology. In opposition to Cartesian philosophy of mind, the Aristotelian account did not consider reason as a unified process working at one time in a cognitive way and at another time in a prescriptive way. The cognitive and the prescriptive modes, so Aristotle argued, were different functions of reason altogether. Theoretical and practical reason each had its own structure, its first principle, and its unique kind of syllogism. MacIntyre suggests that one serious problem with contemporary ethical theory is that the concept of moral agency so central to Aristotelian ethics did not survive through the development of Enlightenment philosophy. The concepts of virtue and moral agency became incompatible structurally with Enlightenment ethics.

MacIntyre, furthermore, argues that once the medieval synthesis disintegrated, the Aristotelian analysis of virtue disappeared conceptually and structurally from Western philosophy. He explicitly states that what he calls 'the failure of the enlightenment project' in moral theory is directly related to the massive rejection of what he refers to as 'the tradition of virtue'. What evolved eventually was the rule theories of normative ethics common to philosophy since the time of Kant. The focus of moral theory centred on the rules to be followed rather than the virtues to be acquired. The Aristotelian tradition in ethics became moribund and largely neglected.

The use of practical reason, the concept of virtue, and the structure of moral agency central to the Aristotelian tradition disappeared in philosophical discourse. The rediscovery of Aristotle forces the philosopher to consider these issues once again. Furthermore, philosophers must grapple with the ontological underpinnings needed to make sense of Aristotelian method in ethics. This search for a metaphysical justification in terms of finding a coherent account of human nature helped bring about the return of the 'philosophical psychology' whose absence Anscombe decried.

In addition to considering practical reason, virtue, and agency afresh, in reading the Aristotelian texts contemporary philosophers had to come to terms with a robust form of ethical naturalism. While similar to some late nineteenth- and early twentieth-century naturalistic accounts, none the less Aristotelian naturalism was far removed theoretically from the classical naturalism common to Bentham and Mill's utilitarianism. Aristotle's naturalism, as interpreted by many philosophers, was based upon a metaphysical theory of essence radically different from the empiricism latent in English utilitarianism. Aristotle and Aquinas's ethical theory is an inquiry based upon their metaphysical theory of the human person. This is expressed in Aristotelian metaphysics as a theory of natural kinds. The common objections to naturalism, expressed by Hume and Kant and later articulated by Moore in his 'naturalistic fallacy' argument, did not apply directly, it was argued, to Aristotelian/Aquinian moral theory. MacIntyre, in particular, goes to great lengths arguing that the factual basis necessary for an Aristotelian account of virtue eliminates the problem of the fact/value dichotomy.

This revival of Aristotelian ethical theory, with its dependence on the concepts of practical reason, moral agency, and virtue — all grounded in ethical naturalism — has influenced moral philosophy to go beyond the limits of rule-laden theories so characteristic of Kantian and utilitarian discussions in contemporary philosophy. What Anscombe proposed, MacIntyre carried out with his analysis of the pitfalls in modern moral theory. This led to what one contemporary philosopher refers to as 'the recovery of Aristotle'.

REVISITING AQUINAS ON NATURAL LAW
THE *TELOS* OF THIS BOOK

The scope, purpose, and design of this book is to lay bare the metaphilosophy and the metaphysics needed to make sense of Aristotelian meta-ethics as seen through the eyes of his most famous medieval commentator, Thomas Aquinas. It is important to be clear from the beginning how these concepts are used in this analysis. Metaphilosophy is a discussion of the activity of philosophy itself. The way Aristotle approached fundamental philosophical problems is different from Cartesian or Kantian approaches. Often the conclusions offered in a philosophical argument are directly connected with the metaphilosophical principles followed. Metaphysics is an inquiry into the nature and structure of the fundamental principles concerning the nature of reality. Metaphysics attempts to articulate the basic categories of reality. Meta-ethics is an inquiry into the nature of moral language, moral argument, and the foundational issues (or lack thereof) determining claims of value. Meta-ethics differs from normative ethics, which is a set of prescriptive norms to be followed and recommendations for virtues to be acquired. These three philosophical concepts will be used frequently in the analysis of Aquinas which follows.

The direction of the philosophical analysis undertaken in this book is in general agreement with Christopher Martin's argument concerning Aquinas's appropriation of the important categories and concepts from the philosophy system of Aristotle. One assumption of this book is that in much of his moral theory, Aquinas is a careful Aristotelian. In his recently published *The Philosophy of Thomas Aquinas*, Martin writes: 'In the first place, St. Thomas is an Aristotelian. His basic concepts and categories are those of Aristotle, and when they are developed beyond the point at which Aristotle left them, they are developed in an Aristotelian manner.'[2]

The central argument in this book offers a close analysis of Aquinas's moral theory as elucidated in his *Commentary on the Nicomachean Ethics* and the *Summa Theologiae*, I-II qq. 90–7. This latter set of texts is often regarded as the classic canon for natural law in Western philosophy. These two works will serve as the textual basis for much of the conceptual analysis undertaken throughout this book. In this section of the *Summa Theologiae* and the relevant passages from the Aristotelian *Commentary*, Thomas Aquinas offers his best analysis of natural law, both for a meta-ethical theory of naturalism and as a foundation for the philosophy of law. Ralph McInerny, in his *Aquinas on Human Action*, suggests much the same position. He writes:

My own view is that which we find expressed if not embraced by Pico della Mirandola: *sine Thoma Aristoteles mutus esset*. I hold that Thomas's commentaries on Aristotle are precious aids for understanding the text of Aristotle ... The Aristotle subsumed within the commodious synthesis of

---

[2] Christopher Martin, *The Philosophy of Thomas Aquinas* (London: Routledge, 1988), 4.

Thomas is the historical Aristotle ... The real test of the relation between Thomas and Aristotle in moral matters is the commentary on the *Nicomachean Ethics*.[3]

That this is a controversial debate in contemporary Aquinian studies is not to be denied. None the less, for our purposes, the moral argument articulated by Aristotle in what has become known as 'virtue ethics' will be used as at least analogously related to what Aquinas argues in his *Summa Theologiae* and in his *Commentary on the Nicomachean Ethics*. Our argument is structural, not textual. None the less, Simon Tugwell writes that 'the commentary on Aristotle's *Ethics*, at least in its final form, seems to be related to the composition of the second part of the *Summa*'.[4] Tugwell refers to the textual analysis on dating the writings of Aquinas undertaken by the Leonine Commission, especially the work of R. A. Gauthier. The second part of the *Summa Theologiae*, where Aquinas's treatise on law is found, appears to have been written and completed by the end of 1270. Tugwell suggests that quite probably Aquinas wrote the Aristotelian commentary while he was at work on the *Summa Theologiae*, I-II. Hence, both major works on his moral theory based on Aristotle's *Nicomachean Ethics* appear to have been written close together during Aquinas's second stay at the University of Paris.

In his 'The *Nicomachean Ethics* and Thomas Aquinas', Vernon Bourke disputes the 1270 dating of Aquinas's commentary.[5] Of course, the matter of the dating of texts is beyond the limits of this inquiry. None the less, recent scholarship suggests that the text of the *Nicomachean Ethics* which Aquinas probably had available for his commentary was a much used but uncritical translation by Robert Grosseteste.[6] Yet there is evidence that Aquinas first began thinking about Aristotle's moral theory from his Cologne days attending the lectures of Albert the Great. The emphasis in this study is on the structural account of a moral theory of Aristotle and of Aquinas

---

[3] Ralph McInerny, *Aquinas on Human Action* (Washington, DC: Catholic University of America Press, 1992), 163–177.

[4] Simon Tugwell, 'The Life and Works of Thomas Aquinas', in *Albert and Thomas* (New York: Paulist Press, 1988), 256.

[5] Vernon J. Bourke, 'The *Nicomachean Ethics* and Thomas Aquinas', in *St. Thomas Aquinas — 1274–1974: Commemorative Studies* (Toronto: Pontifical Institute of Mediaeval Studies, 1974), 239–59.

[6] James A. Weisheipl, OP, *Friar Thomas D'Aquino* (Garden City, NY: Doubleday & Co. 1974), 380.

which does justice to the texts but which is consistent and coherent in itself. To repeat, the argument is structural, not textual.

RENEWED INTEREST IN NATURAL LAW
JURISPRUDENCE SETTING THE STAGE

Twenty years ago, Martin Golding remarked that 'The revival of natural-law doctrines is one of the most interesting features of current legal thought. Recent contributions and criticisms may be found in the journal *The Natural Law Forum*.'[7] While the *Natural Law Forum* has since changed its name to the *American Journal of Jurisprudence*, none the less it has remained one of the principal journals concentrating on natural law jurisprudence. Golding's point is an important one — natural law thinking has witnessed a resurgence of interest both in meta-ethics and in jurisprudence. In their *The Philosophy of Law*, Jeffrie Murphy and Jules Coleman have entitled a major section of their text, 'The Reemergence of Natural Law'. Chapter 2 will provide a sketch of twentieth-century work in natural law in both of these areas, law and ethics. It is important to emphasize, however, that natural law is no longer considered a metaphysical relic to be dusted off only in history of ethics courses or historical overviews of the philosophy of law. In his anthology, *Natural Law Theory: Contemporary Essays*, Robert George writes that 'one finds a remarkable assortment of natural law theories on offer in today's market-place of ideas'.[8]

What accounts for this renewed emphasis in natural law jurisprudence? Following the Second World War, jurisprudential thinking generally moved towards a theoretical interest in natural law justifications. If the Nuremberg trials with their accompanying charges of 'Crimes against Humanity' were to have a theoretical foundation, then one needed a radically different account of the nature of law from that proposed by the then reigning theory, legal positivism. Legal positivism, in many ways, had not advanced beyond the catchy phrase of Justinian's code — 'What pleases the prince has the force of law!' Legal positivism did not offer theoretical grounds to warrant

---

[7] Martin Golding, 'Philosophy of Law, History of', in *Encyclopedia of Philosophy* (New York: Free Press, 1967), 254–64.

[8] Robert P. George, *Natural Law Theory: Contemporary Essays* (Oxford: Oxford University Press, 1992), v.

claims like 'Crimes against Humanity' which were needed to provide justification for the war crimes trials.

Put differently, the positivist view of law steeped in the voluntarist tradition could not make the theoretical case for 'Crimes against Humanity' so central to the war crimes trials. Legal scholars, as a consequence, began searching for rational justifications of law beyond the theoretical accounts common to legal positivism. Often positivist justifications especially as developed in the writings of John Austin, seemed reducible to nothing more than Teddy Roosevelt's 'Carry a big stick' policy. Of course, this position could not distinguish theoretically one legal policy from another. The foundational thrust to legal scholarship caused by the attempt to justify the concept of 'Crimes against Humanity' brought natural law theory into the forefront of legal discussions about the nature of law. Riding the current of these foundational questions came a renewed interest in the texts of Thomas Aquinas, especially the *Summa Theologiae*, I-II qq. 90–7. These eight questions in Aquinas soon gained prominence as the principal canon for Western natural law jurisprudence.

From mid-century onwards, several philosophers of law from different philosophical perspectives produced monographs dealing with different aspects of natural law jurisprudence. While some were developed in more detail and general agreement with Aquinas than others, most referred to Aquinas's account of natural law as the classical foundation for such discussions in Western philosophy. At mid-century, A. P. d'Entréves wrote what became a rather famous account of legal foundationalism entitled *Natural Law* (1951). In this book, d'Entréves developed a thoughtful justification for natural law. Yet his natural law was not the natural law of Thomas Aquinas, although it is unclear if d'Entréves himself realized this difference. In his *Concept Of Law* (1961), H. L. A. Hart wrote about the 'core of good sense' in natural law and spent much time articulating a coherent position on 'natural necessities'. Lon Fuller, in his *The Morality Of Law* (1964), developed the concept of 'procedural natural law' which provided a rational criterion for legal activity. Fuller's emphasis on procedure introduced a theoretical retort to legal positivism. Fuller too considered Aquinas as the harbinger of natural law thinking in Western thought. In the school of philosophy known as classical Thomism, Jacques Maritain, Yves Simon, Thomas Davit, Heinrich Rommen, Thomas Gilby, and Vernon Bourke, among others, all wrote articles and books addressing natural law theory based upon the texts of Thomas Aquinas. Fuller once suggested a distinction 'between a natural law of substantive ends and a natural law concerned with procedures and institutions'. He articulated this distinction because, in his judgment, 'the term "natural law" has been so misused on all sides that it is difficult to recapture a dispassionate attitude toward it'.[9]

In a different context, three authors contributed to the revival of natural law jurisprudence. Leo Strauss asked his readers to rethink classical political writers in order to produce a coherent account of natural law. Strauss's *Natural Right and History* (1953) spells out afresh the demands of reason to acknowledge the natural ends common to human beings. Robert Hutchins and Mortimer Adler, working through the University of Chicago, the Great Books Foundation, and the Fund for the Republic, substantially assisted the renewed interest in natural law theory. The work of John Wild, considering anew Aristotelian realism, prompted serious discussions of Aristotelian philosophy in the mid-part of the twentieth century. Wild addressed natural law issues in his *Plato's Modern Enemies and the Theory of Natural Law*. (1953)

What is important about the above discussion is that it brings to the forefront the role the texts of Thomas Aquinas played, either latently or specifically, in much of the development of natural law jurisprudence in the twentieth century. In *Natural Law and Natural Rights* (1982), one of the most important and influential accounts of natural law jurisprudence, John Finnis notes that 'most people who study jurisprudence or political philosophy are invited at some stage to read Thomas Aquinas's Treatise on Law'.[10] Given this interest and emphasis, a necessary condition for continued fruitful discussion of these texts is a clearly articulated account of Aquinas's theory of natural law. Long ago, Aristotle noted that to become befuddled at the beginning of an inquiry often produces a much larger mistake later. Hence, if Aquinas's texts are to be used and referred to constantly in the development of both meta-ethical works and writings on jurisprudence, then one needs to be rather clear on what Aquinas's theory of natural law amounts to. The texts of Aquinas demand an explication consistent with the expectation of philos-

---

[9] Lon Fuller, *The Morality of Law* (New Haven, Conn.: Yale University Press, 1964), 102.

[10] John Finnis, *Natural Law and Natural Rights* (corr. ed.) (Oxford: Oxford University Press, 1982), 398.

ophers in the analytic tradition. The purpose and scope of this book is to undertake that project.

This is not to deny that work by analytic philosophers has been undertaken on the philosophy of Aquinas in the last thirty years. However, one does not find, in my judgement, the careful analytic treatments of Aquinas's moral theory which exist in other areas of Aquinas's work. Anthony Kenny, for instance, has written perceptively on Aquinas's philosophy of mind. Brian Davies's work on Aquinas's philosophy of religion uses the best analytic techniques in elucidating Aquinas's texts. One need but refer to the careful work of Peter Geach and Elizabeth Anscombe analysing the logical concepts serving as foundations in Aquinas's metaphysics. Christopher Martin's essays on Aquinas's metaphysics in his *The Philosophy of Thomas Aquinas* bring strong analytic insights to our understanding of Aquinas, especially in the light of contemporary metaphysical discussions. Herbert McCabe's discussions of Aquinas's philosophy have been helpful to readers coming untutored in the ways of medieval philosophy to Aquinas's philosophical texts.

Several collections of Aquinas's texts in moral and political philosophy have appeared recently. None the less, one does not find extended conceptual analysis for Aquinas's natural law theory considering both meta-ethics and jurisprudence at the same time. In the 1960s, Jacques Leclercq wrote in the *Natural Law Forum* that 'natural law has never been systematically studied'. Of course, several books have appeared since Leclercq's comment. John Finnis's *Natural Law and Natural Rights* offers a revisionist position of Aquinas's moral theory as related to jurisprudence. Henry Veatch in *Human Rights: Fact or Fancy?* and in several essays published in his *Swimming Against the Current in Contemporary Philosophy* comes closest to considering Aristotle and Aquinas's theory of natural law as related to both law and morality. Thirty years ago, Thomas Gilby published a monograph explicating Aquinas's political theory. Ralph McInerny has completed thoughtful analyses of Aquinas's normative and meta-ethical theories, the most recent being *Aquinas on Human Action*. Alasdair MacIntyre's *Three Rival Versions of Moral Enquiry* contains an interesting analysis of the normative ethics of Aquinas. Yet a detailed analysis of Aquinas's argument on natural law written from the perspective of analytic philosophy directed towards both ethics and jurisprudence has not been produced. The goal of the inquiry articulated herein is to address that need.

The thrust of this book is to provide the analysis necessary to understand Aquinas in the context of contemporary meta-ethics and jurisprudence. This analysis of Aquinas intends to fill the lacuna, at least partially, which Leclercq noted two decades ago. In this way, this study goes beyond but is dependent upon the careful and thoughtful work of Finnis, Veatch, MacIntyre, and McInerny on Aquinas. Without these philosophers and their sustained work on Aquinas's moral and legal theory, this book could not have been written.

This is not, however, a study in speculative or moral theology. Following the insights of Aquinas on doing philosophy, this analysis delves into metaphilosophical, meta-ethical, and metaphysical issues. It is a foundational analysis with arguments and commentary common to such studies written in contemporary analytic philosophy. This analysis and *explicatio textus* purports to be similar in method and scope to what Gustav Bergmann once called the 'structural history of philosophy'. Bergmann's concept of the structural history of philosophy will be explicated later in this book. Moreover, those disputes more common to scholastic philosophy and moral theology – e.g. proportionalism – are not central to this analysis. While attuned to the history and development of natural law theory, this study is not a mere historical account of ethical naturalism in Aristotle and Aquinas. It is a philosophical analysis and explication. This is central to Bergmann's notion of the structural history of philosophy.

OVERVIEW TOWARDS EXPLICATING AQUINAS

Given the expressed goal of providing herein an analytic treatment and *explicatio textus* of Aquinas's theory of natural law in terms of meta-ethics and jurisprudence, the following nine chapters consider at some length issues central to natural law theory in Aquinas. The scope of the book, in addition to providing a thorough analysis of Aquinas on natural law, provides a historical overview of the development of natural law theory in both contemporary jurisprudence and meta-ethical theory. The philosophical problems brought to ethical naturalism in the twentieth century are discussed. A serious objection to natural law theory in Aquinas suggesting its dependence on the existence of God is analysed. Two contemporary reconstructions of Aquinas – those articulated by John Finnis and Henry

Veatch — are considered in some detail. A brief schema suggesting how a theory of natural rights might be developed from this analysis of Aquinas is offered followed by a concluding set of claims suggesting pitfalls for the continued revision and recovery of Aristotelian and Aquinian moral theory.

To be more explicit concerning what follows, Chapter 2 offers a concise summary of the place natural law now occupies in contemporary jurisprudence and meta-ethics. In order to place this book in its proper context, this chapter provides a brief narrative of the major figures in the re-emergence of natural law thinking, especially in English-speaking countries.

Chapter 3 is an extended philosophical analysis in the structural history of philosophy proposing a way to understand Aristotelian naturalism as overcoming the naturalistic fallacy objection common to analytic philosophy in the first half of the twentieth century. The general background materials and content which determined early and mid-twentieth-century analytic meta-ethics, in particular, non-naturalism and non-cognitivism, are considered in some detail. The shadow of Cartesian metaphilosophy is discussed as it applies to contemporary meta-ethics and jurisprudence, especially in the 'good-reasons' philosophers. To help set the stage, the background of Enlightenment philosophy's rejection of Aristotelian naturalism is sketched. This chapter suggests how Aristotelian moral realism emerged as a response to major questions raised in twentieth-century analytic meta-ethics.

The fourth chapter in many ways serves as the core argument in this book. This chapter offers an analytic interpretation and reconstruction of Aquinas's theory of natural law. This is an extended *explicatio textus* of the classical canon for western natural law, Aquinas's *Summa Theologiae*, I-II qq. 90–7. A set of presuppositions that Aquinas needs to justify his natural law theory is developed in some detail. This account will serve as the basis for extending Aquinas's position on natural law into both contemporary meta-ethics and jurisprudence. The chapter discusses the four kinds of law articulated by Aquinas: Eternal Law, Natural Law, Positive or Human Law, and Divine Law.

Chapter 5 considers extensively a classical objection to Aquinas's theory of natural law. Expressed most succinctly in d'Entréves's *Natural Law*, this objection suggests that without a divine being, Aquinas's systematic treatment of natural law cannot be a consistent theoretical account of either meta-ethics or jurisprudence. An interpretation of Aquinas is offered indicating that the concept of essence as 'natural kind' is the central component of Aquinas's metaphysics necessary to natural law, not the existence of God.

Chapters 6 and 7 treat in some detail two contemporary interpretations of Aristotelian and Aquinian naturalism, the reconstructions of John Finnis and Henry Veatch. The discussion in Chapter 6 considers the argument Finnis advances in *Natural Law and Natural Rights* and *Fundamentals of Ethics*. This discussion poses some reservations about the Finnis account of natural law theory in Aquinas. One suggestion put forward is that Finnis, in effect, adopts a Cartesian or epistemological metaphilosophy in his analysis and is not radically different from his colleagues in contemporary jurisprudence and rights theory, such as Ronald Dworkin and John Rawls. Veatch, on the other hand, provides an informative metaphysical underpinning – which Chapter 7 refers to as 'ontological foundationalism' – for his Aristotelian theory of natural law and natural rights.

Chapter 8 offers a proposal for solving several problems common in analytic philosophy and directed against all forms of ethical naturalism, in particular, the naturalistic fallacy, the hypothetical/categorical imperative distinction, and the concept of essence in contemporary philosophy. The ninth chapter suggests a modest schema for deriving a theory of natural rights based on the metaethics of Aquinas as elucidated in Chapter 4. This includes some discussion of the conceptual differences between Aquinas's theory of rights and modern theory. Veatch's suggestion in *Human Rights: Fact or Fancy?* that only so-called 'negative rights' are derivable consistently in Aquinas is addressed.

The final chapter suggests where natural law meta-ethics and jurisprudence may be going in contemporary philosophy and political science. Both prospects and pitfalls are indicated. The chapter concludes with a brief overview of the present re-emergence of natural law theory.

Appendix I contains a freshly translated albeit abridged version of Aquinas's account of natural law from the *Summa Theologiae*, I-II, qq. 90-7. Appendix II discusses the place Aquinas holds in the overall development of legal philosophy. Appendix III is a schematic outline of Aquinas's account of law as developed in the *Summa Theologiae*. There is also a glossary at the end of the book of the technical philosophical terms used.

While at times the clear separation of jurisprudence from meta-ethics is blurred in this book — as often happens in contemporary discussions — none the less a conscious effort has been made to remain cognizant of the different questions asked of natural law in both areas of philosophy. In Aquinas's system, of course, there is no conceptual separation at the foundational level. The jurisprudence follows from the meta-ethics, which in turn is a second-order inquiry based upon his Aristotelian metaphysics of primary substances, which is grounded in a theory of essences of natural kinds. The metaphysical underpinnings of Aquinas's theory of natural law are never far removed from the discussion.

The reader will soon discover that both metaphysics and metaphilosophy are important avenues for understanding the meta-ethics of Thomas Aquinas's theory of natural law. Metaphilosophy, meta-ethics, and metaphysics all serve as important grist for this mill grinding out an analytic interpretation of this theory.

2

Natural Law and
Contemporary Philosophy

IN many areas of contemporary moral and political philosophy and in jurisprudence, natural law theory has sparked a rekindled interest in some ·traditional issues once thought moribund in English language philosophy. It is time now to delve more deeply into these theories of natural law in order to grasp better the scope and latitude of natural law considerations in the mid- and late twentieth century. The following narrative is not to be considered a definitive analysis of the philosophers and legal scholars under discussion. Rather it is an overview account of their respective positions, illustrating how Aquinas's theory of natural law fits into the general scheme of contemporary discussions of natural law theory. In addition, this descriptive analysis indicates the wide diversity of material placed under the umbrella of 'natural law' in present philosophical parlance. While neither definitive nor exhaustive, none the less it is useful to compile a collection of brief philosophical accounts of the many philosophers writing in natural law theory and Aristotelian moral theory. All of these philosophical and jurisprudence accounts have brought natural law discussions onto centre stage in contemporary philosophy and legal theory. In so far as these accounts have discussed natural law jurisprudence and Aristotelian moral theory, they have been generally instrumental in bringing back serious considerations of Aquinas's theory of natural law.

In a more specific sense, this chapter has a twofold goal: (1) a discussion of natural law jurisprudence; and (2) a consideration of natural law meta-ethics. While conceptual connections may overlap in jurisprudence and meta-ethics — and no doubt should — none the less in this chapter, as far as possible, the introductory background

discussions remain separate and distinct. Often, philosophical discussions in law and ethics regarding natural law have been distinct
inquiries. The narrative developed in this chapter abides by this
separation.

Despite the separate nature of legal and moral studies, however,
one general purpose of this book is to suggest the common dimen-
sions of the foundational inquiry in naturalism with special emphasis
on developing an analytic interpretation of Aquinas's theory of natural law. Aquinas's theoretical account of natural law will serve both
his moral theory and his theory of law. In fact, the theory of law is
derived from the moral theory. None the less, the basis for both
morality and law is an analysis of the human person, from which
the moral theory is developed. This moral theory, therefore, is called
a 'second order inquiry'. It is dependent upon the ontological analysis of the human person. Moral theory is thus dependent and not
autonomous.

The first part of this chapter is an extended sketch of twentieth-
century jurisprudence with special emphasis on those philosophers
of law who have suggested a role for moral theory as a necessary
condition for an adequate legal theory. The second major part of
the chapter provides a sketch of the recent work by analytic philosophers who have brought the moral accounts in Aristotle and
Aquinas to the forefront of ethical theory-making in the twentieth
century. Throughout this chapter, the emphasis is on painting a
broad brush-stroke, to help students of ethics and jurisprudence
understand how natural law theory, within the confines of analytic
philosophy, has been brought forward from its moribund stage
earlier in this century.

JURISPRUDENCE

This section of the chapter suggests several twentieth-century
accounts in jurisprudence which have prompted, either explicitly or
implicitly, a renewed consideration of natural law theory. In their
book on jurisprudence, Jeffrie Murphy and Jules Coleman have written that 'many contemporary writers are expressing sympathy for
certain views that are not too misleadingly called natural law in
character'.[1] They deal with several of the philosophers and legal

---

[1] Jeffrie Murphy and Jules Coleman, *Philosophy of Law*, rev. edn. (Boulder, Col.:
Westview Press, 1990), 37.

scholars discussed below, such as H. L. A. Hart, Lon Fuller, and Ronald Dworkin. It will become apparent soon, however, how broadly the rubric of natural law is used in recent jurisprudence. This section concludes with a summary account of what many philosophers of law take to be a set of necessary conditions for natural law jurisprudence. How this set of conditions relates to Aquinas's analysis of natural law jurisprudence is a question requiring a response. Chapter 4 begins that response.

H. L. A. Hart: Reintroducing Natural Necessities

One might plausibly propose that the principal avenue for reconsidering natural law theories in contemporary philosophy of law came via the pen of H. L. A. Hart. For many years, Hart was the Professor of Jurisprudence at Oxford. He published profusely on matters of jurisprudence. A student of ordinary language philosophy, Hart was attracted by the everydayness of much of John Austin's writings in jurisprudence. Bentham also served as the focal point of much of Hart's writings. It was through his *The Concept of Law*, however, that Hart became a household word in contemporary jurisprudence. Hart, in addition, knew philosophy and wrote as a philosopher. Martin Golding once remarked that in the United States, much writing in the philosophy of law is undertaken by law school professors rather than by professional philosophers. Although a member of the Faculty of Law at Oxford, none the less Hart knew his philosophy well. This background enabled him to articulate carefully and consistently the pressing concerns of legal issues to the larger philosophical community. One suspects that even the title of his now famous monograph takes its impetus from Gilbert Ryle's manifesto of ordinary language philosophy, *The Concept of Mind*.

In *The Concept of Law*, Hart ponders what he refers to as the 'core of good sense' in natural law thinking. This he spells out in terms of 'natural necessities', which he refers to as 'the minimum content of natural law'. Like Hobbes before him, Hart considers 'survival' to be the central linchpin in human existence and the 'necessity' which in principle cannot be overridden by the law. Hart attempts to identify certain salient facts about the human species — what existentialist philosophers might call the human condition — which make moral and legal systems understandable and necessary. In addition, Hart proposes that there is some connection, however loosely defined, between the content of some legal and moral rules and certain facts about human nature. Any suggestion of 'facts' about human nature brings to mind immediately both the natural law tradition in general and MacIntyre's discussion of the 'recovery' of the 'way of Aristotle' in particular. In his study of Hart's theory of law, Michael Martin suggests that 'although Hart is opposed to natural law theory in its traditional form, he proposes a theory that he believes rescues what is valuable in the traditional natural law theory'.[2]

In a schematic form, Hart argues for the following five natural necessities, which he claims are contingent facts about human beings as we find ourselves now in the human condition. Hart suggests that these 'simple truisms ... disclose the core of good sense in the doctrine of Natural Law':

1. *Human vulnerability*: humans are vulnerable and liable to various sorts of harm, including harm inflicted by other humans;
2. *Approximate equality*: humans are approximately equal in intellectual and physical abilities; hence, small groups should not dominate the rest;
3. *Limited altruism*: humans are not completely selfish and self-regarding, but take some interest in and concern for the good of their fellow human beings. None the less, humans are limited in their altruism and voluntary co-operation;
4. *Limited resources*: the material resources available to humans are limited and somewhat scarce; all humans need food, clothing, and shelter and have desires for other scarce commodities as well;
5. *Limited understanding and strength of will*: humans are limited in their powers of foresight and self-control; although they vary greatly among themselves in these respects, nonetheless human beings are limited in their self-control based on their knowledge alone.[3]

Given these facts — Hart's 'truisms' — about the human species, Hart suggests that it is necessary, if humans are to live together at all, that there be enacted some rules (laws) protecting their personal safety, property, and promise-keeping. In addition, the social nature

[2] Michael Martin, *The Legal Philosophy of H. L. A. Hart: A Critical Appraisal* (Philadelphia: Temple University Press, 1987), 177.
[3] H. L. A. Hart, *The Concept of Law* (Oxford: The Clarendon Press, 1961), 190–5, *passim*.

of human persons requires rules ensuring some degree of mutual forbearance and respect that will make social living tolerable. These facts about human nature provide the fundamental grounding for the rules of social morality necessary for enacting laws in a legal system. Hart suggests that there is more than a mere accidental connection of these facts of the human condition with our moral and legal language. Of course, the mere mention of 'facts about human nature' suggests some connection with natural law theory, no matter how minimal. The exact role the natural necessities play in Hart's system will decide if his theory is placed justifiably in the category of natural law jurisprudence.

Hart goes on to discuss the theoretical and practical importance of his account of natural necessities:

The simple truisms we have discussed not only disclose the core of good sense in the doctrine of Natural Law. They are of vital importance for the understanding of law and morals, and they explain why the definition of the basic forms of these in purely formal terms, without reference to any specific content of social needs, has proved so inadequate ... We can say, given the setting of natural facts and aims, which make sanctions both possible and necessary in a municipal system, that this is a natural necessity; and some such phrase is needed also to convey the status of the minimum forms of protection for persons, property, and promises which are similarly indispensable features of municipal law. It is in this form that we should reply to the positivist thesis that 'law may have any content'. For it is a truth of some importance that for the adequate description not only of law but of many other social institutions, a place must be reserved, besides definitions and ordinary statements of fact, for a third category of statements: those the truth of which is contingent on human beings and the world they live in retaining the salient characteristics which they have.[4]

Interestingly enough, Hart never argues that these 'natural necessities' are such that civil laws are derivable from them. In the development of his legal machinery, Hart is more of a legal positivist than a natural law philosopher. In *The Concept of Law*, Hart provided what has become an influential definition of law: Law is 'the union of primary and secondary rules'. Primary rules are the natural necessities, while the secondary rules are rules of procedure which are necessary conditions for any mature legal system. Without the secondary rules, there cannot be any legal system at all. Hence, the

---

[4] Harte, *The Concept of Law*, 194–5.

secondary rules determine the existence of civil laws. The secondary rules, according to Hart, are the 'Rule of Recognition', the 'Rules of Change', and the 'Rules of Adjudication'. These are, in effect, meta-rules organizing and ordering the ways a legal system functions. Without these secondary rules, a society lacks any semblance of law in a legal sense. Hence, Hart argues that a mature society only has a legal system when it has adopted the formalized 'meta-rules' which enable it to function with rules. The meta-rules determine the legal system, not the primary rules of behavior based upon the natural necessities.

Hart did not focus attention completely on natural law. In fact, often he argued for the separation of valid law from moral theory. None the less, Hart's insistence on taking seriously the questions of natural necessities and his claim about 'the core of good sense in the doctrine of natural law' prompted much discussion in the direction of natural law jurisprudence. Hart's work stimulated creative responses to his claims about and his interpretations of natural law, especially the 'natural necessities'. The most influential critic of Hart's analysis of natural necessities was Lon Fuller.

Lon Fuller: Procedural and Substantive Natural Law

Probably the principal exponent of natural law among legal scholars in the United States at mid-century was Lon Fuller. While much had been written about natural law in religious-oriented philosophical circles — especially by philosophers conversant with twentieth-century neo-scholasticism and classical Thomism — this body of work appears to have had little impact on the general tenor of secular legal scholarship. On the other hand, Fuller, a member of the Harvard Law School faculty, had a profound influence on the development of natural law thinking in American legal studies. In addition, his books often were read by academics beyond the law school circles. In his *The Morality of Law*, Fuller developed a coherent account of the rational basis for legal reasoning and the craft of lawmaking. Fuller explicitly referred to his theory as one of 'natural law'. Moreover, in 1958, the *Harvard Law Review*[5] published a long debate between Hart and Fuller on the general topic of 'Morality and the Law'. In this extended debate, Fuller again advocated a form of natural law thinking. At mid-century, Fuller's name became

[5] *Harvard Law Review*, 70 (1958), 639–72.

almost synonymous with natural law defence in American jurisprudence.

In *The Morality of Law*, Fuller argues that the making of law is
fundamentally a rational activity with a purpose. He argues that
lawmaking is a craft, and like any other craft, possesses its internal
rules of consistency and coherence. When this 'logic' fails, so too
does adequate lawmaking. If the internal rules are not followed, the
craft does not attain its proper end or goal. Fuller suggests that
his account provides an explication of 'the morality that makes law
possible'. Fuller articulates his rules for successful law making in a
contrasting fashion by showing the eight ways in which a law may
fail. When a law fails, it demonstrates that the craft of law-making
has not been properly pursued. Immediately, one can see that for
Fuller, whatever law is, it cannot be the simple command of the
superior, which is the rankest form of legal positivism. Lawmaking
demands a certain consistency and structure, which Fuller calls the
craft of the activity of lawmaking. It is through this rationally guided
and purposive direction to the legal craft that Fuller introduces his
concept of procedural natural law. According to Fuller, lawmaking
may fail in any of the following ways:

the attempt to create and maintain a system of legal rules may miscarry in
at least eight ways: there are in this enterprise, if you will, eight distinct
routes to disaster. The first and most obvious lies in a failure to achieve
rules at all, so that every issue must be decided on an ad hoc basis. The
other routes are: (2) a failure to publicize, or at least to make available to
the affected party, the rules he is expected to observe, (3) the abuse of
retroactive legislation, which not only cannot itself guide action, but undercuts the integrity of rules prospective in effect, since it puts them under the
threat of retrospective change, (4) a failure to make rules understandable,
(5) the enactment of contradictory rules, or (6) rules that require conduct
beyond the powers of the affected party, (7) introducing such frequent
changes in the rules that the subject cannot orient his action by them, and,
finally, (8) a failure of congruence between the rules as announced and their
actual administration.[6]

Fuller refers to these eight rules as the 'internal morality of the
law'. These rules make up the inner structure of the procedure which
makes law possible. They provide the structure for the 'logic' of

---

[6] Lon Fuller, *The Morality of Law* (New Haven, Conn.: Yale University Press,
1964), 38–9.

lawmaking. This 'logic', so Fuller argues, is incompatible with any form of legal positivism. Fuller emphasized the rational direction and the purposive dimension which are central to this 'logic' of lawmaking. By definition, voluntarism as such is ruled out as a sufficient account of lawmaking. Rationality — i.e. purposive direction — requires more than the mere 'willing' of the person in power. Since legal positivism is essentially a voluntarist theory of law, Fuller believes his procedural natural law has undercut this theory by one huge fell swoop.

What is the relation between Fuller's eight procedural rules for lawmaking and natural law in the classical sense? Fuller himself asks this question:

the first task is to relate what I have called the internal morality of the law to the ages-old tradition of natural law. Do the principles expounded in my [eight rules] represent some variety of natural law? The answer is an emphatic, though qualified, yes.

What I have tried to do is to discern and articulate the natural laws of a particular kind of human undertaking, which I have described as 'the enterprise of subjecting human conduct to the governance of rules'. These natural laws have nothing to do with any 'brooding omni-presence in the skies'. Nor have they the slightest affinity with any such proscription as that the practice of contraception is a violation of God's law. They remain entirely terrestrial in origin and application. They are not 'higher' laws; if any metaphor of elevation is appropriate they should be called 'lower' laws. They are like the natural laws of carpentry, or at least those laws respected by a carpenter who wants the house he builds to remain standing and serve the purpose of those who live in it. . . .

What I have called the internal morality of law is in this sense a procedural version of natural law . . . The term 'procedural' is . . . broadly appropriate as indicating that we are concerned . . . with the ways in which a system of rules for governing human conduct must be constructed and administered if it is to be efficacious and at the same time remain what it purports to be.[7]

Certainly Fuller has added a dimension of rational procedure and purpose into the area of lawmaking. This proposal dramatically goes beyond the command structure of legal positivism. Yet, one might ask, isn't there a set of procedures for ice hockey too? But certainly this set of rules is not called the 'natural law' or the 'inner logic' of ice hockey. Or, to use one of Fuller's own examples, it is unclear

---

[7] Ibid. 96–7.

what the import is of the concept of the 'natural law of carpentry'. Does the mere 'logic' of an operation provide sufficient grounds entailing a natural law position? One suspects not. Fuller's analysis offers an account of natural law in terms of a way of proceeding in the legal process. He is concerned with the directive purpose of lawmaking. But is directive purpose alone sufficient for a natural law theory? When the theory of Aquinas is developed in detail in Chapter 4, the insufficiency of Fuller's position will be contrasted with the ontological underpinnings demanded by Aquinas.

What the above objection suggests is that Fuller probably has not gone far enough in his articulation of a natural law theory. Consistency and coherence, while usually predicates applicable to a rational process, do not alone render a natural law account. In considering the *Summa Theologiae* account in Chapter 4, it will become clear that Aquinas requires more for a theory of natural law than internal consistency in the practice of lawmaking. Put differently, while Fuller's account of internal consistency may be a necessary condition for lawmaking in natural law theory, it is not a sufficient condition.

In another text, Fuller offers a different theoretical link with classical natural law theory. In a critique of Hart's emphasis on survival as basic to natural law theory, Fuller suggests as an alternative a moderate 'substantive' position on natural law. Fuller responds to Hart, who argued in *The Concept of Law* that the 'modest aim of survival' depicts 'the central indisputable element which gives empirical good sense to the terminology of Natural Law'. Fuller, with a reference to Aquinas, noted that survival does not describe any of the characteristics which we deem central to human existence. In the following passage, Fuller criticizes Hart's reliance on survival as the central property determining a moral foundation in human nature:

[Hart] . . . asserts further that in the teleological elements that run through all moral and legal thinking there is the 'tacit assumption that the proper end of human activity is survival'.

. . . Hart is . . . treading . . . dubious ground. For he . . . seems to be saying that (survival) furnishes the core and central element of all human striving. This, I think, cannot be accepted. As Thomas Aquinas remarked long ago, if the highest aim of a captain were to preserve his ship, he would keep it in port forever. As for the proposition that the overwhelming majority of men wish to survive even at the cost of hideous misery, this seems to me of doubtful truth . . .

Hart's search for a 'central indisputable element' in human striving raises the question whether in fact this search can be successful. I believe that if we were forced to select the principle that supports and infuses all human aspiration we would find it in the objective of maintaining communication with our fellows.[8]

Fuller, through this 'morality of aspiration', suggests that the fact of 'communication' — which seems to be reducible to the active engagement of the intellect in the process of understanding — is the fundamental principle based in human nature on which natural law might proceed. Fuller does not develop this insight. None the less, it is arguable whether at this juncture he offered a substantive suggestion proposing content for natural law beyond the procedural dimension of the 'inner morality of the law'. In Chapter 4, the connection of 'communication' with Aquinas's 'rational disposition' will be discussed.

The *Harvard Law Review* debate on law and morality focused attention on the jurisprudential writings of both Hart and Fuller. Fuller argued vigorously against the legal positivist position separating law from morality. In a recently published essay, Russell Hittinger suggests that 'Fuller and Hart were more in agreement than disagreement over what natural law theory should produce: namely, a short list of basic goods that positive law must bear in mind if the system of justice is to have any point'.[9] In his study of Fuller's theory of law, Robert Summers wrote that Fuller and Hart 'jointly and severally rejuvenated the subject of legal theory in our time'.[10] Summers suggests that by 1940, most work in jurisprudence in English-speaking countries had 'come to a standstill'. This changed, Summers argued, due to the thoughtful writings and spirited exchanges of these two philosophers of law, both of whom contributed substantially to the revival of natural law theory.

A. P. d'Entrèves: An Early Reconstruction

In 1951, the first edition of A. P. d'Entrèves's book, *Natural Law*, appeared in the Hutchinson University Library series. This remarkable little treatise was written by a Professor of Political Theory at

---

[8] Fuller, *The Morality of Law*, Ibid. 185. (Fuller's reference to Aquinas is *Summa Theologiae*, I-II, q. 2, a. 5.)

[9] Russell Hittinger, 'Natural Law and Virtue: Theories at Cross Purposes', in Robert P. George (ed.), *Natural Law Theory: Contemporary Essays* (Oxford: Oxford University Press, 1992), 70 n. 56.

[10] Robert S. Summers, *Lon L. Fuller* (London: Edward Arnold, 1984), p. vii.

the University of Turin who also held a position at the University
of Oxford. The book introduced the English-speaking legal community, one not normally knowledgeable about natural law issues,
into the fundamental principles of this theory. The second edition
of d'Entréves's book appeared in 1970, containing three thoughtful
appendices in which d'Entrèves considered some of the current
themes in natural law, especially as related to English-language philosophy. Appendix A, 'The Case for Natural Law Re-Examined', is
a thoughtful *apologia* for the importance of natural law theory. It
also contains several sophisticated proposals d'Entrèves thought
necessary for making natural law theory more acceptable to twentieth-century philosophers. This appendix appeared originally as an
article in *Natural Law Forum*, 1, a journal dedicated to serious discussion of natural law jurisprudence. Appendix B considers different
versions of natural law theory and appendix C is an analysis of Hart's
theory of natural necessities. It is important to note that d'Entréves
knew both Continental and English philosophy well. He was well
versed too in the study of contemporary philosophical issues and in
the history of Western philosophy. Hence, d'Entrèves was a credible
spokesperson, calling for a reconsideration of natural law discussions
in the field of jurisprudence.

As a member of the Oxford faculty, d'Entrèves knew that natural
law theory was not held in high regard by English philosophers.
The tradition of Hume, Bentham, and Mill, together with the prominence of the legal positivist jurisprudence of John Austin, helped
keep natural law discussions out of the mainstream of jurisprudence
work. D'Entrèves notes that even Hart was aware of this issue. In a
survey article discussing jurisprudence in Britain in the decade after
the Second World War, Hart wrote that 'it is surprising to find how
small a contribution to English jurisprudence in these years has been
made by writers in the natural law tradition'.[11]

Through his two editions of *Natural Law*, his work with the
Natural Law Forum, on whose editorial board he served, and his
clear understanding of analytic philosophy, d'Entrèves did much to
make natural law theory an object of philosophical consideration
among English and American legal scholars. Throughout his work,

---

[11] H. L. A. Hart, 'Philosophy of Law and Jurisprudence in Britain (1945-1952)',
cited in A. P. d'Entrèves, *Natural Law*, 2nd rev. edn. (London: Hutchinson University
Library, 1970), 119.

d'Entrèves aspired to render natural law theory consistent within a philosophical system independent of theological principles. That he could not reconcile this goal with his reading and analysis of Aquinas on natural law will become the object of Chapter 5 of this book. None the less, d'Entrèves is a principal spokesperson for the reconsideration and re-examination of natural law theory in English and American secular philosophy.

Jacques Maritain and Yves Simon: Neo-Scholasticism and Natural Law

Following the 1879 publication of Pope Leo XIII's encyclical, *Aeterni Patris*, calling for a rethinking of the philosophy and theology of Thomas Aquinas, much creative textual and critical work was undertaken. An entire school of philosophy, today generally called 'neo-scholasticism' and 'neo-Thomism', emerged in Europe and America. For nearly one hundred years, this philosophy movement embarked creatively and constructively in analysing historical and contemporary problems in Aquinian studies. While primarily connected with Roman Catholic centres of higher education – both in Europe and in the United States and Canada – neo-scholasticism and neo-Thomism appear to have had little direct influence or connection with the dominant mode of analytic philosophy common to English- and Scandinavian-speaking countries. The first critical edition of the entire corpus of Aquinas was begun following Leo XIII's call for a reconsideration of Aquinas's work. Accordingly, this critical rendition of Aquinas's writings is known as the Leonine Edition.

Two prominent neo-scholastic exceptions to this general fact of isolation from the then current mainstream philosophy were the French-born philosophers, Étienne Gilson and Jacques Maritain. Both philosophers, educated in the customary way in France, came to their work in the philosophy of Aquinas later in their academic lives. Neither was educated in the influential centres of classical neo-scholasticism then prominent in Europe. Gilson went on to renown as one of the principal exponents of new studies in the history of medieval philosophy. With the foundation of the Institute for Medieval Studies at the University of Toronto, Gilson directed the course of studies in medieval philosophy for years. His connections at Harvard, both through his visiting lectureships and his invitation to give the William James Lectures in the 1930s, assisted American philosophers in coming to terms with the nature, scope, and diversity of medieval philosophy. Gilson, however, wrote little about the moral and political issues central to this book. He was more interested in classical ontology and epistemology, especially in rethinking the role of 'existence' in the philosophy of Aquinas.

Jacques Maritain, on the other hand, while writing on epistemology, metaphysics, and aesthetics, directed much of his philosophical attention and abilities towards rethinking Aquinas's theory of natural law. His 1951 book, *Man and the State*, offered a reinterpretation of Aquinas's texts in order to make room theoretically for an account of human rights. In discussing the foundational role of individual human rights in scholastic philosophy, Maritain wrote that each human person's 'right to existence, to personal freedom, and to the pursuit of the perfection of moral life, belongs, strictly speaking, to natural law'.[12] Maritain argues explicitly for the existence of individual human rights as derivative directly from natural law. Maritain's writings on natural law were well read by both neo-scholastic and secular philosophers of law. More than anyone else at the time, Maritain brought the concept of 'right' into the mainstream discussions of neo-scholastic accounts of Aquinian jurisprudence.

In *Man and the State*, Maritain suggests that there are two important questions which must be asked about natural law: (1) the ontological element, and (2) the epistemological or 'gnoseological' element. The former issue addresses concern about what Maritain calls the 'normality of the functioning of human nature', which depends upon the 'specific structure and specific ends'. The latter issue considers how natural law is known. At this point, Maritain introduces his own reading of Aquinas by postulating the concept of 'connaturality'. This signifies, so Maritain argues, that knowledge of natural law is 'not rational knowledge, but knowledge *through inclination*'. That this is a controversial analysis of Aquinas is not to be denied. Maritain appeals almost to metaphor while attempting to explicate connaturality. He writes that 'the intellect . . . consults and listens to the inner melody that the vibrating strings of abiding tendencies make present in the subject'.[13] This almost appears to be a direct intuition of an affective dimension of the human person. Ralph McInerny, in particular, is critical of Maritain on this point.

---

[12] Jacques Maritain, *Man and the State* (Chicago: University of Chicago Press, 1951), 100.
[13] Ibid. 91-2.

The account of Aquinas's theory of natural law developed later in this book will avoid this concept of connaturality. None the less, students of natural law dependent on the Maritain analysis often argue for a connatural awareness of the basic inclinations necessary for natural law moral theory.

The concept of right, with its contemporary ramifications for political philosophy, is not articulated explicitly in the texts of Aquinas. None the less, as the discussion in Chapter 9 will suggest, rights are derivable from Aquinas's account. Maritain offered a creative proposal for one form of derivation of human rights in classical neo-scholasticism. In his *The Rights of Man and Natural Law* (1943), *The Person and the Common Good* (1947), and *Scholasticism and Politics* (3rd ed., 1954), Maritain discusses his interpretation of Aquinas's moral theory. In addition, he developed his understanding of the derivation of rights within a Thomist account of human nature.

In *The Person and the Common Good*, Maritain renders a theme similar to our earlier discussion of Fuller's 'morality of aspiration'. In his analysis of the human person, Maritain suggests that a necessary condition of the development of the person is a 'dialogue' in which human agents 'communicate' thoroughly with one another. In Maritain's analysis, rational engagement is a hallmark of individual fulfilment. This account leading to the development of what later philosophers called 'the intellectual life' is a necessary condition for human well-being.

Maritain also contributed much to a contemporary understanding of Aquinian concepts such as 'the common good'. Maritain's analysis distinguishing Aquinas's concept of the common good from the utilitarianism common to Bentham, Mill, and Sidgwick is sophisticated philosophically. Maritain was a harbinger of the criterion developed later by Alasdair MacIntyre articulating the differences between Aristotelian teleology and utilitarian teleology.

Another philosopher central to the neo-scholastic revival of natural law theory was Yves Simon. A member of the faculty at both the University of Chicago and the University of Notre Dame, Simon's work discussed the foundations of natural law theory, especially in Aquinas. His *The Tradition of Natural Law* (1965) is an exquisite account of the metaphysical concepts necessary for understanding natural law theory. In particular, Simon addressed perspicuously the role human essence plays in the natural law theory of Aquinas. Simon wrote with the legal community as his audience. His analysis was directed towards responding to twentieth-century concerns about natural law theory, especially those coming from legal positivism and existentialism. Simon's book also provided an indispensable historical overview of the development of natural law theory in Western philosophy and political science. In several ways, Simon's book may be the best explication of Aquinas on natural law written in the middle part of the century. It appears, however, not to have received a wide audience beyond neo-scholastic philosophers. Like Maritain, Simon appears to have had little knowledge of nor influence on analytic philosophy.

In twentieth-century neo-scholasticism, Maritain probably contributed more to make Aquinas's moral and political concepts known than any other philosopher or legal scholar whose works were either written or translated into English. Both Maritain and Simon, in reworking Aquinas's system, have suggested that a democratic form of government is a justified conclusion drawn from Aquinas's theory of natural law. Of course, this view of democracy would at best be implicit in the texts of Aquinas. Yet Maritain's work, at times, appears to the contemporary philosopher as more dogmatic than analytical and more descriptive than justified through argument. Given these concerns, the influence of Maritain and Simon in analytic philosophy, therefore, has been minimal.

Martin Golding: American Jurisprudence and Natural Law

During the 1974 septicentenary celebrations honouring Thomas Aquinas and acknowledging his contributions to Western thought, Martin Golding presented a paper at the national meetings of the American Catholic Philosophical Association indicating the significance of the writings of Aquinas for the tradition of natural law jurisprudence. Golding wrote that 'the idea of natural law, though the term itself is not always used, is currently enjoying a great revival of interest in ethics and in political and legal philosophy'.[14] Golding also suggested how the insights of Aquinas might contribute to further the contemporary discussions in natural law among scholars of jurisprudence. Golding argues that in the matters of legal effectiveness and legal obligation, there should be some connection. Golding writes: 'The lesson of the natural-law tradition is that both

---

[14] Martin Golding, 'Aquinas and Some Contemporary Natural Law Theories', *Proceedings of the American Catholic Philosophical Association* (1974), 238.

involve attention to human needs, human purposes, and the human good. Whatever the problems of this tradition, we cannot ignore its lesson in trying to understand the law that is.'[15]

Discussing studies in the philosophy of law, Golding offers several suggestions regarding how natural law might overcome the theoretical weaknesses in legal positivism. In response to the classical maxims of the legal positivists, expressed in the famous dictum found in Justinian's Code that 'What pleases the prince has the force of law,' and in John Austin's oft-quoted statement that 'The existence of law is one thing; its merit or demerit another', Golding argues that Natural Law theorists reject both these propositions. Golding writes: 'Natural-law theorists, each with their own particular emphasis, reject these two propositions. They maintain that law making is a rational and purposive activity, so that not every enactment of the legislator need necessarily result in a law; and, second, that there is no sharp distinction between law [what law is] and good law.'[16]

Influenced by Fuller's concept of procedural natural law, Golding places emphasis on the natural law tradition's view of lawmaking as a rational art and as a purposive activity. This process of lawmaking, however articulated, 'cannot be divorced from general human purposes'. This treatment of natural law in terms of 'purposive activity' is characteristic of Golding's writings. In his *Philosophy of Law* (1975), Golding writes that Aquinas's theory 'insists that human laws are means to ends and that they should be reasonable means to those ends'. Golding suggests that both Fuller and Philip Selznick stress this aspect that the 'force of law' comes about only because the law is a 'reasonable direction towards the attainment of a given end'.[17]

In agreement with much Anglo-American empiricism, Golding, however, notes that 'a more searching examination of Aquinas would entail a discussion of the more problematic notions of human nature and the common good'. Chapter 4 responds to this criticism found in Golding's writings — and common among many English-speaking critics of Natural Law theory — concerning the theoretical viability of Aquinas's theory of essence. In one sense, Golding, like Fuller, proposes to undertake natural law discussions without fully investigating the ontological underpinnings, especially in regard to

[15] Ibid. 246.
[16] Ibid. 239.
[17] Martin Golding, *Philosophy of Law* (Englewood Cliffs, NJ: Prentice Hall, 1975), 31.

the role a metaphysical theory of essence plays in Aquinas's system. This terribly important issue will be discussed later in this book.

Among American analytic philosophers of law, probably no one has elucidated and commented more favourably upon Aquinas's contribution to jurisprudence than Golding. Golding has articulated forcefully the need for purposive activity in lawmaking. In addition, Golding brought the discussions of Lon Fuller, Harry Jones, and Philip Selznick to a wider audience of analytic philosophers. More than any other American philosopher of law, Golding has brought the insights of natural law theory into more mainstream jurisprudential discussions. Fuller's work, in particular, appears to have exerted a great influence on Golding's work in natural law theory.

Harry Jones: Legal Realism and Moral Principles

A unique contribution to jurisprudence has been American Legal Realism. Oliver Wendell Holmes, Jun. wrote a groundbreaking essay for the 1897 *Harvard Law Review* entitled 'The Path of Law'. Holmes's principal point was that jurisprudence needed to focus on the processes courts actually undertake in administering the law. This was an urgent call to avoid what Holmes considered excessive metaphysical speculation on the part of legal scholars regarding the nature of law. Holmes probably had the nineteenth-century American Hegelians in mind when he developed his theory about excessive speculation. Moreover, he appears to have held natural law theory, however he may have understood the concept, with particular disdain. Holmes argued that if one wants to understand the nature of law, then one must take what he called 'the bad man's perspective'. In other words, to discover the nature of law, one should become immersed in a legal tangle and see how the law works within the context of the legal system. Speculation, Holmes suggested, told nothing about the structure of law. On the contrary, Holmes argued that this speculative avenue led to a dead-end inquiry. He wanted to direct the emphasis of jurisprudence towards the legal processes exercised in particular court cases. This pragmatic direction helped develop Holmes's account of law as 'the prediction of what the courts will do'.

Obviously, this is a quite pragmatic view of the nature of law. One should remember that Holmes was at Harvard University during the time of the generation and flourishing of American pragmatism in the work of Charles Sanders Peirce and William James. Peirce once suggested that a decent definition of truth was 'a habit of action'. One notes immediately the emphasis on activity and work-manship. Truth comes about through the process of creating and making. Holmes absorbed the tenets of pragmatism and applied them to the legal system and its questions. Hence, to understand the law, one needed to see how it worked, especially in the court system. The best way, furthermore, to observe the court's workings was to take 'the bad man's perspective'. The background of American pragmatism hovers heavily over the writings of Oliver Wendell Holmes, Jun. Interestingly enough, in what might be called post-analytic philosophy, especially the work of Hilary Putnam and Richard Rorty, the influence of the pragmatists, Peirce and James in particular, is quite evident and acknowledged.

Reactions to Holmes's legal realism were many and varied. Philos-ophers in the natural law tradition in particular, saw Holmes's view as abandoning the important moral questions regarding the nature of law. They brought forward the charge that crass expediency replaced the moral foundations of the legal system common to natu-ral law justification. Strongly worded and biting criticisms forged an intellectual chasm between the legal realists and the natural law philosophers.

In his 1956 Riverside Lecture, Professor Harry Jones from the Columbia University Law School Faculty attempted to reconcile the differences between the natural law advocates and the followers of legal realism. Martin Golding once noted that Jones's lecture is notable for its restraint and even-handedness in treating the issues. Adopting the legal realist method of observing the actual workings of a courtroom, Jones argues that a judge, in making an appropriate judicial decision in a difficult case, must consider moral principles. In other words, in determining a decision in a particular case which is ambiguous judicially, the judge cannot very well avoid referring to moral principles for direction in resolution and implementation. Jones argues that this bringing to bear of moral principles in judicial decision-making indicates that natural law directives are at work in the legal system. Hence, Jones suggests that legal realism and natural law jurisprudence are not as distinct conceptually as one might sup-pose. Moral principles, so Jones suggests, always are evident within the process of judicial decision.

The point here, of course, is to determine if Jones's analysis of natural law is adequate conceptually with the tradition. Jones appears to suggest that if moral principles are at work in the process of judicial decision, then this is a sufficient claim for inclusion under the rubric of natural law.

This use of moral principles alone, however, is not sufficient. Natural law theory requires not only a commitment to moral principles but also the acceptance of a set of epistemological and metaphysical principles from which the moral theory is derived. For example, utilitarians such as Jeremy Bentham did not deny that law should have a moral dimension. This moral concern by itself, however, does not entail that Bentham is a natural law philosopher. This matter will be discussed later after considering Aquinas's position in detail. Already one should note how different theories suggest various theoretical commitments for natural law jurisprudence.

Legal realism in the form proposed by Jones is structurally similar to the theory of legal decision put forward by Ronald Dworkin in his influential writings. Both Jones and Dworkin direct attention to the moral principles which determined the context of a judicial decision. Dworkin's account will be considered shortly. The role of moral principles in judicial decision is a hotly contested concept in contemporary jurisprudence.

Ronald Dworkin: Judicial Decision and Moral Principles

Ronald Dworkin, probably the most prominent contemporary scholar of jurisprudence, has raised to a more sophisticated level the debate regarding moral principles within the province of judicial decision-making. Dworkin argues that consistent and justified law is always in accord with the moral principles of the society and the legal framework within which that society operates. His classic 1967 article, 'The Model of Rules', first articulated the central role moral principles play in a consistent account of judicial decision. Dworkin argues that Hart's analysis of law in terms of a 'union of primary and secondary rules' does not provide a sufficient account of legal justification. Dworkin advances the discussion from the meta-consideration of procedural rules characteristic of Hart's analysis to a consideration of the moral principles central to the foundation of a society's legal system. Some critics have suggested that the paradigm for Dworkin's analysis is the United States Constitution.

Dworkin argues that a model of law based on rule-following and rule-application is inadequate conceptually to account for judicial decision. Dworkin appears to adopt Wittgenstein's advice – don't build a theory first; rather, look and see! Following the pragmatists, Dworkin points to actual court cases to see how judicial decisions were rendered. He asks whether strictly following rules, as Hart suggested, renders an unambiguous legal decision. Dworkin selects court cases where the rules were followed completely and to the letter. Everything was correct procedurally. In these cases, however, the court rendered a decision in opposition to the letter of the law as written. This, quite obviously, is in opposition to Hart's theory of law expressed as a 'model of rules'. *Riggs* v. *Palmer* is a classic case that Dworkin uses often to justify his analysis. In this particular case, a young man was to inherit his grandfather's estate. However, in order to move the process along more quickly, the young man murdered his grandfather. Should the fellow inherit his murdered grandfather's estate? The rules for inheritance were followed strictly — i.e. the will had been signed and witnessed according to the laws of the state. None the less, the court ruled that the fact that the grandson had murdered his grandfather contributed a new and significant condition into this case. Dworkin argues that in this case, the court ruled that a higher moral principle is at work; in particular, the court ruled that a person cannot profit in a legal sense from his or her own illegal and immoral actions. This principle, Dworkin argues, is contained within the moral fabric of society's legal system. Such principles have an architectonic function in the process of interpreting legal cases. Dworkin argues that in the so-called 'hard cases' — such as *Riggs* v. *Palmer* — the judge must appeal to moral principles firmly grounded in the fabric of society's system of law. These principles serve as 'reasons' necessary to render valid legal decisions.

Dworkin argues that a theory of law based on rules alone, such as Hart's, is insufficient to explain the resolution of hard cases. Moreover, it is the hard cases which illustrate best, Dworkin suggests, the foundation principles of a legal system. Dworkin's suggestion that a 'right' is a 'political trump' capable of justifying a claim against a particular legal ruling has been influential in contemporary jurisprudence. Dworkin's theory has been further elucidated in his three major works: *Taking Rights Seriously* (1977), *A Matter of Principle* (1985), and *Law's Empire* (1986).

Given that Dworkin suggests the importance of moral principles in determining the law and in the necessity of rational consistency, it has been suggested that he is utilizing a form of natural law investigation. Murphy and Coleman note that because Dworkin argues that judicial decision making 'necessarily involves a moral element, it is not too misleading to see his "natural law" tendencies as dominant in his thinking'.[18] Michael Bayles wrote the following concerning his claim that Aquinas and Dworkin are strikingly similar in matters of jurisprudence: 'To a large extent, the differences between natural lawyers such as Aquinas and Dworkin and positivists such as Austin and Hart stem from the purposes of their theories. Aquinas and Dworkin seek to provide normative theories of obligatory or justifiable law. Austin and Hart [offer] conceptual-explanatory theories.'[19]

In a classic article in the *University of Florida Law Review*, Dworkin wrote the following about the so-called natural law thrust of his position. This illuminating passage indicates both what Dworkin takes to be a contemporary distaste for natural law jurisprudence and his own rather broad understanding of what he takes natural law theory to be.

Everyone likes categories, and legal philosophers like them very much. So we spend a good deal of time, not all of it profitably, labeling ourselves and the theories of law we defend. One label, however, is particularly dreaded: no one wants to be called a natural lawyer. Natural law insists that what the law is depends in some way on what the law should be. This seems metaphysical or at least vaguely religious. In any case it seems plainly wrong. If some theory of law is shown to be a natural law theory, therefore, people can be excused if they do not attend to it much further.

After indicating his theoretical distaste for natural law theory, Dworkin goes on to characterize his own theory, both as to structure and content.

In the past several years, I have tried to defend a theory about how judges should decide cases that some critics (though not all) say is natural law theory and should be rejected for that reason. I have of course made the pious and familiar objection to this charge, that it is better to look at theories than labels. But since labels are so much a part of our common intellectual life, it is almost as silly to flee as to hurl them. If the crude description of natural law I just gave is correct, that any theory which makes the content

---

[18] Murphy and Coleman, *Philosophy of Law*, 40.
[19] Michael Bayles, 'What is Jurisprudence About? Theories, Definitions, Concepts, or Conceptions of Law?', *Philosophical Topics: Philosophy of Law*, 18/1 (Spring, 1990), 38.

of law sometimes depend on the correct answer to some moral question is a natural law theory, then I am guilty of natural law. I am not interested, I should add, in whether this crude characterization is historically correct, or whether it succeeds in distinguishing natural law from positivist theories of law. My present concern is rather this. Suppose this is natural law. What in the world is wrong with it?

Dworkin next illustrates what his theory of 'naturalism' amounts to. In effect, it requires that a judge in judicial decisions form justified positions based on a consistent reading of the principles grounded in the society's constitution:

According to naturalism, judges should decide hard cases by interpreting the political structure of their community in the following, perhaps special way: by trying to find the best justification they can find, in principles of political morality, for the structure as a whole, from the most profound constitutional rules and arrangements to the details of, for example, the private law of tort or contract.[20]

A later part of this book considers if Dworkin's concern with the moral dimension of law, which prompted Murphy and Coleman to suggest that Dworkin should be included as part of the tradition of natural law, is sufficient to classify his work as natural law jurisprudence. In some important respects, Dworkin and Jones appear more aligned structurally than one might suspect. Each demands that the judge have some sense of moral principle working in rendering judicial decisions. The legal realist method and direction are evident throughout Dworkin's writings. It is less evident, however, whether either Jones or Dworkin can be classified as part of the natural law tradition. Dworkin's own words suggest how wide his understanding is regarding natural law categories. Dworkin's analysis raises several questions about the status of natural law inquiries. On what grounds are the principles of political morality based? Is the concept of the human person central to the analysis? Or is the emphasis on the individual rights of the person, the 'trumps' which Dworkin advocates? How is the human good determined? Responses to questions such as these are necessary before one can claim that Dworkin's analysis of legal theory, even with its moral principles, is part of the rubric of natural law jurisprudence.

Before ending this discussion of Dworkin's jurisprudence theory,

---

[20] Ronald Dworkin, 'Natural Law Revisited', *University of Florida Law Review*, 34/2 (Winter, 1982), 165.

it is useful to consider briefly two areas from which serious objections have been raised against Dworkin's account of law: (1) critical legal studies, and (2) feminist jurisprudence.

The critical legal studies movement suggests that the law is infused with, as Andrew Altman has put it, 'irresolvably opposed principles and ideals', which may indicate a deep level of contradiction. This suggests, so the critical legal realists argue, that there exists in law a fundamental legal indeterminacy. This is opposed to Dworkin's argument that in every 'hard case', a resolution is possible through an analysis of rights as determined by the moral principles fundamental to the society's constitution. Moreover, critical legal studies theorists argue that what Dworkin calls 'settled law' is itself the result of political compromise. This compromise, so they argue, is impossible to be considered as 'settled law' with determinate moral principles. The law, they suggest, is a 'patchwork quilt' of irreconcilably opposed ideologies.[21]

Feminist legal theory generally is quite critical of what is termed 'liberal legalism'. This concept entails, so it is argued, an acceptance of the 'separation thesis' and the endorsement of 'moral autonomy'. This criticism is part of the general critique of post-Enlightenment moral theory. However, Robin West directs her critique against what she calls 'masculine jurisprudence' based on what she refers to as 'phenomenological descriptions of the paradigmatically male experience of the inevitability of separation of the self from the rest of the species, and indeed from the rest of the natural world'.[22] This analysis seems to suggest a coextensiveness of 'masculine jurisprudence' with post-Enlightenment moral and political theory.

John Finnis: Revisionist Thomism

Most of the authors discussed above – d'Entréves, Maritain, and Simon being the notable exceptions – while purportedly connected in some way with the natural law tradition, none the less have kept their theories at arm's length from Aquinas's account of natural law. The two philosophers of law to be considered next are less reticent about connecting their theories with Aristotle and Aquinas. Both John Finnis and Henry Veatch, while differing themselves in their

[21] Andrew Altman, 'Legal Realism, Critical Legal Studies, and Dworkin', *Philosophy and Public Affairs*, 15/3 (1986), 220-2.

[22] Robin West, 'Jurisprudence and Gender', *University of Chicago Law Review*, 55/1 (Winter, 1988), 5.

respective analyses of Aquinas's theory of natural law, explicitly argue that their work should be seen as part of the natural law canon found in the writings of Thomas Aquinas.

John Finnis of University College Oxford is the primary British exponent of classical natural law theory as developed in Aristotle and Aquinas. Finnis has produced two books which argue in detail for his revisionist view of Aquinas's theory of natural law. Beginning with his *Natural Law and Natural Rights* (1980), Finnis, along with Germain Grisez and Joseph Boyle, has articulated a version of Aquinas's theory of natural law which attempts to overcome various standard objections to ethical naturalism common in contemporary jurisprudence and meta-ethics. Grisez began this project with his seminal article, 'The First Principle of Practical Reason', which appeared in *The Natural Law Forum* in 1965. Finnis's second book on natural law, *The Fundamentals of Ethics* (1983), is a restatement of the moral principles found in *Natural Law and Natural Rights* but directed towards the philosophical rather than the legal community. Finnis, Grisez, and Boyle have further articulated and defended their revisionist theory of Aquinas in several articles published in the *American Journal of Jurisprudence*. Their *Nuclear Deterrence, Morality and Realism*, which is a structured analysis of the deficiencies central to consequentialist moral theories, appeared in 1987.

It is to the credit of Finnis and Grisez that many analytic philosophers have begun to wrestle once again with the structural issues contained in Aquinas's theory of natural law. Both Finnis and Grisez take seriously the is/ought problem articulated by Hume, developed by Kant, and stated anew through Moore's 'naturalistic fallacy'. Finnis and Grisez argue that a metaphysical interpretation of Aquinas's moral theory is fraught with difficulty because of the objections formulated in modern philosophy. Their concern is similar to MacIntyre's rejection of what he calls Aristotle's 'metaphysical biology' in *After Virtue*. Finnis and Grisez attempt, therefore, to develop a revisionist account of Aquinas which, they argue, evades the theoretical pitfalls found in the is/ought problem and the naturalistic fallacy. Their argument is subtle and often difficult. The argument leads, like Kant, to affirm an autonomous state for moral theory. None the less, it is important to view their revisionist account of Aquinas as an attempt to move Aquinas's theory of natural law around the common objections to ethical naturalism found in modern and contemporary philosophy.

Chapter 6 considers Finnis's revision of Aquinas's theory of natural law in some detail. In that chapter, some theoretical difficulties entailed by the Finnis analysis will be discussed. The principal concern centres on what happens to natural law theory if the Finnis rejection of the metaphysical foundation of that theory is dismissed. Ralph McInerny, Henry Veatch, Russell Hittinger, and Lloyd Weinreb, among others, develop this line of criticism against the Finnis –Grisez account of Aquinian natural law theory.[23] None the less, *Natural Law and Natural Rights* is a philosophical masterpiece as a treatise on natural law theory. The argument is subtle yet comprehensive; Finnis considers with sophistication and aplomb the structure and development of both theories of natural law and theories of natural rights.

Henry Veatch: Ontological Foundationalism

On the American side of the Atlantic, the writings of Henry B. Veatch have been instrumental in providing renewed interest in Aquinas's theory of natural law. Long a student of Aristotelian metaphysics and ethical theory, Veatch has asked penetrating questions about the apparent lack of metaphysical or 'natural philosophy' foundations in contemporary meta-ethics. According to Veatch, the issue is whether meta-ethical distinctions have a basis in nature or in being (the ontological route), or are these distinctions only the result of a consideration of moral language (the linguistic route) or the result of the conditions of knowledge (the epistemological route). Veatch argues vigorously that the ontological route is a necessary condition for understanding Aristotelian and Aquinian moral theory. On these foundations, Veatch argues, normative judgements are based. To deny the importance of the ontological route, which Veatch argues both Finnis and the MacIntyre of *After Virtue* have done, is to misread and misinterpret the natural law theory elucidated by Aristotle and Aquinas.

Beginning with his response to the mid-century *apologia* for existentialism, William Barrett's *Irrational Man* (1956), Veatch's *Rational*

---

[23] Cf. Ralph McInerny, *Aquinas on Human Action* (Washington, DC: The Catholic University of America Press, 1992); Russell Hittinger, *A Critique of the New Natural Law Theory* (Notre Dame, Ind.: University of Notre Dame Press, 1987); Lloyd Weinreb, *Natural Law and Justice* (Cambridge, Mass.: Harvard University Press, 1987). This author also undertook this line of argument in his review of Finnis's *Fundamentals of Ethics*, *New Blackfriars* (June 1984).

Man (1962) provided an Aristotelian analysis for moral decision-making in opposition to the irrationalism of existentialism that Barrett proposed. Yet it is in his two critiques of contemporary ethics and jurisprudence, *For an Ontology of Morals* (1971) and *Human Rights: Fact or Fancy?* (1985), that Veatch vigorously puts forward a defence of natural law which he suggests is in accord with Aristotelian and Aquinian philosophy. As president of both the American Philosophical Association (Western Division) and the American Catholic Philosophical Association, Veatch used his prerogative of office to present a presidential address calling to mind his concerns about the lack of foundations for contemporary moral theory.

Veatch is not reticent about his work in reconstructing Aristotle and Aquinas for contemporary philosophy. In his *Swimming Against the Current in Contemporary Philosophy*, Veatch writes, 'may I simply say that my own program ought perhaps to be regarded as amounting to little more than exercises in dialectic, and in a dialectic directed to the overriding purpose of trying to rehabilitate Aristotle and Aquinas as contemporary philosophers'.[24]

It is clear that Veatch is more centrally connected with the classical tradition of naturalism in Aristotle and natural law in Aquinas than the other philosophers considered above. Veatch wants to reconstruct a viable ontology — what he refers to as 'natural philosophy' or 'Aristotelian physics' — which will serve as an adequate foundation for moral theory. He suggests that the naturalism of Aristotle and Aquinas can serve this role. Given this ontological foundation requirement for natural law, Veatch is opposed theoretically to the revisionist account of Aquinas elucidated by Finnis. This ontological route — what Chapter 7 refers to as 'ontological foundationalism' — goes beyond the limits of the epistemological or the linguistic routes — what Veatch often refers to as 'the transcendental turn' — adopted by many contemporary philosophers of law.

Veatch has written, about his concern for the Finnis/Grisez account of natural law theory, 'in his argument, Finnis is ably seconded by the more than formidable Germain Grisez. Accordingly, my task now becomes one of trying to defuse these Finnis–Grisez arguments, which are designed to show that appeals to nature can never provide proper support for ethics and morality'.[25]

---

[24] Henry B. Veatch, *Swimming Against the Current in Contemporary Philosophy* (Washington, DC: Catholic University of America Press, 1990), 13.
[25] Ibid. 298.

Chapter 7 considers Veatch's foundationalist theory and his response to Finnis in more detail. Veatch offers the most perceptive classical reading of Aristotle's moral theory considered in this book.

Mortimer Adler: Aristotelian Realism

No consideration of recent contributions to natural law theory would be complete without some reference to the work, over half a century, of Mortimer Adler. Adler, both through the Great Books Foundation and through his own voluminous writing, has often emphasized the texts of Aristotle and Aquinas. He has sought to popularize the insights of Aristotle and Aquinas, especially in the area of law and morality. While his work in Aristotle and Aquinas has not had a tremendous impact in the philosophical community, none the less he has kept alive an interest in natural law theory.

Adler's close association with Robert Hutchins, both at the University of Chicago and later with Hutchins's Center for the Study of Democratic Institutions, helped promote a general understanding of the Aristotelian principles of moral and legal theory. Both Adler and Hutchins helped make the University of Chicago a recognized centre for the serious study of Aristotle and Aquinas. Hutchins's institute at Santa Barbara, California, was the scene of much serious research into natural law thinking in the 1950s and 1960s. The results of this multi-faceted research into natural law issues appeared in published form under the title of *Natural Law and Modern Society* (1962). Hutchins himself has an article in this volume entitled 'Natural Law and Jurisprudence'.

Many of Adler's writings have emphasized the importance of Aristotelian principles as a context for discussing pressing contemporary problems. One of Adler's recent books is titled *Aristotle for Everybody* (1978). Adler's recent collection of essays, *Reforming Education* (1990), indicates clearly the consistent Aristotelian/Aquinian dimension to his work for the past fifty years. In an essay in this collection, Adler writes that 'in my judgment, Aristotle's *Nicomachean Ethics* is the only sound, practical and undogmatic moral philosophy in the whole Western tradition'.[26] Adler translated and edited Maritain's *Scholasticism and Politics* (1940).

A clear example of his interest in Aristotelian naturalism can be

---

[26] Mortimer Adler, 'A Sound Moral Philosophy', in *Reforming Education* (New York: Collier Books, Macmillan Publishing Co., 1990), 254.

found in his public broadcasting dialogue with Bill Moyers. Note the following discussion in which Adler focuses attention on the property of human goodness:

I'm using the word 'goodness' in the moral sense of what is good for human beings. Good for them – it makes them good men and women, makes their lives good lives or bad lives.

The only way I can make any moral judgments that have universal validity is if the needs I'm talking about are common to all human beings.[27]

This discussion contains the elucidation of common themes which place Adler squarely in the context of natural law theory. Adler clearly argues that the basis of human goodness is determined by the needs common to human nature. Hence, moral and political prescriptions are justified only in the context of determining the 'good' for the human person. The natural law connections are necessary conditions to Adler's moral theory.

Summary of Recent Work in Natural Law Jurisprudence

The above discussion is intended to provide but a brief overview of some contemporary work in natural law jurisprudence. Certainly it is not nor does it pretend to be complete. One might mention scholastic philosophers such as Vernon Bourke, Thomas Gilby, and Heinrich Rommen, for instance, or the recent work in analytic history of philosophy by Norman Kretzmann and Eleonore Stump. James Ross has addressed the issue of the origin of rights theory in late medieval scholasticism. Fred D. Miller has written on natural law in Aristotle as related to the concept of justice. At mid-century, the work of Philip Selznick gained importance for its consideration of natural law from a social science perspective. In some respects, Selznick's work is allied closely with Fuller's concept of procedural natural law. Lloyd Weinreb's *Natural Law and Justice* (1987) attempts to bridge the gap between natural law jurisprudence and the demands of justice common to political philosophy.

In this chapter, however, emphasis has been placed on those writers in contemporary jurisprudence who have written about classical natural law theory, reinterpreted natural law theory in some way or other, or brought moral principles into discussions of juris-

---

[27] Mortimer Adler, in 'Mortimer Adler and Bill Moyers: A Dialogue on the Nature of Goodness', in Paul Sigmund (ed.), *St. Thomas Aquinas on Politics and Ethics* (New York: W. W. Norton & Co., 1988), 194.

prudence. Some of the philosophers have had greater influence in the general sweep of Anglo-American analytic jurisprudence than others. This chapter uses broad brush strokes to paint the panorama of contemporary natural law jurisprudence. While being a wide picture, this discussion should none the less be useful in at least two ways: (1) it should assist the project attempting to discover the role Aquinas's theory of natural law plays in the context of twentieth-century jurisprudence; and (2) it will help students coming to natural law discussions to understand some of the reasons for the re-emergence of natural law jurisprudence in the last half of the twentieth century. Moreover, this is not an exhaustive account of jurisprudence theories. The purpose of this narrative chapter is to indicate a starting point within the context of contemporary jurisprudence for a serious discussion of Thomas Aquinas's theory of natural law.

Before beginning the next area of discussion — contemporary meta-ethics — it is useful to comment on several common themes for natural law found in the above writers. It should be noted that the term 'natural law' has been used almost as an umbrella concept to cover a wide variety of positions in jurisprudence. At times one gets the impression that some philosophers propose to call almost any theory which demands a moral standard for evaluating positive law a theory of natural law. Martin Golding, for instance, once wrote that Morris Cohen held this exaggerated view. Dworkin appears to offer a similar suggestion. This is entirely too sweeping a category concept. As noted above, given this all-embracing reading of natural law, it would follow that Bentham's jurisprudence, even with its empiricist attack on the concept of 'human nature', would be called a natural law theory. This would render the category of natural law so broad as to make it almost meaningless for serious philosophical discussion and analysis.

What then counts for natural law? Martin Golding probably provides the most thoughtful reflections on what philosophers of law should take to be the necessary conditions for natural law jurisprudence. In reading Golding's account of natural law, he seems to suggest that the following five propositions are in some manner central to adopting a natural law theory:

1. Laws possess directive power;
2. This directive power is based on reason;

3. The will is subservient to reason, in opposition to the legal positivists;
4. Reason ultimately directs laws for the purpose of the common good and for the good of the individual;
5. There is a necessary connection between law and morality.[28]

These propositions contained in Golding's writings focus attention on the rationality of the process of lawmaking. This analysis certainly is useful to assist our understanding of natural law theory. None the less, in a book on Aquinas's explication of natural law, it is important to articulate clearly what Aquinas himself required for a consistent natural law theory. Aquinas will demand more for an adequate account of natural law than Golding's five propositions. The importance Aquinas gives for the metaphysical foundations of natural law theory will become apparent when Chapters 4 and 5 are considered.

It is, moreover, this metaphysical foundation issue which has caused serious reluctance on the part of contemporary philosophers to endorse Aristotelian/Aquinian positions on natural law. There are at least two issues which dominate such criticism: (1) the justification of the concept of human nature or essence; and (2) the dependence or derivation of moral properties from the human essence. In particular, Golding has suggested that Aquinas's reliance on human nature in his theory of ethical naturalism is 'problematic'. Murphy and Coleman, furthermore, have written that contemporary views of natural law 'have no grandiose metaphysical and theological pretensions . . . and (are) much more intellectually modest'.[29] On this metaphysical theory of essence, H. J. McCloskey writes:

However, it is to be noted that difficulties arise for such a theory [i.e., Thomistic theory of natural law] in respect of its theses that there are ends or purposes inherent in human nature, that they are based on inbuilt 'inclinations or appetites' that we have by virtue of our nature as substances, animals, rational beings, and that we have a self-evident right, by virtue of our right to be good as human beings, to align ourselves with these inherent natural ends to attain our natural end and be good as human beings.[30]

The role of essence in Aquinas's theory of moral foundationalism will become clear in Chapter 4. A dispositional view of essence —

---

[28] Golding, *Philosophy of Law*, ch. 2, *passim*.
[29] Murphy and Coleman, *Philosophy of Law*, 37.
[30] H. J. McCloskey, 'Respect for Human Moral Rights', R. G. Frey (ed.), in *Utility and Rights*, (Oxford: Basil Blackwell, 1985), 126.

essence as composed of Aristotelian potentialities — will be elucidated and defended as a coherent and consistent way to analyse
Aquinas's texts discussing this ontological category central to his
metaphysical theory. Chapter 4 will attempt to overcome objections
like those raised by Golding, Murphy and Coleman, and McCloskey.
Later chapters will also suggest how moral properties are grounded
in this account of human nature.

The discussion just completed indicates the wide range of theoretical perspectives which have contributed to the re-emergence of natural law theory in contemporary jurisprudence. The natural law canon
found in the writing of Aquinas often serves as the theoretical backdrop for these discussions. These contemporary texts suggest the
need for a clearly articulated account of Aquinas on natural law.
Chapter 4 begins this process in some detail.

META-ETHICS

Not only recent work in jurisprudence, but also studies in meta-
ethics have witnessed a renewed interest in the ethical naturalism
found in Aristotle and Aquinas. The remainder of this chapter considers several philosophers central to this revival of meta-ethical
naturalism.

Alasdair MacIntyre: After Virtue *and the Recovery of Aristotle*

Recent discussions in meta-ethics have exhibited a vibrant interest
in Aristotle and Aquinas's moral theories. Without a doubt, much
of this revival of interest is due to the creative work of Alasdair
MacIntyre. MacIntyre's *After Virtue* (1981) has literally forced a
'paradigm shift' in meta-ethics, especially among American analytic
philosophers. Prior to the publication of *After Virtue*, most meta-
ethical discussions were centred on the advantages and problems
either with some form of utilitarianism or some form of Kantian
formalism. Aristotelian 'virtue ethics' was considered, for the most
part, only in its historical context. Aquinas's natural law ethics was
virtually dismissed from contemporary ethics discussions. Virtue
ethics was discussed as an interesting but antiquated form of naturalism. MacIntyre, in asking contemporary students of ethics to consider what he referred to as 'the way of Aristotle', has influenced a
whole generation of philosophers to read Aristotle, and, as a consequence, Aquinas, with a care and sophistication beyond what had

been customary in analytic philosophy. MacIntyre's insistence that contemporary meta-ethics was intellectually bankrupt forced philosophers to examine new approaches to meta-ethical discourse. He argues that British utilitarianism and Kantian formalism have reached a dead-end street. He suggests that a rediscovery of Aristotelian virtue ethics will provide a much-needed rejuvenation in contemporary moral philosophy. *After Virtue* literally spawned a 'cottage industry' of philosophical bustle treating Aristotelian ethics with a new vigour.[31]

In *After Virtue*, MacIntyre argues that contemporary ethical theories have reached an intellectual impasse. Moreover, ethical debate had, so he suggests, become 'interminable'. MacIntyre further argues that moral philosophy reached this impasse in the twentieth century because of the Enlightenment's decisive break with Aristotelian teleology. Lacking a concept of virtue, MacIntyre suggests, post-Enlightenment ethical theory is inadequate theoretically and practically. The concept of virtue was replaced by the concept of rule, especially as developed in Kantian formalism. Rules express a list of actions to be undertaken or to be avoided. Virtues emphasize a set of character traits to be acquired. The traits are connected with the well-being of the person. Moral questions directed towards the development of the person and the attainment of well-being were neglected if not avoided in the post-Enlightenment attempt to justify moral rules. Only a recovery of Aristotelian teleology and virtue ethics will rescue the Western ethical tradition.

In a thoughtful analysis of recent work in Aristotelian ethical theory, Russell Hittinger wrote the following account dealing with the influence MacIntyre's work has had on contemporary philosophy:

MacIntyre has been a pioneer figure in what I have elsewhere referred to as the 'recoverist' movement: those who wish to retrieve, in whole or in part, what Alan Donagan has called the 'common morality' of the West.

---

[31] The range of journals in disparate fields publishing reviews of *After Virtue* indicates the breadth of interest MacIntyre's book has stimulated. In the five years following the publication of the first edition, *After Virtue* was reviewed in, among others, the following journals: *Journal of Religion, Contemporary Sociology, Harvard Educational Review, Quarterly Journal of Speech, Partisan Review, Commonweal, Yale Law Review, Sewanne Review*, and *Village Voice*; in addition reviews appeared in many philosophy periodicals. This list suggests the wide range of readers MacIntyre's work on Aristotelian ethics has witnessed.

If nothing else, MacIntyre has made this recoverist project professionally respectable. Less than a decade has passed since its publication, yet many are already prepared to admit that *After Virtue* represents something pivotal.[32]

Hittinger has expressed a position now widely held by contemporary philosophers.

MacIntyre has not limited his work to Aristotle alone. His more recent writing has considered Aquinas's meta-ethics from a new perspective. His Aquinas Lecture in the Marquette University series treats Aquinas with vigour, his *Whose Justice? Which Rationality?* (1988) and *Three Rival Versions of Moral Enquiry* (1990) consider Aquinas's moral theory as one deserving of serious discussion by contemporary students of philosophy. The latter book is the published version of MacIntyre's Gifford Lectures.

Given the immense popularity of MacIntyre's work on Aristotle and Aquinas, it is obvious that much credit for the renewed interest in Aristotelian naturalism is due to his careful and exacting work. More than anyone else writing in meta-ethics, MacIntyre provided the framework within which serious discussions of Aristotle and Aquinas could take place. In summary, therefore, MacIntyre's three books, *After Virtue, Whose Justice? Which Rationality?*, and *Three Rival Versions of Moral Enquiry*, have assisted in the revolutionary reintroduction of Aristotle's moral theory into the roadways of analytic philosophy.

Finnis and Veatch: The Aquinas Connection

Since the work of John Finnis has been discussed briefly above, time will not be spent here with his reconstructed version of Aquinas's meta-ethics. It is important to note, however, that Finnis's work has drawn criticism from several quarters. One of the more complete accounts is Russell Hittinger's *A Critique of the New Natural Law Theory*, which renders a critical analysis of the Finnis revisionist position in the light of classical accounts of Aquinas's moral philosophy. Hittinger suggests that Finnis's reconstruction has more affinity to Kantian meta-ethics than to traditional natural law theory.

Henry Veatch has written extensively on Aristotle and Aquinas both in jurisprudence and meta-ethics. His *Rational Man* and *For an Ontology of Morals* argue cogently for a reconstructed view of Aris-

---

[32] Russell Hittinger, 'After MacIntyre: Natural Law Theory, Virtue Ethics and Eudaimonia', *International Philosophical Quarterly*, 29/4 (Dec. 1989), 449.

totle and, in a derivative sense, Aquinas. In addition to elucidating clearly the texts of Aristotle and Aquinas on moral themes, Veatch has responded carefully to many standard objections to Aristotelian naturalism found in analytic philosophy. Veatch's work has stimulated creative work in the ongoing project of renewed studies in Aristotle and Aquinas. His principal concern has been to consider anew the ontological foundations which he considers as necessary conditions to undertake a sufficient analysis of Aristotle's meta-ethics. In his American Philosophical Association presidential address, Veatch remarked on what he took to be the central issue confronting contemporary moral philosophy: 'the crying need in ethics today would seem to be, not for any language of morals, or logic of morals, or even phenomenology of morals, transcendental or otherwise, but rather for an ontology of morals'.[33]

The work of both Finnis and Veatch has assisted in the present development of Aristotelian ethical studies among English-speaking philosophers. Chapters 6 and 7 consider in some detail the natural law positions articulated and defended by both these philosophers.

Ralph McInerny: Ethica Thomistica

The writings from the prolific pen of Ralph McInerny have also contributed to the renewed interest in Aquinas's moral theory. While steeped in classical Thomism, McInerny has written on issues in the philosophy of Aquinas with a precision and carefulness which has rendered the Aquinian concepts understandable to those philosophers outside neo-scholastic circles. McInerny has written on many themes in Aquinas's philosophy and theology, ranging from analogy and being to God and morality. In the realm of meta-ethics, perhaps his *Ethica Thomistica* (1982) is best known. In this text, McInerny attempts to provide an explanation and defence of Aquinian naturalism in both normative ethics and meta-ethics. McInerny was one of the first scholastic philosophers to respond directly to standard twentieth-century objections to Aristotelian naturalism in the form of Moore's 'naturalistic fallacy'. His recently published *Aquinas on Human Action: A Theory of Practice* (1992) is an astute analysis of Aquinas on action theory, containing an extended commentary on the first sections of the *Summa Theologiae*, I–II, in which Aquinas offers a sophisticated yet complicated analysis of the concept of

[33] Veatch, *Swimming Against the Current*, 156.

undertaking a moral action. McInerny argues that Aquinas's theory of natural law is best understood in connection with his theory of human action. He emphasizes the fact that in Aquinas's writings one finds the following statement: 'Moral actions and human actions are the same' (*Summa Theologiae*, I-II, q. 1 a. 3).

McInerny, moreover, is a staunch advocate of the position suggesting that Aquinas is quite Aristotelian in his philosophical work, especially the moral theory. McInerny is very critical of the position held by R. A. Gauthier that Aquinas's reflections on Aristotle's ethical treatises import a theological dimension missing in the original. In 'Aristotle and Thomas: Père Gauthier', McInerny argues that Aquinas does not misuse or miscarry Aristotle's moral thesis. The point of this rebuttal, centring on the role of 'ultimate end', will be discussed in Chapter 5.

In his *A First Glance of St. Thomas Aquinas* (1990), McInerny considers the conceptual differences between what he calls 'modernity' and the philosophical assumptions characteristic of Aristotelian and Aquinian philosophy. Like MacIntyre and Veatch, McInerny discusses the fundamental differences in metaphilosophical presuppositions between modern philosophy — especially Descartes — and Aquinas. These metaphilosophical differences will be referred to frequently as this book unfolds. Briefly, Descartes begins with an epistemological method. He stresses the role clear and distinct ideas have on the nature of the philosophical inquiry. The result of this beginning determines his foundational analysis. Aristotle and Aquinas, on the other hand, begin with a metaphysical method; their epistemology is built upon their metaphysics. Descartes proceeds in the opposite direction. Considering the method of exposition and argument in Descartes's *Meditations on First Philosophy*, it is the case that Descartes builds his ontological schema of the external world from an epistemological beginning point. Later chapters in this book will consider these metaphilosophical differences in some detail. This argument separates in a radical way many Greek and medieval philosophers from their counterparts in early modern philosophy.

McInerny's writings elucidating Aquinas's moral theory and his creative responses to objections common to analytic philosophy have helped put the work of Aquinas on the desks of many contemporary students of moral theory. Furthermore, McInerny has been a constant critic of the Grisez/Finnis position on practical reason and natural law. His criticism of this revisionist natural law theory has appeared in the *American Journal of Jurisprudence*, among other places.

Martha Craven Nussbaum: Reconsidering Practical Reason

The work of Martha Nussbaum on Aristotelian concepts, especially in the area of reconstructing practical reason, has had an important influence on Aristotelian studies. Her extended analysis of *phronesis* in *Love's Knowledge* (1990) utilizes both her studies in Greek philosophy and her recent work in literary criticism. An earlier work, *The Fragility of Goodness* (1986), discusses her revisionist views of Aristotelian moral theory. Her recent work, especially her essay, 'Non-Relative Virtues' in her edited book, *The Quality of Life* (1993), suggests how Aristotle's moral theory is important for offering creative options for contemporary political issues.

While her interpretations of Aristotelian moral concepts have not been universally accepted, none the less her continued enthusiastic Aristotelian commentaries have contributed to the renewed interest in Aristotelian moral theory. Like MacIntyre and Veatch, Nussbaum appears to be concerned that Kantian moral theory does not begin to approach the theoretical sophistication needed for a successful analysis of moral issues. Nussbaum suggests that rethinking Aristotelian concepts can assist our contemporary moral quandaries on both a theoretical and a practical level. Nussbaum's writings have been influential in helping contemporary students rediscover the insights on 'the kinds of lives we should live' which are found in Aristotelian moral theory. Her work on practical reasoning in Aristotle creatively involves the absorption of literary insights, especially from the writings of Henry James. Nussbaum suggests that literary imagination helps one develop moral insight. But this moral insight is dependent on Aristotelian practical reason rather than on Kantian formalism or rule utilitarianism.

In *Love's Knowledge*, Nussbaum argues that Aristotelian moral theory with its attention directed towards particularity, the noncommensurability of goods, and the role of the emotions in moral decision contributes to the development of a sound theory of moral judgement. She suggests that Kantian formalism based on the categorical imperative removes particularity, non-commensurability, and the emotions from moral decision-making. Aristotle's practical reason focuses attention on the particular nature of moral judgement. Aristotelian moral theory — and Aquinas's theory also — indicates that there are as many goods as there are ends; thus, the goods are non-commensurable. Nussbaum argues that Aristotle allows more play for the emotions in moral decision-making than the Kantian categorical imperative would ever permit.

Nussbaum suggests that literary works, in particular Henry James's *The Golden Bowl*, provide a necessary imaginative contribution which assists moral agents in rendering appropriate judgements. Nussbaum is concerned that the Kantian and utilitarian moral theories are directed centrally towards rule-based moral concepts. This rule-directedness deprives moral theory of some fundamentally sound Aristotelian concepts. Nussbaum argues that the Aristotelian question, 'What kind of life should human beings live?', is the proper beginning point for significant moral theory. Kantian and utilitarian theories miss this fundamentally important question.

In criticizing Nussbaum's account, Hilary Putnam once suggested that Nussbaum's analysis in effect destroyed moral theory. Putnam argued that Nussbaum's revision of Aristotle produced a moral theory whose dependence on rules was so tenuous that it eventually descended to what Putnam called 'Situationist Ethics'. Putnam also worried that Nussbaum's revision of Aristotle removed the central element of obligation from moral theory. This Kantian concept of obligation was replaced, Putnam suggested, by a theory of value alone.

Nussbaum has responded to Putnam by suggesting that her account of Aristotelian moral theory does have a place for moral rules. In a forthcoming article, Nussbaum offers a promissory note that she will treat the foundations of Aristotelian moral theory. One might argue, as Chapter 4 below does, that moral rules are developed from the fundamental concept of human nature central to Aristotle's moral psychology. Given this metaphysical underpinning, Nussbaum might be able to respond to Putnam's criticism. It is unclear how much ontology Nussbaum would accept as a necessary condition for Aristotelian normative ethics.

None the less, Nussbaum's work in reconstructing Aristotelian moral theory within the confines both of analytic philosophy and literary criticism has contributed much to making Aristotle's works accessible to contemporary readers. Her excitement about Aristotelian themes is readily apparent in her many writings. She recently wrote the following about her work with the Aristotelian texts: 'Now the fact that Aristotle believed something does not make it true (though I have sometimes been accused of holding that position!). But it does, on the whole, make that something a plausible *candidate* for the truth, one deserving our most serious scrutiny.'[34]

Paul Sigmund: Political Science and Natural Law Theory

From the area of political science, Princeton University's Paul Sigmund has helped make the natural law theory of Aquinas understandable and useful for contemporary political scientists. His recently published *St. Thomas Aquinas on Politics and Ethics* is an impressive collection of natural law materials. In addition to articulating Aquinas's account of natural law in the context of Western political science, Sigmund has undertaken interesting work indicating the connections between Latin American political philosophy and natural law. In many religious quarters, Aquinas's theory is considered to be in direct opposition to the prevalent 'liberation theology' theory common to Latin American theologians. While Sigmund does not diminish the differences between Aquinas's work and liberation theologians, none the less he has found significant writings in the philosophy, theology, and political theory of Latin America which have used classical natural law insights to offer proposals for some of the severe social and political problems in that area of the globe.

In discussing Aquinas's role in Western philosophy, Sigmund suggests that 'behind the sometimes awkward scholastic format, Aquinas's thought is, on the whole, lucid, logical, and accessible'.[35] Through the writings of Sigmund, Aquinas's thought is known more widely in political science. Sigmund once wrote that 'it would be unfortunate if Thomistic thought no longer gave rise to new social and political formulations'. In his 'Thomistic Natural Law and Social Theory', Sigmund writes the following about Aquinas's appropriation of Aristotelian concepts in the development of his theory of natural law:

In this description of the natural law Aquinas takes a number of Aristotelian concepts and combines them in a way which is different from the way that Aristotle himself used them. Whether or not he was faithful to the spirit of Aristotle may be argued, but a comparison of Aquinas's discussion of natural law with the relevant passages in Aristotle's *Nicomachean Ethics* and *Politics*

---

[34] Martha Nussbaum, 'Non-Relative Virtues', in Martha Nussbaum and Amartya Sen (eds.) *The Quality of Life* (Oxford: Clarendon Press, 1993), 244.
[35] Sigmund, *Aquinas on Politics and Ethics*, p. xiii.

reveals that Aquinas has combined quite disparate elements in Aristotle – the phronesis of the *Ethics*, the description of final causality in the *Physics*, its ethico-political application in the discussions of government, slavery, property, and usury in Book 1 of the *Politics*, the ambiguous treatment of natural justice in Book 5 of the *Politics* – into a new synthesis that makes the determination of natural ends a central consideration in the development of Aquinas's theory of natural law.[36]

Sigmund's work elucidating the Aquinian texts has assisted the general understanding of natural law's relation to concepts central to political science. In his essay, 'Law and Politics', which appears in the recently published *Cambridge Companion to Aquinas*, Sigmund writes the following about Aquinas and natural law theory:

Aquinas's political and legal theory is important [because] ... it reasserts the value of politics by drawing on Aristotle to argue that politics and political life are morally positive activities that are in accordance with the intention of God for man ... (I)t develops an integrated and logically coherent theory of natural law that continues to be an important source of legal, political, and moral norms. These accomplishments have become part of the intellectual patrimony of the West, and have inspired political and legal philosophers and religious and social movements down to the present day.[37]

Summary of Meta-Ethical Naturalism

The purpose of this chapter has been to indicate, however briefly, the various avenues by which the natural law theory of Thomas Aquinas, rooted in Aristotle's *Nicomachean Ethics*, has become important in recent moral and legal theory scholarship. From the areas of both jurisprudence and meta-ethics, the texts of Aristotle and Aquinas, and the concepts and arguments articulated in these texts, have been approached with a new vigour. At times, the legal and moral studies of issues related to natural law have been concurrent but separate developments. In other words, there has not been substantive interaction at the conceptual level between the philosophers

[36] Paul E. Sigmund, 'Thomistic Natural Law and Social Theory', in *Calgary Aquinas Studies*, ed. Anthony Parel (Toronto: Pontifical Institute of Mediaeval Studies, 1978), 69.
[37] Paul E. Sigmund, 'Law and Politics', in Norman Kretzmann and Eleonore Stump (eds.), *The Cambridge Companion to Aquinas* (New York: Cambridge University Press, 1993), 217. This anthology also contains an essay by Ralph McInerny entitled 'Ethics', 196ff.

of law on the one hand and those interested in virtue ethics and Aristotelian and Aquinian naturalism on the other. The works of Finnis and Veatch are notable exceptions. Furthermore, the requirements for natural law, as suggested in many of the texts considered above, appear less than clear.

One purpose of this book, therefore, is to treat Aquinas's natural law theory with an eye towards both meta-ethics and jurisprudence. Since Aquinas is being used in both areas, it seems appropriate to develop an analytic interpretation of the natural law canon capable of being used both in meta-ethics and in the philosophy of law. The goal and structure of this book is to address that need. In addition, this book will articulate the set of necessary and sufficient conditions for natural law as used in the texts of Aquinas. This will, at the very least, provide a philosophical bench-mark which will be useful in comparing and contrasting various versions of natural law theory.

This method of proceeding is consonant with the systematic work of Thomas Aquinas himself. In the *Summa Theologiae* and in his *Commentary on the Nicomachean Ethics*, Aquinas does not separate his legal and moral inquiries. Rather, his moral theory — on which his legal theory depends — is developed from his metaphysical analysis of the human person. Hence, Aquinas's moral theory is a second order philosophical inquiry, grounded on the development of a dispositional view of the human essence. This is a second order inquiry because it follows upon an analysis of the ontological theory of human essence or human nature. Without the metaphysical theory of the human person — the philosophical anthropology — it would be impossible to articulate the demands of the moral theory. Therefore, in Aquinas, both the normative ethical theory and the meta-ethical theory depend upon a prior account of human nature. These concepts, of course, cry out for a thorough analysis, which analysis will occur in Chapter 4 and often throughout the remainder of the book.

3

Beyond the Naturalistic Fallacy: The Rediscovery of Aquinas

THAT natural law theory should rise like a phoenix from the ashes of the cache of criticisms put forward in the first half of the twentieth century is still a surprise to many English speaking philosophers and legal theorists. This chapter is a general attempt to undertake an explication of the structural history of philosophy on moral theory in analytic philosophy. To understand the recent emphasis in Aquinas's natural law ethic of self-actualization, which goes hand in hand with the renewed interest in Aristotelian 'eudaimonism', one needs to grasp the development of meta-ethical discussions in the twentieth century. In the light of the work in meta-ethics from G. E. Moore's *Principia Ethica* (1903) until the present, serious discussion of any form of ethical naturalism was removed theoretically from the analytic tradition of English-language philosophy. The general paradigm within which ethical theories were discussed was characterized by dominant anti-naturalism. Understanding the structure of these anti-naturalist theories in twentieth-century meta-ethics and seeing the objections against these theories helps prepare the way for discussing the re-emergence of natural law ethics and jurisprudence. In particular, these considerations lead to a better understanding of both the arguments recent naturalists in the Aristotelian/Aquinian tradition have constructed and developed and the thrust of the responses made to objections to ethical naturalism common in analytic philosophy. In the end, natural law ethics is based on a consideration of human nature itself and not on the construction or requirements of ethical language.

This chapter begins with a discussion of Hume's arguments on the fact/value distinction. It proceeds to Moore's use of Hume's distinction by means of the naturalistic fallacy argument and the intuitionist theory Moore developed in *Principia Ethica*. The emotivist response to intuitionism becomes important with its corresponding denial of any cognitive basis for moral judgements. Emotivism brings about the significant separation between fact and value. Given the separation of value from fact, any natural law theory is judged to be incomprehensible. Existentialism, with its emphasis on subjectivity and commitment alone, also dismissed naturalism for moral theory. Naturalism was ruled out of the discussions for twentieth-century meta-ethics. But emotivism was challenged by the 'good-reasons' approach to moral reasoning. The question emerged over what counts as a 'good reason' in moral decision-making. One possibility for justifying a 'good reason' is through an appeal to natural law with its requirements for meeting the needs of the human person. This chapter ends with a consideration of the kinds of questions natural law theory might respond to in working out a consistent ethical naturalism. This inquiry is a part of the recent attempt by moral philosophers to transcend the limits of what Alasdair MacIntyre calls 'the enlightenment project' in moral theory. This response to Enlightenment theory is postmodern, but not a part of deconstructionism. It is postmodern, but with a relation of dependence on Aristotle in metaphysics.

TWENTIETH-CENTURY ANTI-NATURALISM
THE SHADOW OF KANT

To understand the anti-naturalism characteristic of twentieth-century meta-ethics, it is important to recall that from the time of Hume, the fact/value dichotomy has been accepted as nearly axiomatic in English-language philosophy. The Humean influence has been directive in determining the limits of analytic meta-ethics. Hume was concerned, of course, with the logical structure of the argument. Is it possible, Hume wrote, to derive an 'Ought' from an 'Is'? Hume responded energetically in the negative. The Humean arguments, both in epistemology and meta-ethics, greatly influenced Kant. *The Critique of Practical Reason* and the *Fundamental Principles of the Metaphysics of Morals*, in many ways, can be read as theoretical attempts to provide an account of obligation without falling prey to the Humean argument. Kant thought that he placed 'obligation' in a realm of its own, independent of any derivation from factual claims.

Ethics becomes an autonomous discipline, devoid and separated from any factual referent. In other words, Kant's theory concludes with two claims, which have determined much of twentieth-century meta-ethics: (1) naturalism cannot serve as the basis for ethical judgements; (2) 'obligation' is independent conceptually from any factual statement. G. E. Moore's intuitionism, which will be considered shortly, is a direct outgrowth of these two propositions.

Interestingly enough, in the second half of the nineteenth century, the British utilitarians derived a meta-ethic which went beyond the limits for ethical discourse and judgement set by Kant. Bentham, Mill, and Sidgwick, among others, argued for a naturalism based upon the production of the greatest amount of pleasure for the greatest number of persons. This hedonistic meta-ethic was congruent, so the utilitarians thought, with the scientific advances made in the mid-nineteenth century. Given the utilitarian account, therefore, 'good' was defined in terms of 'pleasure produced' for the greatest number of persons. In many ways, as MacIntyre has suggested, utilitarianism developed within the context of British empiricism. The ideology of scientism was prevalent in nineteenth century British intellectual circles. The presuppositions of a radical empiricism central to scientism pervaded Mill's thought as well. In developing a social theory based on utilitarian principles, it was assumed that the instances of pleasure could be calculated and measured scientifically and empirically. The influence of Auguste Comte was important in several ways. This scientific methodology determined the limits of utilitarianism as developed by Mill. Given this background, Mill's utilitarian theory can be classified, using the categories of contemporary philosophy, as a cognitivist/definist position. 'Definism' means that an ethical term is capable of being defined; 'cognitivism' means that ethical terms refer to entities in the world. Mill's naturalism based upon 'pleasure' was reducible to a cognitive fact in the world, scientifically measurable — at least in principle. 'Goodness' itself was defined in terms of pleasure produced. Hence, utilitarianism falls into the cognitivist/definist category as used in contemporary meta-ethics.

G. E. Moore and Intuitionism

In writing the *Principia Ethica* in 1903, Moore was concerned that utilitarianism, especially as developed by Mill, rested upon a logical mistake. In many ways, Moore appears to have been influenced by

Kant. While not a Kantian, none the less Moore regarded the ethical term of 'good' as belonging to a non-reductionist category totally independent from naturalist properties. As non-reductive, 'good', as a moral term, was indefinable. Hence, moral language using 'good' was *sui generis*, incapable of being reduced to any piece of language referring to a natural fact. Moore is as insistent as Kant that moral properties are not based upon natural facts in the world. In offering a critique of Mill's utilitarianism, Moore suggests that Mill committed the naturalistic fallacy. This becomes Moore's method rejecting all forms of naturalism in ethics. Moore argued that any attempt to derive a moral property from a natural property embarks upon a logical fallacy. Offering an objection similar to Hume's worries about value issues, Moore suggests that Mill derived a value statement from factual considerations. Moore argues against any form of naturalism by suggesting that naturalism entails committing the naturalistic fallacy.

The naturalistic fallacy is set up, Moore suggests, through use of his famous 'open question argument'. In spelling out his open question argument, Moore brings to our attention the logical character of the term 'good'. This term cannot be definable, Moore argues, by any natural property. Moore adopted the particularist view of simples in his ontology. He argued that for any correct and adequate definition – which is an analytic statement – it is impossible to ask a significant question about whether the definiens is contained in the definiendum. For example, if a 'bachelor is an unmarried person', then if 'Joe is a bachelor', it does not make sense linguistically or conceptually to ask if indeed Joe is married. Of course, Moore's analysis of definition antedates any of the worries Quine raised later in analytic philosophy about the nature of definition and the analytic/ synthetic distinction.

With value statements indicating a definition of a value term with a natural property, however, Moore argues that such an identification of meaning – a strictly analytic connection – never occurs. It is impossible to connect a value term with a natural property analytically. Mill, however, attempted to do just that. Mill suggests that 'good is definable in terms of pleasure'. Moore counters by using the open question argument. He argues that it always makes theoretical sense to ask if a particular instance of pleasure is indeed 'good'. If the statement, 'Pleasure is good', is an analytic statement – which all definitions must be – the open question argument cannot be raised. It does not make sense to ask if Joe is a bachelor, if he is married. That a bachelor is unmarried is not 'open' to the open question argument. But, Moore argues, every value statement falls prey to the open question argument. No matter how a moral property is defined in terms of a natural property, it always makes sense to ask whether the natural property can be ascribed with the moral term. Using Mill's example, it is always possible to ask if a particular instance of 'pleasure' is indeed 'good'. Hence, the relation between 'good' and 'pleasure' cannot be analytic, which all correct definitions must be. 'Good' is not related to 'pleasure' in the same way 'unmarried' is related to 'bachelor'.

A consequence of Moore's open question argument is that any purported naturalist definition of an ethical term is subject to the conditions of this linguistic device. Moore believed he had established conclusively that no definition of a moral term using natural properties can be analytic. It follows, so Moore argued, that it is impossible to have a naturalist ethics. Moore thinks his 'open question' argument entails the conclusion that all forms of naturalism rest on a fundamental conceptual mistake. Because natural law moral theory is based, at least in a minimal fashion, on some natural property or other of a human person, natural law theory too, in the eyes of Moore and his followers in analytic philosophy, falls prey to the open question argument and the naturalistic fallacy. Moore's argument that any form of naturalism is flawed conceptually because of the naturalistic fallacy ruled out natural law ethics from serious consideration in analytic meta-ethics. As a form of naturalism, natural law theory was consigned to the dustbin of refuted philosophical theories. More than anything else in twentieth-century ethical theory, Moore's naturalistic fallacy rendered natural law theory suspect in contemporary English-speaking philosophy.

Moore's own constructive development of meta-ethics evolved into his famous theory of intuitionism. Put simply, his argument for intuitionism saved the independent character of ethical discourse while providing a non-natural basis in reality for ethical judgements. To understand intuitionism requires a glimpse into Moore's ontology, especially his ontology of simple properties. Moore assumed an ontology of simple qualities. Some simple qualities were natural (e.g. red, blue, etc.) while other simple properties were non-natural (e.g. good). Using a reference theory of meaning and a correspondence theory of truth, Moore argues that the statement, 'X is red', is true because the percept 'red' in some fashion corresponds to the 'simple, natural property' of red. In a similar fashion, the statement 'X is good', is true because the concept 'good' refers to the 'simple, non-natural property of good'. Like Bertrand Russell in *Essays on Logical Atomism*, Moore's adoption of a reference theory of meaning and a correspondence theory of truth entails the existence of simple properties. Moore, however, asserts the existence of both natural and non-natural simple properties.

The natural and non-natural properties as simples are never coextensive or conceptually dependent. Each is a distinct ontological category. With this ontology of simples, Moore thus postulates an ontological foundation for statements like 'X is good'. None the less, this foundation is in a non-naturalist realm. There is an ontological foundation for moral properties. But this foundation is non-natural. It is not based on natural properties in any way known through empirical means or method. In his meta-ethical theory, Moore is an anti-naturalist to the core. But he does, however, have an ontological foundation for moral properties. Using contemporary philosophical categories, Moore's theory is a 'non-definist/cognitivist' position. 'Non-definist' indicates that a moral property is incapable of being defined, and 'cognitivist' indicates that moral properties do have an ontological foundation. It is also a 'non-naturalist/cognitivist' position. Good is an indefinable, simple, non-natural property. Yet good does exist as a simple property. Therefore, the theory is cognitivist, but non-naturalist and non-definist.

An epistemological issue comes to the forefront immediately when considering Moore's theory of non-naturalism. Given a non-natural ontological realm, one immediately asks how this non-natural property of 'good' is known? How do we know a non-natural property? Moore responds that moral knowledge of the 'good' is obtained through 'intuition'. 'Good' is the object of an intuitive act of 'direct acquaintance'. While one might worry theoretically about the epistemological status of this intentional intuition necessary for knowing moral properties, none the less it does keep Moore's theory solidly in the non-naturalist camp. Moore appears to have worried less about the epistemological status of intuition than he did about the problems with utilitarian naturalism.

Put differently, Moore's ontology is such that there exist simple properties, some natural and some non-natural. Because of the 'open question argument', Moore argues that simple, moral properties cannot be in the category of naturalist properties. Both natural and non-natural properties are *sui generis*. Good, as a moral property, cannot be defined analytically by a reference to a natural property. Hence, 'good', because of the reference theory of meaning, the correspondence theory of truth, and the open question argument, remains in its distinct realm. The fact/value dichotomy is maintained and no 'ought' is derived from a naturalistic 'is'. Moral theory remains autonomous. But Moore was forced into accepting two claims which would cause concern later in analytic meta-ethics: (1) the existence of an ontological category of non-natural properties; and (2) the existence of a mental act of direct acquaintance which Moore referred to as 'intuition'. The act of intuition is directly aware of simple, non-natural properties.

This view of non-naturalism in meta-ethical theory greatly influenced the course of twentieth century analytic philosophy. In many ways, Moore's insistence on the non-naturalistic character of moral properties kept the Aristotelian and Aquinian theories at bay theoretically for much of the twentieth century. The established paradigm for understanding meta-ethical study was one unfavourable to any version of naturalism. Moore's arguments elucidating the naturalistic fallacy and the open question argument became entrenched principles around which much twentieth century meta-ethics was undertaken. With the arena of ethical discourse and argument so defined, Aristotelian and Aquinian eudaimonistic theories based on the natural development of human essence were removed from mainstream meta-ethical discussions. Because Aristotle and Aquinas were assumed to have committed the naturalistic fallacy, neither the *Nicomachean Ethics* nor the natural law passages in the *Summa Theologiae* were read as having anything to say to contemporary studies of moral theory.

The Development of Non-Cognitivist Meta-Ethics

The epistemological concerns which arose over the intuitionist epistemology of Moore together with the advent of the verification theory of meaning of the logical positivists produced a radically different view of ethical discourse. Moore's intuitionism required two assumptions: (1) the existence of non-natural properties; (2) the direct acquaintance of these non-natural properties through the act of intuitive awareness. The first claim entails the existence of some rather strange metaphysical entities. The second claim demands the

acceptance of a non-empirical epistemological act of direct acquaintance. The logical positivists, with the verification theory of meaning,
criticized both claims. For a statement to be meaningful, it had to
be verifiable. But this only happened through the use of direct sense
observation. This criterion of meaning rooted in sensible verification
refuted the existence of non-empirical metaphysical properties. The
positivists adopted the position that only empirical, factual knowledge was verifiable, and thus meaningful. Therefore, non-natural
properties, as non-verifiable, could not be expressed in meaningful,
significant language. Hence, claims about non-natural properties
were rendered meaningless.

The verification theory of meaning put forward by the logical
positivists eliminated Moore's cognitivist non-definist theory from
theoretical significance. But the positivists did accept Moore's point
that ethical language did not refer to facts in the empirical world.
In other words, value statements are not empirically verifiable. From
this claim evolved what came to be known as 'non-cognitivism' in
analytic ethical theory.

Various aspects of non-cognitivism dominated meta-ethical discussion during the middle part of the twentieth century. While it is
not the purpose here to develop in detail an account of non-
cognitivist meta-ethics, none the less it is important to realize how
much this way of considering ethical discourse hindered a serious
consideration of Aristotelian and Aquinian ethical analysis. The presuppositions of non-cognitivism removed conceptually the possibility of Aristotelian naturalism from consideration. A naturalist theory
must, by definition, be a cognitivist theory. This is more obvious
when one considers that natural law meta-ethics makes sense only
through reference to facts about human nature. Hence, what is
removed from consideration as theoretically possible becomes only
of historical interest. Aristotle and Aquinas were read primarily as
illustrations of outmoded ethical naturalism. Ethical naturalism had
been rejected, first of all, because of the efficacy of Moore's naturalistic fallacy arguments, and secondly, through the development of
non-cognitivism by the logical positivists.

Briefly put, non-cognitivist ethical theory, which became commonly known as 'emotivism', argued that ethical language lacked
any referential status for an ontological foundation, either natural
or non-natural. Various forms of non-cognitivism were espoused
by different philosophers during the middle part of the twentieth

century. None the less, all these theories denied the connection between ethical language and ontological referent. With no referent, the emphasis was directed towards the 'feelings' or 'emotions' present in an agent when in a moral situation. Moral language was neither representative nor descriptive in character. Lacking any referent, moral language was defined in terms of the emotions evoked, a command given, or a recommendation proposed. For example, A.J. Ayer argued that moral statements are nothing more than expressions of emotions. Rudolph Carnap once suggested that ethical judgements are commands. In his *Ethics and Language*, C. L. Stevenson proposed that the function of moral language expresses the speaker's attitude as well as evoking similar attitudes in others.

These early emotivist positions elicited a tendency towards the non-rational. This non-rational emphasis is indicated clearly in the following text from an early analytic philosopher, W. H. F. Barnes: 'value judgments in their origin are not strictly judgments at all . . . They are exclamations expressive of approval.'[1] Emotivism is the most radical non-cognitivist meta-ethical theory proposed in twentieth century ethical writing. Proposing a thorough analysis of moral language, non-cognitivist inquiries were examples of philosophy of language at its most direct.

Without any foundation as the ontological 'glue' or referent for ethical language, it follows that every form of naturalism is removed conceptually from consideration. A non-cognitivist, in the categories of contemporary meta-ethical theory, is a 'definist'. Moral language is defined in terms of non-factual referents evoking feelings, expressing emotions, articulating commands, or urging acknowledgements of approval. Non-cognitivism rules out theoretically any descriptive content for ethical language. Because the content of natural law theory is based upon some form of a descriptive analysis of human nature, natural law theory is rejected by non-cognitivism.

Thus, the twin swords of Moorean non-naturalistic intuitionism and linguistic non-cognitivism rendered Aristotelian naturalism unfit theoretically for meta-ethical discussion. With its foundation in human nature, natural law theory is always a cognitive meta-ethical theory. Moral philosophers accepting Moore's naturalistic fallacy and philosophers accepting any form of non-cognitivism placed natural law theory in a realm beyond philosophical redemption.

---

[1] W. H. F. Barnes, 'A Suggestion about Value', *Analysis*, I (1934), 45.

The Good-Reasons Rejoinder

Following the wide acceptance of non-cognitivism, several moral philosophers became concerned about the connection between non-cognitivism and ethical relativism. Ethical relativism appeared to follow from non-cognitivism because moral language lacks a foundation. The response to these worries about relativism produced a set of theories often referred to as the 'good-reasons' approach to moral language and argument. It is not the purpose here to analyse in detail all of twentieth-century meta-ethical theory. None the less, it is important to consider those components in twentieth-century meta-ethics whose development served to make possible the reconsideration of Aristotelian naturalism. The good-reasons theories play an important role in that process. These theories began the process of asking for a rational justification for moral claims. Asking for such a justification immediately placed the inquiry beyond the non-rational limits of emotivism. This search for good reasons led to an important qualification placed on the limitations central to strict forms of non-cognitivism. One could demand reasons for choices; moral language was not limited to expressions of emotive qualities. One needed a good reason in order to use moral language in an appropriate fashion. It remained unclear, however, what constituted an adequately justified good reason.

The good-reasons approach attempted to provide a consistent and coherent rational justification for making ethical judgements. Ronald Dworkin's theory of jurisprudence is often considered as an example of the good-reasons approach. Rational justification through consistency is the central feature indicating a good reason. One of the early adherents of this method in analytic philosophy was Stephen Toulmin. In his *The Place of Reason in Ethics*, Toulmin writes:

What we want to know is in which of these [non-cognitivist] discussions the arguments presented were worthy of acceptance, and the reasons given good reasons; in which of them persuasion was achieved at least in part by valid reasoning, and in which agreement was obtained by means of mere persuasion — fine rhetoric unsupported by valid arguments or good reasons. And it is over the criteria (or rather the complete lack of criteria) given for the validity of ethical arguments that the most telling objection to this (and any) subjective (or non-cognitivist) theory arise.[2]

---

[2] Stephen Toulmin, *The Place of Reason in Ethics* (Cambridge: Cambridge University Press: 1970), 38.

Toulmin's critique of non-cognitivist meta-ethics is telling. Once good reasons were required for justification, then naturalism once again, at least in the Aristotelian sense, could be considered as theoretically possible. In other words, a good reason might be connected in some way with a natural fact; e.g., the development of the human person. A good-reasons theory does not itself entail a consideration of meta-ethical naturalism. For example, R. M. Hare's 'prescriptivism' developed in his *Freedom and Reason* is a good-reasons theory with a deliberate rejection of any naturalist justification. None the less, Hare's analysis is not coextensive with a good-reasons approach to analytic meta-ethics. Of course, the question demanding resolution is what counts as a good reason. It is at this point that the good-reasons approach is important for the consideration of the re-emerging interest in natural law theory. Naturalism might offer a set of 'good reasons' theoretically cogent and practically efficacious.

G. J. Warnock asked this question forcefully and perspicuously. In his *Contemporary Moral Philosophy*, Warnock wrote that one of the problems with rational consistency alone is that it removes existential and morally relevant content from practical reason. For example, Warnock brought forward the following problems with the good-reasons approach, especially as elucidated in the writings of R. M. Hare:

> For [Hare] is saying, not only that it is for us to decide what our moral opinions are, but also that it is for us to decide what to take as grounds for or against any moral opinion. We are not only, as it were, free to decide on the evidence, but also free to decide what evidence is. I do not, it seems, decide that flogging is wrong because I am against cruelty; rather, I decide that flogging is wrong because I decide to be against cruelty. And what, if I did make that decision, would be my ground for making it? That I am opposed to the deliberate infliction of pain? No — rather that I decide to be opposed to it. And so on.[3]

Warnock demands that a justification be given for moral decision-making other than the fact of the decision itself. This requirement which Warnock suggests as a necessary condition for moral theory is important because it leads one to propose natural law justifications. In other words, what Warnock illustrates in this passage is that in the end there needs to be a foundation for moral theory after all.

---

[3] G. J. Warnock, *Contemporary Moral Philosophy* (New York: St Martin's Press, 1967), 12–13.

Good reasons also require justification. They cannot be arbitrary expressions of whim. Warnock's analysis, for example, suggests room for something like H. L. A. Hart's 'natural necessities' or Martin Golding's 'purposive activity' based on human needs. These natural facts may provide the justification Warnock requires to meet his criticism of the good-reasons approach to ethical theory. What needs to be done now, of course, is to illustrate how naturalism can be consistent theoretically and justified ontologically for meta-ethical discourse. A consistent naturalism still needs to be developed. The goal of the next chapter, with the expressed purpose of reconstructing Aquinas's theory of natural law as a theoretically coherent and ontologically justified form of ethical naturalism, is a first step in that process. Natural law theory in Aristotle and Aquinas requires both a consistency within the theory and a justification for an ontological theory. Theoretical consistency is a necessary but not a sufficient condition for natural law theory.

An Aristotelian Rejoinder

There are at least three ways to proceed in suggesting an Aristotelian and Aquinian response to Moore's intuitionism, the emotivism of the non-cognitivists, and the good-reasons philosophers. First of all, one might hold that Aristotle and Aquinas have theories which, in many ways, can be reconstructed so that they are essentially Kantian and thus circumvent at least Moore's problems. In other words, the moral properties remain grounded in some way in a non-naturalist realm. The is/ought distinction is preserved theoretically and ethical theory remains autonomous. John Finnis and Germain Grisez often appear to treat Aristotle and Aquinas in this way. Finnis, in particular, argues against any form of reductivism in Aristotle and Aquinas. This denial of reductivism claims that moral values are not derived from human nature or from what contemporary philosophers would call a philosophical anthropology. In addition, some of Alan Donagan's work appears to make Aquinas's theory of obligation reducible to a Kantian theory of the categorical imperative.

Secondly, one might follow the suggestions of Alasdair MacIntyre, whose approach to Aquinas in *After Virtue*, while interesting theoretically and very influential in the contemporary 'recovery' of Aristotelian ethical theory, is somewhat idiosyncratic. The exact role essence plays in MacIntyre's version of Aquinian natural law is unclear. In *After Virtue*, MacIntyre rejects the relevance of what he terms Aristotle's 'metaphysical biology'. MacIntyre replaces this metaphysical biology with a cultural and historical position on what counts as 'good' in a particular society. If this analysis entails the rejection of a dispositional view of essence, then the position advocated later in this book will part company with MacIntyre's analysis. In order that a workable Aristotelian ethic might be developed in twentieth-century moral theory, MacIntyre does suggest in *After Virtue* that the metaphysical biology traditionally associated with Aristotelian ethics needs to be replaced with a more cultural and historical view of virtue ethics. In *Three Rival Versions of Moral Enquiry*, however, MacIntyre places emphasis on Aquinas's account of the philosophical psychology which he earlier rejected as out-dated 'metaphysical biology'. MacIntyre writes the following:

What the discussion of good . . . made clear was that when someone identifies a good as being the true good, that is, the end to which by virtue of his or her essential nature moves, he or she, unless hindered or directed in some way, moves towards it. So 'such and such is the good of all human beings by nature' is always a factual judgment, which when recognized as true by someone moves that person toward that good. Evaluative judgments are a species of factual judgment concerning final and formal causes of activity of members of a particular species.

The concept of good, then, has application only for beings insofar as they are members of some species or kind.[4]

These references to 'particular species' and to 'members of some species or kind' do lend a more traditional reading to MacIntyre's version of Aquinas spelled out in *Three Rival Versions of Moral Enquiry*.

Thirdly, an alternative account to both the Finnis/Grisez account and the MacIntyre position in *After Virtue* argues that Moore's theory is basically not applicable to the naturalism developed by Aristotle and Aquinas. Henry Veatch and Ralph McInerny, among others, would take this position. Moral values are derived, in some sense, from an analysis of human nature. In the next chapter, a position similar structurally to that developed by Veatch and McInerny, and quite probably the MacIntyre of *Three Rival Versions of Moral Enquiry*, will be elucidated and defended.

---

[4] Alasdair MacIntyre, *Three Rival Versions of Moral Enquiry* (Notre Dame, Ind.: University of Notre Dame Press, 1990), 134.

A Worry about Existentialism

The third alternative above suggested that natural law theory entails the development of a consistent metaphysical theory of essence. If this is the case, then another objection to natural law ethics needs to be considered, which is twentieth-century existentialism. Most existentialists, rejecting any theory of essence or essential properties in the classical sense, argue against the possibility of a natural law moral theory. If natural law depends upon the concept of an 'essence', and if one of the primary principles of existentialism is 'Existence precedes essence', then it follows that existentialism is not compatible with any moral theory demanding a role for essence. This is, of course, a general point. Particular existentialists may indeed foster some form of a theory of essence. However, if one takes seriously the aspect of existentialism that 'becoming through choice' and 'radical subjectivism' alone determine the essence of a human person without any prior moral content, then existentialism and natural law meta-ethics are opposed to one another. The denial of essence entails the denial of the possibility of natural law. Existentialists, especially Sartre and Camus, are usually seen as denying any content to an essence prior to the act of choosing by the individual. Therefore, eliminating the role of essence in one's ontology entails denying a natural law moral theory.[5]

Until recently, existentialism was the principal Continental philosophical theory prevalent in the United States. The writings of Sartre and Camus have been particularly influential. Given this prevalence of existential writing and its concern for denying the possibility of essences, existentialist thought has contributed to the general lacuna of theoretical considerations for natural law theory. A consistent existentialism denies the moral relevance of natural law ethics.

Nietzsche, it is fair to say, was the nineteenth-century harbinger of things to come in contemporary existentialism. Nietzsche asked about the very grounds of rational discourse. Of course, he denied the possibility of providing such grounds regarding major moral questions. According to Nietzsche, rational justification is impossible. With no rational justification possible, natural law meta-ethics

---

[5] For a thoughtful account of Camus's position on essential properties and how he reacted against the essentialist tradition in Western philosophy, the interested reader might consult Herbert Hochberg, 'Albert Camus and the Ethic of Absurdity', *Ethics*, 75/2 (Jan. 1965), 87–102.

becomes likewise impossible. The radical subjectivism which follows from a Nietzschean analysis entails a denial of natural law possibilities. Nietzsche's influence in the development of existentialism is not to be underestimated in considering the unfavorable environment natural law theory faced during most of the twentieth century.

In his *After Virtue*, MacIntyre considers the direct influence of existentialism on Twentieth Century moral theory. He explicitly argues that, following the demise of Enlightenment meta-ethics, only two alternatives are open to philosophers: the 'Way of Aristotle' or the 'Way of Nietzsche'. MacIntyre takes seriously the charges against reason so central to Nietzsche's existentialism. None the less, MacIntyre argues that a reconstructed version of Aristotle can justify the reintroduction of the concept of virtue and the concept of agency into Western ethical theory. This rehabilitation of contemporary meta-ethics, so MacIntyre suggests, is Aristotelian to the core. As MacIntyre notes, one must respond to the existentialist charge concerning the impossibility of rational justification and hence the claim about the impossibility of a moral theory of virtue.

Among scholastic philosophers, Étienne Gilson responded to the problems existentialism brought to bear against classical Aristotelian realism. In particular, he wrote several articles directed at what he took to be the theoretical weaknesses in both existentialism and Marxism. The thrust of Gilson's own realist philosophy, based on his reading of Aristotle and Aquinas, is central in these critiques. While Gilson's work is important and critically appropriate when considering the existentialist reaction to classical realism in Aristotle and Aquinas, it, however, had little direct influence on English-speaking philosophy.

In summary, the following characteristics of existentialism contributed to the anti-naturalism predominant in meta-ethical discussions for most of the twentieth century: (1) the absence of a role for essence in the analysis of persons; (2) the predominance of 'subjectivity' with the correlative decline in the notion of 'objectivity'; and (3) the emphasis on the role of 'decision-making' and 'commitment' devoid of rationality central to much of existentialism. All three of these characteristics entail the rejection of ethical naturalism in the Aristotelian/Aquinian tradition. Natural law moral theory requires some account of essence, demands a role of objectivity, and places moral decision-making in the context of practical reason and not the will. The 'voluntarism' central to much existentialism is foreign conceptually to moral theory based on Aristotle. In a structural sense, voluntarism is at the core of the existentialist denial of essence, the rejection of objectivity, and the emphasis on commitment. Natural law theory must take the voluntarist analysis seriously.

Late twentieth century postmodern philosophy exemplified in deconstructionism and historically determined philosophical systems tends to dismiss the foundational questions central to natural law theory. At present, there appears to be little dialectical inquiry undertaken between the deconstructionists and the natural law philosophers. However, in ruling out the possibility of metaphysics, many deconstructionists would also rule out natural law moral theory.

THE MACINTYRE REJOINDER

Alasdair MacIntyre's publications on Aristotle and Aquinas have changed the direction of American studies in meta-ethics. His *After Virtue, Whose Justice? Which Rationality?*, and *Three Rival Versions of Moral Enquiry* have brought Aristotelian and Aquinian themes in ethical naturalism back into mainstream philosophical discussion. Among analytic philosophers and existentialists, the term 'virtue ethics' is now part of generally accepted philosophical parlance. In *After Virtue*, MacIntyre argued that the failure of ethical theories based upon enlightenment principles '... is best understood as a sequel to the wrong-headed rejection, in the sixteenth and seventeenth centuries, of what I called the tradition of the virtues'.[6] MacIntyre suggests that this tradition of virtues began in the fifth-century Athenian polis and was developed into a moral theory through the theory and praxis of Socrates, Plato, and Aristotle.

In his work since *After Virtue*, MacIntyre has developed a more far-reaching Aristotelianism. In commenting upon why he now rejects the Nietzsche account, MacIntyre recently said:

A second reason for rejecting Nietzsche is an Aristotelian one. It reflects both a discovery that the narrative of my own uneven intellectual and moral development could only be both intelligibly and truthfully written in Aristotelian terms, and a recognition that in these medieval debates that reconstituted the Aristotelian tradition in Islamic, Jewish, and Christian milieus, Aristotelianism as a political and moral philosophy had both progressed by

---

[6] Giovanna Borradori, *The American Philosopher*, trans. Rosanna Crocitto (Chicago: University of Chicago Press, 1994), 148.

its own standards and withstood external criticism. It finally emerged in its Thomistic version as a more adequate account of the human good, of virtues, and of rules, than any other I have encountered.[7]

MacIntyre's recent work indicates not only his important contribution to the 'recovery' of Aristotle's moral theory in terms of 'virtue ethics', but also indicates the importance his work has given to a reconsideration of the natural law moral theory of Thomas Aquinas.

Earlier in this book, the contributions MacIntyre has made in the 'recovery' of Aristotle have been noted. While *After Virtue* elucidates an Aristotelian position in some detail, it is in his Gifford Lectures mentioned above, *Three Rival Versions of Moral Enquiry*, that MacIntyre brings about a serious reading of the texts of Aquinas on moral theory. MacIntyre calls our attention to Pope Leo XIII's exhortation for a revitalization of Aquinian studies in his encyclical, *Aeterni Patris*. The critical edition of Aquinas's texts began with Pope Leo's interest and backing. Before that time, a critical edition of the Aquinian corpus was non-existent. With its textual work beginning in the late nineteenth century, the Leonine Commission is still completing a critical edition of the entire set of texts generally ascribed as authentic works of Aquinas.

In *Three Rival Versions of Moral Enquiry*, MacIntyre considers afresh the role philosophical psychology plays in Aquinas's moral theory. This is important in the light of the analysis of Aquinas's natural law theory forthcoming in Chapter 4. MacIntyre suggests that he is now more aware of the connection between virtue ethics and the metaphysical foundation of the moral theory than he was when he wrote *After Virtue*.

In addition to the concern about philosophical psychology in Aquinas, MacIntyre calls our attention to the role of reason in matters of meta-ethics which Leo XIII assumed to be found in Aquinas. This twofold analysis of reason is important for understanding Aquinas on natural law. Aquinas's theory of reason is in opposition to the existentialist position steeped in voluntarism discussed above. Moreover, Aquinas's view of rationality is opposed to the paradigm of reason central to nineteenth-century scientism. In many ways, as noted earlier in this Chapter, the paradigm of scientism was central to the naturalism of Mill and his fellow utilitarians. Utilitarian naturalism follows from the empiricism central to scientism. MacIntyre

[7] Borradori, *The American Philosopher*, 149.

considers the differences in meta-philosophy between the naturalism of Mill and the naturalism of Aquinas. Aquinas's naturalism depends on a rationally developed ontology. Mill's utilitarian naturalism depends upon a rationally developed scientific method. These methods in undertaking philosophical analysis are different radically. One is a naturalism whose empiricism is sufficient for philosophical analysis. The other, while demanding empiricism as a necessary condition for naturalism, employs a foundationalist ontology. These metaphilosophical differences used in developing metaphysical and moral theories are not to be dismissed lightly. The way of doing philosophy which results in Aristotelian/Aquinian naturalism is distinct structurally from that used by Bentham, Mill, and Sidgwick. MacIntyre's work articulates these metaphilosophical differences with care. While both have been construed as forms of naturalism, none the less the role empiricism and nineteenth-century scientism play is radically different in each form of naturalism. At the centre will be a theory of essence which Mill's naturalism rejects and which Aquinas's naturalism endorses.

THE VEATCH CRITIQUE BEYOND CARTESIAN METAPHILOSOPHY

For the past thirty years, Henry Veatch has asked us to consider the possibilities of a reconstructed Aristotelian ethical theory. Chapter 7 discusses Veatch's analysis in some detail. None the less, it is important at this point in the discussion to consider one aspect of his critique of modern philosophy and its influence in the development of moral theory. Veatch too has a serious objection to the meta-philosophy adopted by the post-Enlightenment philosophers.

Veatch suggests that modern philosophy has been infected with what he calls the 'transcendental turn'. In effect, this means that a radical mental construct theory has been dominant in modern philosophy. Mental constructs, so the followers of the transcendental turn method tell us, are fashioned in our minds and then applied to interpreting the external world. These constructs interpret our world for us without the benefit of a 'realist' bench-mark against which to check our constructs. This eliminates any possibility of a realist foundation for knowledge. Descartes and Kant, both developing elaborate accounts of innate ideas and a priori categories, determined this modern metaphilosophy. Kant's elimination of any possibility of metaphysics beyond the unknowable noumenal realm is a classic example of what realists see as the shortcomings of the transcendental turn. Veatch in particular is quite concerned about the impossibility of a realist metaphysics which follows from Kant's a priori categories of the human mind.

This radical mental construct epistemology based on the transcendental turn method, Veatch argues, rules out the possibility of doing Aristotelian science, metaphysics, and moral theory. In other words, the transcendental turn used as a metaphilosophical principle directing philosophical inquiry denies the possibility of justifying metaphysical and moral realism. Realism is ruled out at the beginning of the inquiry. Veatch suggests that Aristotelian theory will make sense only if one goes beyond the transcendental turn. 'Mental construct meta-philosophy' must be replaced, Veatch argues, by 'realist meta-philosophy'. In Chapter 7, Veatch's arguments against this mental construct metaphilosophy will be considered in some detail. Simply put, Veatch argues that by accepting the transcendental turn, any knowledge of nature is impossible. Since nature is unknowable, it is impossible that any moral properties can be found as knowable in nature. Even if nature was knowable — i.e. one rejects the transcendental turn — none the less, analytic philosophy, following the impetus of Moore's naturalistic fallacy, would argue that moral properties cannot be found in nature. Veatch argues that in responding to this double set of problems, recent analytic philosophers have turned to an analysis of the requirements of moral language. This can be called a general inquiry into the 'logic of moral language'.

Veatch suggests next that a group of philosophers, which he calls the 'anti-theorists', have developed criticisms against both the transcendental turn and what Veatch has called the 'linguistic turn'. Veatch includes Charles Taylor, Martha Nussbaum, Bernard Williams, and Alasdair MacIntyre in this group of anti-theorists. These philosophers have effectively offered a critique of the fundamental presuppositions of Enlightenment and post-Enlightenment moral theory. MacIntyre, in particular, argues against what he has called the 'enlightenment project' in moral theory.

Veatch next suggests that with the Enlightenment project rejected, the anti-theorists should return to Aristotle's ethical naturalism. Of course, Nussbaum and MacIntyre have done this, but Veatch is unclear about the ontological commitments of either to the metaphysics necessary consistently to explicate Aristotle's ethical natural-ism. Veatch himself develops a theory of what Chapter 7 calls 'ontological foundationalism' in order to fully explicate Aristotle and Aquinas on moral theory. Veatch argues that without an ontological foundation for moral judgements, Aristotelian meta-ethics remains incomplete and theoretically unworkable. To bring Aristotelian theory into the contemporary dialectic on moral theory requires, Veatch suggests, the abandonment of the transcendental turn as a methodological principle of doing philosophy. This leads to what Chapter 7 refers to as Veatch's 'ontological foundationalism'.

THE WHITE PROPOSAL BEYOND CONSISTENCY

An earlier section of this chapter noted the good-reasons approach accepted by many modern philosophers writing in meta-ethics and jurisprudence. This approach suggests that 'rational consistency' alone serves as a sufficient condition for justifying moral and legal principles. Toulmin, Dworkin, Rawls, and Hare all exhibit good-reasons justifications in their writings. As Warnock noted above, however, the good-reasons approach lacks justification grounds beyond the decision procedure itself.

A provocative critique of the good-reasons position has been offered by John and Patricia White in their article, 'Education, Liberalism and Human Good'.[8] The Whites suggest that classical liberalism, as exemplified in many of the good-reasons philosophers, refuses to adopt a particular metaphysical theory about the nature of either the good person or goods for society. According to Dworkin, for example, a primary principle of liberal democracy is that 'the government must be neutral on what might be called the question of the good life'.[9] The Whites suggest that Dworkin's argument indicates that since people differ about what gives value to life, the government cannot favour one group's preferences over another. As the Whites put it, 'Opera must not be subsidized if dog-racing is not.'

---

[8] John and Patricia White, 'Education, Liberalism and Human Good', in David E. Cooper (ed.), *Education, Values and Mind: Essays for R. S. Peters* (London: Routledge & Kegan Paul, 1986), 149.

[9] Ronald Dworkin, 'Liberalism', in *A Matter of Principle* (Cambridge, Mass.: Harvard University Press, 1985), 191.

Dworkin articulates his position in his essay, 'Liberalism', which appears in *A Matter of Principle*:

What does it mean for the government to treat its citizens as equals? That is, I think, the same question as the question of what it means for the government to treat all of its citizens as free, or as independent, or with equal dignity. In any case, it is a question that has been central to political theory at least since Kant.

[P]olitical decisions must be, so far as is possible, independent of any particular conception of the good life, or of what gives value to life. Since the citizens of a society differ in their conceptions, the government does not treat them as equals if it prefers one conception to another, either because the officials believe that one is intrinsically superior, or because one is held by the more numerous or more powerful group.[10]

Given this account put forward by Dworkin, it is clear why his legal writing offers a 'thin' theory of good.

Dworkin is reluctant to have any ontological foundation used to ground moral judgements. Such a foundation, Dworkin suggests, would lead to limiting the freedom of choice. The process of mature reflection, not an ontological theory, is sufficient in determining the goods to be obtained. This is often called a 'thin' theory of good. Its opposite, a 'thick' theory of good, normally depends upon an ontological theory to flesh out the content of good. Dworkin, like many good-reasons philosophers, would fit into Veatch's example of a philosopher adopting the method of the transcendental turn. For Dworkin, the consistency of the argument is sufficient for accepting it. Even though Dworkin considers the moral principles of a society as basic to the justification of a legal theory, the moral principles themselves are not justified by a further appeal to anything beyond consistency.

Rawls holds a similar theory. What counts as 'the good life' on the good-reasons view of meta-ethics is the life which most satisfies one's preferences, whatever these preferences might be. In his *Theory of Justice*, Rawls gives certain conditions which must hold if preferences are to be justified. The two most important conditions are: (1) The preferences to be considered are the hierarchically ordered ends in an individual's life-plan. These ends are chosen only after a process of deliberation in the light of a full knowledge of different options and consequences of adopting them. (2) In Rawls's own

---

[10] Dworkin, 'Liberalism', 191.

words: 'Something is good only if it fits into ways of life consistent with the principles of right already on hand.'[11] Given this restriction, the Whites suggest that, according to Rawls, the 'good life' cannot include the life of a Nero or a Thrasymachus.

The 'veil of ignorance' method by which Rawls determines his list of human rights is another example of the 'good reasons' approach to moral and political methods. What one agrees to commit oneself to in the 'veil of ignorance' and about which one reasons consistently and wills coherently are the necessary conditions for determining fundamental human rights. Considering the implications of Rawls's analysis, the Whites offer the following observations connecting Rawls's suggestion of 'mature reflection' with the good-reasons approach adopted by Dworkin. They write:

If Rawls's restrictions apply to Dworkin's theory then they will both agree that Dworkin's beer-drinking TV addict or Rawls's man who has a passion for counting blades of grass in city squares may each be living the good life, provided that they have chosen these as their most important ends after mature reflection and provided that they are morally decent people.[12]

The Whites present the standard version of the good-reasons theory of justification. 'Mature reflection' undertaken by 'morally decent people' is a sufficient condition for adopting a particular life-plan or view of the good. No substantive theory of the human person and what might count as perfective of that person is necessary. Consistency alone determines validity. Hence, this is a 'thin' theory of the good. This justification procedure eliminates any possible claim that there is a universally applicable content of the good life, no matter how justified theoretically. Of course, the natural law position argues for some content necessary in making moral judgements. What Dworkin calls 'the liberal response' suggests that one cannot distinguish a metaphysical justification from one's own subjective though rationally coherent preference. It is this kind of objection which the natural law theory must treat in some detail. A natural law meta-ethics proposes some version of a 'thick theory' of human goodness based on the concept of a human person. This is opposed to the 'thin theory' adopted by good-reasons moralists such as Rawls and Dworkin.

[11] John Rawls, cited in White, 'Education, Liberalism and Human Good'.
[12] Ibid. 149.

A radical illustration of the lack of content in the good-reasons approach is Hare's example, in *Freedom and Reason*, of the 'moral fanatic'. According to Hare, if any person, including the moral fanatic, wills universally and thus consistently, then the person follows the good-reasons methodology. The moral fanatic is a person who holds an immoral position and undertakes immoral actions and who can, by using Hare's rational method, justify this action. Following Kant, Hare demands that a person, to act morally, must will the action consistently. This demands universalizability. To be consistent requires, Hare suggests, role reversibility. The moral agent must put himself or herself in the shoes of the other person. The similarity with the golden rule is apparent. For example, consider the case of a person adopting the principles of race supremacy. If the race supremacist were to will consistently and universally, then, if the circumstances were reversible, the race supremacist would become the object of bigotry, hatred, oppression, and discrimination. None the less, what if in willing universally, the race supremacist accepted the fact that the bigoted ideology of race supremacy should prevail — even if it meant that the very race supremacist should suffer the cruelties of the victim? This would meet, it seems, the standards of Hare's rational consistency. In other words, if the principles of the race supremacy were willed consistently — which includes the process of role reversal following universalizability — then this consistent willing satisfies Hare's good-reasons theory. Put differently, the role reversal demanded by universalizability is met. The race supremacist is willing to suffer the results of the theory of race supremacy. Hare remarks that it is fortunate that there are few moral fanatics around in our daily world. This example indicates, however, the lack of content in Hare's good-reasons approach to ethical theory. This would be an example of a 'thin' theory of good.

In many respects, what the Whites have suggested is similar structurally to the criticisms Henry Veatch proposed against the moral philosophers subscribing to the Enlightenment project. The good reasons philosophers depend upon the logical structure of moral language and the consistency of moral arguments. The arguments against Hare's moral fanatic, for instance, depend on something more than 'logic' and 'consistency' alone. The structural analysis of the development of recent analytic moral theory has prepared the way, as it were, for a reconsideration of ethical naturalism in general and the natural law theory of Aristotle and Aquinas in particular.

By way of a brief summary, the analysis of the structural development of analytic moral theories undertaken so far in this chapter suggests several important things. Moore's naturalistic fallacy argument, which ruled out naturalism in meta-ethics, is based on a unique account of Moore's ontology of simple properties. None the less, Moore's intuitionism, as developed in response to his critique of naturalism, in turn was rejected by the logical positivists with their verification theory of meaning. This refutation of cognitivist theory in meta-ethics produced the various forms of non-cognitivist emotivism. Emotivism, however, because it was missing any rational foundation for moral judgements, soon succumbed to the charges of irrationalism. With its denial of 'objectivity' and its emphasis on 'subjectivity' and 'commitment', existentialism too falls into the bailiwick of irrationalism. The response to this devastating critique of irrationalism was the advent of the good-reasons theory of justification. This theory looked upon the conditions of linguistic theory, the nature of moral language, and the nature of theory construction itself as sufficient to account for a rationally justified moral theory. Consistency and coherence in the theory were necessary for a moral theory. Yet the nature of what counts as a good reason was brought forward by Warnock, in particular. Moreover, Veatch and the Whites suggest that the thin theory of good elucidated by Hare, Rawls, and Dworkin, among others, eliminates any justification beyond the limits of the theory's consistency. The good-reasons theory would not be a final recourse for moral arguments after all.

What is important here for the discussion of the resurgence of natural law theory in the late twentieth century is to consider what follows consistently from this analysis. One kind of justification for a good reason would be the appeal to the 'natural necessities' which make up human nature. This brings in the possibility of undertaking natural law theory to provide a set of good reasons which are justified beyond the coherence and consistency of the theory itself. Natural law theory articulates what counts as an ontological foundation for moral theory. This ontological foundation, through a theory of essence central to the concept of human nature, suggests a way to develop a 'thick' theory of good beyond the limits of the 'thin' theory common to the good reasons philosophers. This is the direction to which the structural analysis of analytic moral theories points.

COLUMBA RYAN AND THE POSSIBILITY OF LAW

Columba Ryan's analysis of Aquinas's theory of natural law provides a useful bridge going from the questions Warnock, Veatch, and the Whites raised about the good-reasons theory to an account of human nature as the foundation for the possibility of justified moral and legal theory. The possibility for justified normative claims is central to his argument.

Following the work of legal scholars attempting to justify some concept of 'norm' for law in response to the Nuremberg trials, writers familiar with the work of Aquinas proposed that natural law be treated as a concept bringing about the 'possibility of law'. In his fascinating analysis, 'The Traditional Concept of Natural Law: An Interpretation',[13] Ryan offers such a proposal. He writes:

the very possibility of any law being referred to any criterion, even within a legal system, implies that there is, within the legal system, a structure which makes possible critical scrutiny. Or, more simply, the calling in question of the obligatory character of any given law raises the whole problem of the obligatory character of law, and this obligatory character within a legal system constitutes the kernel of the concept of natural law.

Ryan goes on with his account:

in speaking of natural law as a 'law' we should think of it not as lying alongside of, and somehow superior to, all other laws, but as that which is at the heart of, and constitutes the possibility, indeed the obligatory character, of every other law. In other words when we are speaking of natural law, we are in the field of ethics or morality rather than in that of legality in a narrow sense.

Ryan notes that the theory of natural law as proposed by Aquinas is a 'theory of what makes laws laws, not an easy substitute for making laws, for legislating'. Ryan brings our attention to the claim that natural law is not an item in the 'hearts of human beings', in 'the mind of God', or wherever. Rather, natural law is a philosophical concept providing a response to the question of what makes laws possible at all. In other words, natural law is not a method for making laws. It is the ontological foundation in human nature which explains the possibility of a moral theory and of lawmaking in the first place.

[13] Columba Ryan, OP, 'The Traditional Concept of Natural Law: An Interpretation', in Illtud Evans, OP (ed.), *Light on the Natural Law* (Baltimore: Helicon Press Inc., 1965), 13–35.

The issue Ryan raises is a modified Kantian question. Ryan asks about what is necessary theoretically in order to make some X possible. The analysis offered as a response, however, is not a Kantian response. It is an Aristotelian response grounded in a theory of human nature. In the next chapter, the systematic analysis begins by suggesting how Aquinas offers a theory of natural law which provides both for the possibility of moral theory and for the possibility of law. That there is a connection between a moral theory and a legal theory should not be surprising. In Aquinas's system, a justified legal theory is only justified in so far as it is derived – in some sense of 'derived' as yet unexplicated – from the moral system. Aquinas outrightly denies the claim of Austin that 'law is one thing – its merit or demerit another'. There is a necessary connection between the demands of a moral theory and the requirements for justified lawmaking.

Ryan's suggestion considering natural law as a philosophical theory explicating the condition for the 'possibility' of law is a fruitful way to approach Aquinas's concept of natural law. This manner of considering natural law in Aquinas helps one move around some of the more quickly articulated objections to natural law – i.e. 'It's not helpful in lawmaking;' 'It's vague;' 'It's too general;' 'It's unworkable.' What Ryan suggests is that any metaphysical foundation is general, theoretical, and responds to basic questions about presuppositions. To expect more is like expecting a philosopher of science to undertake laboratory experiments rather than consider the basic concepts foundational to the scientific enterprise. Natural law meta-ethics is a foundational inquiry – an inquiry to the core of what makes moral judgements and justified laws possible. That this inquiry demands an ontological commitment to realist foundation theory will become apparent as this discussion develops.

It is in adopting and explicating this 'possibility' proposal offered by Ryan that the process begins, in the next chapter, of elucidating an analysis of Aquinas's theory of natural law.

4

Aquinas's Theory of Natural Law:
A Reconstruction

IT is always a challenge to render significant the issues and problems which are centred in texts from an earlier philosophical time. Yet this challenge must be met if the theory of natural law put forward by Thomas Aquinas is to help advance the discussions in contemporary moral, political, and legal philosophy. This chapter attempts to unpack the texts and thus elucidate clearly the metaphysics underlying Aquinas's moral theory. The approach to these issues in Aquinas's account of natural law is an example of what both Gustav Bergmann and Henry Veatch call 'the structural history of philosophy'. According to Veatch, structural history of philosophy means that often philosophical insights and theories articulated by philosophers involve structural implications and requirements. At times, so Bergmann suggests, philosophers themselves are not always aware of these presuppositions and entailments. Often, Bergmann once wrote, these issues are not stated clearly in the written record of the history of philosophy. Structural history of philosophy suggests providing analysis and interpretation. Often the methods common to the practice of analytic philosophy are used in elucidating the principal issues in the history of philosophy. The *explicatio textus* undertaken in this chapter follows the general themes for doing structural history of philosophy articulated first by Bergmann and then elaborated upon by Veatch.[1]

The structural history of philosophy undertaken in this chapter is an important exercise in meta-ethics. The analysis of the texts

---

[1] Henry B. Veatch, *For an Ontology of Morals* (Evanston, Ill: Northwestern University Press, 1971), 4.

considers the following issues central to the moral theory in natural
law:

1. The presuppositions of the theory ;
2. The structure of the argument;
3. The place of Aquinas's ethical naturalism in contemporary
   meta-ethics;
4. Some traditional objections and their responses to this form of
   ethical naturalism.

The completion of this kind of philosophical analysis should ensure
that studies in the history of philosophy, in meta-ethical naturalism,
and in natural law jurisprudence considering Aquinas's theory of
natural law will be better served. The result will indicate how
Aquinas's moral realism transcends what MacIntyre has called the
Enlightenment project in moral theory.

This is a discourse into metaphysics, epistemology, and metaphilosophy. It is metaphysical in so far as an analysis is offered of the
ontological categories of essence, causality, dispositional property,
and synthetic necessary properties as found in the writings of Aristotle and Aquinas. It is epistemological in that it discusses Aristotle
and Aquinas's way of becoming aware of essential properties. It
raises metaphilosophical questions by discussing the differences in
approaching philosophical issues in medieval and early modern
philosophy and how these differences are important in comparing
Kantian and Aquinian moral theories.

This exegesis, in the manner of an *explicatio textus*, is not an
attempt to do normative ethics. The purpose of this book is not to
offer practical applications of natural law theory to contemporary
moral issues, such as human rights, nuclear warfare, abortion, liberation theology, or any of the cluster of issues sometimes associated
with natural law theory. Not that these issues are unimportant; but
if natural law ethics is to make sense, its presuppositions and ontological commitments must be stated clearly and articulated concisely.
If they are not, one is conceptually confused right from the beginning. This chapter, therefore, is an exercise in elucidating the metaphysics necessary to ground the moral naturalism in Aquinas's ethical
theory, especially his meta-ethics. It is a conceptual analysis which
Aquinas would regard as a philosophical exercise propaedeutic to
moral commitment and praxis. Aquinas, moreover, argued for a
realist ontology. None the less, the method of conceptual analysis

common to analytic philosophy will assist in the process of understanding the realist foundation for Aquinas's metaphysics.

An earlier chapter noted Martin Golding's suggestion that 'the revival of natural law doctrines is one of the most interesting features of current legal thought'. While Golding had in mind a reference to the conceptual work of H. L. A. Hart's *The Concept of Law* and Lon Fuller's *The Morality of Law*, none the less the impact of natural law on contemporary moral and legal theory has been substantial and beyond that provided by Hart and Fuller.

Most contemporary statements of natural law meta-ethics and jurisprudence refer to the position elucidated by Thomas Aquinas as the *locus classicus* for Western natural law theories. In particular, the texts of Aquinas's *Summa Theologiae* I-II qq. 90–7, are the principal articles in which Aquinas's theory of natural law is articulated. Furthermore, these texts in the *Summa Theologiae* are dependent structurally on Aquinas's treatment of Aristotle's moral theory in his *Commentary on the Nicomachean Ethics*.

Because so many writers refer to Aquinas's theory as a paradigm for natural law jurisprudence, it is important for contemporary students of meta-ethics and jurisprudence to have a clear idea of the structure of Aquinas's arguments on these matters. Therefore, in providing a contemporary *explicatio textus* of Aquinas's account of natural law in the *Summa Theologiae*, this chapter and the ones immediately following can assist philosophers and legal scholars to understand an important piece of classical moral theory, a piece, moreover, which has in some quarters been misunderstood and articulated without care. Given these issues, Aquinas's classical theory of the meta-ethics of natural law can benefit from a careful reconsideration and reconstruction.

THE FUNDAMENTAL PRINCIPLES OF AQUINAS'S THEORY OF NATURAL LAW

Gustav Bergmann once wrote that 'in what a great philosopher says there is a pattern. It all flows from one source, a few fundamental ontological ideas. In the light of this source and only in this light, it can all be understood'.[2] In developing his account of natural

---

[2] Gustav Bergmann, 'Inclusion, Exemplification and Inference in G. E. Moore', in E. D. Klemke (ed.), *Studies In the Philosophy of G. E. Moore* (Chicago: Quadrangle Books, 1969), 82.

law, Aquinas uses various assumptions or principles which serve the function Bergmann notes above. It is important conceptually to consider these principles at the beginning of this kind of textual analysis of Aquinas's meta-ethics. The major philosophical presuppositions in Aquinas's natural law theory are the following:

1. A realist metaphysics is possible;
2. Essential properties are possible;
3. Essential properties are found only in the natures of particular individuals;
4. Essential properties fundamentally are dispositional in character;
5. The dispositional theory of essential properties entails a metaphysics of finality;
6. 'Truth' is the correspondence between mind and thing: 'Veritas est adequatio rei et intellectus';
7. Moral 'properties' are based upon dispositional or developmental properties;
8. A 'metaphysics of morals' is possible;
9. The rational (reason) takes theoretical precedence over the affective (will);
10. Divine commands must be in accord with the rational demands of the eternal law.

These ten statements serve as foundational principles in Aquinas's theory of natural law. Each requires further explication. A good bit of explication and analysis takes place in this chapter. To begin this process of conceptual elucidation, the following brief gloss on the above ten propositions is offered.

1. *A realist metaphysics is possible*: The proposition stating that 'metaphysics is possible' is not a claim about possible worlds. Rather this proposition asserts that for Aquinas it made perfectly good sense philosophically to consider metaphysics as significant cognitively. Aquinas is a realist, not in the sense of Platonic realism, but in the Aristotelian sense. This Aristotelian position affirms the real existence of individuals, which both Aristotle and Aquinas refer to as 'primary substances'. Moreover, it is possible theoretically to consider real distinctions and categories in the world of individual primary substances. Like most philosophers in the thirteenth century, Aquinas did not believe that he had to defend the possibility of metaphysical inquiry. Christopher Martin once noted that

Thomas 'is a metaphysician; and he uses the concepts of Aristotle to systematize the unconscious metaphysics that we all share.'[3] Metaphysics considers those concepts which apply generally to beings; e.g., essence, disposition, cause, individual, etc. Metaphysics, therefore, is a consideration of the fundamental categories of reality. This book does not use the concept of metaphysics in a restricted scholastic sense by referring only to transcendental claims about being. Rather a more contemporary application of the concept is utilized.

2. *Essential properties are possible:* This proposition states that in Aquinas's metaphysics, it is meaningful to talk about essential properties which determine a natural kind. In a manner akin to Kripke and some of Putnam's earlier writings, Aquinas would concur that the name for an essential property is not an arbitrary definition but 'rigidly designates' a natural kind. Michael Ayers once argued that 'there is some awareness at least that the [Kripke/Putnam] view is not so new as all that, since it is not at all unlike Aristotelian Doctrine'.[4] The point is that Aquinas's account of an essential property or of a set of essential properties is what determines a natural kind. Natural kinds are the particular species in the external world, but they occur only in particular individuals.

3. *Essential properties are found only in the natures of particular individuals:* Aquinas believes that essences, other than in their exemplar role in the divine mind, are existent only in individual concreta, which are the primary substances of Aristotelian ontology. A primary substance is an individual – 'Marianne', 'Bernard', 'Fido', 'Boots', 'This particular oak tree', 'This particular lump of coal', etc. Christopher Martin has argued that Kripke's analysis of 'our unconscious metaphysics' has brought attention to the theory of essence in Aristotle and Aquinas. An essence determines the nature of a particular individual belonging to a natural kind. The essence determines the natural kind of the species, but the species is a collection of individual primary substances brought together through the properties of the natural kind.

4. *Essential properties fundamentally are dispositional in character:* A dispositional property, by definition, is a potentiality directed

[3] Christopher Martin, *The Philosophy of Thomas Aquinas* (London: Routledge, 1988), 5.
[4] Michael Ayers, 'Locke versus Aristotle on Natural Kinds', *Journal of Philosophy*, 78/5 (May 1981), 248.

towards a specific development or 'end'. A disposition is a capacity to 'do something' which an object possesses. Like most Aristotelian terms, there are analogical uses of disposition, ranging from a concept (an acquired disposition to understand), to a sense faculty such as the eye (a natural disposition to see), to an innate property such as growth (a natural disposition to utilize food and transform energy). Yet throughout this discussion, a disposition is always a potentiality or a capacity to undertake or to develop towards a specific end. The 'end' is called an 'act', which is the fulfilment or completion of the potency. Aristotelian teleology makes sense only in terms of the attainment of a *telos*, which is the end or goal of the dispositional property. Aquinas, following Aristotle, suggests that potency and act are the two fundamental categories of all being. In Aquinas's ontology, the dispositional paradigm holds only for temporal essences. It would not hold for the divine or angelic essences. Neither God nor angels, so Aquinas thought, developed. Hence, dispositional properties are not applicable to these essences. This chapter is concerned only with temporal essences, except when considering the relation of concrete essence to the divine mind.

5. *The dispositional theory of essential properties entails a metaphysics of finality*: In his Aristotelian commentary, *La Morale d'Aristote*,[5] R. A. Gauthier uses this concept of 'the metaphysics of finality' to distinguish the teleology inherent in Aristotelian moral theory from that common to many nineteenth- and twentieth-century teleological theories. Henry Veatch develops this concept in his analysis of natural law. The metaphysics of finality suggests that the ends appropriate to human nature are built into the very nature or essence which determines a human person. The end is not a 'non-moral good' to be attained which is common to many teleological theories such as classical utilitarianism. The end is a constitutive aspect of the very nature of a dispositional property. This is the act/potency relation so often articulated in Aristotle and Aquinas. Aquinas's account of obligation depends on this concept of the metaphysics of finality. The analysis of obligation and obligatory ends in Aquinas will occur later.

6. *'Truth' is the correspondence between mind and thing*: Like many

---

[5] R. A. Gauthier, *La Morale d'Aristote* (Paris: Presses Universitaires de France, 1959), 47–48, cited in Henry Veatch, *Swimming Against the Current in Contemporary Philosophy* (Washington, DC: Catholic University of America Press, 1990), 101.

medieval philosophers, Aquinas adopted a modified correspondence theory of truth. A relation of *adequatio* or 'proportion' holds between the concept and the thing. When this relation holds, a proposition is true. While there are different senses of *adequatio*, none the less in its simplest sense it expresses a version of the correspondence theory of truth. *Adequatio* is a relation of proportion obtaining between the mind and reality. When the relation holds between proposition and thing, 'truth' holds.

7. *Moral 'properties' are based upon dispositional or developmental properties:* Following Aristotle's suggestion in the *Nicomachean Ethics*, Aquinas defined the 'good' in terms of an 'end'. In the *Summa Theologiae*, I-II, q. 94 a. 2, Aquinas writes that 'good has the intelligibility of end and evil has the intelligibility of contrary to end'. Following Aristotle, Aquinas adopts the fourfold theory of cause: material, formal, efficient, and final causality. From (4) above, it follows that the final cause, in the case of a temporal essence, is the end of the development of the dispositional properties which make up the formal cause. Of course, in the hylomorphic theory of Aquinas, the substantial form is always connected with a 'chunk' of prime matter. From (3) above it follows that only individual concreta or primary substances as members of a natural kind exist.

8. *A 'metaphysics of morals' is possible:* In a manner strangely akin to but certainly not identical with Kant, Aquinas suggested that it is possible cognitively to unpack the metaphysical issues which are necessary for an elucidation of a moral theory. The result is a non-Kantian 'metaphysics of morals'. Of course, Aquinas's metaphysics is beyond the phenomenal realm of Kantian epistemology. None the less both philosophers transcend the limits for meta-ethical discourse delimited by the non-cognitivists. In other words, rationality is a category applicable to the moral sphere. One can develop moral arguments which are justifiable rationally. It is important to note that Aquinas's metaphysics is realist in nature and not transcendental. Aquinas adopts the epistemological principle that reality is knowable. Aquinas rejects any form of Kantian noumena. Metaphysical categories are realist in character and not mental constructs. Aquinas does not adopt the 'transcendental turn' method which Henry Veatch ascribes to much modern and contemporary philosophy. In Aquinas's philosophy, the moral theory is dependent upon the metaphysical theory. It is in this sense that Aquinas develops a 'metaphysics of morals'.

9. *The rational (reason) takes theoretical precedence over the affective (will)*: In opposition to the dominant Franciscan tradition in the thirteenth century, Aquinas argued that the intellect has a hierarchical value above the will. This assumption will become important in understanding the difference between Occam and Aquinas on natural law. In addition, it will become a key proposition removing Aquinas's natural law jurisprudence from the arena of legal positivism and existentialism.

10. *Divine commands must be in accord with the rational demands of the eternal law:* This proposition is a corollary to (9).

The above gloss on the ten principles Aquinas assumes in his articulation of natural law should help one understand the metaphysics underlying his moral theory. More analysis, of course, needs to be undertaken. The remainder of this chapter offers a major part of the required explication and analysis. This argument is fundamentally an extensive *explicatio textus*, which is nothing more than an unpacking of the concepts central to Aquinas's account of natural law moral theory.

AQUINAS'S DEFINITION OF LAW

The eight questions of *Summa Theologiae*, I-II qq. 90–7, comprise the classical canon of Aquinas's theory of natural law. While it is true that Aquinas discusses moral theory elsewhere, none the less these eight questions comprise the clearest account of Aquinas's natural law ethics. In many ways, this account is derivative from and dependent on Aristotle's eudaimonistic naturalism as spelled out in the *Nicomachean Ethics*. Aquinas's commentary on this Aristotelian treatise is in harmony philosophically with the natural law theory developed in the *Summa Theologiae*.

In beginning the discussion reconsidering and reconstructing Aquinas's argument on natural law theory, the following issues need to be discussed:

1. The nature of the four kinds of law;
2. The relation of eternal law to natural law;
3. The role of a dispositional theory of essence in determining a theory of value;
4. The structure of the is/ought distinction as applicable to Aquinas's ethical naturalism.

All four issues above will be addressed within this book, and the method of analysis will follow a modified sequential order. This chapter will consider (1) and spend much time with (3). Chapter 5 considers in some detail (2), i.e. the relation of eternal law to natural law in Aquinas's theory. Chapter 8 offers a few suggestions on providing an interpretation of Aquinas's theory of obligation (4) which, while limited, may shed some light on the role of obligation and the is/ought controversy in this theory.

Fundamentally, this chapter and the next are both pieces of metaphysical analysis offering a reconsideration and reconstruction of how contemporary analytic philosophers might read Aquinas's texts on natural law. This reading depends upon a conceptual analysis of some important items central to Aquinas's metaphysics: (1) the theory of essence; (2) his theory of how we acquire knowledge of essences; (3) what we need to know in order to understand an essence; and (4) what implications his metaphysics and epistemology have for his theory of natural law.

In discussing his account of law in the *Summa Theologiae*, Aquinas offers this definition of law: 'Law is the reasonable ordinance or prescription which is promulgated, is for the common good, and comes from the one who has charge of the community' (I-II q. 90 a. 4). Using this definition, Aquinas offers the following fourfold division of law:

1. Eternal law (*lex aeterna*);
2. Natural law (*lex naturalis*);
3. Human or positive law (*lex humana vel positiva*);
4. Divine law (*lex divina*).

The first three kinds of law are interrelated conceptually within the ontological scheme Aquinas proposes. The fourth, divine law, refers to what Aquinas understood as 'revelation', which is the set of statements found in the biblical texts. Put simply, the first three kinds of law are philosophical in nature, while divine law — which must not be confused with eternal law — is theological in character. Divine law refers to the moral imperatives found in the biblical texts and whose justification is divine authority. Divine law as rooted in a divine command theory is beyond the limits of a philosophical inquiry.

This chapter proceeds in a rather systematic way to unpack these four kinds of law. In addition, this analysis offers an interpretation regarding the interconnections of these specific categories of law as enunciated by Aquinas. In the end, several suggestions will be made noting how Aquinas might respond to some traditional objections to his position. While this chapter discusses in some way all four kinds of law proposed by Aquinas, the next chapter considers in detail how eternal law fits in conceptually with a secular reconstruction of natural law in Aquinas. Moreover, the issues relating to the role God plays in Aquinas's systematic account of natural law are discussed in the following chapter.

ETERNAL LAW AND PLATONISM

What is eternal law? How could this ontological concept become significant to a modern person living in an age so heavily influenced by the existentialists? Most contemporary philosophers have read Hume's *Dialogues*, Sartre's *Existentialism as a Humanism*, and have taken for granted Dostoevsky's claim that 'If God is dead, everything is possible!' Furthermore, Camus and Russell have offered convincing arguments that absurdity results from the attempt to explain the world through a divine plan. Even some existentialist theologians have given up on the possibility of understanding theoretical concepts such as these.

It is no accident that this discussion of natural law begins with existentialist claims. Even MacIntyre in *After Virtue* considers what he calls the 'way of Nietzsche' as an opposing theory to Aristotelian virtue ethics – what he calls the 'way of Aristotle'. Aquinas's concept of eternal law is the affirmation of what Camus, Sartre, Nietzsche, and Russell have denied. These philosophers deny the possibility of an ultimate metaphysical explanation of reality.[6] To be more exact, this analysis proposes that for Aquinas, eternal law functions as an ontological principle of explanation. Eternal law plays a role similar to what Plato attempted in his ontology through the world of the Forms. This book argues, furthermore, that Aquinas could provide an account of natural law without any reference to eternal law. There is a conceptual secularism to his theory of natural law. Of course, this point demands a careful elucidation and theoretical exegesis.

[6] Herbert Hochberg, 'Albert Camus and the Ethic of Absurdity', *Ethics*, 2 (Jan. 1965), 87–102. This article is an excellent discussion of the denial of the possibility of metaphysical explanation in the writings of Camus.

Given the above claims, what then is eternal law? In order to understand eternal law, one might begin by thinking of the function classically given to Plato's world of the Forms. In Aquinas's ontology, one must take the world of the Forms schematically and place it into the divine mind. Those familiar with the history of medieval philosophy will recognize this as an Augustinian metaphysical move. In another sense, it is similar structurally to the function of the Demiurgos and the Forms in the *Timaeus*. In that Platonic dialogue, the Forms function as the archetypes after which the temporal realm is patterned. One of Plato's more persistent metaphors when considering the role of the Forms is 'pattern'. Following Aristotle, Augustine, and most of the early medieval philosophers and theologians, Aquinas read Plato in this way. What Aquinas meant by eternal law is the set of archetypes, analogous to the world of the Forms, which are found as the divine ideas in God's mind.

Another point to remember when reading Aquinas's philosophy is that he rejects categorically Tertullian's irrationalism. Tertullian is famous for articulating the theological maxim that 'Credo, quia absurdum est'. In other words, one believes a theological proposition because the content of the proposition transcends the ability of human reason.[7] One might argue that Tertullian and the logical positivists offered positions structurally similar regarding the cognitive significance of such theological propositions. In *The Myth of Sisyphus*, Camus articulates the same philosophical conclusion arguing that metaphysical discourse is meaningless. None the less, such ontological scepticism was as foreign to Aquinas as it was to Plato and to Scotus, and is to David Lewis and Saul Kripke.

---

[7] Aquinas divides the possibility of propositional knowledge in a threefold fashion: (1) Those propositions capable of being understood by the human intellect alone; e.g. science, mathematics, and so forth; (2) Those propositions capable of being known by the human intellect but also part of the set of propositions revealed by God; e.g. the existence of God, the immortality of the soul, the natural moral law; (3) Those propositions which refer to the uniquely Christian mysteries which transcend the limits of the human intellect for complete understanding; e.g. the Incarnation, the Resurrection, the doctrine of Grace, and so forth. For Aquinas, only (3) above contains propositions which, for the purpose of discovery and demonstration, transcend the limits of the human understanding. In effect, (2) contains metaphysical propositions; but these propositions are discoverable and demonstrable, so Aquinas argued, by reason alone. Of course, neither Kierkegaard nor Tertullian would accept (2) in any form. Furthermore, Aquinas believes that the propositions in (3) are capable of analysis, explication, and philosophical 'unpacking'. This is the object of one of the uses of the activity of philosophy. Tertullian would not accept this either.

Recalling the list of principles suggested above, Aquinas assumes that 'Veritas est adequatio rei et intellectus': this is translated as 'truth is the correspondence or adequation between the mind and the thing'. Of course, this is similar to one formulation of a correspondence theory of truth. In addition, Aquinas accepts the claim that the Scriptures, which would be the written form of God's revelation to human beings, are significant cognitively and, of course, expressible in a propositional mode. One such proposition found in the Scriptures suggests that human beings are 'made in the image and likeness of God'. It is important to realize that Aquinas accepted a propositional mode of faith. The content of faith statements can be expressed in propositional form. Hence, there are philosophical issues to be discussed both for the truth of these propositions and for their analysis. Aquinas was not a non-cognitivist in regard to theological claims. The totality of these propositions is the set of revealed statements accepted as true on the word of God who has revealed them. Faith is not reducible to a commitment or emotional attachment, which is a common interpretation of faith among contemporary religious writers.

Given the truth of these propositions of faith — which he does not question — Aquinas asked how these propositions might be articulated and analyzed. In his commentary on the *De Trinitate* by Boethius, Aquinas suggests that one of the functions of philosophy is to 'make known those statements that help one to understand better the claims of theology'. In this sense, Aquinas used an analytical method similar to what C. D. Broad early in the twentieth century called 'critical philosophy': 'the analysis and definition of our fundamental concepts, and the clear statement and resolute criticism of our fundamental beliefs'.[8] In the mind of Aquinas, it is not impossible rationally to explicate these propositions found in the Scriptures. Aquinas and Tertullian — and, *a fortiori*, Kierkegaard — radically part company at this juncture. One aspect of the philosophical enterprise for Aquinas is a process analysing the meaning of propositions already known to be true. In an important way, this process is similar to Moore's conception of 'philosophy as analysis' and Broad's 'critical philosophy'. This use of philosophical method in Aquinas is strikingly similar to the analytic method articulated by early twentieth-century British philosophers. This does not mean that Aquinas

---

[8] C.D. Broad, *Scientific Thought* (London: Routledge & Kegan Paul, 1927), 18.

saw analysis as a sufficient account for philosophical activity. But he did not dismiss this activity either.

Following Augustine, Aquinas, using a method of analysis, realizes that he must explain the proposition found in the biblical text which states that 'human beings are made in the image and likeness of God'. He does this by suggesting that the divine mind contains the divine archetypes as divine ideas. The temporal world, therefore, is patterned after these archetypes. This is the most plausible account explicating what Aquinas meant by the concept of eternal law. Eternal law is fundamentally a metaphysical explanation of 'what there is'. It serves as a metaphysical schema or pattern of the beings which exist.

Another way to consider the role eternal law plays in the metaphysical explanations Aquinas offers is to consider his definition of truth. Recall principle (6) above: 'Truth is the correspondence between mind and thing.' The correspondence comes about if a 'measure' or 'adequation' holds between mind and thing. In theoretical or speculative reason, Aquinas suggests that the mind is measured by the thing. In practical or productive reason, the thing is measured by the mind. Hence, when the chemist understands the formula for hydrochloric acid (HCl), the mind, so Aquinas suggests, is measured by the structure of 'HCl' in the external world. On the other hand, when a person is exercising a craft – pottery, for example – the thing is measured by the idea or model in the mind of the person undertaking the craft – in this case, the potter. The *adequatio* holds, therefore, in both speculative and practical reason. However, what holds as the standard or measure differs. In the former, it is in the thing; in the latter, it is in the mind as idea or exemplar.

In an interesting passage from the *De Veritate*, Aquinas considers how the categories of speculative and practical reason apply to the divine mind.

natural objects from which our mind gains knowledge [i.e. speculative reason], measure our mind or intellect. Yet these objects are themselves measured by the Divine Mind, in which are all created objects – just as all works of art [i.e. practical reason] find their origin in the mind of an artist. The Divine Mind, therefore, measures and is not measured; our minds, on the other hand, are measured [i.e. in speculative reason] and measure [i.e. in practical reason] only artifacts, not natural objects in the world.

This passage from *De Veritate* indicates how Aquinas appropriated

Aristotelian terminology to explain a metaphysical view theoretically akin to Plato's world of the Forms. This passage also indicates how the concept of *adequatio* holds for both speculative and practical reason, albeit differently.

With eternal law described in the manner of Plato's archetypes, Aquinas, like his Greek predecessor, is doing a piece of metaphysical analysis. He offers an explanatory principle. God, in a manner akin to a person practising practical reasoning, models the created world after the content of the divine archetypes. Hence, Aquinas is not like Tertullian; to speak rationally and descriptively through metaphysical discourse about the eternal law, and, accordingly, about an ontological first principle, is neither absurd nor beyond the possibility of human reason and discourse. Eternal law, then, is the set of divine archetypes after which God has created the world. The most important archetype is that of human nature. The archetype of human nature is exemplified in existing human beings. This becomes important in an analysis of natural law. Eternal law is not natural law, but the archetype in the divine mind after which human beings have been created. This account indicates how Aquinas used Aristotelian theory for his own purposes in developing an explication of philosophical concepts central to his system.

NATURAL LAW IN AQUINAS

Following the insight suggested by Columba Ryan and noted at the end of the preceding chapter, Aquinas suggests the possibility of a metaphysics of morals. This is not a Kantian use of 'metaphysics of morals'. There is a fundamental difference in that Aquinas argues for a type of realist ontology which Kant denied explicitly. None the less, like Kant, Aquinas suggests that a metaphysical theory will have something to say about a moral theory. That there are major differences in the metaphysical theories is not to be denied. In reading Aquinas's account of natural law, one must remember that Aquinas thought it possible to explicate a metaphysical foundation for moral theory. Furthermore, both argued for consistent moral theories independent of a divine being. In other words, while God plays a part in Kant's moral theory — as a postulate making morality possible — so too does God have a role in Aquinas's theory. The role for God in Aquinas's theory, however, is one of the final propositions in the system. Aquinas will argue for a 'humanist' account of moral theory based upon reason alone, much in the systematic way Kant did. The systems are radically different, but the humanist thrust is the same. Again, this is not to suggest that there are not fundamental differences between Kant's meta-ethics and Aquinas's meta-ethics. None the less, one must not ignore the similarities either. The next chapter discusses in some detail the role God plays in Aquinas's theory of natural law.

HUMAN NATURE AS A SET OF DISPOSITIONAL PROPERTIES

In order to understand Aquinas's theory of natural law, one must acknowledge a theory of natural kinds. Aquinas's ontology is a necessary presupposition for his moral theory. It does not go the other way around. Moreover, the essential properties which determine the natural kinds are dispositional in mode. Put differently, the philosophical anthropology Aquinas adopts is based upon a metaphysical theory of essences, whose structure is composed of dispositional properties. Aquinas is very much a developmental psychologist and metaphysician. His concept of an essence in an individual primary substance is one containing developmental, dispositional properties. A 'static' essence is quite foreign to his mind. Furthermore, the essence is always found in an individual primary substance, the principal existent in Aquinas's ontology.

Before considering Aquinas's concept of essence as a set of dispositional properties, it is useful to consider the concepts of essence as used in twentieth-century analytic philosophy. In discussing essences or universals, most contemporary philosophers have been influenced by the writings of Russell, Moore, and Quine, all of whom contributed significantly to the development of twentieth-century analytic philosophy. Russell's paradigm for a universal is a mathematical property. In other words, a mathematical class is determined by a property. There is nothing more static and unchangeable than the concept of a class determined by a mathematical property. As Yves Simon once noted, a mathematical class or property is not similar to an Aristotelian essence. Simon wrote the following: 'we may not attribute to it [i.e. a mathematical property] a dynamism, a tendency to force its way in a world of becoming.'[9] Furthermore, contempor-

---

[9] Yves Simon, *The Tradition of Natural Law* (New York: Fordham University Press, 1965), 44.

ary philosophers often transfer the notion of class and universal from Russell, Moore, and Quine to Plato, Aristotle, and Aquinas.[10] At any rate, in opposition to almost every philosopher in the early analytic tradition, Aquinas does not consider an essence to be a static class concept or a set of strictly limited, changeless properties. Henry Veatch suggested that the tendency to consider a universal as a changeless entity arose with Descartes and the rise of the new science.[11] Gilson has written about the mathematical paradigm determining Cartesian metaphilosophy while the biological paradigm determines Aristotelian metaphilosophy. The Cartesian revolution in philosophy destroyed the concept of disposition as a significant ontological category. Without this category, Aristotelian and Aquinian accounts of essence fall by the wayside.

What then is an essence for Aquinas? It is a 'supreme set of dispositional properties'. Using terminology gained from Aristotle, Aquinas argues that a temporal essence is made up of matter and form. A form is what specifically differentiates one kind of a thing from another kind of a thing. This is Aquinas's concept of a 'substantial form'. The properties which make up a substantial form, which in turn specify the content of an essence, are developmental or dispositional in character. They are not static. To reconstruct Aquinas's view of essence demands reintroducing the concept of disposition into the discussion. The model of a tulip bulb developing during the spring is closer to Aquinas's concept of essence than the definition of a triangle. A verbal definition of a class – what logicians call analytic a priori propositions – does not reflect this dispositional character of the properties which determine an essence. As Yves Simon once suggested, there are no Aristotelian essences in the ontology of Descartes. The Cartesian paradigm, in so far as it has influenced modern and contemporary philosophy, has ruled out the Aristotelian concept of a dispositional essence.

In contemporary metaphysics, the Kripke/Putnam view of natural kinds suggests the possibility of essentialism within the confines of

[10] Were space available, I would argue that Aquinas makes a category distinction between essence and universal. The former is a first intention referring to the content of a substantial form. The latter is a second intention referring to the content of the first intention.

[11] Henry B. Veatch, 'Telos and Teleology in Aristotelian Ethics', in Dominic J. O'Meara (eds), *Studies In Aristotle* (Washington: Catholic University of America Press, 1981), 279–96. See also his *For an Ontology of Morals* and *Swimming Against the Current in Contemporary Philosophy*.

analytic philosophy. Students of the history of philosophy realize that Aristotelian essentialism had been widely rejected both by the British empiricists and later by the twentieth-century logical positivists and some ordinary language philosophers. The clarion call of the verification theory of meaning affirmed the fundamental 'nonsense' of essential claims. Using the theory of rigid designators, the Kripke/Putnam position has brought about the possibility of a reconsideration of Aristotelian essentialism. Considering the relation and structural similarities of contemporary essentialism to Aristotelian essentialism, Michael Ayers writes:

> Saul Kripke and Hilary Putnam and others have changed the scenery somewhat in the last ten years. The names 'gold', 'tiger', etc. have their meaning, it is said, not by being tied to an arbitrary definition or to an idea or mental concept, but simply by being the name of, or, more technically, by 'rigidly designating', a natural kind. Membership of the kind is determined by the presence of a presumed underlying common nature which may be unknown to us, rather than by the satisfaction of a definition consisting of a list of those properties which we happen to use as criteria for identifying things as members of that kind.[12]

This is a *de re* argument suggesting that the external reality in all possible worlds is such that natural kinds are necessary conditions to explain the semantic content of our scientific and commonsense views of reality. It is theory about truth, about 'what there is', in terms of the categories of reality. A common name rigidly designates an essence; a theory of descriptions is not sufficient to explain the ontological requirements for an adequate theory of meaning. Aquinas's concept of an essence is, I suggest, structurally similar to the metaphysical requirements of a natural kind ontology. Chapter 8 will consider in more detail the natural kind ontology as found in the writings of Kripke and the early Putnam.

Kripke does suggest that the concept of 'necessity' is neither identical with nor coextensive with the concept of 'a priori'. Kripke argues for the possibility of 'necessary a posteriori' knowledge. In this analysis, I suggest that one contemporary way to consider the set of properties which make up an Aquinian essence is as a set of synthetic necessary or synthetic a priori properties. 'A priori' suggests, following the work of Everett J. Nelson, that the metaphysical category of essence is not itself directly perceivable. Yet it is neces-

---

[12] Ayers, 'Locke versus Aristotle', 248.

sary because it holds for all instances of the natural kind. On this point, the account of 'a posteriori' will not fit with the general treatment of Aquinas's account of essential properties.

At this point in the discussion, Aquinas's concept of teleology must be considered. Teleology, for Aquinas, is not similar to this concept as proposed by the eighteenth-century deists. In Aquinas, to quote from his *Commentary on Aristotle's Physics*, teleology means that 'Nature acts for an end'.[13] This means that in any developmental process in an individual, there is at least a statistical average for a terminal point. The properties determining the essence have 'tendencies' or 'abilities' to develop in a structured way. For example, two hippos mating produce another hippo, and not a horse; tulip bulbs produce tulip plants with blooms, and not geraniums; acorns develop into oak trees, and not blue spruces or blue herons; and so forth. While Aquinas is not so modern as to claim that the universe is nothing more than a statistical probability, none the less his notion of nature acting for an end does not entail that nature has a conscious purpose. Neither Ralph Waldo Emerson – and similar pantheists – nor William Paley – and similar deists – developed or defended the type of teleology with which Aquinas would concur. Aquinas would probably reject the teleology proposed by the pantheists or the deists. In the Aristotelian and Aquinian systems, the end or 'telos' is the point at which the dispositional properties in the primary substance reach their development or perfection. The individual, therefore, now functions well as a member of a species or natural kind. In Aquinian terminology, the potency or disposition has reached a state of actualization. This is not a conscious direction on the part of the properties themselves. The acorn is not 'consciously driven' to become an oak tree.

It is impossible to consider the structure of a disposition without bringing the concept of teleology into the discussion. A disposition, of its very nature, is tending towards a *'telos'* or end. Teleology as the account of the development or actualization of the disposition is neither identical nor coextensive with teleology as is evidenced in the writings of pantheists or deists. It is a much more sanguine metaphysical concept.

[13] For an interesting account of Aristotle's theory of teleology, cf. Alan Gotthelf, 'Aristotle's Conception of Final Causality', *Review of Metaphysics*, 30/2 (Dec. 1976), 226–54.

In the *Summa Theologiae*, I-II q. 94, Aquinas suggested that a human being is composed essentially of a set of dispositional properties divided into three generic sets — living, sensitive, and rational. This account is based on Aristotle's philosophical anthropology as developed in the *De Anima*. Each of these properties in the three sets develops through a process towards a particular end or terminal point. Following Aristotle, each end, by definition, is a good. Hence, there are as many goods as there are ends, and there are as many ends as there are dispositional properties to be developed in an essence. The concept of good is incommensurable in Aquinas's meta-ethics. There is no one content which every instance of good has beyond its ontological status as an end.

Even though Aquinas does use the concept of end in his ethical theory, his theory is not structurally similar to the standard paradigm of a teleological theory as used in recent analytic philosophy. Aquinas is not interested merely in the attainment of a goal, but rather in reaching an end as determined by the dispositional properties central to human nature. Aquinas is not a teleologist in the utilitarian schema of naturalism. Aquinas would better be defined as a 'deontologist' than a 'teleologist'. The end to be attained is always determined by the properties of the human essence or human nature.

Henry Veatch once suggested that one ought to call Aristotle and Aquinas 'teleologists' but distinguish two kinds of teleology: one with non-moral ends to be attained, which is common to utilitarianism, and the other with moral ends to be attained depending on the essence of the human person, which is appropriate for natural law theories. Introducing the concept of human essence, however, probably aligns natural law theory more clearly with a deontological than with a teleological account. None the less, what is important here is to note that the categories which William Frankena and others have used to classify normative moral theories do not fit neatly onto the naturalism of Aristotle and Aquinas.

THE *SUMMA THEOLOGIAE* TEXT ON NATURAL LAW

The following text from q. 94 a. 2, considers the many kinds of incommensurable goods as ends of dispositional properties.

Insofar as good has the intelligibility of end and evil the intelligibility of contrary to end, it follows that reason grasps naturally as goods (accordingly, as things to be pursued by work, and their opposites as evils and thus things to be avoided) all of the objects which follow from the natural inclinations or dispositions central to the concept of human nature.

First, there is in human beings an inclination or disposition based upon the aspect of human nature which is shared with all living things; this is that everything according to its own nature tends to preserve its own being. In accord with this inclination or natural tendency (i.e., disposition), those things (actions, events, processes) by which human life is preserved and by which threats to human life are met fall under the natural law.

Second, there are in human beings inclinations or dispositions towards more restricted goods which are based upon the fact that human nature has common properties with other animals. In accord with this inclination or disposition, those things are said to be in agreement with the natural law (which nature teaches all animals) among which are the sexual union of male and female, the care of children, and so forth.

Third, there is in human beings an inclination or disposition to those goods based upon the rational properties of human nature. These goods are uniquely related to human beings. For example, human beings have a natural inclination or disposition to know the true propositions about God and concerning those necessities required for living in a human society. In accord with this inclination or disposition arise elements of the natural law. For example, human beings should avoid ignorance and should not offend those persons among whom he or she must live in social units, and so on.

Schema 1 illustrates the dispositional properties discussed in the above text.

Schema 1.

HUMAN NATURE AS A SET OF DISPOSITIONAL PROPERTIES

1. Dispositions or inclinations towards living
   to continue in existence
   to seek nutrition and growth

2. Dispositions or inclinations towards sensory apprehensions
   to have sense experiences
   to care for offspring

3. Dispositions or inclinations towards rational cognitivity
   to understand (rational curiosity)
   to live together in social communities

Martin Golding once referred to the living dispositions as the 'basic requirements of human life', the sensitive dispositions as the basic requirements for the 'furtherance of the human species', and the rational dispositions as the basic requirements for the 'promotion of (a human person's) good as a rational and social being'.[14] This is a contemporary analysis of the fundamental human characteristics which Aquinas argues are necessary conditions for an adequate explication of natural law theory. In his discussion of Aquinas's natural law theory, Columba Ryan writes of these three general assets of dispositional properties as 'the good of individual survival, biological good, and the good of human communication'.[15]

In her essay on Aristotelian moral theory, Martha Nussbaum suggests eight properties, which she claims 'we can none the less identify [as] certain features of our common humanity, closely related to Aristotle's original list'. Using the terminology developed in this chapter, we might argue that Nussbaum's eight characteristics are like dispositional properties. Her list includes the following: (1) mortality; (2) the body; (3) pleasure and pain; (4) cognitive capability; (5) practical reason; (6) early infant development; (7) affiliation (a sense of fellowship with other human beings); (8) humour.[16]

The point here is that Golding, Ryan, and, in a sense, Nussbaum have developed a set of dispositional properties which each suggests is central to the foundational issues for establishing an ethical naturalism. All of this is similar structurally to what Aquinas suggests in his classical account of human nature.

Because of this developmental view of essence, Aquinas consistently can define the good in terms of an end. In other words, the completion of a developmental process – the natural termination point – is a good. In *De Veritate*, Aquinas writes that 'omne id quod invenitur habere rationem finis, habet et rationem boni'. Translated, this proposition reads that 'all things found to have the criterion of an end at the same time meet the criterion of a good' (21 1) The end – i.e. the good – is built into the very process of development. Using Aristotelian terminology, the final cause (end) is related to the formal cause (dispositions or structure). This is the root explanation of Aquinas's appropriation of *eudaimonia* from Aristotelian moral theory; Aquinas calls this end *beatitudo*. To function well

[14] Martin Golding, 'Aquinas and Some Contemporary Natural Law Theories', *Proceedings of the American Catholic Philosophical Association* (1974), 242–3.
[15] Columba Ryan, 'The Traditional Concept of Natural Law', in Illtud Evans (ed.), *Light on the Natural Law* (Baltimore: Helicon Press, 1965), 28.
[16] Martha Nussbaum, 'Non-Relative Virtues', in Martha Nussbaum and Amartya Sen (eds), *The Quality of Life* (Oxford: Clarendon Press, 1993), 263–4.

means to reach the developmental potential of one's essential properties. This relation is important in offering an analysis of Aquinas's theory of obligation, which will be considered later in this book. Once again, the incommensurability of good in the texts of Aquinas is obvious. The passage from *De Veritate* indicates that there are as many goods as there are ends. The extended passage from question 94 above indicates that the goods — ends — result from the development of the set of dispositional properties which make up the human nature or essence. This is the realist foundation for Aquinas's natural law theory. This realist foundation, moreover, renders Aquinas's ethical theory deontological rather than teleological in structure.

THE PRINCIPLES OF META-ETHICAL NATURALISM

Using this analysis of a human essence or human nature, Aquinas articulates his theory of ethical naturalism. The following nine principles help explicate this developmental or self-actualization moral theory:

1. A dispositional property is developmental in character;
2. The natural bent of a dispositional property is towards the completion of the developmental process;
3. The well-being of a human person is determined by the harmonious completion of the dispositional properties, which determine the content of a human essence;
4. The end — i.e. well-being — is, by definition, a good;
5. There are as many goods as there are ends;
6. The concept of good is incommensurable; this follows from (5) above;
7. The hindering of any developing process frustrates that process;
8. To frustrate a natural process in a human being denies the possibility of attaining human well-being;
9. The source and foundation of the concept of morality is a fully functioning human person.

These nine principles contained within and underlying the text of q. 94 a. 2, contribute to a clearer elucidation of Aquinas's metaphysics of morals. This metaphysics of morals is a metaphysics of finality based upon the developmental character of human nature.

A concept central to this analysis of natural law is 'disposition'. In considering Aquinas's account of essence, a fruitful way to translate Aquinas's Latin terms *inclinatio* or *appetitus* is 'the development of dispositions'. These terms are used often to describe the properties central to a human essence. In analysing the concept of *inclinatio* as disposition, a disposition is not, of itself, a conscious drive or the object of consciousness. It can become the object of consciousness when the mind, reflecting upon the human experience, decides upon a certain construct as a possible explanation of the concept of human nature. But a disposition in and of itself is not necessarily a conscious drive. Translating *inclinatio* as 'disposition' avoids misinterpreting this concept as an intentional act or a conscious drive.

On this scheme of meta-ethical naturalism, it follows that an immoral action is the hindering of the natural developmental process based upon the dispositional properties common to human beings. Morality has its foundation in human nature. An act is morally wrong, not because God commands that 'A is wrong', but rather because the act prevents the completion – the self-actualization, as it were – of the dispositional properties which determine the content of human nature. While it is true that God has commanded that some acts are wrong, none the less the act is wrong structurally because an immoral act prevents the self-actualization of human beings. An act is wrong, not on account of God's command, but because the act hinders the development of the human dispositions. This is the fundamental normative position based upon a metaphysical theory of essence which is central to Aquinas's moral theory. The concept of 'human flourishing' used recently by Phillipa Foot and John Finnis[17] is a perspicuous way to account for Aquinas's concept of self-actualization. This is the end of the development of the dispositional properties which determine a human essence in the individual person.

This theory has a contemporary analogue in the writings of the existentialist psychologist, Carl Rogers. Rogers once suggested that there is an organismic base in the human person from which the activities leading to self-actualization emerge.[18] Self-actualization is coextensive with 'well-being', the Aristotelian *eudaimonia* and the Aquinian *beatitudo*. All of these terms are coextensive with the con-

---

[17] John Finnis, *Fundamentals of Ethics* (Oxford: Clarendon Press, 1983).
[18] Carl Rogers, 'The Valuing Process in the Mature Person', *Journal of Abnormal and Social Psychology*, 2 (1969), 160–7.

cept of 'human flourishing'. The relation of Rogerian psychology to Aquinian natural law ethics will be considered in Chapter 9.

There are interesting connections between Aquinas's set of dispositions and the accounts of natural necessities in Hart and Fuller. Hart's analysis of survival is similar to what Aquinas means in part by the living dispositions. The central point of the 'living disposition' is 'to continue in existence'. Fuller's account of 'communication', moreover, in his theory of the morality of aspiration, is recognizable as part of what Aquinas includes in his rational dispositions. Part of the 'rational disposition' is to engage in language with other persons. Aquinas's account of the content of human essence is more complete and inclusive than the theories proposed by either Hart or Fuller. None the less, in both cases from twentieth-century jurisprudence, there are structural similarities with the naturalism developed by Aristotle and Aquinas.

The central issue in Aquinas's theory of natural law, therefore, is to elucidate clearly his account of an essence which determines a natural kind. Aquinas argues for the possibility of this kind of metaphysics. In other words, he asks two ontological questions: (1) what is the ground for a human essence? And (2) how do we determine the content of the human essence? These are the metaphysical and epistemological issues necessary to natural law. When the essence of a human person is determined, then this becomes the normative ground for what human beings are to be and to become. It is the foundation for *eudaimonia*, which is the functioning well of the essential properties common to the individual in a specific natural kind.

An example from contemporary metaphysics may illustrate this discussion. To paraphrase what Everett J. Nelson suggested in his 1967 American Philosophical Association presidential address, [19] the question of essence in Aquinas is really the question of synthetic a priori or synthetic necessary properties. Following Nelson's suggestion, a contemporary way of considering Aquinas's theory of essence is as a set of synthetic a priori dispositional properties. This 'metaphysical glue' is necessary for Aquinas to establish his theory of causality in the world. An essence accounts for the regular causal relations existing in nature. Furthermore, Aquinas can account for

[19] Everett J. Nelson, 'The Metaphysical Presuppositions of Induction', presidential address, (American Philosophical Association Western Division), Chicago, 5 May 1967; found in *Proceedings and Addresses of the American Philosophical Association* (1966–7) (Yellow Springs, Ohio: Antioch Press, 1967), 19–33.

this analysis of the concept of essence with or without God. The next chapter considers this issue in some detail. Hence, Aquinas's account of natural law — which is in effect an account of moral properties based upon an account of an essence of human nature — is independent conceptually from his account of eternal law. One need not know the eternal law prior to knowledge of the natural law. Natural law makes sense in terms of a consideration of the development of the dispositional properties. The synthetic necessary properties serve as the causal basis for this account of essence Aquinas adopts as central to his metaphysical system. Given this causal dimension to an essence, the concept of *eudaimonia* so central to Aristotelian ethics becomes more clear. The role of self-actualization is the causal production of the end — which Aquinas has defined in terms of a good — which comes about through the development of the synthetic necessary causal properties.

Utilizing another example from contemporary metaphysics, the Aquinian individual of a natural kind is similar structurally to what Harré and Madden called a 'powerful particular' in their book, *Causal Powers*. The Aquinian ontology is one of 'powerful particulars', each an individual primary substance whose essence is determined by a set of synthetic necessary dispositional or causal properties. This metaphysical dimension, therefore, renders Aquinas's theory of natural law classifiable as a cognitivist/definist meta-ethical theory. Human nature is both a fact in the world and is capable of definition.

It is the argument of this book that Aquinas can elucidate the concept of essence or human nature — the set of synthetic a priori dispositional properties — without an appeal to the Divine Mind, which contains, in the manner of divine archetypes, the eternal law. In other words, Aquinas's epistemological machinery — the *intellectus agens* or agent intellect with its abstractive process — is so structured that a human knower can be aware of an essence without a direct reference to the eternal law. Aquinas includes the divine mind, as the next chapter indicates, only because it provides the ultimate explanation for his ontology. A human knower does not need to know the eternal law in order to form a concept of an essence through the abstractive process of the *intellectus agens*. A knowledge of the essence of a human person is all that is necessary for understanding the concept of natural law in Aquinas.

THE METAPHYSICS OF FINALITY AND A
THEORY OF OBLIGATION

Given this view of dispositional properties and the role that develop-ment plays in the actualization of the essence, it is important to be clear how Aquinas relates this aspect of teleology to a theory of obligation. From the start, one must realize that Aquinas is not considering teleology in a manner akin to that of Bentham or Mill. This point was developed earlier in considering MacIntyre's dis-cussion of nineteenth-century naturalism. Utilitarianism — and most other teleological theories — consider that moral theories are justifi-able in terms of the ends developed. In his classic treatment of modern ethical theory, William Frankena argues that teleological theories are determined by the attainment of non-moral ends or goods. Hence, the realm of value is determined by the process and the attainment of certain ends, which ends themselves are morally neutral. Given this neutrality, most ends considered in teleological theories are determined by the subjective wants, interests, or desires of the human agents. Of course, a critical question concerns the moral value of these personal aspirations, however they might be described.

The Aristotelian 'metaphysics of finality', a concept suggested by R. A. Gauthier and Henry Veatch, argues against the subjective characterization of human aspirations. To avoid identification with this subjective aspect of human nature and its potentialities common to teleological ethical theories, this analysis of Aquinas continues to use the term 'disposition' to translate *inclinatio* and *appetitus*; both terms could be translated as 'inclination' and 'appetite' or 'drive' respectively. These latter translations lead directly into the hornet's nest of subjective desires so commonly criticized in many teleological theories.

The metaphysics of finality, on the other hand, argues that an end is to be attained, not because of a subjective desire or wish on the part of the agent, but because the end itself determines the well-functioning of the human person. The disposition has, as a part of its very nature, a tendency towards a specific end. This end, when realized, contributes to the well-being of the individual. This is the crux of natural law moral theory. Nature has 'determined', as it were, the ends which lead to the well-being of the individuals of the natural kind. 'To have been determined', however, means only that these particular ends are part of the development of the individual's essence. This does not entail that God necessarily established human beings in this way. The present stage of human development could just as easily have been the result of evolutionary theory. While the origin of the essence is not a trivial issue, it is not central to elucidating Aristotle's theory of a metaphysics of finality.

The theory of obligation, therefore, enters Aquinas's moral theory through his theory of dispositional essence. A human nature, of its very being, is composed of a set of dispositional properties metaphysically directed towards development. This is the kernel of teleology Aquinas develops in his account of human nature in the passages from the *Summa Theologiae* discussed and analysed above. The 'value' as end is not added on to the essence like paint to a bench. The value, as end, is the realization of the dispositional process. End is to disposition as act is to potency. The concept of end is built into the very concept of the disposition. This is the significance of Aquinas's often-used passage that 'the good is an end'. If this end is what perfects the essence and if the perfection is what one means by 'well-being' or *eudaimonia*, then what does not lead to well-being hinders the development of the natural dispositions. The value is not derived from the fact. The value is built into the fact as actualization is built into potency.

Reason is a necessary condition in determining a theory of obligation. The obligatory end, then, is part of what the development is. To reach the obligatory end determines the nature and content of a human duty. Theoretical reason determines the content of human nature. This analysis is in terms of a set of dispositional properties. The end is what it is only because of the dispositions. Practical reason determines the obligation to undertake the actions which lead to *eudaimonia*. The obligatory end in Aristotle is dependent necessarily on the metaphysics of finality. This produces a naturally obligatory end. These ends are what Aristotle and Aquinas spell out through their philosophical anthropology. The ends — the human *telos* — are not arbitrary but rather determined by the dispositional properties which make up a human nature. These ends are, therefore, objective goods. These goods are desirable in themselves. They are not good only because they happen to be desired or serve as objects of interest here and now. The metaphysics of finality determines the set of objective ends central to human perfection, which is what Aristotle and Aquinas called *eudaimonia* and *beatitudo* respectively.

Aristotle and Aquinas's theory of obligation, in so far as one can glean this modern moral concept from their writings, depends upon human nature. Human nature has rationality as an essential property. Aristotle and Aquinas both argue that rationality is what distinguishes human persons from the rest of the natural world. This rational disposition is to be used according to its function. Of course, it has two functions: theoretical and practical. Reason's function is to act rationally, in both the theoretical and the practical spheres. When undertaking appropriately rational actions, some Aristotelian commentators refer to this as exercising 'right reason'. Practical reason pursues the goods which lead to human well-being. To do the opposite would be to act irrationally. Acting irrationally is opposed to the rational disposition central to the essence of the human person. Furthermore, this is opposed to what we are as human beings. Hence, the ends which make up the human essence, determined by theoretical reason and pursued by practical reason, establish the obligatory actions for human beings. This is, in effect, Aquinas's way around the criticisms of both the naturalistic fallacy and the is/ought distinction. Chapter 8 will consider these two issues in more detail.

In contrasting Aquinas's account of natural law with theories developed in renaissance scholasticism, in particular Vasquez and Suarez, Finnis suggests that when Aquinas writes that law 'is an act of the intellect', he argues that 'it is intelligence that grasps ends, and arranges means to ends, and grasps the necessity of those arranged means; and *this is the source of obligation*'.[20] Finnis will differ on the relation of 'good' or 'end' to essence; however, he would agree that the foundation of obligation is grounded in the functioning of practical reason undertaking ends to be pursued. As Gauthier and Veatch argue, human moral agents have a 'duty to be happy'!

POSITIVE LAW BRIEFLY CONSIDERED

The role of positive law in Aquinas now needs to be considered, albeit briefly. The theoretical implications are rather simple, once the concept of natural law has been elucidated. Aquinas suggested that there must be a moral foundation for law, and writes thus about the moral foundation of positive law:

[20] John Finnis, *Natural Law and Natural Rights* (corr. edn.) (Oxford: Oxford University Press, 1982), 54–5 (italics mine).

The force of a law depends on the extent of its justice. In human affairs, a thing is said to be just because it is right, which means that it is according to the rule of reason. And the first rule of reason is the law of nature . . . Thus, each human law (positive law) has as much of the nature of law as it is derived from the law of nature. However, if at any point it deflects from the law of nature, it is no longer a law but a perversion of law.

(Summa Theologiae I-II q. 95 a. 2.)

Aquinas continues this discussion:

Law may be unjust . . . by being contrary to the human good. This can happen as the following discussion indicates: Although being opposed to the things mentioned above [i.e. the discussion about the development of the dispositional properties central to the concept of human nature], a law may be contrary to the human good in the following ways: a) in regard to the end, for example, when the person in power imposed on the subjects burdensome laws which are not conducive to the common good, but rather to the leader's own desire or vainglory; b) in regard to the author of the law, for example, when a person makes a law that goes beyond the rightful power ascribed to the ruler; and c) in regard to the form, for example, when burdens are imposed unequally on the community — even with a view towards the common good.

These instances are indeed acts of violence rather than laws, as Augustine warns: 'A law that is not just seems to be no law at all.'

These purported laws, therefore, do not bind in conscience.

(Ibid. q. 96 a. 4)

This position has come down in the history of jurisprudence as the cluster of issues generically called 'law and morality'. But it is important not to confuse the issues in this cluster. Aquinas is not concerned about the problem of what immoral actions ought also to be proscribed by the legal machinery in a given society. In fact, some textual evidence suggests that Aquinas was somewhat of a legal conservative in regard to the scope of law. He wrote in one place that the principal function of law is to protect the innocent from actions by those persons insensitive to the demands of human well-being.[21] Aquinas writes, about the role of virtue, coercion, and voluntary following of the law:

Humans who are well disposed virtuously to good work are led willingly to virtue through being admonished rather than through coercion. However,

---

[21] For a recent analysis of this set of issues in a contemporary context, see Samuel Fleischacker, 'On the Enforcement of Morality: Aquinas and Narcotics Prohibition', *Public Affairs Quarterly*, 4/2 (Apr. 1990).

humans who are disposed towards undertaking evil actions need to be restrained and compelled. This is done so at least such persons might refrain from undertaking evil actions and thus leave the virtuous citizens in peace . . . The kind of habit formation which is compelled through fear of punishment is what makes up the discipline of law. Thus, so that human persons might have peace and virtue, it is necessary for positive laws to be made.

(Ibid. q. 95 a. 1)

In replying to an objection in this section of the *Summa Theologiae*, Aquinas writes that 'human persons who are disposed to undertake evil actions are usually not led to the path of virtue except through being compelled and coerced'. Furthermore, Aquinas did not seem warm to the idea of changing society through the courts. Aquinas's concern here is about the function of law – what is necessary to make justified positive law possible.

In considering the relation between law and morality, as suggested in the passages noted above, Aquinas is concerned with the moral foundation of law. He suggests that it is unsatisfactory theoretically to have as a law any proscription or prescription which goes against the developmental properties common to human nature. Whether Aquinas had determined the correct set of properties common to human nature is one issue. However, and perhaps more important for legal theory, he provided a theory entailing a denial of the possibility of legal positivism. Of course, at its starkest, legal positivism removes any connection between law and morality. Aquinas suggests much more about the nature of law than merely 'what pleases the prince has the force of law', to quote again the classic phrase from Justinian's code.

Aquinas suggests that the proper establishment of law demands a foundation in the very depths of human nature. Put differently, valid human laws are judged valid only in so far as they affect human beings. The procedural element so prevalent in contemporary jurisprudence is of secondary importance. This could be translated in modern terms as suggesting that laws must be subservient to basic human needs. Hence, Aquinas, agreeing with Augustine, holds that arbitrary repressive laws are not, in fact or theory, laws at all. As noted above, Aquinas writes that if a law 'deflects from the law of nature, it is no longer a law but a perversion of law'. In principle, there is no distinction between good law and bad or unjust law. An unjust law, in Aquinas's eyes, is no law at all; it lacks the foundation for law. That Aquinas was less concerned than most moderns about procedure and the formal rules or 'pedigree' for legality is obvious. None the less, he considered that his theory was a rational justification for the possibility of law. It explains what must be necessary if law is to be possible at all. It is not a descriptive account of the legal codes in different nations or cultures. Nor is it a method for making laws or rendering quick judicial decisions. Aquinas himself, as the texts often suggest, was aware of cultural diversity regarding mores. None the less, as many jurisprudence texts continue to mention, the concept of 'crimes against humanity', so common in the trials following the Second World War — and the grounds for charging Henry Wirz, the commandant of the infamous Andersonville Prison during the American Civil War — makes little sense without some foundation of basic human rights apart from the individual nation state. This is one part of the 'core of good sense' in any theory of natural law.

DIVINE LAW AS REVELATION

The concept of divine law is the last component to be considered in this analysis of Aquinas's account of law. The first thing to remember is not to confuse eternal law with divine law. Eternal law is the set of divine archetypes contained in the divine mind. Divine law is nothing more than the theological notion of revelation as applied to moral situations. Aquinas writes that since the moral development of human persons is essential for their happiness and flourishing — their ultimate *beatitudo* — and since a thorough grasp of the natural law with all its metaphysical implications is quite difficult, God has a 'moral responsibility' to reveal to human beings the basic principles necessary in order to make human morality possible. Aquinas suggested in various places that the possibility of grasping essences cognitively is certainly not an easy task.[22] Chapter 5 discusses this point in more detail. Furthermore, divine law is necessary in order

---

[22] Aquinas often indicated the difficulty human knowers have in coming to terms with the content of an essence. The following passages illustrate this concern: 'The essential differences are unknown to us' (*De Anima*, I lec. 1); 'Essential differences are unknown to us' (*De Veritate*, q. 4 a. 1 ad. 8); 'We are ignorant of many of the properties of sensible things, and in many cases we are unable to discover the proper nature even of those properties that we perceive by the senses' (*Summa contra Gentiles*, 1, 3). In his translation of the *Summa Theologiae*, I qq. 84–9, Paul T. Durbin provides an informative discussion of these issues. Cf. app. 2, vol xii, 'Human Intelligence' (London: Eyre and Spottiswoode, 1968), 170–2.

for human beings to become aware of the supernatural end through baptism. A consideration of this theological topic is, of course, beyond the possibility of a rational inquiry alone. None the less, Aquinas adopts the covering principle that 'grace perfects nature'. Hence, theological requirements will be in accord with the demands of reason and not *per se* contradictory. The next chapter discusses the role of a supranatural ultimate end and how it is related to Aquinas's philosophical account of natural law. Once again, Aquinas is neither a Tertullian nor a Kierkegaard.

Put simply, Aquinas argues that the Ten Commandments are basically sound rational moral principles derivable from an analysis of human nature. However, since it is difficult to undertake this inquiry through reason alone, Aquinas suggests that it is in some way incumbent upon God to make knowledge of the moral system and of the supernatural end part of revelation. In fact, Aquinas did the same thing when he developed his proofs for the existence of God. One needs to consider briefly the early structure of the *Summa Theologiae*, I, where the classic 'Five Ways' are found. Divine law serves a function analogous to a recommendation Aquinas made in discussing the preamble to the Five Ways, his 'demonstrations' for the existence of God. Aquinas suggests that because it is difficult to establish metaphysically a first ontological principle, and further-more, because a knowledge of God is important for human beings, it is once again incumbent upon God to share this knowledge with human beings. Hence, the need for revelation. Likewise, because an adequate moral theory is centrally important for human well-being, and because this knowledge is equally difficult to obtain, it is equally important and incumbent that God reveal this knowledge to human persons. This is the structural role divine law plays in Aquinas's theory of law.

What is interesting here for the history of philosophy is that Aquinas is not afraid to follow consistently the demands of his ontol-ogy. For Aquinas, reason and the principles of rational organization are central to understanding the universe. God too follows some version of rationality. Aquinas suggests that since God created human beings in a certain way – i.e. through the divine archetypes in the eternal law, after which human nature is patterned – then it follows, so Aquinas argues, that the moral principles commanded must be in accord with the moral principles derived from the dispo-sitional analysis of human nature. It would be inconsistent, therefore, for God to have commanded moral prescriptions which would go against the natural law. To do this would entail that God acted inconsistently, going against the content of a human essence as defined foundationally in the divine archetype. This is what some Aquinas scholars have called a 'moral necessity'.[23]

From this analysis, it follows that in the area of meta-ethics, Aquinas is different conceptually from William of Occam. Occam argued that what makes an act right is that God commands it. This is what might be called a 'theological definist' position. A 'right action' is defined by 'what God commands'. To the contrary, on these matters Aquinas has an unequivocal response to the famous Euthyphro question. To paraphrase the text of the *Euthyphro* modestly, an act is right, not because the gods command it, but the gods command it because it is a right action. Aquinas rejects any form of divine prescriptivism or theological definism. What makes an act right or wrong is that it is either in accord or not in accord with the fundamental developmental properties central to the concept of human nature.

Interestingly enough, William of Occam's position is identical structurally with the legal positivist. Both justify the nature of law through the 'act of commanding'. Aquinas, on the other hand, is neither a prescriptivist nor a non-cognitivist on these matters. This follows from his assumption that the intellect is superior to the will, even as this affects God. The demands of rational consistency and justification play a far greater role in Aquinas's moral theory than in Occam's. Aquinas is a rationalist, not a voluntarist. Commenting on Occam's theological definism, Frederick Copleston once wrote the following analysis:

It is the divine will which imposes the moral law which man is obliged to obey. 'By the very fact that God wills something, it is right for it to be done.' Ockham, indeed, gives a traditional view of morality when he says that 'nothing is dear to God unless it is good;' but he insists that it is good because God wills it. And he was quite prepared to draw the logical consequences from this position . . .

[23] In the *Summa Theologiae*, I q. 1 a. 1, Aquinas wrote: 'Necessarium igitur fuit, praeter philosophicae disciplinas, quae per rationem investigantur, sacram doctrinam per revelationem haberi.' The Marietti edition of the *Summa Theologiae* has an interesting footnote explicating these passages: 'Necessitate finis seu hypothetica, sed non stricta (necessitate morali seu ad bene esse . . .' I suggest that in discussing the need for revelation regarding God's existence, Aquinas's concept of 'moral necessity' as applied to God 'for a good end' (*ad bene esse*) is equally transferable to his concept

His position was ... that the present moral order depends on God's choice. God could, absolutely speaking, have imposed a different moral law; but in fact He has imposed the one which actually obtains.[24]

Aquinas would not accept this voluntarist account of the human moral law. An act is right, Aquinas argues, because it is in accord with the requirements of human nature, not because it is reducible to a divine command. That God may have created the structure of human nature differently is not the issue. Of course that could have taken place. But once human nature had been established, certain moral rules follow from the divine archetype of human nature.

This concludes a major portion of the *explicatio textus* of Aquinas's account of natural law. While there are other important sections of Aquinas's writings in which he considered moral theory, the analysis of this chapter has focused attention upon the *Summa Theologiae*, I-II qq. 90-7. In the history of Western philosophy, these texts have served as the classical canon for Aquinas's treatment of natural law meta-ethics and jurisprudence. This *explicatio textus* should help contemporary philosophers and legal scholars better to understand the theory itself, the presuppositions of the theory, and implications of Aquinas's writings on natural law. For Aquinas's theory of natural law is important both as a historical position in the canon of Western philosophy and as a statement expressing the possibility of a consistent theory of ethical naturalism.[25]

---

of divine law. This would hold no matter how one might analyse the proposition that God can be said to have an obligation.

[24] Frederick C. Copleston, *Medieval Philosophy* (London: Harper & Row, 1961), 133.

[25] As I mentioned earlier in this chapter, I am not suggesting that there are no important differences between Kant and Aquinas on moral theory. Rather, to charge too hastily that Aquinas, by definition — because he is a natural law philosopher — commits the naturalistic fallacy, fails to notice the structure of the role of end and good — which, in effect, reduces to the relation between final cause and formal cause. Aquinas is certainly not a naturalist in the same sense as Mill, Spencer, or any other nineteenth-century naturalist against whom Moore directed his charge of the naturalistic fallacy. (Chapter 8 will consider this fallacy in detail.)

5

Aquinas and God:
The Question of Natural Kinds

THE question of the relation of the existence of God to a consistent account of natural law theory, especially in the writings of Thomas Aquinas, has often baffled philosophers. The nature of the relationship between natural law and eternal law is open to conceptual confusion. Moreover, the analysis proposed suggested that such confusion has occurred often in recent discussions of Aquinas's theory of natural law. Ultimately, the main confusion rests on the claim that the natural law is so connected intrinsically with the eternal law that one cannot know the natural law without knowing the eternal law. Since most contemporary meta-ethics is agnostic at least, any theory entailing a relation to a divine being is suspect theoretically. Furthermore, this claim amounts to an interpretation rendering Aquinas's moral theory an instance of theological definism.

The task of this chapter is to suggest how one might make sense conceptually and structurally of Aquinas's account of natural law without implying a necessary relation to eternal law. Like the previous chapter, this present analysis continues the *explicatio textus* of Aquinas's writings on law in the *Summa Theologiae* with attention here paid to the connection of natural law with eternal law. Like the preceding chapter, this is an inquiry into the metaphysics which underlie Aquinas's moral theory.

DENTRÈES ON ETERNAL LAW IN AQUINAS

In his analysis of Aquinas's account of natural law, A. P. d'Entrèves once suggested that Aquinas's theory necessarily entailed the existence of a divine being. Without a divine being, Aquinas's theory of natural law, so d'Entrèves wrote, is unintelligible. This an alternative to the interpretation put forward by phil as d'Entrèves. The intelligibility of Aquinas's account interpreted in terms of a theory of natural kinds as elucidateu previous chapter, can be rendered conceptually consistent without the purported dependence upon a divine being.

In order to offer a rejoinder to d'Entrèves's account, one must offer an analysis of a rather tricky text in Aquinas's classic canon of natural law in the *Summa Theologiae*. This text reads that 'natural law is a participation in the eternal law.' The Latin is as follows: 'Unde patet quod lex naturalis nihil alilud est quam participatio legis aeternae in rationali creatura' (I-II q. 91 a. 2). Reading this passage, contemporary commentators such as d'Entrèves have suggested that Aquinas cannot account for natural law without appealing to eternal law. Moreover, as the analysis in the previous chapter indicated, eternal law is nothing more than the divine mind functioning as an explanatory principle in a manner akin to Plato's Forms. Since many contemporary philosophers are theoretical offspring of the French Enlightenment and thus imbued with atheism or agnosticism, the need for eternal law as a necessary condition for natural law indicates a serious problem for Aquinas's theory of natural law. This is the precise criticism d'Entrèves directs against Aquinas's theory. In his classic jurisprudence treatise, *Natural Law*, d'Entrèves writes:

Now it seems to me that in our divided world the first and most serious stumbling block to the Thomist conception of natural law lies precisely in its premise . . . of a divine order of the world, which St. Thomas recalls at the very beginning of his theory of law, and from which he infers, with unimpeachable logic, the most detailed and specific consequences: *supposito quod mundus divina providentia regatur, ut in primo habitum est*. Once that premise is granted, the whole majestic edifice of laws can be established on it: eternal law, the natural law, human law, and divine law. All are ultimately based on and justified through the existence of a supreme benevolent being.

Continuing with his commentary, d'Entrèves writes:

For the agnostic jurist of the present day . . . it will be very difficult to accept the notion of natural law, if that acceptance is made conditional on the acceptance of the metaphysical premise: *supposito quod mundus divina providentia regatur*. This, to my mind, is the first difficulty for the 'ontological' theory of natural law . . .[1]

---

[1] A. P. d'Entrèves, *Natural Law*, 2nd rev. edn. (London: Hutchinson University Library, 1970), 153–4.

In appendix B of *Natural Law*, d'Entrèves reiterates his claim about
the role God plays in Aquinas's type of natural law theory:

In order to conceive of these different laws as normative or ought-
propositions, it will be necessary to postulate the existence of a divine creator
who has allotted to each creature its part.[2]

D'Entrèves, moreover, is not alone in rendering this interpretation
of Aquinas. In his *Aquinas and Natural Law*, D. J. O'Connor offers
the same appraisal: 'this way of looking at the nature of law depends
upon establishing the existence of a provident God who planned and
guides the universe. St. Thomas, of course, believed that he had
done this.'[3] In a recent article, Vincent M. Cooke, while accepting
the claim that a metaphysical theory of human nature is a necessary
condition for explicating natural law theory, none the less argues
that an account of moral obligation requires a creative God who
designed human nature in a particular way. Cooke writes:

The position I am arguing for is that a metaphysics of nature is quite
sufficient to provide both a *ratio essendi* and *ratio cognoscendi* of moral obligation, but that a metaphysics of nature, i.e., the position that things in general,
and a fortiori human beings, have a *telos* or purpose other than one which
they conceptually set for themselves, is thoroughly implausible unless one
posits a Creator God.[4]

Given this passage, it appears that Cooke agrees with the d'Entrèves
position. Furthermore, Cooke claims that in an agnostic world-view,
the only sense of *telos* which human beings might have is determined
by ones which 'they conceptually set for themselves'. An important
theme necessary to natural law theory concerns the ability to transcend this kind of objection. This depends upon an analysis of obligatory end which is central to Aquinas's metaphysics of finality. The
metaphysics of finality determines what ends are obligatory beyond
what individual agents 'conceptually set for themselves'. Cooke's
analysis is reducible to what Veatch calls a 'desire ethic'.

In contemporary jurisprudence, Alf Ross inveighs against this transcendental dimension he considers necessary for any theory of natural law. He writes: 'Natural law seeks the absolute, the eternal . . .

---

[2] D'Entrèves, *Natural Law*, 179.
[3] D. J. O'Connor, *Aquinas and Natural Law* (London: Macmillan, 1967), 60.
[4] Vincent M. Cooke, SJ, 'Moral Obligation and Metaphysics', *Thought*, 66/260
(Mar. 1991), 70.

The source of the transcendent validity of law has been sought in a magical law of fate, in the will of God, or in the insight of absolute reason.'[5] One can find similar claims arguing against the possibility of natural law theory in the writings of Hans Kelsen and Joseph Raz, among others. In R. G. Frey's *Utility and Rights*, Alan Ryan argues unequivocally that without God one cannot make sense of natural law: 'Once God was dead, natural law was dead, natural duties were dead, and natural rights were dead. A secular natural-law theory is simply incoherent, and a secular natural-rights theory is therefore incoherent too.'[6]

The kind of argument presented by Ryan and Ross offers the strongest case asserting the dependence of natural law theory on the existence of God. These claims, moreover, have been accepted to a greater or lesser degree by many English-language philosophers. Recall the passage from Ronald Dworkin quoted in Chapter 2 above stating that natural law theory 'seems metaphysical or at least vaguely religious. In any case it seems plainly wrong.'

In his Gifford Lectures, *Three Rival Versions of Moral Enquiry*, Alasdair MacIntyre reports on a passage found in Adam Gifford's treatise, 'The Two Fountains of Jurisprudence', in which Gifford wrote: 'there is an eternal and unchangeable system and scheme of morality and ethics, founded not on the will, or on the devices, or in the imagination of man, but on the nature and essence of the unchangeable God'.[7] This is a clear illustration of the theological definist position for natural law indicating that the essence of God alone determines the natural law.

REMOVING THE TRANSCENDENTAL FROM
NATURAL LAW

It is on this point, however, that many historians of philosophy, moral philosophers, and philosophers of law such as d'Entrèves, Cooke, O'Connor, Ross, Ryan, and Gifford, are, I suggest, mistaken conceptually in considering Aquinas. Recall what d'Entréves wrote

[5] Alf Ross, from *On Law and Justice*, cited in Michael Golding, *The Nature of Law* (New York: Random House, 1966), 69.

[6] Alan Ryan, 'Utility and Ownership', in R. G. Frey, *Utility and Rights* (Oxford: Basil Blackwell, 1985), 180.

[7] Alasdair MacIntyre, *Three Rival Versions of Moral Enquiry* (Notre Dame, Ind: University of Notre Dame Press, 1990), 25.

about Aquinas's system of law: 'eternal law, the natural law, human law, and divine law. All are ultimately based on and justified through the existence of a supreme benevolent being.' And recall Ryan's resolute claim: 'A secular natural-law is simply incoherent . . . '

It is correct that some natural law theorists have proposed a meta-ethical account which no doubt relies on the divine realm. This dependence, however, is not a necessary condition for Aquinas's theory of natural law. In opposition to d'Entrèves, this chapter suggests that Aquinas's account of natural law can be elucidated consistently without being 'ultimately based on and justified through the existence of a supreme benevolent being'. The issues central to elucidating the concept of natural law in Aquinas are not theological with regard to establishing or interpreting the existence of a divine being. On the contrary, the principal issues in understanding Aquinas's theory of natural law, as discussed in the preceding chapter, are common discussions in metaphysics and epistemology. The concepts Aquinas requires as necessary conditions for a consistent account of natural law are the following:

1. The possibility of essences or natural kinds;
2. A dispositional view of essential properties determining the content of a natural kind;
3. A metaphysics of finality determining the obligatory ends central to human well-being;
4. An adequate epistemological apparatus providing an awareness of essences or natural kinds in the individual;
5. A theory of practical reason undertaking the ends to be pursued in terms of human nature.

The existence of God is, in a structural sense, neither a relevant concept nor a necessary condition for Aquinas's account of natural law. While the texts do indicate, as d'Entrèves suggested, the participation of the natural law with the eternal law, this participation follows from a second order metaphysical question. This chapter articulates the position that one can provide a consistent account of the content of natural law without appealing to the eternal law. The core issue concerns the analysis of human nature, which, of course, is the natural kind. If d'Entrèves, O'Connor, Ross, and Ryan, among others, are correct, then the following proposition holds: In Aquinas's ontology, every account of an essential property or natural kind demands an appeal to a divine being. Or, in terms of Aquinas's theory of law, natural law entails a strict explanatory relation to eternal law.

There are two issues which appear to dominate the discussions concerning the relation of natural law to eternal law: (1) the issue concerning the relation of the content of human nature, as expressed in natural law theory, to the eternal law; and (2) the foundation of a theory of obligation within the theoretical limits of natural law ethics. Both of these issues are interconnected structurally.

In regard to the first point, this chapter suggests, contrary to d'Entrèves and others, that the issues Aquinas faced in constructing a theory of natural law are similar to those found in any attempt to establish the possibility of natural kinds. Natural law depends upon natural kinds, which is a metaphysical issue resolved in terms of Aquinas's ontology, not his theology. Therefore, a consistent account of Aquinas's theory of natural law is independent conceptually of the proposition that God exists.

Regarding the second point, Chapter 4 articulated an account of the metaphysics of finality. This view of metaphysics is a necessary condition for explicating Aquinas's theory of obligatory ends. Most philosophers considering Aquinas's theory of natural law are concerned about attributing the concept of obligation to human nature. Vincent Cooke states the issues quite clearly above when he writes that for 'human beings (to) have a *telos* or purpose other than one which they conceptually set for themselves, is thoroughly implausible unless one posits a creator God'. Cooke, as most contemporary analytic philosophers, can make sense of obligation in natural law theory only within the bounds of a theological definist position. In other words, obligation comes about because of the 'command of God'.

In response to this position, one needs to articulate Aquinas's natural law moral theory in terms of a metaphysics of finality. Using practical reason working with the will accounts for Aquinas's view of action theory. This provides Aquinas's position on how human agents undertake actions. In this view, a moral agent acts rationally only if the agent prescribes those actions which develop the dispositional properties common to human nature. This is the role of practical reason. To act in a contrary fashion entails acting irrationally, and hence, immorally. The metaphysics of finality builds into the set of dispositional properties the obligatory ends which are necessary for well-being. This sense of obligatory end depends upon the dispositional theory of human nature. Practical reason pursues the actions developing the human goods. To act otherwise is to act irrationally and thus to act contrary to our rational nature.

The general objective of this chapter, then, is to explicate the metaphysical underpinnings necessary to account for our understanding of natural law. Aquinas's account of intentionality with its structured awareness of the active and passive intellects necessary to explicate the process of understanding is, to be sure, far more complicated than the epistemology normally associated with British empiricism. To acquire an understanding of essential properties depends upon the epistemological structure of Aquinas philosophy of mind. Of course, this analysis transcends the limits of classical empiricism.

Writing on Aquinas's metaphysics and epistemology, Christopher Martin offers the following observations concerning the impact Aquinas's metaphysics and epistemology has had on some of the issues central to contemporary analytic philosophy:

The lesson has been slowly re-learned by some this century that our ordinary language and indeed all our ordinary thought presuppose the Aristotelian–Thomistic view of knowledge, and the metaphysics which lies behind it. No matter how much we may profess empiricist or positivist ideas, we cannot express them in the language that we normally use, and cannot, either, do more than sketch – with very broad strokes, sometimes – the language that would be appropriate to them.

Martin goes on to suggest how Aquinas's themes have been reiterated by Frege and Kripke:

This century, philosophers have been coming to see the bankruptcy of empiricism. But old habits die hard. The brilliant puzzles of Hume are still set for study of undergraduates, and no alternative system is given which will explain and organize the unconscious metaphysics that we all use, the metaphysics that Hume seeks to expose as unfounded. So philosophers continue to be influenced by empiricism. This is where the value, and the difficulty, of the study of Aquinas become evident. He is not an empiricist, and indeed largely ignores the epistemological questions to which empiricism seeks to give an answer. He is a metaphysician: and he uses the concepts of Aristotle to systematize the unconscious metaphysics that we all share. He represents a step forward, as it were, on the road at whose beginning we are standing. Frege and Kripke, among others, have brought us to the start of this road: the one by relegating problems of epistemology to their rightful place, the other by drawing attention to our unconscious meta-

physics. What we need to do is to develop and systematize that metaphysics
... Our unconscious metaphysics has a presumptive correctness, but that
presumption can be defeated. But it can also be defended, and should be:
it is not enough merely to draw attention to it.[8]

Martin suggests the importance of reading Aquinas seriously when
considering metaphysical and epistemological problems. It is in
offering an analysis of essence as a natural kind that Aquinas's metaphysics bears on the issues common to natural law theory.

ESSENCE AS NATURAL KIND

The previous chapter offered an analysis of Aquinas's theory of
essence in terms of a dispositional view of natural kind. The role of
a dispositional theory of essence is crucial in determining Aquinas's
naturalist theory of value. In the preceding chapter, the explanation
of eternal law indicated that this aspect of Aquinas's account of law
is reducible to a theory of archetypes in the divine mind. Similarly
to Plato in the *Timaeus*, Aquinas argues that individuals existing in
the temporal realm are patterned after the archetype in the divine
mind. The eternal law is, on this analysis, the set of archetypes in
the divine mind after which the world of experience is modelled.

Aquinas's account of eternal law follows from his theory of truth.
Aquinas, like most medieval philosophers and probably all Aristotelians, adopted a version of the correspondence theory of truth. Assuming that the proposition found in the Scriptures is correct which
asserts that 'human beings are made in the image and likeness of
God', Aquinas wonders how to explicate and offer an analysis of
this proposition. Aquinas explained this proposition in the following
manner. Eternal law is a metaphysical explanation of reality, or, as
Quine once put it, of 'what there is'. Primary substances have essential properties because they are patterned after the archetypes in the
divine mind. Aquinas wrote elsewhere in the *Summa Theologiae* that
'the eternal law is nothing more than the exemplar of divine wisdom'.
With eternal law analysed in the manner of Plato's archetypes,
Aquinas undertook a piece of metaphysical analysis. This is not a
form of theology. He offered an explanatory analysis in a Platonic
mode accounting for a proposition he took to be true. To reiterate

[8] Christopher Martin, *The Philosophy of Thomas Aquinas* (London: Routledge,
1988), 4–5.

a theme from the previous chapter, when considering the divine archetypes, Aquinas's method of doing philosophy is strikingly similar to G. E. Moore's distinction between 'truth' and 'analysis'. Aquinas does not doubt the truth of the proposition. But he does realize that the meaning of the proposition is not clear. Hence, he subjects the proposition to analysis in order to make it as clear as possible. This helps us understand the proposition's meaning; it does not establish the truth of the proposition. Moore's account of philosophy as analysis is very similar structurally.

Aquinas does write that the natural law participates in the eternal law. D'Entrèves and O'Connor remind us of this text often. The question to be considered now is in what sense does the natural law depend upon the eternal law? If it is a strict entailment relation, then d'Entrèves and O'Connor are correct. It would follow that Aquinas's theory of natural law cannot be separated conceptually from eternal law.

An alternative analysis of these texts suggests a reading of the texts which avoids the theological pitfalls d'Entrèves and O'Connor claim is inherent in Aquinas theory of natural law. In his philosophical anthropology and, accordingly, in his ontology, Aquinas proposed a developmental view of essence. This point was discussed and developed in the previous chapter.

Moreover, Aquinas adopted Aristotle's fourfold theory of causality. Without a developmental analysis of essence, Aquinas could not elucidate consistently the concept of final cause. Following Aristotle in the *Nicomachean Ethics*, Aquinas defined the 'good' as an 'end': 'Quia vero bonum habet rationem finis . . .' (*Summa Theologiae*, I-II q. 94 a. 2). Hence, there are as many goods as there are ends. Once again, this indicates the incommensurability of the concept of good in Aquinas's writings. An end – the final cause – is the full development or 'actualization' of a dispositional property. An essence, which is composed of a set of dispositional properties, determines those ends which are to be obtained. In Aristotelian language, this is the relation between the formal cause and the final cause. The natural law, in the mind of Aquinas, is nothing more than the determination of the ends – read final cause – of the dispositional properties of the essence – read formal cause – of the human person. By using theoretical reason, the moral agent comes to understand the content of human nature. This content, in terms of essential properties, is determined by the form. The agent then determines that actions need to be undertaken in order to develop these dispositions. Practical reason determines the actions needed to reach the 'obligatory ends'. Not to strive for the development of these dispositions is to act irrationally. To reach the end is to reach the final cause. The final cause, in other words, refers to the set of properties as developed which determine the essence. As act to potency, the final cause is the 'act' of the 'potency', the act which is the completion of a disposition.

Aquinas's theory of natural law, therefore, depends necessarily on his theory of essence. This theory of essence is nothing more than a dispositional account of natural kind. This dispositional theory of natural kinds is a necessary condition for Aquinas's rendition of natural law. Determining the ends as goods is a second order inquiry based on his philosophical anthropology. This anthropology determines the ends as the completion of the natural kind. It is these concepts which Aquinas needs to explicate in order to render his theory of natural law consistent.

In discussing Aristotle on essence in the previous chapter, reference was made to Michael Ayers's suggestion that an essential property, in a manner akin to Kripke and the earlier Putnam, 'rigidly designates' a natural kind: 'there is some awareness at least that the (Kripke/Putnam) view is not so new as all that, since it is not at all unlike Aristotelian doctrine'.[9] Ayers's suggestion applies equally well to Aquinas. Hence, what Aquinas needs for his theory of natural law is a dispositional theory of natural kinds, not a divine being. Following Christopher Martin's suggestion from the passage referred to above, Kripke's metaphysics of natural kinds may well have important connections with Aquinas's theory of essence. Hence, Aquinas's metaphysics is not totally removed from the mainstream concerns of contemporary analytic philosophy. It is these mainstream metaphysical concerns, moreover, which are necessary for a coherent account of Aquinas's theory of natural law.

[9] Michael Ayers, 'Locke Versus Aristotle on Natural Kinds', *Journal of Philosophy*, 78/5 (May 1981), 248.

The next part of this investigation considers the nature of the
relation between eternal law and natural law. Given the analysis just
proposed, it follows that Aquinas did not first ask his readers to
accept the existence of God before understanding the concept of
natural law. Rather, he asked them to consider the possibility of a
metaphysics of natural kinds. As a philosopher talking about natural
kinds, Aquinas asked, first of all, what is necessary to ground an
essence? Secondly he asked, how do we determine what is the content of an essence, which is the metaphysical construct from which
we derive the set of ends or goods? These are the metaphysical and
epistemological issues – the natural kind and our awareness of its
content – necessary to natural law. This is what Aquinas needs to
explicate his metaphysics of finality. The existence of God and the
role of eternal law do not comprise the first set of questions to be
considered in Aquinas's rendition of natural law theory. Following
the analysis offered in the previous chapter, the essence is determined by a set of synthetic a priori causal connections. This essence
is known through the abstractive process of the *intellectus agens*. In
other words, Aquinas's epistemological account of how a knower
becomes aware of the content of an essence or nature – what Aquinas
called 'having a concept' – depends on the role of abstraction
through the active intellect. The exact analysis of this process of
abstraction is beyond the limits of this inquiry.[10]

Aquinas can provide an account for this analysis of the concept
of essence, moreover, with or without God. The analysis of an
essence in terms of a set of dispositional properties as put forward
in Aquinas's metaphysics is independent conceptually from an argument for the existence of God. Hence, Aquinas's account of natural
law – which is in effect an account of moral properties based upon
a dispositional view of human nature – is independent conceptually
from his account of eternal law. The metaphysics of finality with its
concept of an obligatory end is separated structurally from the eternal law. One need not know the eternal law prior to gaining knowledge of the natural law, because one need not know that God exists

---

[10] The interested reader may consult many of the writings of Peter Geach and
Anthony Kenny in order to discover first-rate analytic accounts of Aquinas's philosophy of mind.

prior to acquiring knowledge of an essence or natural kind. If this were not the case, then in principle an atheist or an agnostic could not acquire knowledge of an essence. Aquinas would find this claim incomprehensible. His entire account of the acquisition of a knowledge of essences never mentions such a claim. Therefore, it is possible theoretically to determine the concept of an essence without asking any questions about God's existence or God's providence.

In his *Natural Law and Natural Rights*, John Finnis suggests a similar account. Finnis writes that 'for Aquinas, there is nothing extraordinary about man's grasp of the natural law; it is simply one application of man's ordinary power of understanding'.[11] Moreover, Finnis also suggests that his own analysis is 'a rather elaborate sketch of a theory of natural law without needing to advert to the question of God's existence or nature or will'.[12] Commenting on Finnis's theory of natural law, Charles Covell writes the following on the possibility of a 'secular' analysis of natural law theory in Aquinas:

[In] *Natural Law and Natural Rights*, [Finnis] claimed that the principles of natural law admitted of an entirely secular derivation, which involved no metaphysical assumptions regarding the existence, nature or will of God. Indeed, he emphasized that it had been an essential feature of the Thomist system that, for Aquinas, the first principles of natural law were self-evident to human reason, whereas the knowledge that union with God ranked as the final human end could be acquired only through revelation.[13]

That Finnis will not endorse the need for an essence, which theory he calls 'reductivism', in his account of Aquinas on natural law will become apparent in Chapter 6. None the less, Finnis would agree with the central claim in this chapter suggesting that the existence of God is not a necessary condition for an explication of Aquinas on natural law.

Furthermore, this knowledge of an essence – in this case, the human essence – is all Aquinas needs to begin his discussion of natural law. D'Entrèves, O'Connor, and the other philosophers mentioned earlier in this chapter, are mistaken structurally in suggesting otherwise. In addition, historians of medieval philosophy realize that

[11] John Finnis, *Natural Law and Natural Rights*, corr. edn. (Oxford: Oxford University Press, 1982), 400.
[12] Ibid. 49
[13] Charles Covell, *The Defence of Natural Law* (New York: St Martin's Press, 1992), 222–3.

Aquinas rejected both the divine illumination epistemology proposed by Augustine and its later counterpart, the separated existence of the *intellectus agens*, postulated by Avicenna and Averroës. Both Augustine and the two Arabian philosophers postulated an epistemology which required divine activity in some way or other in order for human knowers to acquire a knowledge of essences. Aquinas emphatically denies such a claim.

GOD AS A NECESSARY BEING

But, one might reasonably ask, why does Aquinas write about eternal law as that in which the natural law participates? Aquinas, it appears, uses eternal law as the solution to a second order metaphysical question. With regard to the nature and function of God, Aquinas is not a modern philosopher. This is not merely the assertion of a chronological proposition. Aquinas is separated conceptually from philosophers such as Descartes, for instance, who argue to the existence of God before suggesting anything about the nature of the external world.[14] Descartes's ontology of the external world is in terms of individuals made up of two distinct and separable items – extended matter and a spiritual mind. Aquinas's ontology, following the Aristotelian insights, is in terms of individuals of a natural kind. The natural kind is determined by a set of synthetic necessary dispositional properties. All of this is rooted in Aquinas's hylomorphic ontology of matter and form. This ontology is all Aquinas needs, therefore, to begin his consideration of natural law. Philosophically, one might not accept this account entailing the existence of synthetic necessary properties which determine the content of an essence and the metaphysics of finality. But that is another question. Aquinas did accept this metaphysical schema. It is through this schema, moreover, that he developed his theory of natural law. Given this analysis, it seems clear that Aquinas can determine the content of an essence without appealing to a divine being.

---

[14] In his *A First Glance at St. Thomas Aquinas*, Ralph McInerny suggests that this Cartesian attitude should be labeled as 'modernity'. In several of his writings, but most significantly in *For an Ontology of Morals*, Henry B. Veatch calls this the 'transcendental turn' in philosophy. Both philosophers direct their attention to the epistemological beginnings of Cartesian philosophy with its negative effects on interpreting Aristotelian/Aquinian realism. This important metaphilosophical direction of modern philosophy should not be underestimated.

Furthermore, elsewhere Aquinas argued that it is impossible theoretically to know the nature of God. This is why Aquinas admits validity only to a posteriori arguments for God's existence. While acknowledging divine simplicity, the eternal law is an aspect of the divine mind and must be construed as a 'component' of the divine nature. Aquinas's agnostic claims about the possibility of knowing God's nature should make one become suspicious when reading a suggestion that one must know the eternal law prior to the natural law. Aquinas would think such a cognitive project humanly impossible.

In considering the relation between God and temporal essence in Aquinas, one has to recall the structure of Aquinas's proofs for the existence of God. These proofs, which are the classic 'Five Ways' in the *Summa Theologiae*, I, point to the existence of a first metaphysical principle. This is the conclusion of Aquinas's 'demonstrations' when he embarked upon a rational or philosophical theology within the confines of the *Summa Theologiae*. Metaphilosophically, however, Aquinas reached these conclusions only after reflection upon the existential limitations of temporal essences. In other words, all primary substances are contingent beings dependent existentially on a being beyond themselves. Aquinas is at least latently Platonic when considering the proofs for the existence of God, especially regarding God as the source of all being through the bestowal of existence.

The 'third way', the 'proof' from contingent to necessary beings, is perhaps the crucial *demonstratio* in Aquinas's writings about the rational ways of establishing God's existence. Frederick Copleston once wrote that contemporary Aquinas scholars 'often assert that the third proof, bearing directly on the existence of things, is fundamental'.[15] One argues to an act of existence, which must be subsistent and independent, only to explain the acts of existence found in temporal essences. This is one of the final questions in Aquinas's metaphysical inquiry. The acts of existence in temporal essences are not subsistent but extrinsic to that contingent essence. For a primary substance, existence is always external to the individual's essence. Existence is never part of the set of dispositional properties which determine the essence. Existence is 'added on', as it were. Of course, this is the definition of a contingent being: one whose essence does not contain existence as a constitutive property. It is only at this

---

[15] F. C. Copleston, *Aquinas* (London: Penguin Books Ltd., 1955), 122.

level that Aquinas comes to a notion of a first being, first cause, necessary being, or whatever else anyone might call the God of the philosophers. It is the result of a reflective analysis on the constitutive character of a temporal essence, which is of its very nature contingent. This analysis, Aquinas argues, suggests that existence is never an essential property of a primary substance. This is why the essence/existence distinction is so important to Aquinas. It is only at this level of a second order, reflective metaphysical question that eternal law becomes necessary for natural law. The 'necessary being' handles a question about the nature of a contingent essence, not a question about the content of the essence itself. This becomes clear in the phrases in Aquinas which Gilson articulated so forcefully: the question about 'what' something is is different from the question 'that' something is. The 'what' refers to the content of an essence. The 'that' refers to its existence. The question about existence is beyond the question about the content of the essence itself. It is only the latter issues which Aquinas needs to consider in determining the foundation of human nature for natural law theory

Given this analysis, Aquinas could provide a consistent account of the concept of essence in terms of a set of synthetic necessary dispositional properties without appealing to the divine mind containing the eternal law. In other words, Aquinas argues that his epistemological machinery—the *intellectus agens* and its role in 'abstraction'—is sufficient to provide an explanatory account of our knowledge of an essence without a direct reference to the eternal law. Aquinas included the divine mind only because it provided the ultimate or capstone explanation for his ontology. God as the 'necessary being' accounts for why there is something rather than nothing. God provides the existence to the temporal essence whose structure is contingent. But an analysis of this relation of existence dependent upon the necessary being is not itself a necessary condition for understanding the content of a temporal essence.

If one does not arrive at this ultimate explanation in the necessary being, however, then one has, so Aquinas thought, only an incomplete metaphysical theory, not a false metaphysical theory. One can render a consistent conceptual account of essence without an appeal to the eternal law. A knower does not need the eternal law in order to form a concept through the abstractive process of the *intellectus agens*. Again, Aquinas rejects the epistemological position of illumination in any of the modes favoured by Augustine, Avicenna, or

Averroës. An essence is dependent ontologically on a first cause only if one accepts Aquinas's theory of contingent and necessary beings. But this is a second order metaphysical question. It follows from an analysis of the contingent nature of a finite, temporal essence. It is one of the last steps in Aquinas's ontology. It is never the first step. Aquinas considers the natural world before he begins a consideration of the divine realm. Regarding the role of God in his ontology, Aquinas is not a Cartesian by any stretch of the imagination.

Furthermore, this analysis of essence is compatible with an evolutionary account postulating the development of essences over time. That Aquinas argued for a necessary being ontology and a divine archetype position is a second order metaphysical issue. None the less, a human knower can be aware of the set of synthetic necessary properties making up an essence, no matter how this set of properties came to be. The set of properties could have come about through evolutionary development, through the *rationes seminales* which Augustine proposed, or through another form of divine interaction. But this is a separate ontological question beyond that which determines the content of finite essences. The intentional structure of the active intellect accomplishes the act of knowing sufficient to acquire a concept, which is knowing an essence. The structure of the essence in terms of a metaphysics of finality, and becoming aware of that essence, therefore, are the necessary conditions for offering an account of Aquinas's theory of natural law. The existence of God is not a necessary condition for knowing an essence.

AQUINAS ON THE ULTIMATE END FOR HUMAN BEINGS

In discussing Aquinas's moral theory, the issue of the ultimate end of human beings must be considered. As a philosopher/theologian in the Christian tradition, Aquinas holds a different view of the content and structure of the ultimate end from that which is found in the texts of the *Nicomachean Ethics*. The ultimate end in both Aristotle and Aquinas is referred to as 'happiness', which is the common translation for *eudaimonia*, *beatitudo*, and *felicitas*. Happiness as the ultimate end, however, does have a distinct meaning in the account of each philosopher. In Aristotle, *eudaimonia* means 'an activity of reason in accord with virtue'. Aristotle does express some ambiguity about the nature of the 'activity' which constitutes *eudaimonia*. In discussing the moral virtues throughout most of the *Nicom-*

achean Ethics, he brings our attention to the activities undertaken through the 'mean' which help human agents function well as human beings. In those troubling passages in the tenth book of the *Nicomachean Ethics*, however, he changes direction and stresses the role the intellectual activity of contemplation plays in bringing about the actualization of our rational disposition. The activity of contemplation is in accord with the acquired virtues of speculative reason.

In appropriating Aristotelian moral theory as the structural paradigm for the development of the moral arguments in the *Summa Theologiae*, Aquinas draws heavily upon the role of contemplation which Aristotle developed in book 10 of his *Ethics*. Aquinas, working within the structure of Christian theology, argues that the ultimate end for human beings is a contemplative awareness of God. Human happiness, therefore, consists in an intellectual exercise directed towards an object which transcends the ordinary experiences of human beings.

What makes this issue more difficult is the fact that Aquinas demands some transnatural or supernatural states which are necessary conditions for attaining Christian beatitude:

1. As an object of knowledge, God is beyond the possibility of limited, finite human awareness;
2. A supernatural aid, the 'light of glory', enables the human intellect to become directly aware of God;
3. Grace is a necessary condition enabling human beings to embark upon the path of eternal salvation.

These necessary conditions would appear to bring about an unbridgeable chasm between the demands of Aristotelian moral theory and the corresponding requirements of Aquinian moral theory. In *Summa Theologiae*, Aquinas writes:

When the human intellect is directly aware of the essence of God, that very divine essence becomes the form through which the human intellect understands. Therefore, there must be some assistance given to the human understanding which is beyond its own nature so that it can be elevated to this ability. Since, as we have shown, the natural ability of the human understanding is not sufficient to be directly aware of the essence of God, this power of the understanding must come to it by divine grace. This elevation in the ability to understand is called the 'illumination' of the human mind; in a like manner, the intelligible form is spoken of as 'light'.

(I q. 12 a. 5)

Given this expansion of the Aristotelian paradigm by Aquinas, the question that arises immediately is that of the compatibility of the Aristotelian moral theory with the ultimate end as discussed by Aquinas. Some critics, such as R. A. Gauthier, suggest that the incompatibility is so severe that any reconciliation is structurally impossible.[16] Ralph McInerny argues against the Gauthier account and offers an analysis which suggests a compatibalist theory for Aristotle and Aquinas on the theory of ultimate end. In his excellent account of the life and works of Aquinas, Simon Tugwell writes, concerning the Gauthier thesis: 'Gauthier argues that Thomas' concern was always theological, even in his "philosophical" writings, but his critics have pointed plausibly enough to signs that Thomas did have a serious philosophical purpose and that he was interested in clarifying Aristotelian philosophy in its own right.'[17]

The following analysis attempting to establish the compatibalist position on the ultimate end discussions of Aristotle and Aquinas depends very much on the arguments put forward by McInerny and Brian Davies.[18] In order to resolve this difficulty in interpretation of Aristotle and Aquinas, one must distinguish between the 'natural' or 'temporal' ultimate end and the 'supernatural' or 'transnatural' ultimate end. Aquinas refers to this difference as the 'imperfect' and the 'perfect' ultimate end. Aquinas writes that 'perfect happiness requires the human mind to be aware of the essence of the first cause' (*Summa Theologiae*, I-II q. 3 a. 8). He says much the same thing earlier in this part of the *Summa Theologiae* when he writes that 'the human intellect attains perfection in so far as it knows the essence of a thing . . . perfect happiness requires that the intellect reaches the very essence of the first cause' (ibid. a. 3). Elaborating on this distinction, he says:

A human person is actualised through virtue towards these actions by which he or she moves towards happiness . . . None the less, human happiness is twofold . . . One is proportionate to human nature; human beings can aquire

---

[16] For an extended discussion of this issue, the interested reader should consult Ralph McInerny, 'Aristotle and Aquinas: Père Gauthier', which is ch. 7 in McInerny's *Aquinas on Human Action*, (Washington, D C, Catholic University of America Press, 1992).

[17] Simon Tugwell, 'The Life and Works of Thomas Aquinas', in *Albert and Thomas* (New York: Paulist Press, 1988), 257–58.

[18] Brian Davies, *The Thought of Thomas Aquinas* (Oxford: Clarendon Press, 1992), chs. 12 and 13; Ralph McInerny, 'Aristotle and Thomas: Père Gauthier', 161–177.

this happiness through their own resources. The second form of happiness, which transcends human nature, can be attained only by the power of God. This happens through a kind of participation of the God-head. Therefore, it is written that by Christ we are made 'partakers of the divine nature' (2 Peter 1:4). Because this happiness transcends the natural ability of human nature, the natural resources by which human persons are able to act well according to human nature alone are not adequate to direct them to this higher form of happiness. And thus, in order to be directed to this supernatural happiness, it is necessary that human persons need to be divinely assisted through some additional principles of activity. These additional principles are like the native dispositions, which direct humans to their connatural end, yet always with God's help. These principles of action are called theological virtues. (*Summa Theologiae*, I-II q. 62 a. 1)

Writing again on this issue when discussing the differences between human and angelic knowledge, Aquinas states:

The ultimate end or perfection of rational or intellectual beings is twofold: in the first case, the perfection which humans can attain through their natural dispositions; this is called 'happiness' (*beatitudo vel felicitas*). In this sense, Aristotle suggested that the ultimate end for human beings is the highest contemplative activity, which is the knowledge which is possible to the human mind in this life (*Ethics* 10). But beyond this happiness there is another, to which human beings look forward in the next life, which is the happiness of 'seeing God as He is'. This is beyond the cognitive possibility of any created intellect. (I q. 62 a. 1)

Given these texts, certainly serious questions arise concerning the role a theological perspective plays in Aquinas's understanding of Aristotelian *eudaimonia*. Aquinas completes the above passage by stating that 'this happiness is beyond the nature of our created intellect'.

PERFECT AND IMPERFECT HAPPINESS

Aquinas gives evidence of having thought deeply about Aristotle's account of *eudaimonia* and how to reconcile the suggestions on the ultimate end considered in the *Nicomachean Ethics*, especially the tenth book, with Christian theology. The issue may be constructed in terms of the concepts of 'perfect' and 'imperfect' happiness. There are two parts to the problem:

    1. Imperfect happiness is what Aristotle discussed in the *Nicomachean Ethics*. Fundamentally, this is the activity of theoretical reason

supported by the virtuous life attained through the exercise of the moral virtues in practical reason. Perfect happiness, on the other hand, is the complete satisfaction of the intellect and the will through the intellectual attainment of knowledge of God.

2. Imperfect happiness, even as discussed by Aristotle, is never completely attainable in this life. In the *Nicomachean Ethics*, Aristotle suggests that *eudaimonia* in terms of contemplation is attained by human beings infrequently. To appropriate a term McInerny uses in this context, human happiness as experienced by human agents is at best an 'episodic' condition. It is never complete, stable, and without interruption. Contemplative activity, Aristotle writes, is a rare occurrence experienced by only a few human persons. Furthermore, contemplation depends upon the successful practising of the moral virtues.

The analysis of this distinction, therefore, indicates two things. First of all, Aquinas suggests that Aristotelian *eudaimonia* is a terrestrial activity depending on the development of the human 'function' (*ergon*), especially that of reason. This activity, which is imperfect happiness, is contemplation. Perfect happiness, which is the direct awareness of God, goes beyond the limits of Aristotle's terrestrial *eudaimonia*.

The principal point of Aquinas's reflection on these matters, however, is not merely to suggest the distinction between terrestrial *eudaimonia* and trans-terrestrial *beatitudo*. Of course, Aquinas does make this distinction. None the less, the structure of the argument points to a deeper issue regarding the nature and structure of the concept of *eudaimonia* as put forward in the Aristotelian texts. Aristotle realized the limitations of human beings regarding the attainment of *eudaimonia*. This attainment is, as McInerny suggests, at best an episodic attainment. Aquinas picks up on this limitation in Aristotle's use of *eudaimonia*. He suggests that there exists the possibility of a trans-terrestrial *eudaimonia*, which he calls *beatitudo*. This trans-terrestrial happiness will meet the requirements of Aristotle's account but also will transcend the limitations. This is what Aquinas calls perfect happiness, *vera beatitudo*. This state of perfect happiness is attained only through a direct and permanent awareness of God as the first cause of all things and as the ultimate source of Good. God becomes the object of the human intellect and the human will, satisfying both human faculties without deficiency. In this way,

Aquinas once again views his theology as an instantiation of the principle that 'grace perfects nature'. The attainment of the everlasting life promised to those who follow the gospel message is not antithetical to the best naturalist account of human well-being. Rather, it is perfective of that naturalist account.

Aquinas considered that Aristotle's *Nicomachean Ethics* provided the best account of moral theory put forward by Western philosophers. This 'best account', as determined by Aristotle himself, was seen as providing only an episodic attainment of the activity central to the ultimate end for human moral agents. Working within this Aristotelian structure of moral naturalism, Aquinas develops his theological interpretation of the ultimate end, perfective of, yet dependent upon, naturalism. Given this interpretation of the ultimate end in Aquinas, it is not that Aquinas used Aristotle for his own purposes, which were theological in nature and scope. Aquinas did not, as Gauthier suggests, do 'violence to Aristotle's thought by forcing it into the Procrustean bed of Christian theology.'[19]

What this analysis of ultimate end tells us about Aquinas's theory of natural law morality is its dependence on a naturalistic account of *eudaimonia*. Furthermore, it suggests that distinctions must be made. It suggests that moral theory, as envisioned by Aristotle, has built-in limitations. But it assumes that Aristotelian moral theory is the best naturalist account available. It is as if Aquinas, when reading Aristotle's moral theory, were to quote an American television beer commercial, 'It doesn't get any better than this!'

GRACE NATURE AND THE MORAL LIFE

Given our discussion on the theological interpretation of the ultimate end, the question arises concerning the role natural law theory has in the purely philosophical realm. Once again, Aquinas will offer a distinction between the purely secular virtuous person and the person whose virtue has been modified by means of grace. As a Christian theologian, Aquinas will, of course, emphasize the importance of the theological virtues of faith, hope, and charity. These virtues are given to human persons only through the divine activity of grace. Yet, because of Aquinas's theological axiom that grace perfects nature, one cannot attain the benefits of the theological

---

[19] As cited in McInerny, 'Aristotle and Thomas', 161.

virtues without having some semblance of moral accomplishment in the natural realm.

Aquinas argues that the realm of Christian virtues has as its principal methodological virtue charity rather than prudence, which is Aristotle's methodological moral virtue. Hence, as prudence enables the moral agent to choose the mean virtuous action, so charity enables the moral agent to act virtuously within the Christian context. However, natural virtue still is attainable. But the historical situation, Aquinas believes, has been determined by the Christian context. Hence, holiness is an important Christian end. None the less, Christian virtue is not antithetical to naturalism in virtue. Were there no trans-terrestrial ultimate end for human beings, the Aristotelian account as modified through Aquinas's theory of natural law would be sufficient for an adequate moral theory.

A SET OF CONDITIONS FOR NATURAL LAW THEORY

By way of a schematic summary, the five central necessary conditions for natural law theory in Aquinas are:

1. A theory of essence or natural kind;
2. An interpretation of natural kind containing dispositional and not static necessary properties;
3. A metaphysics of finality determining the obligatory ends;
4. An epistemological machinery adequate to provide veridical intentional content of an essence or natural kind;
5. A theory of practical reason undertaking the ends to be pursued in terms of the requirements of human nature.

The existence of a divine being is neither centrally important nor a necessary condition for an awareness of the content of an essence in Aquinas's epistemology. Since his theory of natural law, as argued in the last two chapters, depends upon his account of essence in space-time, eternal law is not a necessary condition for understanding the content of natural law.

The history of natural law theory — both in meta-ethics and jurisprudence — has often reached conclusions regarding Aquinas's theory similar to those offered by d'Entréves and O'Connor. This interpretation, however, neglects to read the texts as based upon a developmental theory of essence or natural kind. This natural kind view, so this book argues, is central to understanding Aquinas's

ontology of natural law. Aquinas's metaphysics can account for the
content of a human essence, the natural kind, without an appeal to
the eternal law. There is no need, therefore, to appeal to a divine
being. Natural law depends upon natural kinds, which is a metaphysical issue resolved in terms of Aquinas's metaphysics, not his theology. What Aquinas needs for his natural law theory is an account
of essence in terms of dispositional properties. It is this ontology
that his theory is 'ultimately based on and justified [by]', *not* 'through
the existence of a supreme benevolent being'.

Before concluding this chapter, it is important to note that
recently John Finnis has articulated a different account of the foundation of natural law in Aquinas. Chapter 6 considers the Finnis
rejoinder to the analysis as proposed in the last two chapters. It is
important at the end of this chapter, however, to realize that the
account of Aquinas's moral theory based upon a philosophical
anthropology of natural kinds has been questioned by Finnis and
others. In his *Natural Law and Natural Rights* and *Fundamentals of
Ethics*, Finnis rejects what he calls the 'reductivist' account of Aquinas
based upon a philosophical anthropology. Finnis, none the less,
would agree that God is not necessary to explicate Aquinas's theory
of natural law. The following chapter considers Finnis's non-
reductionist account in some detail.

6

The Finnis Reconstruction

IN Saul Bellow's novel, *More Die of Heartbreak*, the principal narrator, Kenneth, a student of Russian history and culture, expresses this worry: 'An apparent ethical logic drew him on. But by and by it became evident that the metaphysics that had long supported the ethical order had crumbled away. To me, this similarity with St. Petersburgh was a stimulus. There were intoxicating analogies.'[1]

Bellow addresses, unbeknownst to him to be sure, the issue addressed in this chapter. In the passage, Bellow indicates a persistent worry contemporary philosophers often bring to discussions of natural law ethics. This issue, the crumbling of the metaphysical edifice normally associated with natural law ethics, has determined the boundaries within which John Finnis attempted his reconstruction of natural law moral theory. In a radical way, Finnis undercuts the functional view of Aristotelian ethics by suggesting that the metaphysical support normally used to interpret natural law in Aristotle and Aquinas is misguided. Hence, Finnis would reject the general thrust of the analysis of Aquinas discussed in Chapters 4 and 5 above.

In two well-argued and subtle books, *Natural Law and Natural Rights* (1980) and *Fundamentals of Ethics* (1983), Finnis elucidates a view of natural law ethics which denies that the 'functional view' of essence is a necessary condition for explaining that theory. Finnis asserts that Aristotle's defence of the function view is an 'erratic boulder' and suggests that natural law ethics is neither 'deduced nor inferred from metaphysics or anthropology' (*Fundamentals of Ethics*, 17–22). Finnis is concerned that the function view of Aristotelian ethics entails the naturalistic fallacy.

Chapters 2 and 3 indicated the recent revival of Aristotelian moral

[1] Saul Bellow, *More Die of Heartbreak* (New York: Morrow, 1987), 187.

theory and the role Alasdair MacIntyre's *After Virtue* has played in generating much creative work under the guise of 'virtue ethics'. Aristotle's ethics has served as a focal point of much of that discussion, dismissing through MacIntyre's forceful pen the tradition of Enlightenment ethics, especially Kantian deontology. Readers of *After Virtue* are familiar with the poles of opposition MacIntyre presents: Aristotle or Nietzsche. Moreover, Henry Veatch has long articulated the concepts central to Aristotelian ethics and has defended Aristotle's moral insights with provocative critiques of both analytic and existentialist meta-ethical theories.

Into this fray, Finnis presented his freshly formulated reconstruction of Aristotle and Aquinas. Commenting on this reconstruction, Veatch, writing in the *American Journal of Jurisprudence*, referred to Finnis's analysis as 'a book that bids fair to being the one really definitive treatment of natural law in the present day'.[2] On another occasion, Veatch remarked that 'John Finnis's achievement in his book, *Natural Law and Natural Rights*, is nothing if not truly remarkable!' Veatch argues, however, that Finnis appears to omit the core concepts which are essential to the natural law theory of Aristotle and Aquinas. Veatch worried lest Finnis lose the necessary element in natural law ethics, which is the role human nature plays in this form of ethical naturalism. Can one have Aristotelian meta-ethical theory without a consistent metaphysics of human nature? Veatch articulates his worry in the following way:

For it really isn't necessary, [Finnis] seems to say, that so-called natural laws in law and ethics should be laws of nature at all, or in any sense discoverable in nature. No, and as if to puzzle and perplex his readers even more, Finnis apparently wants to claim no less a one than St. Thomas Aquinas as being on his side in this regard. For St. Thomas, Finnis suggests, was one who was never taken in by any such notion as that one might be able to derive ethical principles from nature, or that one would ever need to suppose that ethics had to be based on metaphysics. Yes, it is almost as if Finnis would go so far as to say that St. Thomas never even thought that *bonum* was to be understood in terms of *ens*.[3]

This is the question Finnis poses to readers of Aquinas and the

[2] Henry Veatch, Review of *Natural Law and Natural Rights*, *American Journal of Jurisprudence*, 26 (1981), 247–59.
[3] Henry B. Veatch, 'Natural Law and the Is–Ought Question: Queries to Finnis and Grisez', in Veatch, *Swimming Against the Current in Contemporary Philosophy* (Washington, DC: Catholic University of America Press, 1990), 293.

response philosophers such as Henry Veatch and Ralph McInerny suggest about the Finnis analysis. This chapter addresses this cluster of issues central to contemporary readings of natural law theory in some detail. In developing this analysis of Finnis's account of natural law theory, this chapter proceeds with the following five tasks:

1. To elucidate carefully Finnis's Theory of natural law ethics;
2. To indicate the differences between Finnis and philosophers such as Veatch and McInerny;
3. To provide a critique of Finnis's reconstruction of natural law;
4. To suggest why Finnis proceeds the way he does with Aristotle and Aquinas;
5. To hint at a metaphilosophical difference between Aristotelian philosophy and most modern philosophy.

This analysis is important because, as Chapter 4 argued, if natural law moral theory is to make sense in the contemporary discussions of virtue ethics, one must be clear about the presuppositions and principles from which the theory proceeds. Finnis's theory needs a careful elucidation and analysis. This is a vexing and difficult philosophical journey. In particular, to sort out precisely where Finnis differs from much of the Aristotelian tradition is a difficult investigation. None the less, the thrust of this chapter attempts such an inquiry.

FINNIS ON NATURAL LAW ETHICS

While Finnis is careful never to claim that he is offering a defence of Aristotle and Aquinas, none the less he has written that 'Aristotle and Aquinas, I believe, both accepted the thesis [on practical reason] I have just put forward' (*Fundamentals of Ethics*, 12). Moreover, one need only look at the structure of Finnis's arguments to see the close affinity with what classically has been referred to as the Aristotelian manner of doing normative ethics: 'But ethics is precisely and primarily ("formally") practical because the object one has in mind in doing ethics is precisely my realization in my actions the REAL and TRUE goods attainable by a human being and thus my PARTICIPAT-ING in those goods'. (ibid. 3).

Finnis writes that the end of the moral process is the attainment of 'flourishing', which is his translation for Aristotle's *eudaimonia*; this also means 'to function well as a human being'. Likewise, this is Finnis's translation for Aquinas's term, *beatitudo*. In a 1984 convention paper, Finnis referred to this 'end' or *telos* as 'integral human fulfillment'.[4] In considering this eudaimonistic dimension of a teleological ethic based on some form of naturalism, Finnis is prima facie in the Aristotelian and Aquinian tradition of doing meta-ethical writing.

FINNISS RECONSTRUCTION OF NATURAL LAW ETHICS

Writing on the eudaimonistic ethics central to Aristotelian/Aquinian natural law, the following three issues concern Finnis:

1. Reductivism in normative ethics is false;
2. Moral judgments are 'objective';
3. Rejecting excessive metaphysical baggage renders a more perspicuous case for natural law ethics.

Regarding the first point, the heart of Finnis's reconstruction of natural law ethics centres on reductivism. Early on in the *Fundamentals of Ethics*, Finnis writes: 'So the temptation is powerful, and rarely resisted, to envisage ethics reductively. One reductive strategy eliminates the RADICAL practicality of ethics, by envisaging ethics as a reduction from metaphysical or general anthropology (the descriptive knowledge of human nature), or as an intuition of non-natural properties of agents and actions' (p. 4). Following the thrust of mid-century non-cognitivist criticism in meta-ethics, Finnis thus rejects reductivism in its naturalism and intuitionism forms. By 'reductivism', Finnis means the theoretical explication of moral concepts in terms of a metaphysical, cognitive foundation. A moral theory is 'reduced' or 'falls back on' a metaphysical basis in order to have normative validity. In the above passage, Finnis argues that (1) naturalism is the attempt to 'reduce' moral judgements to properties found in the natural world; and (2) intuitionism is the attempt to 'reduce' moral judgements to simple properties found in a non-natural realm. Mill's utilitarianism is an example of the former, while Moore's intuitionism is an example of the latter. Both theories offer as an explanatory principle of justification some aspect of reality — empirical properties of pleasure or the non-natural property of goodness.

---

[4] John Finnis, 'Practical Reasoning, Human Goods and the End of Man', *Proceedings of the American Catholic Philosophical Association*, 58 (1984), 23–24.

This denial of reductivism, however, promptly evokes comment from students of natural law theory. Traditionally, the concept of human nature or human essence has played a central role in determining the list of goods that are to be sought. Natural law philosophers, Veatch in particular, ask if the dependence on human nature for the determination of the goods is eliminated, then what is the ground for these ends or goods? Put differently, what is the connecting link between the basic goods to be sought, the cognitive awareness of those goods, and the human person? Finnis rejects the philosophical anthropology usually associated with natural law moral theory.

In approaching natural law this way, however, is Finnis omitting a necessary component of Aristotle and Aquinas's theory of essence, and, *a fortiori*, of primary substance? Each individual in Aristotle's metaphysics is a primary substance. The conception of good – the end or *telos* – as discussed by Aristotle and Aquinas is derived from the human essence or human nature. The concept of an Aristotelian human essence, as suggested in Chapter 4, is best elucidated in terms of a set of dispositional properties. In Aristotle and Aquinas, the human goods, as ends, are connected with the structure of the human person. The relation of final cause to formal cause holds here. It is not possible, in the eyes of Aristotle and Aquinas, to determine the final cause without knowing the formal cause. Early in the twentieth century, the late Professor Mure strongly argued the position considering the reduction of final to formal cause, but not vice versa. The formal cause determines the function (*ergon*) of the essence. The *telos* as end is the fulfilment or actualization of this function in the human person. Without an analysis of the formal cause, one cannot know the final cause. This is a fundamental principle of Aristotelian metaphysics. Finnis differs from many Aristotelians over the nature of this relation between final cause and formal cause.

The account presented in Chapter 4 suggests that an analysis of essence in terms of dispositional properties saves the teleology inherent in Aristotelian ethical naturalism. A disposition, by definition, is a potentiality or capacity. Most modern philosophers, on the other hand, consider essence as a class of inert, static properties. As static properties, they lack any possibility of growth or actualization. The essence, on the modern reading, does not 'tend towards' an end which indicates its completion and fulfilment. A dispositional view of essence, therefore, is a necessary condition for discussing the ethics of Aristotle and Aquinas based on human nature. Essence as a set of dispositional properties saves the teleology necessary for Aristotelian ethics. This is a summary of the argument presented in detail in Chapter 4.

Now to the second point. Rejecting reductivism, Finnis asks a different kind of question. Finnis needs a way to substantiate his claim that, without reductivism, his reconstruction of natural law ethics remains at a level beyond subjectivism and relativism. Finnis does this by suggesting that the concept of 'objective' can handle this issue. Therefore, Finnis places emphasis on the concept of 'objectivity' rather than on the concept of 'nature'. Consider this passage where Finnis discusses this issue: 'In replacing the word 'nature' with the word 'objective', wasn't I shuffling out of sight the claim of classical ethics to be founded on NATURE and on a true metaphysics or descriptive knowledge of nature – the claim which to some is the chief merit and to others the all-vitiating fallacy of pre-enlightenment ethical theories?' (*Fundamentals of Ethics*, 10).

Finnis places himself in the latter camp while it is hard not to place Aristotle and Aquinas, of course chronologically but more importantly, structurally, in the former. Recently MacIntyre reminded us of this radical bifurcation in the history of Western ethical theory. Of course, the shadow of the is/ought problem and the naturalistic fallacy hovers over Finnis's rejection of reductivism. Finnis believes that the is/ought problem formulated by Hume and defended by Kant is correct. Finnis sees no way to derive an 'ought' from an 'is'. Reductive naturalism, Finnis assumes, violates the separation of the 'is' from the 'ought'. This is a case of 'reducing' an ought statement to a fact. This would be a form of cognitivism which Finnis assumes would violate the canon of the naturalistic fallacy.

Finnis quotes Aristotle's *De Anima*, and refers to Aquinas's *Commentary* on that Aristotelian treatise, in this way: 'We come to understand acts by understanding their objects, and capacities by understanding their actualization' (ibid. 25). Finnis comments that, of course, one knows the essence by knowing the capacities, but one only comes to know the capacities or dispositions by coming to know the acts of those dispositions. An old scholastic maxim is that we know something only through its act. A knowledge of potency or disposition is, in effect, a reductive form of knowledge. On this issue Finnis writes:

In the 'ontological order', no doubt, 'the essence of the soul grounds the potencies, the potencies ground the acts, and the acts ground knowledge of objects'. But if you ask how we come to know human essence or nature, the order will be stated by Aristotle himself: one must first know the objects, and thus one can fully know the characteristic human acts, and THUS the human potentialities, and THUS the human essence or nature. And the object(ive)s of human acts are the intelligible goods that make sense to someone choosing what to do. (ibid. 21)

In determining the list of human goods, Finnis distrusts any form of reductive ethics. Hence, he rejects the process of going from a philosophical anthropology to a set of moral prescriptions. Finnis questions our ability to determine what the human essence is without first considering the goods to be obtained. More traditional Aristotelians, on the other hand, argue that without knowing what the essence is, how can we be sure that the ends are indeed human goods? In *Human Rights: Fact or Fancy?*, Veatch suggests that his *'Euthyphro* principle' applies to this problem. What reasons determine the inclusion of any characteristic into the class of the uniquely human goods or ends?

Finnis suggests that the mental process of determining the goods renders them 'objective'. The goods to be obtained are self-evident — what Aquinas refers to as *per se nota* propositions. Since the propositions are *per se nota*, they are not reducible to facts about human nature. The denial of reducibility entails that reductivism is false. Later in this chapter this account of 'objective' and its method will be considered in more detail.

FURTHER COMMENTS ON REDUCTIVISM

Lest one think Finnis is not serious about removing his reconstruction of natural law ethics from the reductivist camp, the following passages indicate clearly his theoretical bent:

it is simply not true that 'any form of natural law theory of morals entails the belief that propositions about man's duties and obligations can be inferred from propositions about his nature'.

(*Natural Law and Natural Rights*, 33)

The fact is that Aristotle is not a neo-Aristotelian who believes that ethical truths are attained by an inventory (or any description) of aspects of human nature. (*Fundamental of Ethics*, 14)

Ethics is not deduced or inferred from metaphysics or anthropology.
(Ibid. 22)

Aquinas considers that practical reasoning begins not by understanding this
nature from the outside, as it were, by way of psychology, anthropology, or
metaphysical observations and judgments defining human nature ...
(*Natural Law and Natural Rights*, 34)

The 'function' argument is not the deep structure of Aristotle's ethical
method; it is an erratic boulder. (*Fundamentals of Ethics*, 17)

Aquinas asserts as plainly as possible that the first principles of natural law
... are not inferred from speculative principles ... They are not inferred
from metaphysical propositions about human nature, or about the nature
of good and evil, or about 'the function of a human being.'
(*Natural Law and Natural Rights*, 33)

Such references to what is (humanly) natural NEED not be regarded as an
appeal to, or expression of, some independent, 'value free' investigation of
the sort that Veatch would call (Aristotelian) physics, and that we might
call general anthropology. (*Fundamentals of Ethics*, 20)

Nor, usually, do such facts about the natural order play a role in Aristotle's
argument.   (Ibid. 17)

Given his argument, Finnis suggests that our grasp of what it takes
to understand the fulfilment of a human nature is the conclusion of
moral reasoning, not the principles from which the process begins.
The reductivists thesis, so Finnis suggests, approaches Aristotle and
Aquinas in a backwards fashion. The following passages indicate
what Finnis takes to be the philosophical starting point in understanding Aristotle and Aquinas on natural law:

The whole argument of the *Ethics* concludes to a proposition about what is
natural to man, in the sense of truly appropriate to and fulfilling for human
beings; but that is the conclusion, or a way of expressing the conclusion,
and the arguments for it are found elsewhere.   (Ibid.)

Finnis also argues in the following way:

Now any thesis about what is in this sense supremely good for you or for
me, or any other human being, can helpfully be expressed in various sorts
of ways. It can be expressed as a thesis about what a human being should
do or be; or what it is the business (not necessarily the PECULIAR function)
of a human being to do or be; or what fulfills a human being; or what
actualized the potentialities of human nature; or what is in keeping with
human nature ... These last formulae, referring explicitly to human nature,

can thus be a way of expressing the conclusions of an openly evaluative, practical, ethical investigation.   (Ibid. 20)

In a recent restatement of his reconstruction of natural law theory, Finnis, along with Germain Grisez and Joseph Boyle, asserts afresh the opposition to the reductivist thesis. This passage indicates also the importance that the is/ought problem plays in the Finnis analysis of ethical theory: 'The theory we defend also departs from classical models — at least, as many have understood them — by taking full account of the fact that the moral ought cannot be derived from the is of theoretical truth — for example, of metaphysics and/or philosophical anthropology.'[5]

Finnis argues explicitly that any reference to human nature or essence is the conclusion of a natural law ethical inquiry. Human nature is not the starting point of a natural law inquiry. Hence, reductivism is false. This denial of reductivism entails a denial of the metaphysics of finality, which Chapter 4 suggested as central to understanding the concept of an obligatory end in natural law theory. This is the unmistakable thrust of Finnis's reconstruction of Aristotle and Aquinas on natural law theory. Given the denial of reductivism, the concept of 'objectivity' becomes very important in the Finnis analysis.

In rejecting reductivism, Finnis believed he was providing a more perspicuous analysis of natural law ethics while at the same time removing this theory from the twin towers of twentieth-century objections to ethical naturalism, the naturalistic fallacy and deriving an 'ought' from an 'is'. Denying the reductivist thesis, Finnis suggests, frees natural law theory from the excessive metaphysical baggage which rendered it unacceptable theoretically for twentieth-century analytic ethics.

WHAT HAS FINNIS DONE TO ARISTOTLE AND AQUINAS

Having explicated Finnis's reconstruction of natural law ethical theory, two questions require a response:

---

[5] John Finnis, Germain Grisez, and Joseph Boyle, 'Practical Principles, Moral Truths, and Ultimate Ends', *American Journal of Jurisprudence*, 32 (1987), 99–151. In an extended bibliography following this excellent account, Finnis writes that his position is closer to Aquinas's account than to Grisez's. In this article, while not committing themselves to reformulating Aquinas's theory, none the less there is the strong sense that any reductivist reading of either Aristotle or Aquinas is misguided

1. Is Finnis correct in suggesting that the role of human nature is not a necessary condition for natural law ethics? Or, put differently, is the metaphysics of finality inconsistent with natural law ethics?
2. Does Finnis's method of doing ethics lead to a confusion between practical and theoretical reasoning in Aristotelian ethics?

To the first question. How might Aristotle and Aquinas respond to Finnis? The argument to be developed, following the analysis produced in Chapter 4, suggests that Aristotle and Aquinas would agree with the line of argument endorsing the concept of a metaphysics of finality. Human essence is important for considering moral theory. At this point in the analysis, it will be useful to recall a theme developed in Chapter 4. A perspicuous way to understand an Aristotelian essence is as a set of dispositional properties. The formal cause, in this analysis, is the ground for the set of dispositional properties which determine the content of a natural kind. The final cause, therefore, is the exemplification of the completed or actualized set of dispositions in the individual person.

Moreover, in the *Summa Theologiae*, I-II q. 94 a. 2, Aquinas indicates the importance human nature plays in providing the foundations for moral philosophy. His arguments establish a metaphysics of morals in terms of a metaphysics of finality serving as a foundation for natural law moral theory. In his treatise, *De Veritate*, Aquinas addresses the matter of *bonum*, the translation of 'good', as connected conceptually with, and intelligible only in terms of, *ens*, the translation of 'being'. The good, moreover, is specific to the individual of a natural kind. An individual's *ergon* determined by the substantial form reaches completion or actualization by the development of the dispositional properties common to the essence or nature. This is the meaning of *eudaimonia*. Aquinas writes: 'Bonum est in rebus, ut Philosophus dicit.' Translated, this is rendered as 'Good is found in things, as the Philosopher [i.e. Aristotle] indicates.' Commenting on this passage, Veatch suggests that 'in the *De Veritate* . . . St. Thomas seems to give the unmistakable impression that ethics must discover its own principles directly in being and in the context of the discipline of metaphysics'.[6]

---

theoretically. That the is/ought problem hovers over this reconstruction of natural law theory is clearly articulated.

[6] Veatch, *Swimming Against the Current*, 256.

What Chapter 4 suggested as the metaphysics of finality is certainly the common interpretation of book 1 of Aristotle's *Nicomachean Ethics* and of the relevant passages in Aquinas's *Summa Theologiae* and the *Commentary on the Nicomachean Ethics*. In his historical commentaries on Aquinas's philosophy, Étienne Gilson once noted how in his moral theory, Aquinas held that 'moral philosophy blends with metaphysics'.[7]

Other philosophers argue in a similar vein. For example, in her commentary on Aristotle's ethics, 'The Function of Man', in *Aristotle's De Motu Animalium*, Martha Nussbaum writes that 'Aristotle appears to be saying that if we know what a man is, we will know how he should behave; he seems to be deriving behavioral norms from factual observations concerning human nature.'[8] In his analysis of Aristotelian and Aquinian ethics, 'Natural Law, Human Action, and Morality', Alan Gewirth argues that 'it is ... the ontological feature [i.e. human nature] that especially differentiates the Aristotelian-Thomist version of natural law theory from alternative versions'.[9] Furthermore, in his 'Moral Obligation and Metaphysics', Vincent M. Cooke explicitly argues against the Finnis/Grisez analysis of Aquinas on natural law. Cooke writes:

The conclusion that I draw is that modern moral philosophy and particularly the Neo-Aristotelian movement that is currently in the ascendancy are wrong in their attempts to do moral philosophy without also doing metaphysics. The judgments we reach about what is real profoundly affect the judgments we make about what we experience and how we ought to live. The reverse is surely also the case, as witnessed by Plato and Kant: convictions about the kind of life worth living frequently give rise to elaborate metaphysical systems. Metaphysics and moral philosophy are properly inseparable.[10]

In his *The Tradition of Natural Law*, Yves Simon suggested that a

[7] Laurence K. Shook, *Étienne Gilson* (Toronto: Pontifical Institute of Mediaeval Studies, 1984), 192.

[8] Martha Craven Nussbaum, *Aristotle's De Motu Animalium* (Princeton, NJ: Princeton University Press, 1978), 102.

[9] Alan Gewirth, 'Natural Law, Human Action, and Morality', in Rocco Porreco (ed.), *The Georgetown Symposium on Ethics: Essays in Honor of Henry Babcock Veatch* (Lanham, Md.: University Press of America, 1984), 68. Gewirth is critical of this type of natural law theory which he attributes to Aristotle and Aquinas, suggesting while it might be a necessary condition for normative ethical theory it is theoretically inconsistent for a sufficient account.

[10] Vincent M. Cooke, 'Moral Obligation and Metaphysics', *Thought*, 66/260 (Mar. 1991), 73.

theory of universals, or essences, is a necessary condition for an elucidation of the concept of natural law:

Let us confess that it is meaningless to argue seriously about natural law without having ever raised the question of universals ... It is obvious that the theory of natural law is opposed by the nominalist tendency and probably would be made impossible by a strictly and consistently nominalistic philosophy, if such could exist.[11]

In *Man and the State*, Maritain argues explicitly for the concept of essence as a necessary condition for understanding Aquinas on natural law. He writes:

What I am emphasizing is the first basic element to be recognized in natural law, namely the *ontological* element; I mean the *normality of functioning* which is grounded on the essence of that being: man ... Let us say, then, that in its ontological aspect, natural law is an *ideal order* relating to human actions, a *divide* between the suitable and the unsuitable, the proper and the improper, which depends on human nature or essence and the unchangeable necessities rooted in it.[12]

The above passages indicate several philosophers in the Aristotelian/ Aquinian tradition of natural law ethics whose writings suggest agreement with the metaphysics of finality articulated in Chapter 4. Of course, what is necessary is to lay bare the argument indicating the role essence plays in natural law theory. The passages above suggest the necessary role essence plays in that theory; yet this is at best an argument from authority. The final test is in the analysis of the texts of Aristotle and Aquinas indicating that without a dependence on essence, the metaphysics of finality necessary for natural law theory cannot be justified.

ON KNOWING ARISTOTELIAN ESSENCES

Of course, a difficulty arises. How does one know the content of an essence? Put differently, how does one know the structure of the essence which is determined by the formal cause? How is the set of

---

[11] Yves Simon, *The Tradition of Natural Law*, ed. Vukan Kuic (New York: Fordham University Press, 1965), 7–8.

[12] Jacques Maritain, *Man and the State* (Chicago: University of Chicago Press, 1951), 87–88.

dispositional properties determined? Aristotle, and Aquinas following, provided an elaborate epistemological machinery to explicate
the acquisition of concepts. A concept is discussed in terms of knowing an essence. Through a process of abstraction using the agent
intellect (*intellectus agens*), a concept is formed in the understanding.
This is, however, a long, involved and complicated process. Much
trial and error accompany the acquisition of concepts. Probably both
Aristotle and Aquinas would agree with Finnis that one needs to
consider the possible results of activities in order to develop an
awareness of the content of an essence. As Finnis noted, dispositions
are known through their acts, and acts through their objects. This
is a traditional axiom common to much scholastic philosophy.

Briefly one should note the following parenthetical comment on
the process of knowing Aristotelian essences. It is worthwhile
recalling that in commenting upon the acquisition of concepts in
Aristotelian epistemology, Aquinas thought it extremely difficult for
human knowers to understand the content of an essence. In fact,
the following brief selections suggest that Aquinas was almost agnostic about this possibility of knowing essences:

The essential principles of things are unknown to us. (*De Anima*, 1 lec. 13)

Essential differences are unknown to us. (*De Veritate*, q. 4 a. 1 ad. 8)

We are ignorant of many of the properties of sensible things, and in many
cases we are unable to discover the proper nature even of those properties
that we perceive by the senses. (*Summa contra Gentiles*, 1, 3)

In his recent work on Aristotle and natural kinds ontology, David
Charles rendered an analysis of the differences in doing natural kind
metaphysics between Aristotle on the one hand and Kripke and
Putnam on the other. In this analysis, Charles offered similar agnostic suggestions regarding Aristotle's ability to know the content of
an essence easily and completely.[13] What this indicates, however, is
that the epistemology needed to be aware of the content of a natural
kind in contemporary metaphysics is not Aristotelian epistemology.

Aristotle and Aquinas, however, do not discount the possibility of
knowing essences through the abstractive process of the agent intellect. They merely argue that it is a difficult process. Paul Durbin's
excellent commentary on the acquisition of concepts in Aquinian
texts in the *Summa Theologiae* points out the difficulty yet the possi-

---

[13] David Charles, 'Aristotle and Natural Kinds', a paper delivered to the American
Philosophical Association (Central Division), 3 May 1986.

bility of concept formation in Aquinas's philosophy of mind.[14] For
Aquinas, the intellect continues to strive for a less general though
more specific awareness of an essence. This account of mental act
is based on Aristotle's *Posterior Analytics*.

MORAL PHILOSOPHY AS A SECOND ORDER ACTIVITY

Moral philosophy for Aristotle and Aquinas, given the analysis in
terms of a metaphysics of finality proposed in this book, is a second
order philosophical inquiry. Moral theory is based on the nature of
the human person. In other words, first Aquinas expects the metaphysical account of essence to be developed. Only then, as a second
order inquiry, is the philosopher ready to develop a normative
theory. The normative issues are developed from and dependent
upon the ontological issues. Hence, it is a 'second order inquiry' in
so far as it depends for its very nature on another inquiry, namely,
an ontological one. The dispositional properties which make up an
essence – the formal cause – provide the necessary ground for moral
philosophy. Furthermore, using the categories of Aristotelian epistemology, theoretical reason is the means, through the process of
abstraction, by which a knower becomes aware of the content of an
essence. Because a form is known by its actualization, Finnis suggests
correctly that a knower comes to be aware of an essence by considering the completion or perfection of that essence. This is, however,
a methodological issue which does not undercut the need for an
essence as the metaphysical ground for moral philosophy.

Put differently, because we know acts before we know potencies or
dispositions, it does not follow that the dispositions are not centrally
important in determining what the acts are in the first place. The
'potency/act' distinction implies a complementary relation in
Aquinas, and not a relation of opposition. Finnis appears to over-
simplify this opposition. When a human knower comes to understand the content of a human essence – to have even a provisional

---

[14] Paul Durbin, *Commentary on Summa Theologiae*, xii, *Human Intelligence*, Black-
friars ed. (New York: McGraw Hill Book Co. 1967), 170–2. For analytic philosophical
accounts of Aquinas's philosophy of mind, see Peter Geach, *Mental Acts* (New York:
Humanities Press 1953); Anthony Kenny, 'Intellect and Imagination in Aquinas', in
Aquinas: A Collection of Critical Essays (Garden City, NY: Doubleday, 1969); and
Anthony J. Lisska, 'Deely and Geach on Abstractionism in Thomistic Epistemology',
Thomist, July 1973.

understanding such as Aristotle considers in the *Posterior Analytics* – this understanding helps to elucidate what the acts – or ends – are to be attained.

In rejecting reductivism in natural law ethics – and Finnis thinks many contemporary commentators on natural law are reductivists – Finnis argues that ethics is principally a practical activity. Aristotle and Aquinas of course would agree. But would they agree with Finnis's unique analysis of ethics as a practical activity? Finnis writes that ethics, as practical, is a determination of the goods or acts which will help bring about 'flourishing', i.e. *eudaimonia*, for human agents. How do agents determine these goods? By asking, Finnis suggests, certain kinds of questions. Finnis calls this the analysis of the pre-philosophical experience of human moral agents. This point he argues in the following passage:

The goal of ethical inquiry is identification of and participation in the true human good. The primary and, in my view, the proper function of those appeals to what we or others (or 'everyone') would say or choose is to PROMPT or REMIND us (the participants in the inquiry) firstly, of our own and others' pre-philosophical experience, and secondly, of our own and others' practical and pre-philosophical grasp of good(s). (*Fundamentals of Ethics*, 18)

Finnis, moreover, suggests that Aristotle embarked upon a questioning method in meta-ethics which is similar to the 'experience machine' made famous by Robert Nozick.[15] This philosophical 'thought experiment' has been used extensively in analytic philosophy. Finnis uses it in his analysis of Aristotle and Aquinas. In explicating his experience machine, Nozick wonders if, given the choice, one would agree to have one's brain put into a vat for all time, even if the vat contained a biochemical solution which would produce pleasurable sensations in the brain for ever and ever. Nozick, by asking a set of questions about the nature of this 'brain in the vat existence', concludes that a rational agent would reject this possibility. In other words, such an existence, Nozick argued, is not what humans consider a normal humanly structured existence to be. The 'vat state' is not a desirable. Human persons want more out of life than the 'brain in the vat' state of existence. Finnis comes to the same conclusion. Finnis believes he has developed an 'objective'

---

[15] Robert Nozick, *Anarchy, State and Utopia* (New York: Basic Books, 1974), 42–5.

reason why this choice cannot be undertaken. Rational agents refuse to accept the experience machine as a successful model for *eudaimonia*. One sees parallels with Rawls's method of questioning in the 'veil of ignorance'. The point to emphasize is that both Nozick and Finnis use a rational method alone as sufficient to determine normative issues. Finnis suggests that Aristotle and Aquinas develop the *per se nota* propositions of natural law in much the same way. This gives Finnis his 'objective' character to the *per se nota* propositions. The similarity with Nozick and Rawls is striking.

What does one make of this argument? The point remains, however, even if Aristotle did ask these kinds of questions, and proceeded in a rational manner, it does not follow that he rejected an ontological underpinning for his ethics. Or, put differently, it does not follow that the ontological ground in terms of a metaphysics of finality does not serve as an important principle in his metaphysics of morals. The consideration of the use of a method alone does not exclude the need for an ontological foundation. To suggest that the opposite holds in Aristotle's philosophy is to confuse epistemology with metaphysics. Nozick, Rawls, and Dworkin – and Finnis too – on the other hand, appear to claim that embarking on a rational method is sufficient to provide justified, 'objective' claims. This is an example, I suggest, of the 'good-reasons' approach discussed in Chapter 3.

In his analysis, it appears that Finnis has used a Cartesian-like method common in analytic philosophy. He raises an epistemological question first: 'What might the acts be which will contribute to my flourishing?' Or, put differently: 'Wouldn't any responsible and reasonable person agree to this?' This method gives Finnis his 'objectivity'. We won't hook ourselves up to the 'experience machine' no matter what! This is, Finnis argues, an 'objective' reason. Once again, the similarities with the analysis of the 'good-reasons' approach in Chapter 3 above are striking. In considering Finnis's use of 'objective', Aristotelian commentators holding the metaphysics of finality account would respond in the following manner: 'Well, yes, this method is useful and you may be saying something about "objectivity", but this alone does not undercut the need for an ontological ground.' This ground, of course, is human nature.

Human nature as a set of dispositional properties constitutes the human essence. Human nature as an essence exists outside the mind in a primary substance. Human nature is not a mental construct. To use Everett Nelson's suggestion indicated in Chapter 4 above, this human essence serves as the ground for counterfactual conditional propositions.[16] A proposition indicating the set of synthetic necessary properties making up an essence is a nomic universal and not an accidental universal statement. A nomic universal proposition cannot refer only to a mental construct. It must refer to a causal feature of reality. The importance of the Nelson analysis for natural law theory is that nomic universals, like Aristotelian essences, must be ontological categories in reality.

For Aristotle and Aquinas, therefore, the method determining the properties central to the essence is different from the question of whether or not one needs the essence as the ground for moral judgements. The final cause is the actualization of the dispositions which make up the formal cause. But just because one begins with the final cause – through an epistemological method – it does not follow that the formal cause is unimportant theoretically. Appropriating Nelson's categories, the formal cause grounds the nomic universal. This is the core of the ethical naturalism central to natural law as elucidated by Aristotle and Aquinas. This core demands more than only using a method to determine objectivity. Finnis uses only a method and rejects the core. Using Finnis's language, natural law ethics demands more than indicating the necessary conditions for exercising 'practical reasonableness'.

Finnis appears concerned, moreover, about Aristotelian commentators such as Mortimer Adler who describe the content of a human essence as a set of 'drives' or 'desires'. In this regard, Finnis poses a fundamental problem in elucidating the content of an essence. To reiterate a suggestion from Chapter 4, a far better way to translate *inclinatio* in the Aquinas texts is as 'disposition'. Structurally, a disposition is neither a conscious drive nor is it necessarily an object of consciousness. It is nothing more than a capacity grounded in an essence which tends towards some kind of actualization or development. One might refer to this quality as a 'dispositional tendency'. The ontological structure of a dispositional property is by its very nature to 'tend towards' its developmental end or terminus point. This analysis renders meaningful the formal/final cause distinction. The final cause is the state of development of the dispositions constituting the structure of the formal cause. This is the cash value of Aristotle and Aquinas's analysis of essence as a set of dispositional properties.

---

[16] Everett J. Nelson, 'The Metaphysical Presuppositions of Induction', presidential address, American Philosophical Association (Western Division), 5 May 1967, in

PRACTICAL VERSUS THEORETICAL REASONING IN
FINNIS AND ARISTOTLE

Because Finnis removes a role for essence in natural law ethics, the second question noted above arises: does Finnis confuse the concepts of practical and theoretical reasoning as used by Aristotle and Aquinas? Finnis renders practical reason more theoretical in its structure, it would seem, than either Aristotle or Aquinas would accept. One does, as Finnis suggests, consider what kinds of activities would best develop one's human nature. But is this not a form of theoretical reason? One considers reflectively the kinds of activities which best develop the dispositions comprising a human essence. Practical reason enters once this has been accomplished. One uses practical reason in considering how best to undertake an action in a particular set of circumstances. Both Aristotle and Aquinas insist that the conclusion of the so-called 'practical syllogism' is a particular action, a 'piece of doing'. To consider the goods as end falls under theoretical reason. To undertake an action pursuing a good falls under practical reason. Practical reason is directed towards undertaking particular actions here and how, or, as Aquinas writes, *hic et nunc*!

Due to the fact that Finnis has removed essence as the starting point for moral discussion, the consideration of the kinds of activities needed to develop one's 'nature' becomes an exercise of practical reason. But this use of practical reason by Finnis is, it appears, nothing more than theoretical reason. Finnis seems to slip from a discussion of 'knowing and doing' to merely 'knowing' alone as an intellectual grasp of what is to be done. He writes that 'what I do assert is that our primary grasp of what is good for us is a practical grasp' (*Fundamentals of Ethics*, 12). This grasping, although about an end to be attained, is reducible in Aristotelian eyes to a 'knowing' alone rather than a 'doing'. This is a form of theoretical reasoning used in determining the actualization – the final cause – of the dispositions – the formal cause – which make up an essence. Finnis seems to use the concept of 'practical grasp' to become aware of the ends to be attained. This is self-evident, *per se nota* knowledge. But it is knowledge and not action. It is a 'piece of knowing', not a 'piece of doing'. Practical reason concerns actions to be undertaken, not a knowledge of ends. Knowing is a function of theoretical reason.

Proceedings and Addresses of the American Philosophical Association, 1966-1968 (Yellow Springs, Oh.: The Antioch Press, 1967), 19–33.

Action is a function of practical reason. To determine the content of a final cause depends on knowing the formal cause. These questions belong in Aristotle and Aquinas's epistemology, under the rubric of the exercise of theoretical reason.

Finnis blurs, it appears, the distinction between theoretical and practical reasoning because of his unique method used in determining the appropriate 'goods' or 'ends'. But this method helps the agent to know an essence — i.e. the final cause as the end of the dispositional properties making up the formal cause. This is, however, a form of theoretical reason, not practical reason.

Put differently, if Finnis's rejection of reductivism denies the role essence traditionally played in natural law discussions, there is neither room nor role for theoretical reason. What role could *theoria episteme* have if there is no object to be known? Structurally, it is no surprise that Finnis claims that ethics is primarily a practical activity — i.e. *phronesis*. Using Finnis's method, one considers, with an almost Cartesian indubitability, how, as a moral agent, one goes about determining what is good for the agent as a human person. The importance of the 'experience machine' follows necessarily from Finnis's reductivism rejection. In addition, the person of practical wisdom in Aristotle (*phronismos*) seems to be the person whose moral experience has been entrenched through the acquisition of virtuous habits. It is unclear how this person of Aristotelian practical wisdom fits into Finnis's account of Aristotelian moral theory. The role habit or 'acquired disposition' plays in Finnis's analysis seems oblique at best and irrelevant at worst.

FINNIS AND INTUITIONISM

Without a philosophical anthropology, how does Finnis arrive at his particular list of basic goods? What is the structure of the 'practical grasp' which Finnis suggests is the 'primary grasp' of the basic goods? In his *Fundamentals of Ethics*, Finnis argues explicitly that he is not an intuitionist. He reiterates this claim in his 1987 *American Journal of Jurisprudence* essay, 'Practical Principles, Moral Truths, and Ultimate Ends'. In *Natural Law and Natural Rights*, Finnis provides the following list of what he has called 'the basic aspects of my well-being' and 'the basic forms of good for us': Life, knowledge, play, aesthetic experience, friendship, practical reasonableness, and religion.

It is unclear structurally how Finnis justifies this particular list.

Since Finnis rejects a philosophical anthropology, Veatch, for instance, uses his *Euthyphro* principle in order to ask about the ground for Finnis's specific list as opposed to another list. In reading Finnis, one recalls the method of an earlier Aristotelian commentator, Sir David Ross, determining the 'prima facie duties' in *The Right and the Good*. This would be a practical grasp, it is true; but ultimately it is a form of a moral intuition. Without an object for theoretical reason, it is unclear what else, despite his protestations to the contrary, Finnis might use for 'moral knowledge' but a form of intuition under the guise of practical reason. This is, it should be noted, a form of intuition similar to that proposed by Ross. It is not, to be sure, akin structurally to Moore's intuition of non-natural properties. None the less, it appears that Finnis's denial of reductivism forces him into adopting a concept of 'practical grasp' of basic goods which is self-evident because it is a prima facie intuition. The 'basic forms of good' are similar structurally to 'prima facie duties'. This is, it appears, the cash value of Finnis's interpretation of practical reasonableness through the self-evident, *per se nota* propositions central to his analysis of natural law theory.

In *Natural Law and Natural Rights*, Finnis argues that the number of basic goods has been firmly established: 'But I suggest that these other objectives and forms of good will be found, on analysis, to be ways or combinations of ways, of pursuing (not always sensibly) and realizing (not always successfully) one of the seven basic forms of good, or some combination of them' (p. 90).

Finnis assumes that, upon 'cool reflection', clear-thinking human persons will come to the same set of 'basic goods'. Like Ross's prima facie duties, the basic goods are those which reasonable persons would accept, given thoughtful, sober consideration. This provides Finnis with his concept of 'objectivity'. Undertaking this reflective approach to practical reasonableness is what Finnis has asked his readers to do. Yet this appears strikingly different from Aristotelian moral agency undertaken through practical wisdom. The problem many natural law philosophers have had with Ross — and with Hare's good-reasons theory and Rawls's 'veil of ignorance' method — is that such theories lack an ontological basis on which to build a moral theory of human virtue. This is, of course, the reductivist's principal worry with Finnis's reconstruction of natural law theory.

THE EPISTEMOLOGICALONTOLOGICAL DISTINCTION

In his essay, 'Natural Law and Human Nature', Robert George responds to the criticisms philosophers have made to Finnis and Grisez's analysis of natural law. In particular, George has Lloyd Weinreb, Ralph McInerny, and Henry Veatch in mind. All three of these philosophers argue that the Finnis/Grisez account removes the import of human nature from their reconstructed position on Aquinas's theory of natural law.

George denies the cogency of this kind of objection to the Finnis/Grisez account. George argues three points in his analysis:

1. The is/ought problem is too quickly dismissed by Finnis/Grisez critics, especially McInerny and Veatch;
2. Finnis/Grisez have not denied the significance of human nature;
3. Finnis affirms a distinction between epistemology and ontology which must be acknowledged if one is to understand his account of natural law in Aquinas.

Regarding the first point, George is concerned that critics of the Finnis/Grisez position have not taken seriously the logical demands of the is/ought problem and the naturalistic fallacy. George writes that, 'according to Grisez and others, natural law theory need not — and a credible natural law theory cannot — rely on this logically illicit inference from facts to norms'.[17] Furthermore, he asserts that 'Grisez and his followers are correct in maintaining that our knowledge of basic human goods and moral norms need not, and logically cannot, be deduced, inferred, or . . . derived from facts about human nature.'[18] George takes seriously the charges brought forth against naturalism by Moore's naturalistic fallacy.

Secondly, George emphatically argues that not deriving norms from human nature in the reductivist manner does not entail that human nature is not significant in the Finnis/Grisez account of Aquinas. George writes that 'contrary to what their critics claim, the natural law theory advanced by Grisez and his collaborators does not entail the proposition that basic human goods or moral norms have no connection to, or grounding in, human nature'.[19]

Thirdly, George suggests that recognizing a distinction between

---

[17] Robert P. George, 'Natural Law and Human Nature', in Robert P. George, (ed.), *Natural Law Theory: Contemporary Essays* (Oxford: Clarendon Press, 1992), 33.
[18] Ibid.
[19] Ibid.

an 'epistemological' and an 'ontological' mode of analysis renders the Finnis/Grisez account clear enough so that the critics will realize that their position does not detach values from the concept of human nature. George argues that the Finnis/Grisez critics 'have assumed, gratuitously, that anyone who maintains that our knowledge of human goods is not derived from our prior knowledge of human nature must hold that human goods are not grounded in nature'.[20] Furthermore, he argues explicitly that 'the proposition that our knowledge of basic human goods and moral norms is not derived from prior knowledge of human nature does not entail the proposition that morality has no grounding in human nature'.[21] It follows from the George analysis that our knowledge of human well-being in the classical Aristotelian and Aquinian sense may be underived and self-evident. Furthermore, this knowledge may still remain knowledge of human well-being and fulfilment. In other words, the knowledge is underived and thus not based on human nature but none the less in accord with the requirements of human nature. This is what Finnis and George call the 'epistemological' as opposed to the 'ontological' mode of analysis. Human moral agents have a direct, underived (*per se nota*) awareness of the human goods without deriving them through a reductivist ontology. The 'ontological' mode of analysis is the reductivist position. George suggests that Aquinas — and Finnis and Grisez following the 'true' Aquinas — have brought to light the epistemological position. Those who adopt the 'ontological' position have the process used by Aquinas and Aristotle backwards. Hence, reductivism is a 'backwards' account.

One can respond to George's critique in the following manner. One needs to begin with the third point first, the 'epistemological/ ontological' distinction. What Finnis has done is, in effect, to adopt a method of argument common to contemporary analytic philosophy. Finnis is centring his energies on what counts for a good argument. This is what he refers to as finding moral claims to be 'objective'. This is similar structurally to the method used by Rawls and Dworkin and considered earlier in this chapter. This is connected directly with George's second point. George assumes that one can have this self-evident knowledge which is not opposed to those 'goods' which will provide *eudaimonia* and *beatitudo* for human moral agents. One

[20] George, 'Natural Law', 35.
[21] Ibid.

still asks the question – how is this possible? George appears to hold to an intuitionist position. One intuits the basic 'goods' and it just happens that this set of goods corresponds to human well-being. But what establishes this causal relation? What the ontological position offers over the epistemological position is that this Aristotelian *aporia* is, at least in principle, resolvable. The causal dilemma can be answered. The state of well-being is the 'final cause' based on the structure of the 'formal cause', which is the set of dispositional properties determining the content of the essence. What George fails to do is to provide a justification for the connection between the human goods and the human person. According to Finnis/Grisez and George, this just 'happens'. This appears, however, to be reducible to the prima facie duty account developed by Sir David Ross fifty years ago. It is intuitionist to the core.

The response to the naturalistic fallacy charge will be considered in Chapter 8 in some detail. The reader has a promissory note for that important discussion. Suffice it to say now that the naturalistic fallacy is endemic to what MacIntyre has called the 'Enlightenment project' in moral theory. Natural law theory is, if anything, not part of this moral theory project.

WHY FINNIS RECONSTRUCTED NATURAL LAW IN THIS WAY

Before concluding this analysis of Finnis's reconstruction of natural law ethics, it may be useful to offer a suggestion concerning why Finnis undertook this particular revision of natural law. This suggestion follows from the structure of his natural law analysis. It appears that two issues have driven Finnis as he reconsidered Aristotle and Aquinas:

1. The is/ought distinction;
2. The modern view of essence or substance.

These two issues are, moreover, interrelated. First, like most contemporary philosophers, Finnis has worried about the is/ought dichotomy so forcefully articulated by Hume and reinvested with authority, as Chapter 3 argued, through Moore's telling naturalistic fallacy. Finnis notes that Germain Grisez's analysis of the first principle of practical reason influenced his own reconstruction of Aristotle and Aquinas. In rethinking Aquinas on the foundations of moral theory, Grisez addressed explicitly the naturalistic fallacy issue. Finnis, Grisez, and George suggest that any reductivist position ascribed to Aristotle or Aquinas entails deriving an 'ought' from an 'is' based upon a natural property. In a response to a critical comment raised by Ralph McInerny, Finnis and Grisez made this claim, one strikingly similar to those of Hume, Kant, and Moore: 'There can be no valid deduction of a normative conclusion without a normative principle, and thus ... [the] first practical principles cannot be derived from metaphysical speculations'.[22] Finnis is convinced that reductivism entails adopting the is/ought problem of deriving an 'ought' prescription from an 'is' proposition.

Secondly, this problem brings in the modern view of essence. In Chapter 4, this issue was discussed briefly. Since the time of Descartes, an essence has been considered, for the most part, as a static collection of properties. In the twentieth century, Russell and Quine's analysis of class through defining properties is part of the Cartesian legacy. Of course, this scheme fits in nicely with the Cartesian quest for 'clear and distinct ideas'.

On the contrary, the argument elucidated in this book claims that the Aristotelian/Aquinian position on essence can be described perspicuously as a set of dispositional properties. A disposition is, by definition, tending towards its completion or end. Metaphysically, a disposition is inherently fuzzy. Hence, dispositional essences are structurally an intrinsic affront to Cartesian ontology. Finnis assumes that reductivism entails the naturalistic fallacy, which in turn entails deriving an 'ought' from an 'is'.

Yet, if one takes seriously what can follow from a dispositional view of essence, one has a way around the naturalistic fallacy. With a static view of essence, a value necessarily is added to a fact. The fact is the set of defining properties. The value is added as an additional component to the fact. In effect, this is what Moore claimed with his 'open question' argument. That a value was added to a natural fact, so Moore observed, destroyed the possibility of any form of ethical naturalism. Put simply, how did one know which value to add? And what was the justification of the addition? With a dispositional view of essence, however, the value is the terminus of the development of the dispositional properties. It is not an extrinsic

---

[22] John Finnis and Germain Grisez, 'The Basic Principles of Natural Law: A Reply to Ralph McInerny', *American Journal of Jurisprudence*, 26 (1981), 24.

property joined to a fact. On the contrary, the value is built right into the fact as end or perfection to the disposition or potency.

The Aristotelian response to the naturalistic fallacy will be discussed at some length in Chapter 8. Briefly, however, a dispositional view of essence with the *telos* being the actualization of the dispositional properties renders the naturalistic fallacy inapplicable and irrelevant. This account depends, however, on adopting an ontology of natural kinds determined by dispositional properties. The standard Cartesian view of essence will not do the job. Moore's naturalistic fallacy is dependent upon an ontology of simple properties which are static and do not develop. Each property is self-contained. That this is incompatible with a dispositional account of essential properties should be apparent.

Despite his talk of capacities and potentialities, it appears that Finnis, in the end, does not break radically from his Cartesian forebears on the matter of essence. Furthermore, Finnis, it seems, lacks the metaphilosophical machinery to develop a coherent view of a rich Aristotelian theory of essence, and of primary substance, in terms of dispositional properties.[23] Therefore, a dispositional view of essence in Aristotle and Aquinas provides the basis for an analysis of meta-ethics as a second order inquiry which avoids the naturalistic fallacy problem and also bypasses Finnis's worries about reductivism. Chapter 8 considers the is/ought problem and the naturalistic fallacy in more detail.

A SHORT HISTORICAL POSTSCRIPT

At issue in the debate between Finnis and Grisez and at least some of the philosophers whom they call reductivists, may be a theme which in a limited way demarcates much Greek and medieval philos-

---

[23] In private conversation, Finnis suggested once that a consideration of human goods makes sense only in so far as they shed light on the 'real' development or flourishing of a human person. In fact, he noted that he wrote *Natural Law and Natural Rights* with the purpose, not to convince the Aristotelians and the Thomists around, but rather the Oxbridge-trained philosophers common to twentieth-century British and American philosophical circles. Given this audience, he downplayed any suggestion of an essence. He then expressed some mild surprise when many natural law philosophers of the traditional Thomist school offered him so much criticism, when all along he considered himself to be aligned philosophically with them. Of course, one must see if indeed the arguments Finnis provides do mesh structurally with Aristotelian and Aquinian theory, or whether, as Veatch and others suggest, they undermine the whole role of essence in traditional natural law moral theory.

ophy from modern philosophy. Does one approach philosophy only through an epistemological method, as Finnis has done in his reconstruction of natural law ethics? Certainly George emphasizes this epistemological method. Or does one, even though using epistemology, argue for the possibility of metaphysical properties? Nelson and Veatch, while holding different ontologies, none the less ask for real categories outside the mind in order to ground their metaphysical propositions. These are important metaphilosophical differences which distinguish pre-Enlightenment from post-Enlightenment philosophy. Each metaphilosophical position entails a different way of articulating the natural law ethics and the philosophy of law associated with Aristotle and Aquinas. It is useful at this juncture in the discussion to realize how these differences have entailed, in the example of Finnis's reconstruction of natural law ethics and George's defence of this reconstruction, a radically different way of articulating the philosophy of natural law associated with Aristotle and Aquinas. The Finnis analysis is, it would seem, part of the Enlightenment project, especially regarding metaphilosophical method.

The following chapter argues that modern philosophy is characterized by what Veatch refers to as 'the transcendental turn'. Briefly put, this metaphilosophical method begins by articulating a conceptual schema which then is used to interpret a particular state of affairs. This modern method was developed with a vengeance by Kant. It has determined much contemporary jurisprudence and is illustrated in Rawls's 'veil of ignorance', Nozick's 'experience machine', Dworkin's method in *Law's Empire*, and also Finnis's account of 'objectivity'. Finnis is dependent upon the method of the transcendental turn as he explicates his reconstruction of Aquinas's natural law.

In opposition to this modern metaphilosophy, Aristotle and Aquinas — and Veatch and Vincent Cooke too — argue that metaphysics is possible. In their philosophical anthropologies, a discussion of essence as dispositional is significant cognitively. This ontology provides a theoretical ground in reality for moral judgements independent of the canons of reason or objectivity characteristic of the Cartesian modern method. There can be no doubt that Aristotle and Aquinas argue that metaphysics is possible. This becomes the backdrop of their meta-ethical naturalism, a theory dependent upon this analysis of essence.

It should be clear now why the argument of this book claims that meta-ethical questions, therefore, belong to a second order inquiry based upon the ontological content of a human essence. This second order meta-ethical inquiry based upon a dispositional account of essence is the 'core of good sense' which H. L. A. Hart once suggested is central to natural law ethics. But it is the core beyond Hart's limits, and a core which, because of a metaphilosophical move common to modern philosophy, Finnis omits in his reconstruction of natural law moral theory.

7

The Veatch Rejoinder:
Ontological Foundationalism

THE reductionist position eliminating the dependence of metaphysics, especially a theory of essence, from Thomas Aquinas's theory of natural law requires a response. In particular, it is concerned with unpacking the concepts central to the moral theory of Henry Veatch. That Veatch will adopt a metaphysical realism structurally similar to that of Aristotle and Aquinas as an ontological underpinning for his naturalist meta-ethics, a position suggested in the preceding chapter, will become apparent as this chapter develops. To help understand the moral naturalism of Henry Veatch, I intend to tease out the concepts he has used as presuppositions and to indicate how his method – his metaphilosophy – differs from much contemporary philosophical activity in analytic ethical theory. Veatch's method in approaching foundation questions in ethics differs radically from Finnis's metaphilosophy. The differing ways of approaching normative and foundational issues determines the theory as elaborated and developed.

To begin with, it is useful to recall Gustav Bergmann's suggestion that in understanding the works of a philosopher, 'there is a pattern' and one must discover the 'few fundamental ontological ideas' or principles from which the whole system flows and through which it can all be understood. This chapter is an attempt to unpack the basic pattern, the presuppositions, and the ontological ideas common to Henry Veatch's moral realism. In undertaking this project, concepts touching upon metaphilosophy issues and also issues pertaining to the content of Veatch's meta-ethics of naturalism will be considered. Using distinctions which became part of the philosophical canon through the writings of William Frankena, meta-ethics is an analysis of the set of questions, both foundational and linguistic, about the nature of normative ethics. Normative ethics is a set of moral rules or reasons why one ought to act in such and such a way. Throughout his investigations, Veatch is concerned about the foundational issues common to questions Frankena would classify as meta-ethics.

At the end of this chapter, Veatch's metaphilosophy will be contrasted with that used by Finnis and discussed in the previous chapter. Metaphilosophy, it will be recalled, refers to the basic presuppositions which direct the philosophical inquiry itself as undertaken by a particular philosopher. These differences in meta-philosophy determine how Finnis and Veatch, for example, offer differing interpretations of Aquinas on natural law. In addition, these differences illustrate the theoretical structures utilized in offering competing accounts of Aquinas on natural law. This should assist in understanding the fundamental differences between Finnis and Veatch in providing opposing accounts of the role human nature and practical reason play in the natural law theory of Aristotle and Aquinas. That Finnis and Veatch differ in their accounts of Aristotelian moral theory is obvious. Where and why they differ, however, are difficult questions to bring to resolution. This chapter attempts, among other things, to spell out these differences in some detail, and furthermore, illustrates the fact that metaphilosophical differences determine differing accounts of Aristotelian ethical theory.

FOUNDATIONALISM AND MODERN PHILOSOPHY

Since the time of Descartes and the dawn of modern philosophy, the term 'foundationalism' has been common in studies of Western philosophy. In the *Discourse on Method* and in his *Meditations*, Descartes focused on the analysis of the foundations of knowledge. From the time of these Cartesian exhortations, the philosophical emphasis on knowing and on the foundations of knowledge has occupied the serious study of many philosophers and determined the course of most Enlightenment and post-Enlightenment philosophy. Much modern philosophy can be characterized as foundational regarding questions concerning the way knowledge is ultimately justified.

The analysis of Henry Veatch's account of Aristotle and Aquinas, however, focuses attention on a different sense of 'foundationalism'. Veatch's writings have drawn attention to these issues for the past thirty years. Seizing on themes common to the Aristotelian tradition, Veatch has asked contemporary philosophers to redirect their thinking away from the Cartesian slumbers and move to Aristotelian realism. At the present, when Aristotelian studies are flourishing and the fabric of the Enlightenment project seriously questioned, it should be recalled that one philosopher has been urging a rethinking of Aristotle — and of Aristotle's primary medieval exponent, Thomas Aquinas — for the better part of the past thirty years. The analysis in this chapter spells out the metaphilosophy and the metaphysics which have directed the significant work in natural law meta-ethics and jurisprudence of Henry Veatch.

Veatch is not bashful about indicating the direction and scope of his philosophical work. In his recently published collection of essays, *Swimming Against the Current in Contemporary Philosophy*,[1] he writes forcefully about the nature of his philosophical efforts thus: 'With respect, then, to this present volume and the essays and discussions that follow, may I simply say that my own program ought perhaps to be regarded as amounting to little more than exercises in dialectic, and in a dialectic directed to the overriding purpose of trying to rehabilitate Aristotle and Aquinas as contemporary philosophers.'

Given that the content of this book is steeped in the analysis of the Aristotelian and the Aquinian natural law tradition, it is appropriate to consider a contemporary philosopher who has directed the general thrust of his philosophical pen to issues coextensive with, if not substantially identical with, many of the concerns discussed in this book on Aquinas's theory of natural law. The similarities in philosophical method and content with the account of Aquinas developed in Chapters 4 and 5 of this book will become apparent as this chapter unfolds.

CARTESIAN SLUMBERS

Until recently, the philosophy of Descartes dominated the direction of much modern philosophy. It is no accident that often Descartes is referred to as the 'parent' of modern philosophy. In the last part of the twentieth century, however, a gradual shift away from Cartesian issues began to take place in Western philosophy. One might

[1] Henry B. Veatch, *Swimming Against the Current in Contemporary Philosophy* (Washington, DC, Catholic University of America Press, 1990), 13.

argue that indeed a Kuhnian paradigm shift has occurred. The demand for certainty as central to the philosophical enterprise, which is so prevalent in the Cartesian corpus, has been seriously questioned. In the analytic tradition, the writings of Wittgenstein, Austin, and Ryle, among others, and the general thrust of ordinary language philosophy, have contributed to overturning the Cartesian hegemony in Western philosophy. Even Continental philosophers, some of whom witnessed the continuing of Cartesian worries through existentialism, have begun changing their focus of attention. Some historians of philosophy suggest that deconstructionism has sounded the death-knell for twentieth-century existentialism.

Obviously, some serious metaphilosophical questions about the change in the nature of philosophical inquiry at the end of the twentieth century have arisen. What accounts for this shift in the direction of philosophical inquiry? While this is an important question, it is, of course, well beyond the limits of the issues discussed directly here. None the less, this chapter attempts to concentrate on the metaphysical issues central to the structural revolution against foundationalist theories in which Veatch participated, particularly in moral theory. This is one avenue of the revolution against Cartesian philosophy and its dominance in modern thought.

Of course, Veatch is not the only philosopher considering afresh the insights of Aristotelian philosophy. Earlier chapters mentioned the publication of Alasdair MacIntyre's *After Virtue*, *Whose Justice? Which Rationality?*, and *Three Rival Versions of Moral Enquiry*, and Ralph McInerny's *A First Glance at St. Thomas Aquinas*, *Ethica Thomistica*, and *Aquinas on Human Action*. Both philosophers articulate serious worries about the Cartesian way of doing philosophy. In language strikingly reminiscent of MacIntyre's analysis of the state of twentieth-century analytic ethics in *After Virtue*, Veatch, in *For an Ontology of Morals*, writes, 'Could it be that contemporary ethics has just about reached a dead end?'[2] Of course, Wittgenstein's *Investigations* and the ordinary language work found in the writings of Ryle and Austin helped clear the ground of Cartesian overgrowth. Seeing these connections related to the work of Thomas Aquinas, Christopher Martin, in *The Philosophy of Thomas Aquinas*, argues forcefully about the Aristotelian and Aquinian insights contained in

[2] Henry B. Veatch, *For an Ontology of Morals* (Evanston, Ill.: Northwestern University Press, 1971), 3.

discussions found in recent analytic philosophy. Even some recent work in artificial intelligence has rethought its earlier acceptance of Cartesian criteria for knowing and intelligence. In this context, for some thirty years, Veatch has persisted as a harbinger of Aristotelian discussions continually asking probing questions about what analytic philosophers would call metaphysics, meta-ethics, and metaphilosophy.

In the 1930s, Étienne Gilson offered a comparative analysis between Cartesian method and Aquinian method. This was part of an extensive project in what Gilson called an analysis of *la méthode thomiste*. Gilson notes that in what is here referred to as Aquinas's metaphilosophy, the method of proceeding is *ab esse ad nosse valet consequentia*, ('from being to knowing is a proper logical connection or consequence'). The Cartesian method is just the opposite: *a nosse ad esse valet consequentia* ('from knowing to being is a valid deduction or consequence'). Gilson pointed to the opposite properties of each version of metaphilosophy. He argued that, for Aquinas, if there is no account of reality, then it is not possible to develop a theory of knowledge. Scott MacDonald recently articulated a similar view: 'Aquinas does not build his philosophical system around a theory of knowledge. In fact, the reverse is true: he builds his epistemology on the basis provided by other parts of his system, in particular, his metaphysics and psychology.'[3]

This way of proceeding philosophically is in direct opposition to the Cartesian method developed in the *Meditations*. Furthermore, the emphasis Descartes placed on epistemology is evident in his insistence on the primacy of the 'Rules for the Direction of the Mind'. Commenting on these differences between medieval and modern philosophy, Gilson wrote, in *The Unity of Philosophical Experience*, that 'there is more than one excuse for being a Descartes, but there is no excuse for being a Cartesian'.[4] Veatch, along with other contemporary analytic philosophers, especially Gustav Bergmann, shares these Cartesian metaphilosophical worries with Gilson. From positions such as these expressed by Gilson, it is not difficult to derive the philosophical worries which Veatch has articulated in his arguments against what he calls the 'transcendental turn'.

[3] Scott MacDonald, 'Theory of Knowledge', in Norman Kretzmann and Eleonore Stump (eds.), *The Cambridge Companion to Aquinas* (New York: Cambridge University Press, 1993), 160.

[4] Étienne Gilson, *The Unity of Philosophical Experience* (New York: Charles Scribner's Sons, 1937), 7.

THE TRANSCENDENTAL TURN

Why has Veatch rallied against Cartesian foundationalism? A better picture of Veatch's philosophical concerns and his lifelong interest in Aristotelian philosophy becomes evident by considering briefly some of his earlier works. In the early 1960s when nearly every introductory philosophy class in the United States and Canada was reading and discussing William Barrett's *Irrational Man*, Veatch wrote a monographic response entitled *Rational Man*.[5] This book, subtitled *A Modern Interpretation of Aristotelian Ethics*, indicates Veatch's long-term interest in Aristotelian moral theory. The issues Veatch addressed in this book focused his attention and energies directly on Aristotelian moral theory and its relation to questions in contemporary ethics. The role of reason determining human values based on human nature determined Veatch's response to Barrett in particular and to existentialists in general.

In his 1973 *For an Ontology of Morals*, Veatch directed his philosophical argument against what he termed 'the transcendental turn'. The argument developed in this book — and in much of Veatch's later writings — he referred to as an 'analysis and . . . account of the structural history of linguistic ethics'.[6] This argument against the transcendental turn is a clear statement of his attack on the Kantian way of doing epistemology, and, *a fortiori*, on Cartesian foundationalism. What worried Veatch was that criteria expressed in terms of mental consistency and clearness alone said precious little about the truth claims of propositions — in metaphysics or morals. Veatch suggested that this transcendental turn, massaged in Kant's *Critique*, denied the possibility of any objective foundation for knowledge. Kant's contention is that a human knower cannot ever know things as they are in themselves. Rather, our knowledge is always 'filtered' through the categories of the mind and the forms of intuition. This inability to understand things as they are, of course, renders impossible any knowledge of a human essence containing necessary properties. Given this result, Aristotelian moral theory as discussed in Chapters 4 and 5 would be impossible theoretically. And, of course, this is what Kant argued.

Veatch suggests that there are two aspects of this transcendental

[5] Henry B. Veatch, *Rational Man: A Modern Interpretation of Aristotelian Ethics* (Bloomington, Ind.: Indiana University Press, 1962).

[6] Veatch, *Swimming Against the Current*, 155–6.

turn in philosophy: (1) its use as 'a transcendental means of justification', and (2) its use as 'a transcendental surrogate for ontology and
metaphysics'.[7]

Veatch argues that these two senses are related. The first sense
suggests that through the transcendental turn, philosophers can provide a way to justify their philosophical first principles. The paradigm
here is Kant's first *Critique* where Kant argued for his transcendental
mode of justifying a priori truths. These a priori principles – the
'pure forms of the understanding' – were justified as the very conditions for a knower's having any experiences at all. It is through
these first principles that a human experience comes to be ordered
and structured so that it is a 'genuine experience'. Therefore, this
first sense of the transcendental turn suggests that rational judgements are determined by the conceptual schemes that reason alone
projects upon reality – whatever reality might be.

The second aspect of the transcendental turn follows from the
first. The transcendental means of justification removes the possibility of considering metaphysics as a necessary part of philosophy.
Metaphysics is no longer about the categories of reality, because
the categories by which human knowers understand anything are
determined by the conceptual schemes through which the human
understanding itself works. Hence, metaphysics or ontology is
removed from the province of philosophy.

In his 1985 *Review of Metaphysics* article, 'Rorty's Would-Be
Deconstruction of Analytic Philosophy', Veatch writes this analysis
of the transcendental turn:

All the same, it does begin to look as if both contemporary philosophy and
contemporary science have allowed themselves to be led down the garden
path, as a result of their having made what has sometimes been termed the
Kantian 'Transcendental Turn'. For the import of making such a turn is
that neither science nor philosophy can any longer claim to be in any way
a knowledge of things in themselves – i.e., of things as they really are.[8]

In his 1971 American Philosophical Association (Western Division) presidential address, Veatch wrote that a major presupposition
of contemporary meta-ethics 'is no less than a kind of transcendental
turn or perhaps a transcendental argument in virtue of which (to
quote Kant) the understanding is enabled not so much to draw its

---

[7] Veatch, *For an Ontology of Morals*, 52.
[8] Veatch, *Swimming Against the Current*, 92.

laws from nature, as rather to prescribe them to nature'.[9] The transcendental turn has been an object of Veatch's philosophical concern for some time. It is the major metaphilosophical principle against which he has directed much of the force of his arguments.[10]

In considering the good-reasons moral philosophers — Hare, Foot, and Searle, among others — Veatch suggests that they have used what he calls 'the linguistic turn' as a way to justify the rational character of moral judgements. This linguistic turn, Veatch argues, suggests that the rules of moral language — what might be called the 'moral language game' — entail certain linguistic requirements in order to maintain consistency. Moral justification is, therefore, reducible to the requirements of moral language. Veatch writes, about what he takes to be the linguistic turn:

we might say that the linguistic rules that govern the moral or ethical language game are no less than 'the conditions *a priori* of the possibility of (moral) experience', and that these same rules being thus the conditions *a priori* of the possibility of moral experience are at the same time the sources from which all the reasons and universalized laws of ethics may be derived.[11]

The linguistic turn is a derivative of the transcendental turn. Both deny the necessity of what Veatch calls an 'ontological commitment' for justification.

The good-reasons philosophers, therefore, are subsumed, Veatch argues, under the rubric of the transcendental turn. This transcendental turn entails that there is no ontological foundation for moral theory. Given this result of the conceptual scheme position, there is no possibility to consider seriously any theory of naturalism which depends in some way or other on a metaphysical foundation. Aristotle and Aquinas thus have their moral theories of natural law assigned to the dustbin containing theoretically irrelevant philosophical theories. Doing his structural history of twentieth-century ethics, Veatch assigns blame to the transcendental turn as the metaphilosophical principle dooming natural law ethical theory.

In their 1991 article, 'Does the Grisez-Finnis-Boyle Moral Philos-

---

[9] Ibid. 143.

[10] In a different century — namely the 19th — Veatch's worries could well have been articulated by Pope Leo XIII in his call challenging philosophers to bring scholasticism into the modern world. Recall that one of Leo's worries was the excessive internality of Kantian philosophy, which in effect ruled out knowledge beyond the phenomenal realm.

[11] Veatch, *Swimming Against the Current*, 149.

ophy Rest on a Mistake?', Veatch and Rautenberg list what they claim to be five principles central to recent analytic ethics. They refer to this account as 'the theory' which is articulated and defended in various ways in the writings of 'Sidgwick, Moore, Prichard, Hare, Donagan, Nagel, and any number of others'.[12] These five principles can be summarized in the following way:

1. Moral knowledge cannot be based on any fact of nature;
2. Moral knowledge is reducible to the 'logical grammar' of moral language;
3. 'Universalisability' is a necessary condition for that 'logical grammar';
4. Terms like 'good' and 'value', considered as 'desire words', do not belong to moral language;
5. 'Impartialism' is a necessary condition for the 'logical grammar', entailing that no moral term may be 'agent-related'.[13]

Veatch and Rautenberg argue that these five principles rule out any possibility that the moral theory of Aristotle and Aquinas meets the set of criteria deemed necessary for moral theories. These five principles constitute what most good-reasons theories require. Hence, one notes immediately the theoretical tension between natural law theories on the one hand and good-reasons theories on the other. Furthermore, the criteria of 'the theory' is an extension of the Enlightenment project for doing moral philosophy.

In his American Philosophical Association, Veatch indicates what he takes to be the serious consequences of adopting the transcendental turn as one's metaphilosophical principle: 'And unfortunately, a transcendental turn in ethics, however one chooses to interpret it, either strictly or more loosely, would seem to commit one, either to a certain arbitrariness in one's ethics, or else to a pretty hopeless relativism.'[14] In *Human Rights: Fact or Fancy?*, Veatch reiterates this claim: '[from] a Kantian transcendental turn, it must inevitably follow that any attempt to find a proper justification for morals and ethics will thereby become hopelessly compromised'.[15]

It is true that Kant's transcendental moral theory did not lead to

---

[12] Henry Veatch and Joseph Rautenberg, 'Does the Grisez-Finnis-Boyle Moral Philosophy Rest on a Mistake?', *Review of Metaphysics*, 44 (June 1991), 810.

[13] Ibid. 810–18

[14] Veatch, *Swimming Against the Current*, 156.

[15] Henry B. Veatch, *Human Rights: Fact or Fancy?* (Baton Rouge, L.: Louisiana State University Press, 1985), 241–2.

relativism. Kant based his theory on the formal requirements of reason itself. This is the philosophical import of the categorical imperative. The existentialists and the good-reasons philosophers lack the theoretical structure Kant accepted which enabled him to go beyond the arbitrariness and the relativism Veatch mentions in the last passage. Veatch's philosophical worry is that a metaphilosophy using the transcendental turn entails adopting a 'construction' of reality theoretically disconnected with the nature of reality.

THE ONTOLOGICAL TURN

In his *For an Ontology of Morals*, Veatch argued that this 'phenomenal' aspect of knowledge played itself out in the good-reasons moral theory, in existentialism, and in any deontological formalism of a Kantian variety. Dependence on the requirements of a conceptual scheme renders the good-reasons argument removed from any ontological foundation. The subjectivity inherent in existentialism together with the denial of the possibility of essence entails the acceptance of the transcendental turn. The Kantian denial of any epistemological access to reality entails the same conclusion. All three philosophical theories are rooted in a transcendental metaphilosophy which has placed a premium on the canons of knowing or of using language rather than on the canon of understanding reality. It is at this juncture that Aristotle and Aquinas part company with their transcendental successors in the Enlightenment. Kantian philosophy, the good-reasons moral philosophy, and existentialism are the theoretical results of the transcendental turn. Once a philosopher rejects knowing anything beyond the phenomenal, then what grounds, Veatch asks, does one have to make consistent judgements? Veatch is concerned that the conceptual scheme, the moral language game, or the existential decision itself, may all be arbitrary. The transcendental turn engenders a claim that the mind itself or the conceptual scheme itself is in some way sufficient. The Aristotelian tradition rejects this claim. The Kantian position suggests that things must conform to the human categories in the mind or those necessary to language, whereas the Aristotelian position suggests that the categories used in understanding must conform to things. This account illustrates a profound metaphilosophical difference. Interestingly enough, MacIntyre arrived at a similar set of conclusions in *After Virtue*.

One might argue that the existentialists, in suggesting that objectivity is a matter of historical currency only and hence irrelevant for contemporary philosophy, at least are consistent on this matter. In *For an Ontology of Morals*, Veatch refers to Frederick Olafson's account of existentialism in *Principles and Persons: An Ethical Interpretation of Existentialism*. Olafson writes that existentialists, in particular Heidegger and Sartre, deny the possibility of moral knowledge beyond the dimension of the moral decision itself. The analysis Olafson renders argues that a moral judgement is an act of decision or commitment made by the individual moral agent for which there is no counterpart beyond the agent. Given this account, Veatch, therefore, renders existentialism equally dependent on the transcendental turn.[16] Thus, subjectivity reigns supreme!

This subjectivity characteristic of existentialism, the relativism of the conceptual schemes of the good-reasons philosophers, and the transcendental nature of Kantian philosophy, Veatch suggests, bring about an Aristotelian *aporia*. An *aporia* is a mental stumbling-block or a philosophical dilemma which needs to be overcome. The *aporia* is the apparent moral relativism caused by the lack of connection with reality. This *aporia* dependent on the transcendental turn can be overcome successfully, Veatch argues, through redirecting our metaphilosophical presuppositions away from the transcendental turn and towards the ontological foundationalism of Aristotelian metaphysics. This is the direction in which Veatch suggests contemporary philosophical analysis must go if it is to overcome the Aristotelian *aporia* — the relativism — resulting from the transcendental turn.

Veatch worries even more that the internal consistency demanded by the transcendental turn philosophers remains strangely silent about the foundation for moral truth. In this regard, Ralph McInerny, in his *A First Glance at St. Thomas Aquinas*, suggests that 'modernity' is the proper name to refer to Cartesian foundationalism. McInerny argues that Aristotle — and Aquinas following him — have structural ways which reject 'modernity' and its canons of rational consistency devoid of any ontological connection. Veatch is in total agreement. Quoting from his presidential address once again, Veatch argued that 'the nonobjective character of ethics is not rec-

---

[16] Veatch, *For An Ontology of Morals*, 60-1 n. 6.

oncilable with its rationality after all'.[17] In considering the role of good reasons in twentieth-century analytic ethical theory, Veatch raises the same question about rationality and foundationalism:

Nevertheless, what is interesting for our present purposes about this almost unanimous determination on the part of more recent meta-ethicists to try to preserve a rational basis for our moral and ethical judgments is that it seems never to have occurred to them that if there were to be a rational basis for ethics there would presumably need to be an objective basis as well . . . [The linguistic philosophers have] been at some pains to show that there can be perfectly good reasons for calling something good or right, even though neither goodness nor rightness is ever an objective feature of the world.[18]

This is, Veatch suggests, an Aristotelian *aporia*. Veatch states the *aporia* in the following way: 'How could moral principles, to say nothing of ethical norms and standards generally, be at once nonobjective and at the same time universal and necessary?'[19] In other words, rationality demands an objective character to ethical judgements. The absence of an ontological foundation, Veatch argues, destroys the possibility for rational justification.

Succinctly put, Veatch seeks to find a foundation in reality for the truth of both metaphysical and moral terms. In language used in Chapter 4, it appears that Veatch needs metaphysical categories in order to establish regularity in nature. Nelson's synthetic a priori causal connections in the external world offer ontological insights on how this requirement might be determined in a realist metaphysics. More will be suggested about this reading of Veatch's theory later in this chapter.

At a root metaphilosophical level, Veatch is bothered about the realist foundation for the truth conditions of terms and propositions. This is where one of his main metaphilosophical principles enters: the *Euthyphro* question. Veatch refers often in his works to this method of operating. Recall the question Socrates put to the young Euthyphro: 'Is something pious because it is loved by the gods, or is it loved by the gods because it is pious?' The former question leads to the transcendental turn – the gods could easily determine for themselves what makes something pious. But the latter question

---

[17] Veatch, *Swimming Against the Current*, 156.
[18] Ibid. 144–5.
[19] Ibid. 156.

indicates that there is something about the nature of the 'pious' which entails that the gods indeed love it. This, Veatch suggests, points to the need to have reasons reflect something about the nature of reality. The transcendental turn, with its a priori elimination of any connection with reality, *a fortiori* eliminates any possibility of answering the *Euthyphro* question. The *Euthyphro* question is a major metaphilosophical principle at work in the philosophy of Henry Veatch. It indicates the necessity for having a realist, rational foundation for our language. Without this realist foundation, one cannot escape beyond the *aporia* dependent upon the transcendental-turn philosophers.

Veatch and Rautenberg discuss the *Euthyphro* principle thus:

> There is no better way, we think, to point out the sort of ambiguity that attaches to the notion of 'good' or 'value' than simply to apply what we ourselves have been wont to refer to as the *Euthyphro* test — a test that is borrowed from Plato's dialogue by that name, and that poses the question: is a thing to be pronounced 'good', simply because it is what people like or desire, or is it something that people like or desire because they see it is good — that is, truly, or objectively good.[20]

Using the *Euthyphro* principle, Veatch suggests that if any X is held to be good for no other reason than a human agent happens to like it, then any judgement of universalisability is removed theoretically. On the other hand, using the second alternative of the *Euthyphro* principle, if any X is held to be good because it is recognized, and justified, as an objective good, then it is possible theoretically to have a judgement of universalitability. Without this second alternative, Veatch argues that moral judgements indeed become relative. This argument, so Veatch suggests, indicates the necessity of accepting an Aristotelian moral realism. The *Euthyphro* principle also indicates the fundamental problem with any 'desire' ethic.

CONTEMPORARY PHILOSOPHY OF LAW

One area where Veatch best illustrates his concern for realism transcending formalism is in his critique of contemporary jurisprudence. In his *Human Rights: Fact or Fancy?*, Veatch adroitly argues for a foundation for human rights beyond what he considers the unsub-

---

[20] Veatch and Rautenberg, 'Grisez–Finnis–Boyle Moral Philosophy,' 828.

stantiated claims of contemporary philosophers. Veatch has Rawls, Dworkin, and Nozick in mind. It would be useful here to consider briefly why Veatch believes these three important figures in contemporary jurisprudence have serious deficiencies in their respective theories of human rights.

Veatch considers that most modern philosophers, influenced by Enlightenment philosophy, have been infected with some form of the transcendental turn. What follows from adopting the transcendental turn is that a metaphilosophy dominated by a conceptual scheme has been accepted, at least latently. This entails, so Veatch argues, that any foundationalist ontology is ruled out definitionally or a priori. Simply put, it follows, so Veatch argues, that the transcendental turn destroys the possibility of metaphysics, and *a fortiori*, of any ontologically significant meta-ethics. Kant so argued, Veatch reminds us, in the *Critique of Pure Reason*. Rawls, Nozick, and Dworkin all adopt, in some form or another, this conceptual scheme metaphilosophy steeped in the transcendental turn.

Consider for a moment the theory of John Rawls. His concept of the 'veil of ignorance' has been significant in the development of contemporary American jurisprudence and political theory. Veatch refers to Rawls's position as 'contractarianism'. Rawls asks us to think about what rights — as rational, self-interested agents — we would accept were we grouped together and asked to form a livable society. The 'veil of ignorance' postulates that all members of the discussion group on the foundation of rights bring no prior knowledge to the discussion other than the use of reason itself. Hence, there is no blatant self-interest. Out of this arrangement, so Rawls suggests, come the classic rights of Western liberalism: freedom, religion, pursuit of happiness, and so forth. Rawls suggests that given 'cool, reflective reason', this is what we, as rational agents considering what rights we would adopt, would all agree to. That we reach agreement depends upon the consistency in the arguments of the individuals considered. Briefly, Nozick, with the 'night watchman' theory of rights, argues in much the same manner. Dworkin, with his form of the 'good-reasons approach', gives a similar kind of justification. In none of these cases does one need an ontological foundation to justify a particular claim about the nature of human rights.

Dworkin is quite clear in suggesting that the kind of Western liberal theory he, Rawls, and Nozick adopt, all hold that any definition of the ontological character of either the 'good' or of a 'human person' is impossible conceptually. Dworkin rejects any particular theory of human excellence which might be derived from an account of human nature. In his 'Liberalism', Dworkin writes that 'government must be neutral on what might be called the question of the good life'.[21] Consider Dworkin's argument:

I did say that we [Rawls, Nozick, and Dworkin] were all 'working the same street', but I want to make plain that we each have very different theories. My point was that we were each offering a conception of liberalism – an account of what follows from the basic liberal idea that justice must be independent of any idea of human excellence or of the good life ... But we are all together, as I said, in accepting the liberal attitude which insists that government must not force a conception of the good life upon its citizens, or justify political decisions by preferring one vision of human excellence to another.[22]

This passage indicates why Dworkin rejects any realist foundation for human excellence or the good life. His liberalism rejects the possibility of any set of values being forced upon the lives of citizens in the liberal state. Of course, one must distinguish between an ontological foundation for rights and justice and the forced adherence to any particular set of values. An ontologically grounded set of values does not entail the forced acceptance of those values. While certain historical situations, in which ontological commitments to value existed, have engendered a lack of tolerance for difference, none the less this is not a necessary condition following from an ontologically based moral theory. The same historical event might occur from Finnis's self-evident analysis of the *per se nota* goods in natural law theory, considered in the last chapter. Ontology and governmental pressure are distinct concepts and should not be confused. Dworkin has, it seems, confused these two.

In considering the liberalism of Dworkin, Rawls, and Nozick, Veatch asks structurally what makes internal consistency or successfully engendered good reasons sufficient conceptually to ground a moral theory. Of course, his response is that neither can offer an appropriate justification. 'Consistency' and/or 'good reasons' do not

---

[21] Ronald Dworkin, 'Liberalism', in *A Matter of Principle* (Cambridge, Mass.: Harvard University Press, 1985), 191.
[22] Ronald Dworkin, interview, in Bryan Magee, *Men Of Ideas* (New York: Viking Press, 1978), 259.

satisfy the demands of the *Euthyphro* question. There is no reference to reality. Recall Nozick's famous 'experience machine' example. Veatch reminds his readers that just because human agents might not substitute their living experiences for putting their brains in the experience machine vat does not sufficiently answer the *Euthyphro* question. The natural law argument would be that the experience machine is rejected because it violates the process of reaching *eudaimonia*. The metaphilosophical move behind the 'experience machine' is insufficient conceptually because it does not refer to the development of the human person. The *Euthyphro* question has forced the philosophical analysis to go beyond the demands of language alone or the canons of rationality alone. The demands of human fulfilment in terms of *eudaimonia* become important at this point in the discussion. The *Euthyphro* question requires that something be said about the nature of reality. Rawls, Nozick, Dworkin, and Finnis, in rejecting any form of reductivism, cannot answer Veatch's *Euthyphro* question. A consideration of the conditions of language or the laws of reason do not inform about the nature of things. Veatch, following Aristotle and Aquinas, argues that without a knowledge of the nature of human beings, it is impossible to attain justified knowledge about how we ought to lead humanly satisfying lives.

In his discussion of the differences between natural law as understood by Aquinas and natural rights as elucidated by Hobbes, Veatch writes, about the nature of justification:

on the basis of the more traditional natural law theory (Aquinas), all human duties and human rights may be reasonably adjudged to be duties and rights only in so far as they can be justified, and thus shown to be duties or rights, in the light of man's natural end and perfection. Take away, then, this notion of a natural end or a natural perfection of human life, and there would no longer be any ground on the basis of which rights or duties of any kind might be rationally justified.[23]

Referring directly to Rawls, Dworkin, and Nozick, Veatch asks about the nature and limits of rational justification as proposed in these three distinct yet structurally similar theories of human rights:

For these rights that Rawls, Dworkin, and Nozick have been so vigorous in championing are not held to be natural rights; nor are the various duties

[23] Veatch, 'Natural Law: Dead or Alive?', in *Swimming Against the Current*, 265.

and side-constraints, that are correlative with the asserted rights or individuals, to be regarded as having any foundation in nature.

Yet if rights and duties cannot be shown to have any basis in nature or in fact, what reason is there to suppose that they have any basis at all? True, we may feel strongly about them; and nothing is easier than to get human beings to warm to affirmations of their individual rights and freedoms. But mere warmth of feeling can hardly be a substitute for rational justification. And if rights and duties are not held to be natural rights and duties, what is there that is rational about them?[24]

In his *Human Rights: Fact or Fancy?*, Veatch offers a similar critique of Kantian formalism and utilitarianism — what he refers to as 'duty ethic' and 'desire ethic'. In this and other writings, Veatch offers much the same calibre of criticism against 'duty' and 'desire' ethics.[25] Both are exemplifications of a transcendental-turn metaphilosophy in modern moral theory.

GRAPPLING WITH FOUNDATIONALISM

In responding to proponents of the transcendental turn and those refusing to accept ontological foundationalism, Veatch argues dialectically for a consideration of Aristotelian essence. This project began in *For an Ontology of Morals* and continued in *Human Rights: Fact or Fancy?*.

Veatch begins with Moore's classic 'open question' argument, a linguistic argument discussed in Chapter 3 above. Recall Moore's objection against any form of naturalism: we can always, so Moore suggests, ask about any property which is described or defined as 'good': 'Well, is it really good?' Any claim that a property is defined as 'good' fails the test of the open question argument. In other words, any purported definition of 'good' is never analytic. What Moore suggested, of course, was that utilitarian accounts of good in terms of 'happiness' or 'pleasure' were insufficient. One can always ask about an instance of pleasure — 'Is it an instance of good?' The open question argument leads to Moore's conclusion that the concept of good is indefinable. Veatch responds that the open question argument holds true only of definitional claims regarding clearly articulated simple concepts, e.g. simple geometric concepts. Again,

---

[24] Veatch, 'Natural Law', 273.
[25] Veatch, *Human Rights: Fact Or Fancy?*, see Chs. 1 and 2.

Cartesian overtones become apparent in that a true concept is defined as a 'clear and distinct idea'.

Veatch asks his readers to reconsider the Aristotelian role of essence in terms of a set of dispositional or potential properties. A dispositional property – an Aristotelian potency – is defined in terms of a 'becoming'. Hence, it is not subject to the 'clear and distinct' criterion. A disposition is a property with a developmental tendency. It is complex. A disposition cannot meet the clear and distinct criterion established by Descartes for meaningful discourse. This Cartesian criterion entails conceiving nature 'purely statically'. Veatch argues, to the contrary, that 'to conceive human nature . . . largely on the model of the nature of purely geometrical figures'[26] destroys the possibility of developing a coherent theory of natural law. As Anthony Kenny once pointed out, what Descartes forgot from his La Fleche scholastic training was the concept of Aristotelian potentiality. In other words, the concepts of act and potency so central to Aristotelian metaphysics are not part of the Cartesian metaphysics. With a rejection of the act/potency distinction came a rejection of final cause. Aristotelian ethics requires an account of final cause. Hence, modern philosophy's rejection of the act/potency distinction entails the dismissal of natural law theory as properly understood.

Veatch argues that the concept of good can make sense if one accepts the concepts of act and potency into one's ontology. Veatch refers to Aquinas's disputation, *De Veritate*, in which Aquinas considers the concept of good to be articulated in terms of the completion of a potency. As the discussion in Chapter 4 indicated, this analysis depends upon the concepts of formal and final causality. Formal cause determines the structure of an essence and final cause determines the development or perfection of the dispositions or potencies in the essence. Both of these metaphysical concepts are necessary conditions in the analysis of Aristotelian essence.

In considering the differences between Aristotle and Mill, Veatch offers a perspicuous quotation from R. A. Gauthier: 'it is entirely accidental to the supreme good in Aristotle's sense that it should be called happiness; the determination of its nature owes nothing to this word, but rests entirely on a metaphysics of finality'.[27] Gauthier

---

[26] Veatch, *Swimming Against the Current*, 301.
[27] Ibid. 101.

wants to disassociate Aristotelian teleology from any connection with utilitarian consequentialism. Gauthier's suggestion is right to the point. While both engage in teleology, Aquinas's teleology based on human nature is different conceptually from Mill's 'production of pleasure' teleology as an end of actions.

Both Aristotle and Aquinas refer to the concept of good as a kind of end. This is the root analysis of Aristotelian teleology. In Veatch's judgement, teleology in Aristotle is not anthropomorphically determined, but ontologically determined. Teleology is not the result of human desires, but rather determined by the concept of human nature as a set of dispositional properties. This is the cash value of the 'metaphysics of finality' necessary to elucidate the Aristotelian moral theory. In his 'Telos and Teleology in Aristotelian Ethics', Veatch writes: 'Isn't it high time, then, that we returned once again to something like an Aristotelian telos or a naturally obligatory end? For what else can give meaning to our lives as we actually live them and in terms of the actual purposes and projects to be pursued and striven for?'[28]

Veatch quotes Aquinas on this issue: 'Bonum est in rebus, ut philosophus dicit.' Commenting on this philosophical proposition, he notes that in the *De Veritate* (q. I a. 1), Aquinas 'specifically addresses himself to the matter of *bonum* as being inseparable from, and intelligible only in terms of, *ens*'. Veatch goes on to write that in the *De Veritate*, 'St. Thomas seems to give the unmistakable impression that ethics must discover its own principles directly in being and in the context of the discipline of metaphysics.'[29] This passage is in clear opposition to the non-reductivist theory that Finnis proposed, covered in the previous chapter.

By way of summary, the following items are necessary in order for Veatch to develop successfully his ontological foundationalism. These four principles are similar conceptually to the analysis of Aquinas's natural law theory explicated in Chapter 4 above.

1. The possibility of natural kinds. In order for Veatch to argue for a systematic ontology in the manner he does, he needs to have an ontology of natural kinds. A natural kind engenders the appropriate potentialities and actualities necessary to make sense of the concept of *bonum* as an end specific to a nature.

[28] Veatch, *Swimming Against the Current*, 116.
[29] Ibid. 289.

2. A dispositional theory of essence as a natural kind. Veatch rejects the Cartesian view of substance as a collection of inert properties. A dynamic view of essence in terms of a theory of dispositional properties directed to fulfilment is a necessary condition for his account of the Aristotelian/Aquinian theory of human essence. This set of dispositional properties might be called a set of synthetic a priori causal properties which determine the content of a natural kind. This is the causal category of essence found in the individual.

3. A version of 'final causes' bringing out the development of the potentialities in the essence. This point follows from (1) and (2). A final cause as end, the *telos*, is a necessary condition for a developmental scheme: the final cause is based upon the formal cause, which would be the determining set of dispositions common to a natural kind.

4. Normative Ethics as a second order activity or inquiry based upon the prior ontological account of essence as a dispositional natural kind. This point follows from (1), (2) and (3) above.

These four principles, it should be obvious, are strikingly similar conceptually and structurally to the *explicatio textus* provided in Chapter 4. In other words, the ontological foundationalism attributed to Veatch's meta-ethical theory is congruent structurally with the analysis of Aquinas's theory of natural law. In fact, of all the contemporary philosophers, both in jurisprudence and in meta-ethics, considered in this book, the work of Henry Veatch is most similar to the position suggested in these pages as a correct and adequate conceptual analysis of Aquinas on natural law.

VEATCH ON PHILOSOPHY

At this time, a summary of the metaphilosophy Veatch has used in his analysis of natural law might be both helpful and useful:

1. Veatch assumes that the subjectivity entailed by the transcendental turn forces contemporary ethics into an Aristotelian *aporia*;
2. By using a dialectic method, Veatch argues that subjectivity can be countered successfully;
3. The dialectic forces one into acknowledging the importance of the *Euthyphro* question;
4. The only response conceptually sufficient to the *Euthyphro* question argues for ontological foundationalism.

Propositions (1)–(4) elucidate the metaphilosophical principles Veatch thinks necessary to develop an adequate metaphysics of morals. These principles are compatible theoretically with the analysis of Aquinas's theory of natural law developed in Chapter 4.

FINNIS AND VEATCH ON NATURAL LAW

Through his critique of the transcendental turn, Veatch has called attention to the role of metaphysics in moral theory. He has developed a metaphysics which serves as a foundation for normative claims. Veatch rejects the Kantian/Cartesian method establishing the rational possibility of moral theory in terms of consistency. Veatch accepts the Aristotelian position of moral theory as a second order activity dependent upon the role of human essence. A theory denying the possibility of essence entails the conceptual impossibility of Aristotelian moral theory.

Before concluding, one difference between what Veatch asserts in reconstructing Aristotle and Aquinas for contemporary philosophy and some other attempts to rethink Aristotelian/Aquinian natural law meta-ethics should be noted. In particular, as suggested earlier, Veatch's position is in opposition to the revisionist version of Aristotelian ethical theory considered in the previous chapter, elucidated by John Finnis, Joseph Boyle, and Germain Grisez. In his *Natural Rights and Natural Law* and *Fundamentals of Ethics*, Finnis adopts, as suggested in the previous chapter, a form of Cartesian metaphilosophy in determining the so-called 'human goods'. Finnis's analysis is congruent structurally with Dworkin and Rawls – what must be the case for a human person, as a coolly dispassionate thinker, to adopt intellectual equilibrium and accept such a property as 'good'? Veatch wants more than this transcendental turn meta-philosophy, as the above analysis suggested. While this section will not repeat the Finnis revision of Aristotle and Aquinas, suffice it to say that Finnis – like Dworkin, Rawls, and Nozick – has assumed the 'transcendental turn' method. Given this, it is impossible in Finnis's revisionist theory of Aristotle and Aquinas to undertake a metaphysical analysis sufficient to elaborate realist moral properties. Finnis denies outright that a philosophical anthropology is a necessary condition for doing Aristotelian ethical theory. Given the 'ontological foundationalism' attributed to Veatch's analysis, it is rather easy to see why Veatch has argued that the Finnis reconstruction, when the chips are down, really undercuts the moral realism essential to Aristotelian normative ethics. Veatch once wrote a review of Finnis's *Natural Law and Natural Rights* containing this rather strong critique: 'Could it be that he [Finnis] was somehow tempted by the devil, so as to seem to say that natural law doctrines are not really based on a knowledge of nature after all!'[30]

Finnis appears to have accepted this account of Aristotle and Aquinas regarding the dismissal of metaphysical knowledge as foundational for moral theory.

This discussion of Finnis and Veatch ends our journey into the metaphilosophy of Henry B. Veatch. Veatch argues for a realist ontology — a metaphysics of finality — which can overcome the radical subjectivism which he sees as endemic to modern moral theory. His meta-ethics driven by his metaphilosophy produces a metaphysics of morals. Accordingly, the ontological foundationalism in opposition to the transcendental turn common to most contemporary foundationalists has been, in the mind of Veatch, articulated and defended.

[30] Ibid. 292.

8

Natural Law Revisited

THE place of natural law theory in the continuing discussions of ethical naturalism requires that the conceptual account of several vexing problems in moral and legal theory be analysed in some detail. The *explicatio textus* of Aquinas's classic account of law from the *Summa Theologiae*, I-II qq. 90–7, comprised Chapter 4. The role of eternal law in relation to the development of natural law made up Chapter 5. Chapters 6 and 7 discussed two contemporary analyses of Aquinas, the former by John Finnis and the latter by Henry Veatch. Having completed this part of the task, it remains to suggest how natural law ethical theory might fit into the programme of contemporary moral and legal discussions. Quite obviously, this is principally a discussion of meta-ethical issues in natural law theory.

AQUINAS AND CONTEMPORARY META-ETHICS

The analysis put forward in this chapter will indicate how Aristotle and Aquinas might resolve the is/ought problem and transcend the naturalistic fallacy. Before that takes place, however, it is time to summarize the fundamental principles in this traditional, albeit reconstructed, natural law theory contained in the texts of Aquinas's *Summa Theologiae*. This summary argument, which belongs to the general discussion of meta-ethical naturalism, will also indicate how the argument elucidated in this book compares with the analyses put forward by Finnis, MacIntyre, and Veatch.

In order for Aquinas's theory of natural law to be a consistent theory of ethical naturalism, the *explicatio textus* and the structural argument proposed in this book suggests that Aquinas needs to assume the following principles:

1. A theory of natural kinds;
2. A theory of essence composed of dispositional properties;
3. A metaphysics of finality determining the obligatory ends;
4. Ethics as a second-order activity based upon the development of the dispositional properties in the individual that make up an essence;
5. A conjunction of 'good' with 'end' as the terminal point of the natural process;
6. A consistent theory of practical reason.

Given the above principles, the account of natural law Aquinas develops in the *Summa Theologiae* can become a consistent, coherent, and theoretically interesting version of ethical naturalism.

The six principles suggested above as necessary conditions for natural law theory in Aquinas entail a metaphysical foundation which goes beyond the reconstructed versions articulated by Finnis in *Natural Law and Natural Rights* and MacIntyre in *After Virtue*. Finnis, in denying what he calls the 'reductivist thesis', rejects the metaphysical foundation for a moral theory which Chapters 4 and 5 argue as necessary conditions for a succinct and complete analysis of natural law theory. Finnis's position cannot respond to the *Euthyphro* question. Finnis's position, in terms of what he calls 'objectivity', appears to be reducible to a form of the transcendental turn. Without accepting the ontological foundation necessary for grounding moral judgements, it is unclear how Finnis believes his position is connected foundationally with the tradition of natural law.

MacIntyre's account in *After Virtue*, furthermore, at times appears to undertake an Aristotelian analysis which, like Finnis, denies the reductivist thesis. In this way, there is at least a marginal structural similarity with the reconstruction articulated by Finnis. While the ontological underpinning of MacIntyre's analysis is at times difficult to sort out thoroughly, none the less, in *After Virtue* he does argue that the 'metaphysical biology' that Aristotle thought necessary is now obsolete for a consistent reconstruction of Aristotelian moral theory. Denying the metaphysical biology seems to deny the function view of essence. This entails that the moral theory is independent conceptually from an ontology of essence or human nature. It is not immediately obvious that MacIntyre's virtue ethics is part of the Aristotelian tradition if indeed he does deny a role for human nature as the ontological foundation of that theory.

In *Three Rival Versions of Moral Enquiry*, however, MacIntyre argues for a position interpreting Aristotle and Aquinas which clearly considers the role human nature and speculative philosophy play in natural law morality. This is a progressive move from the rejection of what he termed the 'outmoded metaphysical biology' in Aristotle to the need for a ontological foundation in human nature. In his 'MacIntyre's Postmodern Thomism: Reflections on *Three Rival Versions of Moral Enquiry*', Thomas Hibbs argues that 'in *After Virtue*, MacIntyre sought to rehabilitate Aristotle's ethics by substituting social for natural teleology'.[1] Concerning the role essence and human nature play in his more recent analysis of Aristotle and Aquinas, MacIntyre writes: 'Evaluative judgments are a species of factual judgments concerning the final and formal causes of activity of members of a particular species. The concept of good, then, has application only for beings insofar as they are members of some species or kind.'[2]

MacIntyre considers his analysis of the need for human nature in order to explicate properly Aristotle and Aquinas on natural law in the following passages:

For an Aristotelian, whether Thomist or otherwise, what is good or bad for anyone or anything is so in virtue of its being of a certain kind, with its own essential nature and that which peculiarly belongs to the flourishing of beings of that kind.

Take away the notion of essential nature, take away the corresponding notion of what is good and best for members of a specific kind who share such a nature, and the Aristotelian scheme of the self which is to achieve good, of good, and of pleasure necessarily collapses ... So metaphysical nominalism sets constraints upon how the moral life can be conceived. And, conversely, certain types of conceptions of the moral life exclude such nominalism.

So an anti-nominalist philosophical psychology provides the basis for an account of these dispositions which, perfectly possessed, are the distinctively human perfections, the virtues.[3]

Given the above arguments elucidated by MacIntyre, it is clear that

---

[1] Thomas Hibbs, 'MacIntyre's Postmodern Thomism: Reflections on *Three Rival Versions of Moral Enquiry*', *Thomist*, 57/2 (Apr. 1993), 279.

[2] Alasdair MacIntyre, *Three Rival Versions of Moral Enquiry* (Notre Dame, Ind.: The University of Notre Dame Press, 1990), 134.

[3] Ibid. 138–9.

the once outmoded metaphysical biology has returned in terms of his consideration of human nature and human essence. Yet Mac-Intyre insists that Aquinas's account is beyond the limits which Cartesian modernity placed upon the nature of philosophical inquiry. MacIntyre argues for the compatibility of the rational and the social in the natural law texts of Aristotle and Aquinas. The search for the rational is always, MacIntyre suggests, within the context of the social and the historical narrative. Yet in *Three Rival Versions of Moral Enquiry*, MacIntyre places much more emphasis on philosophical psychology and human nature than in his account of similar issues in *After Virtue*. In fact, Hibbs, in his account of MacIntyre's work, argues that MacIntyre has developed a 'constructive, postmodern Thomism'.[4]

In a 1991 interview, MacIntyre said this about his view of metaphysics and its connection with Aristotelian moral theory:

This complex conception of virtues received its classical statement from Aristotle in a form that requires not only the justification of the central theses of his political and moral philosophy, but also that of the metaphysics which those theses presuppose. This latter connection between virtue and metaphysics I had not understood when I wrote *After Virtue*.[5]

In this interview, MacIntyre explicitly suggests that in order to understand natural law theory, a connection is needed between the moral claims of the theory and the metaphysical propositions which serve as the foundation of that theory. In this respect, the later MacIntyre's account of Aristotle and Aquinas is more akin to the analysis provided in this book than it is to the non-reductivist interpretation put forward by Finnis. This later account suggested by MacIntyre renders his moral theory less associated with postmodernism and more connected with classical Aristotelianism.

Finnis, and the MacIntyre at least of *After Virtue*, appear to ground their reconstructions of Aristotelian moral theory in the conditions of the theory itself. MacIntyre appeals often to the social and political context in which Aristotle developed his theory in the *Nicomachean Ethics* and the *Politics*. It is not clear that his denial of a metaphysical biology, which this book has often referred to as a philosophical anthropology, is replaced sufficiently with a normative theory

---

[4] Hibbs, 'MacIntyre's Postmodern Thomism', 277.
[5] Giovanna Borradori, *The American Philosopher*, trans. Rosanna Crocitto (Chicago: University of Chicago Press, 1994), 148.

constructed around the demands of a social and political theory. MacIntyre's position in *After Virtue* probably would not pass the test of the *Euthyphro* question. The historical conditions appear to determine the context in which the moral theory is articulated.

Hence, it appears that both Finnis and the MacIntyre of *After Virtue* have developed accounts reconstructing Aristotelian ethics that fail to take into consideration the metaphysical requirements of this theory. Chapter 7 suggested that the ontological foundationalism proposed by Veatch is more akin to the Aristotelian position as classically understood than either Finnis's account or that proposed by MacIntyre in *After Virtue*. The theme of this book is that both Aristotle and Aquinas, in developing a moral theory based on a metaphysical theory, made meta-ethics and normative ethics into second order inquiries. This second order dimension is meaningless without the prior first order development of an ontological theory. Aquinas and Aristotle developed their respective theories of essence, cause, essential property, disposition, primary substance, and *telos* in metaphysical discussions. For moral theory, this developed into what is called the metaphysics of finality. These metaphysical discussions, however, are necessary conditions for constructing the normative and meta-ethical theories. In Aristotle and Aquinas, no metaphysical theory entails no moral theory. That is the bottom line argument in this book. The position articulated over the years by Veatch comes closest to the theory argued in these pages.

Given this thematic summary, it is now time to consider several problems with natural law theory as expressed in the writings of Aristotle, Aquinas, and most of their realist commentators.

THE METAPHYSICS OF MORALS

In this context, the concept, 'metaphysics of morals', refers to the real existence of ontological categories. It is not the Kantian use of the transcendental deduction of the categories or the a priori development of the categorical imperative. The foundation for moral concepts is realist and not transcendental *a priori* in the Kantian sense. Of course, the realist nature of this analysis is opposed to any postmodernist interpretation of Aristotle and Aquinas.

In the mid-part of the twentieth century, it would have seemed theoretically irresponsible to be writing about the metaphysical foundations of a moral theory. There was a double curse on this kind of inquiry: (1) the rejection of metaphysics, and (2) the acceptance of non-cognitivist positions in meta-ethics. Non-cognitivism, which followed from the scientism of logical positivism, reigned supreme. The analysis of ethical language in terms of various forms of emotivism and prescriptivism served as the normal paradigm for undertaking moral analysis. Any factual basis for moral judgements was held in theoretical disrepute. The naturalistic fallacy strongly articulated by Moore in response to the nineteenth-century utilitarian naturalists was, furthermore, held with such theoretical conviction that any form of naturalism was dismissed quickly from meta-ethical discussions. Beyond the confines of moral discourse, metaphysical questions were often relegated to history of philosophy discussions strangely irrelevant to the then contemporary direction of philosophy. To consider either an ethical naturalism or an ontological theory, or worse still, a metaphysics or an ontology of morals, was considered beyond the norm of sophisticated philosophical conversation.

But metaphysics did return, almost with a vengeance. One need but consider recent discussions in possible-worlds ontology or in the metaphysics of natural kinds to realize the force of the return of metaphysics in analytic philosophy. Along with this return has come a renewed interest in discussing the foundations of moral theory. Writing in the *American Philosophical Quarterly*, Paul J. Dietl observed, about the rise of metaphysical and meta-ethical concerns from the ashes of logical positivism: 'Some of the most remarkable turns in recent philosophical discussion have been the resurrection of issues original readers of *Language, Truth and Logic* would have thought forever dead. [Among other philosophical claims] . . . ethics is considered cognitively significant in respectable circles.'[6]

While it certainly does not follow that the rejection of non-cognitivism entails the acceptance of natural law moral theory, none the less its rejection, along with the demise of logical positivism, did encourage the possibility of discussions in metaphysics and in normative theories based on metaphysical foundations. Natural law philosophers, furthermore, must establish that the conditions of language alone do not justify normative conclusions. This is the role Veatch's *Euthyphro* question plays in this analysis. In other words, natural law philosophers must transcend the position that the con-

---

[6] Paul J. Dietl, 'On Miracles', *American Philosophical Quarterly*, 5 (1968), 130.

ditions of either language or theory-making are sufficient to account for normative judgements. A natural law theory, in the Aquinian mode, requires a realist ontology as a foundation. Language and consistency alone will not satisfy the realist demands. In their recent article, 'Does the Grisez–Finnis–Boyle Moral Philosophy Rest on a Mistake?'[7] Veatch and Rautenberg argue against the sufficiency of language conditions alone to solve normative foundational questions.

Moreover, certain practical issues in normative ethics, ranging from medical ethics to liberation theories to gender issues to self-fulfilment pop-culture, among others, helped bring about the demise of non-cognitive meta-ethics. Moral issues demand discussion, and this discussion points to the need for foundational analysis. In the previous chapter we saw that Henry Veatch continually asks the *Euthyphro* question in his meta-ethical discussions. A foundational analysis is the only way to render a response sufficient to meet the demands of the *Euthyphro* question. In other words, the *Euthyphro* question requires that there are some aspects of nature — or in realist ontology — which provide grounds for justified normative judgements.

Metaphysical discussions are important once again in contemporary philosophy. Furthermore, an offshoot of this discussion has been a reintroduction of questions regarding the metaphysical foundation of moral theories. At mid-century, Rommen wrote: 'The idea of natural law obtains general acceptance only in the periods where metaphysics . . . is dominant. It recedes . . . when the essence of things and their ontological order are viewed as unknowable.'[8]

Rommen, of course, realized that his metaphysical claims required more than the conditions necessary to establish a theory. In the classical sense of the term, Rommen expected that the metaphysical foundations did reach to the categories of being or reality in some sense or other. Rommen is paradigmatic among scholastic philosophers in suggesting that metaphysics is real and not conceptual. This is the classical way Aquinas's ontology has been considered.

Moreover, the classical paradigm for a metaphysical foundational theory of morality is Aristotle's *Nicomachean Ethics*. That metaphysical analysis was foreign to neither Aristotle nor Aquinas is obvious.

---

[7] Henry Veatch and Joseph Rautenberg, 'Does the Grisez–Finnis–Boyle Moral Philosophy Rest on a Mistake?', *Review of Metaphysics*, 44 (June 1991), 807–30.

[8] Heinrich A. Rommen, *The Natural Law*, trans. Thomas R. Hanley (B. Herder Book Co.: St Louis, M. 1947), 161.

The role essence plays in Aristotle's moral theory entails that ethics itself is a second order philosophical inquiry. The meta-ethics follows from the analysis of essence, and not the other way around. Normative inquiries are second order to the first order metaphysical inquiry. Moral philosophy is dependent upon the metaphysical analysis of a theory of essence. This book has attempted to indicate that Aquinas's theory of natural law is, when analysed appropriately, structurally similar to the metaphysical foundationalist theory Aristotle suggested in his *Nicomachean Ethics*. Aquinas's theory of natural law entails more content than the procedural natural law Fuller proposes, offers a wider sense of human 'natural necessities' than found in Hart, is less Kantian and Cartesian than Finnis suggests, and provides a structured sense of the human person which Dworkin and others have denied.

None the less, several problems remain to be considered. This chapter attempts to bring to closure some of the issues which have been raised in twentieth-century philosophy as substantive objections to Aquinas's theory of natural law.

AROUND THE NATURALISTIC FALLACY

Now that we have explicated in some detail Aquinas's moral theory of natural law, it is time to consider how this revised theory might stand up against the two principal objections to ethical naturalism in the twentieth century: (1) the naturalistic fallacy, and (2) the hypothetical/categorical imperative issue. Henry Veatch articulated this worry forcefully when he noted: 'From the point of view of many thinkers in the nineteenth century and even after, the entire doctrine of natural rights and natural law would appear to rest on nothing less than a patent logical fallacy.'[9]

Veatch writes that any argument for either natural law or natural rights was considered 'to commit this fallacy of trying to infer an ought from an is or a value from a fact, or, as G. E. Moore was to term it years later, it involves the naturalistic fallacy'.[10]

Students familiar with meta-ethical discussions realize that since the time of Hume the naturalistic fallacy problem has been para-

---

[9] Henry B Veatch, 'Natural Law: Dead or Alive?', in *Swimming Against the Current in Contemporary Philosophy* (Washington, DC: Catholic University of America Press, 1990), 268.

[10] Ibid.

mount in philosophical discussions of moral issues. Hume was concerned greatly that from a fact one could not validly derive a value statement. Hume's point is that, as every elementary student of logic knows, one cannot have more in the conclusion of a deductive argument than is contained in the premises. If a value is not contained in the premiss or premisses of a factual statement, then it cannot be derived validly from that statement about the world. Hume argued that, in effect, every meta-ethical position of naturalism violated this basic logical maxim. Hence, the charge against naturalism in ethics is that it derives a 'value' from a 'fact'. Put another way, however one might define a statement, naturalism derives a 'value statement' from a 'factual statement'. This is what Moore referred to as the essence of the naturalistic fallacy in the *Principia Ethica*.

From our earlier discussions of Aristotle and Aquinas, it is obvious that the meta-ethical theories of both philosophers illustrate a form of ethical naturalism. Both offer cognitivist/definist theories. Moral terms are defined through general statements about human nature, which are 'natural' facts about the world. Given this, what can Aristotle and Aquinas say by way of a response to the fact/value problem? Or, put differently, can Aristotle and Aquinas refute the charge that their theories commit the naturalistic fallacy?

In response to the fact/value dichotomy issue, one needs to remember the dispositional view of essence discussed in Chapter 4 above. Recall that an essence for Aristotle and Aquinas is best elucidated in terms of a 'set of dispositional properties'. Each disposition or potency is a property 'tending towards' a completion as its 'normal' end. An essence is not a set of inert, static properties with the properties complete in and of themselves.

There are two questions central to the issue of the relation of a metaphysical theory to a value claim:

1. Is it possible to derive a value claim from any proposition referring to a factual claim – or any reference to being?
2. Does the fact/value dichotomy expressed in Moore's naturalistic fallacy assume a particular kind or theory of ontology?

In responding to (2), a general response to (1) will become evident. The point of this discussion is that Moore assumed a particular ontology of properties which, in turn, determined the way he developed the open question argument.

A response to (2) will be given first. In considering the ontology underpinning the naturalistic fallacy, as Moore elucidated the issue, it appears that the fact/value dichotomy assumes as a theoretical presupposition, an ontology of simple, discrete, complete properties. Recall Moore's analysis of simple properties as discussed in Chapters 3 and 7. Moore assumed ontologically that there existed both simple natural and simple non-natural properties. The properties were in some way fundamentally simple entities. This theory of ontological simples probably emerges from the psychological atomism of British empiricists such as Berkeley and Hume. Basic, discrete properties were perceived as 'psychological or intentional atoms', and from these 'atoms' were composed the complex intentional ideas which make up our mental awarenesses of the world. The point is that simple objects in the mind refer in some way to simple objects in the world. Much English and American philosophy from the time of Hume until the mid-part of this century appears to have accepted this version of metaphysics in some form or another. A good example would be Russell's *Essays on Logical Atomism*. Russell's ontology depends upon the blending of a reference theory of meaning with an intentionality theory of psychological atomism.

Given this ontology, a 'fact' is reducible fundamentally to a complex of 'simples'. If a 'simple' is complete in and of itself, there is no sense theoretically that can be made of the concept of a disposition or of a potentiality. On the other hand, if one needs the concept of a disposition to resolve the fact/value difficulties, it is obvious that Aristotle and Aquinas, incorporating the concept of disposition, come to these matters with a different set of metaphysical assumptions. Neither Aristotle nor Aquinas assumes an ontology of simple entities as essential properties.

In attempting to resolve this fact/value issue, one must moreover recall that moral philosophy in the Aristotelian/Aquinian tradition is a second order activity. It is based upon the concept of a human nature, which is dependent upon a theory of ontological essence. From the analysis in the preceding chapters, the concept of essence in Aristotelian ontology is determined as a 'set of dispositional properties'. The moral theory is rooted ontologically in the theory of dispositional essence. Moral theory, therefore, is in some sense derivative from the metaphysical theory. Of course, Hume, Kant, Moore, most intuitionists, all non-cognitivists, and many other critics object that this indeed is the very nature of a violation of the fact/value dichotomy. The thrust of the 'second order' nature of

Aristotelian moral theory renders it suspect, in modern eyes, to the naturalistic fallacy as the 'reduction' of a value claim to some factual referent. This is what Finnis often refers to as the 'reductivist thesis'.

The ontology of 'simples' held by most philosophers in the Anglo-American tradition forces these philosophers into asserting the fact/value dichotomy precisely because of this ontology. If a natural property – whatever it is – is complete and self-sufficient, then it would require something to be added to it in order to be classified as a different kind of property. The fact/value dichotomy assumes that a 'value' is added in some way to a 'fact' in order to render a value statement true. But this does demand, as the critics have observed, that something is in the conclusion which was not in the premiss. Of course, this violates a basic rule of deductive arguments. The claim expressed here is that the fact/value problem in modern philosophy arose because an ontology of simple properties replaced the then prevalent Aristotelian ontology of dispositional properties.

In order to respond to this objection, one must consider for a moment what a dispositional view of property does to the fact/value dichotomy. If a natural property can be dispositional in character, then it is involved in a process 'naturally' – or from its very nature. It is disposed towards some goal or fulfilment, which is its end. The tulip bulb is directed 'naturally' towards becoming a tulip plant and not a hippopotamus. A hippopotamus embryo is structured 'naturally' towards becoming a certain kind of an animal, and not a palm tree or a corn plant. Individuals in natural kinds tend towards the ends or 'perfections' which are built into their dispositional properties. In effect, this is the structural analysis for the concept of natural kinds in Aristotle and Aquinas. Using the concepts Aristotle developed in his account of causality, the set of dispositional properties which determine the substantial form serve as the formal cause. When these dispositions are actualized, this illustrates the attainment of the final cause. Both formal and final cause when predicated of a natural object are dependent on the substantial form, which in turn determines the structure of the natural kind itself.

Given this dispositional view of properties – which set of such properties make up a human essence – the Aristotelian/Aquinian theory suggests claiming that the end of the developmental process is what is defined by the 'good'. Aquinas writes that 'the end is, by definition, a good'. This claim can make sense only if one accepts the ontology of a dispositional view of properties. Given this view, the 'good' is not something added to a property. Rather, the 'good' is the terminal point, however construed, which is the end of the process of development common to the natural process in the dispositional property itself. There is no fact/value dichotomy because the 'value' — in this case, the 'end' of the natural process — is the result of the normal development of the 'fact' — in this case, the dispositional property. There is no radical bifurcation between fact and value because the value — i.e. the 'good' — is nothing more than the development of the process structured by the nature of the set of dispositions. It follows, therefore, that a value is not derived from a fact through the process of 'adding' the value to the fact. The value is another way of referring to the completed state of the dispositional property in the individual. This is the end process of the transformed or developed dispositional property. The value as end (final cause) is connected to the fact as dispositional property (formal cause). The relation of final cause to formal cause renders insignificant the claim that a value is added to a fact. The value as fact is a state of completion of the disposition as fact. This is an important consequence of Aristotelian/Aquinian natural kind essence theory. A dispositional view of natural kinds is, therefore, a necessary condition in rendering the fact/value question inapplicable to Aristotelian/Aquinian moral theory. Once again, the metaphysical implications of the theory of essence are centrally important for issues arising in the moral theory.

While Moore and his followers might claim that the Aristotelian moral argument, rooted in a realist ontology, still commits the naturalistic fallacy, the Aristotelian can respond that the ontology of complex dispositional properties side-steps structurally the force of the open question argument. It is incoherent to ask about an end, as an actualized disposition, whether or not it is good. It is good analytically, because that is the definition of the concept of 'good' as analysed in terms of the Aristotelian act/potency distinction. The claim articulated and defended here is that without an ontology limited to simple properties, the open question argument as formulated by Moore will not work.

What results from this analysis is that the fact/value dichotomy is overcome theoretically because of the metaphysics of natural kinds composed of dispositional properties which is common to the Aristotelian/Aquinian ontology. The 'fact' evolves into the 'value', all on the natural level. The act is the developed disposition, which is the final cause. There is no radical bifurcation of levels of reality, as Moore proposed. Aristotelian naturalism suggests a unity to fact and value through the analysis of a dispositional property reaching its determined end in the individual. Aristotelian teleology, therefore, skirts the issues involved in the naturalistic fallacy.

In *After Virtue*, MacIntyre argues that the fact/value problem is not applicable to Aristotelian moral theory. MacIntyre's argument is different from the one expressed above. None the less, there are some structural similarities. MacIntyre argues that a functional view of human nature can ground successfully a value claim with a factual referent. Along with the demise of the Aristotelian functional view at the time of the rise of the new science, moral terms changed their meaning, at least to some degree. MacIntyre suggests that accepting the fact/value problem assumes that no moral theory could be consistently functional. In addition, MacIntyre suggests that the historical dimension of the rise of modern ethical theory is important as one sorts out the fact/value dichotomy thicket. He writes:

So the 'No ought conclusion from is premises' principle becomes an inescapable truth for philosophers whose culture possesses only an impoverished moral vocabulary ... That it was taken to be a timeless logical truth was a sign of a deep lack of historical consciousness which then informed and even now infects too much moral philosophy. For its initial proclamation was itself a crucial historical event. It signals both a final break with the classical tradition and the decisive breakdown of the eighteenth-century project of justifying morality in the context of the inherited, but already incoherent, fragments left behind from tradition.[11]

MacIntyre rests his argument on the demise of Aristotelian functionalism. This is certainly correct. However, the argument articulated above goes further than MacIntyre's claim. The argument asserts that a particular view of the ontology of properties was also a part of the rise of the new science and the advent of modern philosophy. Cartesian ontology rejects the possibility of the concept of disposition. One suspects that this is part of the Cartesian criterion of clear and distinct ideas. If one cannot have dispositional properties in one's ontology, then one cannot have Aristotelian functionalism. For Aristotelian functionalism, based on the *ergon* or 'function' of the human person, establishes the teleology necessary to make the

---

[11] Alasdair MacIntyre, *After Virtue*, 2nd edn. (Notre Dame, Ind.: University of Notre Dame Press, 1984), 59.

functionalism possible. The *ergon* is determined by the substantial form. But this teleology is only possible within the context of the acceptance of dispositional properties. To deny dispositional properties entails the rejection of Aristotelian functionalism. Hence, the argument put forward above goes one step beyond that expressed by MacIntyre in *After Virtue*. Functionalism is only possible for Aristotle and Aquinas because the ontology accepted for natural kinds is dispositional in character and structure. In connecting functionalism with dispositional properties, this argument goes a tad further than MacIntyre's analysis of the is/ought problem in Aristotle and Aquinas.

AROUND THE HYPOTHETICALCATEGORICAL IMPERATIVE PROBLEM

The analysis to be undertaken next considers a response to the 'hypothetical/categorical imperative' problem, which, like the naturalistic fallacy, is often attributed to the moral theories of Aristotle and Aquinas. This is another side of the coin treating issues central to the is/ought problem. It is time to consider how the reconstructed view of Aquinas on natural law might meet this ever-present hypothetical imperative objection to meta-ethical naturalism. Suggesting a solution for Aquinas's theory regarding this famous objection from Hume brings forward an interesting link with Kantian ethics.

To put the question succinctly, does Aquinas, as many twentieth-century critics have claimed, derive the 'ought' from an 'is'? In considering Aquinas on natural law, every person conversant with twentieth-century meta-ethical theory from Moore onwards will raise this kind of worry. In his analysis of Aquinas on natural law, D. J. O'Connor writes:

The whole discussion seems to confuse two senses of 'good' as (i) what *is* sought after, and (ii) what *ought to be* sought after. What reason is there to suppose that there is any coincidence between happiness and virtue? . . .

Granted that the good life for man must somehow be grounded in human nature, how do we argue from the *facts* of human nature to the *values* of morality? As Hume notoriously showed, the gap between fact and value cannot be bridged by logical argument.[12]

---

[12] D. J. O'Connor, *Aquinas and Natural Law* (London: Macmillan, 1967), 23–4.

Moreover, if the 'ought' is derived from the 'is', a common objection is that the argument is reducible to a hypothetical imperative at best. This is a classic twentieth-century objection to Aristotelian naturalism. Even if one could bring an imperative to bear on the theory, so the criticism of Aristotle and Aquinas goes, at best this would be a hypothetical imperative and never a categorical imperative. The proposition takes the following form: 'If one wants to reach a state of *eudaimonia*, then one must act in such a way to promote self-actualization.' This would be the hypothetical imperative. Martin Golding raises this objection from the perspective of jurisprudence: 'One of the criticisms that has been leveled at this aspect of Aquinas's theory is that it fails to explain why laws have the authority of obligation. For law making, on this theory, involves what Immanuel Kant called "hypothetical imperatives" . . . Clearly, such hypothetical imperatives do not give rise to obligations.'[13]

In these discussions reducing Aquinas's moral imperative to the hypothetical rather than the categorical, two underlying assumptions appear to be at work:

1. Following Kant, a moral imperative must be categorical in order to establish obligation;
2. Aristotelian functionalism leads only to a hypothetical imperative.

In order to respond to this kind of objection, suggesting that Aquinas's theory lacks any adequate account of obligation through a categorical imperative, one might begin fruitfully by considering an interesting link with Kantian ethics. The 'philosophical hunch' of this section is that if Kant can get around the is/ought problem through the development of a categorical imperative, then so can Aquinas. This, obviously, is a rather limited claim. It is important to note that the claim articulated here is not that there are no important differences between Kant and Aquinas on moral theory. There are, of course, many. Rather, the claim is that to charge too hastily that Aquinas, by definition because of the naturalist meta-ethics expressed in his theory of natural law, derives an 'ought' from an 'is' only by a hypothetical imperative, fails in an important sense to notice the structure of the role of end and good. This is, to reiterate, reducible to the structure of the relation between final cause and formal cause.

[13] Martin Golding, *Philosophy of Law* (Englewood Cliffs, NJ: Prentice-Hall, 1975), 31.

Aquinas is certainly not a naturalist in the same sense as Mill, Spencer, or any other nineteenth-century naturalist against whom Moore directed his charge of the naturalistic fallacy. The preceding chapter noted the passage from Gauthier indicating the incommensurability of teleology between Aristotle and Aquinas on the one hand and the utilitarians such as Bentham and Mill on the other.

This section does not propose to demonstrate on independent grounds that Aquinas can transcend the Humean dilemma. It offers a much more limited claim. Rather, if one considers Kant's moral theory to transcend successfully the is/ought problem by the categorical imperative — and most historians of philosophy seem to accept this claim — then this account proposes reading Aquinas on an obligation of imperatives in a way congruent with Kant. In other words, the proposed resolution requires reconstructing Aquinas's account of moral obligation in a modified Kantian fashion. Or, to consider the other side of the coin, this discussion suggests considering Kant's theory of obligation in modified Aristotelian categories. Both have very interesting similarities through the structure of the categorical imperative.

To attempt this reconstruction, one must first consider how Kant established the concept of obligation. In his *Fundamental Principles of the Metaphysics of Morals*, Kant asserts that an immoral action fundamentally is a contradiction. Just as human agents ought to avoid a contradiction in their speculative reason, so ought such moral agents avoid this kind of 'problem' in their practical reason. A human person, as a rational agent, must avoid engaging in contradictions. Aquinas too uses the same categories of speculative and practical reason, as earlier chapters in this book noted. Aquinas, furthermore, writes explicitly that 'in matters of human action, something is said to be just because it is right, according to the rule of reason' (*Summa Theologiae*, I-II q. 95 a. 2) Here, reason plays an important role in both the Kantian and the Aquinian accounts of moral justification.

In the Kantian scheme, why is a contradiction to be avoided? Not because of any hypothetical imperative, so Kant argued. Rather, a contradiction is to be avoided because it strikes fundamentally at the very root of rationality itself. A consequence of Kantian ethical theory is that what constitutes immorality in an action is that it renders the human agent less than human. Put differently, an immoral action goes against what we are as human beings. In other words, immorality strikes against the very humanity of a human person.

In the Kantian scheme, in so far as rational beings engage in the process of moral deliberation, a contradiction – being fundamentally irrational – strikes against what human beings are in their very existence; i.e. rational beings. To choose to act immorally entails acting on a contradiction. This contradiction is contrary to the very structure of reason itself. Hence, it goes against reason. Since a human person as a rational agent must exercise the canons of rational consistency, an immoral action, as inconsistent and contradictory, goes against what rationality requires. This contradictory action, therefore, entails going against the very structure of the human person as a rational agent. Of course, any human agent can do this. That is what constitutes freedom and moral choice. This is the cash value of 'ought implies can'.

The argument put forward here is that it is possible for Aquinas to make a similar structural suggestion, at least analogously. In so far as an immoral action in Aquinas's moral theory is what it is because it strikes against the developmental properties of a human person, it prevents that person from reaching a state of 'functioning well' or 'flourishing'. This denial serves at least an analogous function to what 'engaging in a contradiction' does for Kant. Therefore, using Kantian ethical categories, Aquinas is not offering a hypothetical imperative for moral obligation, as so many of his critics have suggested. He is doing much more than merely suggesting that if a moral agent wants to attain human well-being, then she or he ought to act in such and such a way. On the contrary, just as Kant thought he had grounded morality in human nature alone – i.e. in rationality alone – so too Aquinas thought he had grounded morality in human nature alone – i.e. not only in reason, but also in the sensitive and living dispositional properties. The set of dispositions which determine the content of human nature determines the scope of moral theory. To undertake an action against the dispositions is to undertake an action against reason. To fail to undertake actions which develop the basic dispositional properties is to engage in a self-defeating activity. This strikes at the foundation of human nature in the same way that holding contradictory maxims strikes at the foundation of rationality itself. It is not a matter of the hypothetical imperative. It is categorically necessary that the practical reason undertake those actions which lead to *eudaimonia*. One is not free to decide on the nature of the good, just as, for Kant, one cannot determine arbitrarily the structure of a contradiction. Both kinds of self-defeating activities have an objective structure determining their function. For Aquinas, this is the purpose of the 'metaphysics of finality'.

The concluding suggestion from this analysis is, quite obviously, if one grants Kant success in getting around the is/ought problem by invoking the categorical imperative, then too one ought to grant Aquinas the same consideration. In this one area, both philosophers have put forth a strikingly similar central theme. Immorality consists in striking at the very roots of one's humanity. Both arguments have an important structural similarity, a similarity which has been overlooked in contemporary studies in the history of philosophy as well as in meta-ethical analysis.

The above argument is limited at best. It points to an interesting foundational similarity in Aquinas and Kant. This argument, however, is not adopting a 'Whiggish' attitude towards historical studies in philosophy. Rather, it indicates a conceptual account which appears to be common to both Aquinas and Kant. If the argument fails for Kant, it also fails for Aquinas. But if it holds for Kant, then there is the structural possibility that it will hold for Aquinas too. What this entails is that Aquinas's naturalism may transcend the standard objection that the only theoretical structure natural law theory might establish regarding obligation is through the development of a hypothetical imperative. The interpretation suggested above provides a way to consider a modified Kantian categorical imperative as applicable to Aquinas's natural law system.

Alan Donagan once offered a similar Kantian interpretation of Aquinas's theory of obligation. Donagan, however, used the Aquinian texts on 'Human Acts' at the beginning of the *Summa Theologiae*, I-II. He did not refer to the natural law texts in qq 90–7 considered in this book. Donagan argued that Aquinas's account of the nature of human action in the context of biblical obligation could generate successfully a form of the categorical imperative. He was worried lest Aquinas's moral theory be perpetually entrenched in the criticism of providing only a hypothetical imperative.[14]

---

[14] Donagan argued this point during his period as a lecturer at the NEH (The National Endowment for the Humanities) Seminar at the University of Notre Dame in June and July 1985. It is unclear whether Donagan would have accepted the analysis argued in this book.

It is important to realize that the conclusions of a theory of natural law in terms of what can be justified are limited and moderate at best. Columba Ryan once suggested that natural law is like the general rules built into the nature of a manufactured object which help an observer determine how the object will work and function well. A washing machine, for instance, comes with a set of instructions so that the machine might be used efficiently and efficaciously. Transferred to the human condition, this is an illustration of Aristotelian/Aquinian *eudaimonia*. As noted above, *eudaimonia* is often translated by contemporary philosophers as 'flourishing' or 'self-actualization'. Yet humans do not come into this world with a printed set of instructions as does the washing machine purchased from the local appliance store. Only by undertaking the reflective analysis of human nature can a human agent determine the structure of *eudaimonia*. The analogy is striking, but limited. None the less, a defensible account of the concept of essence is a necessary condition for elucidating any account of natural law theory in Aristotle and Aquinas. We must now consider the defensibility of the concept of essence for contemporary philosophy.

THE DEFENSIBILITY OF THE CONCEPT OF ESSENCE

One empiricist objection often raised against natural law theory centres on how one determines the metaphysical need for a theory of essence. Work in contemporary metaphysics suggests two ways to respond to this objection. The first is a consideration of the Kripke Putnam view of natural kind ontology, and the second is a discussion of nomic universals as put forward by Everett Nelson. Both theories have been mentioned earlier in this book.

The Kripke/Putnam Position on Natural Kinds

One might argue that contemporary analytic philosophy in the arguments of Kripke and the early Putnam has established that a theory of natural kinds makes coherent, theoretical sense. A natural law theorist, in a rudimentary way, can argue that the contemporary reconstruction of Aquinas's theory readily accepts some of the structure of the ontological arguments used by natural kinds philosophers. In other words, with the acceptance of natural kinds in the arguments of Kripke and Putnam, the natural law theorist can appeal to their work and use it as a presupposition for natural law meta-ethics. A natural kind ontology is necessary for natural law theory. Hence, one can use the arguments of others to help make sense of this theory of natural kinds for dispositional essences.

The important similarity between what has come to be known as the Kripke/Putnam position on natural kinds and Aquinas's account of essence would centre on the nature of essentialism itself. The Kripke/Putnam view suggests that a common name for an essence — what Aquinas would refer to as a set of dispositional properties — 'rigidly designates' the set of essential properties which determine the structure and content of a natural kind. In considering the meaning of a 'rigid designator', Kripke appears to argue for the following two claims:

1. A term rigidly designates the same kind of object in all possible worlds;
2. In any possible world where the object of the kind does exist, the 'designator' term in question does indeed 'designate' that kind of object.[15]

We might put the Kripke/Putnam theory in the following way:

> For any possible world W, and for every individual S in W, S is a kind of an individual (i.e. a member of a species), if and only if S has the same fundamental structure and constitution as S in our actual world.

This is a metaphysical analysis of what is necessary to explain the 'depth semantics' of our language of science and common sense. An essence breaks the world 'where the natural joints are', as Plato suggests in the *Phaedrus* (265d–e). Aquinas's account of an essence seems compatible structurally with this twentieth century essentialism. It suggests an ontological claim about the nature of reality. Ultimately, the nature or essence of any object is reducible to the exemplar in the divine mind, which would pertain to Aquinas's account of eternal law as elucidated in Chapter 5. Given the role of the exemplar in the divine mind, which determines the content and structure of any essence, any individual of that kind would be the same in all possible worlds.

---

[15] Saul Kripke, 'Identity and Necessity', in Milton K. Munitz (ed.), *Identity and Individuation* (New York: New York University Press, 1971), 144–6. Kripke also considers this issue in his more famous essay, 'Naming and Necessity'.

It is one question to consider how a name itself may be determined rigidly to designate a natural kind. It is another question to consider the nature of the constitution of reality needed to explain the objective reference of the rigid designator. Aquinas would accept the second issue. This is his foundation for the structure of reality determined by a substantial form whose dispositional properties constitute the content of an essence. The metaphysical structure of a natural kind seems to be structurally similar to the natural kind essentialist conclusions articulated by Kripke and Putnam. Put differently, the Kripke/Putnam view on natural kinds has two fundamental claims:

1. A realist account arguing that natural kinds exist independently of any act of intentionality on the part of a knower.
2. A linguistic theory of direct reference for natural kind terms.

In so far as these two claims are articulated in terms of the metaphysical constitution of reality, Aquinas would appear to accept both. Like Kripke and Putnam, Aquinas argues for a *de re* and not a *de dicto* account of the necessity of essential properties determining an essence. Aquinas might not accept the exact formulation of a reference theory of meaning through rigid designation as postulated in the Kripke/Putnam model. None the less, his theory of meaning would necessarily demand some form of rigid designation. Aquinas does not adopt the transcendental turn which is characteristic of much modern and contemporary philosophy.

One objection might be that the natural kind ontology as proposed by Kripke and the earlier Putnam is not easily reconcilable with a natural kinds theory needed in order to explicate Aristotelian metaphysics. An earlier chapter noted that David Charles suggested this problem. In his 'Natural Kinds: Direct Reference, Realism, and the Impossibility of Necessary A Posteriori Truth', Chenyang Li suggests some of the same conclusions articulated by Charles.[16] Both Charles and Li criticize the Kripke/Putnam position on natural kinds — and Charles in reference to his own reading of Aristotle, especially the *Posterior Analytics* — by suggesting that an Aristotelian natural kind is always in some sense indeterminate. Given this indetermination, it cannot be an appropriate object of a rigid designator which the Kripke/Putnam model assumes.

A quite modest response to this kind of objection is that the

---

[16] Chenyang Li, *Review of Metaphysics*, 47 (Dec. 1993), 261–76.

philosophical jury is not yet in. Certainly Kripke and the earlier Putnam offered a persuasive case for natural kinds as necessary conditions for understanding science and language. Chapter 4 indicated a passage from the writings of Michael Ayers suggesting that the Kripke/Putnam model of natural kinds was not that different from Aristotelian theory. If Ayers is correct, then it seems that Aristotle, in treating natural kinds, was working the same side of the street. While Aristotle grounded a natural kind in the substantial form, none the less the substantial form seems to serve much the same function in science and language which natural kinds do for contemporary philosophers. At issue may be a distinction regarding the epistemological requirements for identifying a natural kind through rigid designation and the ontological demands for a natural kind in order to ground the regularity needed for science and language. Aquinas would accept, I suggest, the ontological demands; he would, however, establish the epistemological requirements through the abstractive function of the *intellectus agens*. This is an issue which certainly requires more discussion and its resolution is beyond the limits of the present inquiry.

The Nelson Account of Nomic Universals

The arguments put forward by Everett J. Nelson discussing the role of contrary-to-fact conditionals in establishing nomic universals are relevant to a reconstructed version of Aquinas's theory of essence. Nelson argues that a nomic universal, through the methodological use of a contrary-to-fact conditional, can render a category distinction between an accidental universal and a nomic universal. The nomic universal entails, so Nelson argued, the existence of the categories of substance and causality. Nelson used these arguments to establish his theory of the metaphysical foundations for induction. An Aristotelian/Aquinian dispositional essence functions in the same way as Nelson's nomic universal for physical objects. Furthermore, the formal cause and the final cause are indeed causal structures found in an individual primary substance of a natural kind.

Nelson argued that the method of finding the presuppositions necessary to ground counterfactual propositions entailed the existence of nomic universals. Furthermore, these nomic universals, so Nelson argued, could be explained sufficiently only if one accepted the existence of the synthetic necessary categories of substance and causality. These necessary categories belong to the structure of reality. In other words, a scientific law, which Nelson considered to be a nomic universal, needed an ontological foundation beyond what an accidental universal itself could provide. The synthetic necessary categories establish this ground in reality. Nelson's two principal ontological categories were those of substance and causality. Aquinas, following the Aristotle of the *Categories*, would have a world of primary substances — the individual substances — whose nature was determined by the substantial form — the foundation for causality in Aristotelian science. The argument expressed here is that Aquinas can easily appropriate the Nelson 'ontological machinery' to help elucidate some of the ontological items in Aristotle's and Aquinas's metaphysics. Nelson's analysis provides a sharp rejoinder to the prevalent empiricist objection to an ontology of essential properties. Aquinas would reject, however, the intuitive grasp of direct awareness which Nelson suggested was a necessary condition for knowing the categories of substance and causality. The arguments of Christopher Martin noted earlier on the role of Aquinas's metaphysics in contemporary analytic philosophy are worth remembering here.

The above discussion suggests that the contemporary work of Kripke and the earlier Putnam in natural kind ontology and the research of Everett Nelson into nomic universals can be used to assist in rendering a coherent *explicatio textus* for Aquinas's metaphysical underpinnings for his theory of natural law. Using contemporary metaphysical categories, Aquinas needs a nomic universal — the principle of causality in the individual primary substance — rooted in a natural kind. In interesting and fascinating ways, recent metaphysical work enlightens Aristotelian ontology.

Commenting on his own metaphilosophy, MacIntyre, in considering his differences with Richard Rorty, recently said, 'Unlike Rorty, I believe that there are strong and substantive conceptions of truth and rational justification — Aristotelian and Thomistic conceptions — that remain unscathed by his critique of epistemological foundationalism.'[17] Aquinas — and both Kripke/Putnam and Nelson — demand an ontological foundationalism beyond the limits of any epistemological foundationalism.

---

[17] Borradori, *American Philosopher*, 151.

EMPIRICISM AND ESSENCE THREE RESPONSES

Assuming that a contemporary philosopher of natural law can make sense theoretically of a natural kind ontology and a nomic theory of universals, one still must respond to another variety of empiricist objection. The objection states that cross-culturally, there appear to be different dispositions which make up human nature. Sociologists suggest that there are sufficient cultural differences to repudiate the claim of essential properties determining a human essence. This would be the gist of the contemporary social science argument against accepting natural kinds for human beings. In 'Natural Law and Sociology', Philip Selznick states this case explicitly: 'Among modern sociologists, the reputation of natural law is not high. The phrase conjures up a world of absolutisms, of theological fiat, of fuzzy, unoperational, "mystical" ideas, of thinking uninformed by history and by the variety of human situations.'[18] Yves Simon put this empiricist question in its starkest format; the legal positivist retort claims that 'if there were such a thing as natural law, it would be known to all [humans] at all times, in all societies, in an equal degree of perfection'. Also, Simon notes another form of the objection: 'If there were a natural law, there would be more uniformity in ideas about the right and the wrong, and in the customs and institutions which embody these ideas'.[19]

A threefold response to this objection might be suggested:

1. a consideration in Aquinas's meta-ethics of the particular and contingent nature of practical judgements using practical reason;

2. A consideration of the biological work determining a specific unity to human beings as members of a natural kind; there may be more unity than cultural anthropologists have been wont to admit;

3. A consideration of the psychological unity which appears in constant studies of human behaviour. Carl Rogers has suggested similarities in his discussion of self-actualization theories of human development.

[18] Philip Selznick, 'Natural Law and Sociology', in Robert M. Hutchins (ed.), *Natural Law and Modern Society*, (Cleveland, Ohio: World Book Publishing Co. 1966), 154.
[19] Yves Simon, *The Tradition of Natural Law*, ed. Vukan Kuic (New York: Fordham University Press, 1965), 3–4.

The explication of each response to these three points will be developed below.

The Contingent Nature of Practical Judgements

The first response revolves around the role of practical reason – *phronesis* – in Aristotelian moral theory. Earlier in this book, the differences between speculative and practical reason were discussed. Three points need to be considered in this discussion: (1) the structure of practical reason is not isomorphic with the structure of theoretical reason. Both kinds of reason have distinct first principles and distinct operations. (2) The conclusions of speculative and practical reason are fundamentally different in kind. Speculative reason arrives at propositions to be known, while practical reason arrives at actions to be undertaken. (3) The propositions derived in a speculative syllogism have a necessity and certainty about them. The actions determined in a practical syllogism are always contingent, specific, and tailored to a particular set of circumstances.

In commenting upon the distinction Aquinas affirms between speculative reason and practical reason, Columba Ryan suggests that it is a mistake to turn 'practical reasoning into just another piece of theory'. Ryan remarks that Aquinas often refers 'to the conclusions of the practical reason as actions — not just as decisions to act, still less as conclusions about what ought to be done'. The conclusion Ryan suggests should be taken as 'a piece of doing – the outcome is action'.[20]

In the *Summa Theologiae*, I-II q. 90 a.1 ad. 2, Aquinas refers to the practical syllogism as a *quodam syllogismo*, which translates as 'a kind of' or 'a sort of' or 'a close approximation of' a syllogism, directed towards actions to be undertaken (*in operabilibus*). In this same passage, Aquinas goes on to write that 'in the practical reason, something is related to actions as in the speculative reason, a proposition is related to conclusions'. Clearly Aquinas affirms a category distinction between the workings of speculative reason and the workings of practical reason. In another place in the *Summa Theologiae*, Aquinas also refers to the practical syllogism as a *quodam syllogismo* (I-II q. 76 a. 1). In this article, Aquinas writes that 'actiones autem in singularibus sunt; unde conclusio syllogismi operativi est singularis'.

---

[20] Columba Ryan, 'The Traditional Concept of Natural Law', in Illtud Evans (ed.), *Light on the Natural Law* (Baltimore: Helicon Press, 1965), 25.

Again, the particular nature of actions and the specific action to be undertaken as a conclusion of a practical syllogism are noted explicitly. Furthermore, in his *Commentary on the Nicomachean Ethics*, Aquinas writes that 'the understanding of practical matters concerns ... the particular and the contingent' (VII lec. 9, n. 1247).

The conclusion of a speculative syllogism – the Aristotelian demonstration – is a general statement applicable for all members of a class. But the conclusion of a practical syllogism is, on the contrary, the undertaking of a specific action in a particular set of circumstances. The following two passages from the *Summa Theologiae* indicate again the differences between theoretical or speculative reason and practical reason.

it is proper to the human person to act according to reason. It pertains to reason, however, to proceed from common principles to more specific conclusions, as Aristotle noted in the *Physics*. Concerning this process, speculative reason and practical reason are structured differently. For the speculative reason is concerned principally with necessary propositions, which cannot be otherwise than they are. Thus, without any mistake, speculative reason discovers truth in the specific conclusions just as it discovers truth in its more common principles.

On the other hand, practical reason is concerned with contingent matters, which belongs to the domain of human actions. Therefore, it follows that there is some necessity in the common principles, but the more we descend to specific cases, the more readily can a mistake be generated.

(I-II q. 94 a. 4)

I suggest that practical reason is concerned with actions to be undertaken. These actions are singular and contingent. They are not about necessary matters, which is the province of speculative reason. From this it follows that human law cannot have the certainty which is found in the conclusions of the demonstrative sciences.   (I-II q. 91 a. 3 ad. 3)

A practical syllogism as 'syllogism' in Aristotelian moral theory is really a misnomer. It is not a syllogism in any sense of a demonstrative argument. Rather, it is a prescription indicating an action to be undertaken in a particular context. Given this particular dimension and specific set of circumstances to a 'conclusion' of a practical syllogism, there is always a context of uncertainty and individuality to the conclusion. In one sense, what the existentialists call 'subjectivity' regarding particular decision-making holds true of what Aristotle and Aquinas consider necessary for moral reasoning. In other words, there is always the particular context and situation in which the action is to be undertaken. This situation and context are relative to the individual person found in those circumstances. It is not axiomatic nor deductively evident in a cognitive sense what kind of action is to be undertaken. The implementation of practical reason demands more for its explication than the suggestion that it is theoretical reason used in a practical context. The structure of practical reason is different from theoretical reason. At times, discussions of practical reason by both modern and analytic philosophers appear to reduce practical reason to theoretical reason, but theoretical reason being used in a moral situation. This is a legacy of Humean epistemology.

However, this Humean account of practical reason is not isomorphic with practical reason in Aristotle and Aquinas. Practical reason in the Aristotelian scheme is structurally distinct from theoretical reason. The former has an 'action' as its end, while the latter has a 'true proposition' as its end. Both kinds of reason have their unique first principles which also ensure their distinctness. It will be useful to recall an Aquinas passage noted earlier in this book considering speculative and practical reason:

A theoretical or speculative inquiry is distinguished from a practical inquiry in that the former is directed towards discovering truth considered in itself. The latter, on the contrary, is directed towards the doing of something. Thus, the purpose of speculative inquiry is truth, while the purpose of practical inquiry is action, in the area of actions in our capacity to undertake. The goal of a speculative inquiry is not about determining ends – i.e. actions to be undertaken. (*Commentary on the De Trinitate of Boethius*, 16. 5.1)

In the *Summa Theologiae*, moreover, Aquinas writes that 'as the speculative reason discusses the theory of things, so the practical reason deliberates about the undertaking of actions'. To undertake specific actions is the goal of the practical reason. It is not a form of speculative reason used in moral situations. Speculative reason is 'to know' whereas practical reason is 'to do' or 'to undertake'. Furthermore, the undertaking of an action is always determined by the particular context in which the agent is found. The conclusion of a practical syllogism, therefore, is always contingent. In his *Commentary on the Nicomachean Ethics*, Aquinas writes explicitly that 'thus, it is evident that moral matters are variable and divergent, not having the same certitude each time' (I lec. 3 n. 34).

Thomas Gilby, the English philosopher who translated, edited, and commented upon many Aquinas texts in the middle part of this century, once offered the following translation of Aquinas's insights on the contingent nature of moral matters. This passage is from Aquinas's *Commentary on the Nicomachean Ethics*. It stresses the non-universalized character of natural law moral theory regarding particular judgements:

Disquisitions on general morality are not entirely trustworthy, and the ground becomes more uncertain when one wishes to descend to individual cases in detail. The factors are infinitely variable, and cannot be settled whether by art or precedent. Judgment should be left to the people concerned. Each must set himself to act according to the immediate situation and the circumstances involved. The decision may be unerring in the concrete, despite the uneasy debate in the abstract. Nevertheless, the moralist can provide some help and direction in such cases. (II lec. 2)

This is an explicit statement regarding the contingent nature of individual moral decision-making. Shortly, a longer passage from lecture 2 will be discussed. Furthermore, Aquinas repeats this point often in his *Commentary on the Nicomachean Ethics*. Comparing the undertaking of moral actions with the exercise of different crafts, Aquinas writes that 'the matter of moral study is of such a nature that perfect certainty is not suitable to it' (I lec. 3 n. 32). Natural law theory is not Kantian in terms of rule-generation or rule-following. The particularity and contingency of the practical reason conclusion indicates unequivocally that practical reason is not just theoretical reason used in moral or practical conditions. It is a use of reason with its own distinct first principles. On this point, Aquinas writes, in his discussion of natural law in the *Summa Theologiae*:

The precepts of the natural law are to the practical reason what the first principles of demonstrations are to the speculative reason . . .

Now, a certain order is found in those things that human knowers apprehend and know. That which first falls under the rubric of human awareness is being. In everything which a human knower understands, being manifests itself in some form or other. On this account, the first indemonstrable principle of speculative reason is 'the same thing cannot be affirmed and denied at the same time'. This principle of non-contradiction is grounded on the concepts of being and non-being. As Aristotle writes in the *Metaphysics*, all other speculative principles are based on this indemonstrable principle.

Now, as being is the first thing which falls under the apprehension or awareness when we consider these aspects of intentionality in themselves, so good is the first thing which falls under the apprehension of the practical reason. Practical reason is directed towards action; this is the case, since every agent acts for an end, and this and every end has the nature of good. Given this analysis, the first principle necessary for the functioning of the practical reason is rooted in the nature of the concept of good. This is: 'Good is that which all things seek after.' Therefore, the first principle of practical reason is the following: 'Good is to be done and promoted and evil is to be avoided.' All other principles of the natural law are based upon this first principle. Thus, all actions which the practical reason undertakes are perceived as belonging to the human good – this in terms of actions to be done and actions to be avoided. (I-II q. 94 a 2)

Given this extended passage, one can understand better the role of first principles in both speculative and practical reason. The principle of non-contradiction provides the possibility of theoretical reason. The principle of *synderesis* provides the possibility for practical reason. Just as the structure of theoretical reason cannot be utilized (i.e. things cannot be known) without at least the tacit acknowledgement that one must avoid contradictions, so too the structure of practical reason cannot be utilized (i.e. actions cannot be undertaken) without the possibility of considering ends to be attained. Separate principles for operation entail separate functions of reason. Aquinas discusses this difference in his *Commentary on the Nicomachean Ethics* where he suggests that in moral matters, the moral agent must keep three things in mind: (1) moral truth is to be brought forward in a rough outline; (2) moral claims are at best approximations to the truth; and (3) moral events are to be considered as they happen in the majority of cases. This radical contingency is a necessary part of understanding Aquinas on moral matters.

How, then, does one undertake a particular action? It is here that the role of 'prudence' becomes important. Prudence is the virtue which assists the virtuous person to determine the proper action to be undertaken here and now. In every situation facing a moral agent, prudence determines the 'mean' action between the extremes. This is the common understanding of Aristotle's account of virtue. Prudence is the moral methodological virtue which serves as the vehicle in determining what action is to be done here and now. In the *Commentary*, Aquinas defines prudence as 'a habit of action with right reason directed toward the good for the human agent' (VI lec. 4 n. 1171). The action, however, is always in the context of developing the dispositional properties which make up the human essence. Hence, while similar to the subjectivity of the existentialists, none the less the content of human nature – the set of dispositional properties – determines the general boundaries of the actions to be undertaken. Aquinas discusses this point at some length in his *Commentary on the Nicomachean Ethics*:

Any discussion treating actions to be undertaken must be given in a general way, as a 'precedent' or 'as likely', but never definitively . . . This is so because philosophical discussions always need to be carried out according to the nature of the subject matter . . . We see that matters pertaining to moral actions and materials useful to such actions – e.g. external goods – do not have in themselves anything fixed by way of necessity; rather everything is contingent and changeable.

The same thing takes place in works relating to the art of medicine, which are concerned with health; this is so because the body's disposition or capacity to be healed and the remedies administered to produce a cure are indeed changeable in many ways.   (II lec. 2 n. 258)

The discussions on the general aspects of moral matters are uncertain and variable. None the less, still more uncertainty is found when we, as moral agents, render a decision in particular cases. Moral science does not fall under either art or tradition, because the causes of particular actions to be undertaken are infinitely diversified.

Given this, moral judgement in particular cases is left to the prudence of each moral agent. The moral agent, in acting prudently, must attentively consider the action to be undertaken at the present time, but only after all the particular circumstances have been taken into consideration. In this kind of way, a medical doctor must act in order to bring about a cure, and a ship's captain in guiding a ship.   (Ibid. 259)

Martha Nussbaum, in discussing what she calls 'non-relative virtues' in Aristotle, writes as follows:

What I want to stress here is that Aristotelian particularism is fully compatible with Aristotelian objectivity. The fact that a good and virtuous decision is context-sensitive does not imply that it is right only *relative to*, or *inside*, a limited context, any more than the fact that a good navigational judgment is sensitive to particular weather conditions shows that it is correct only in a local or relational sense. It is right absolutely, objectively, anywhere in the human world, to attend to the particular features of one's context; and the person who so attends and who chooses accordingly is making, according to Aristotle, the humanly correct decision, period. If another situation should ever arise with all the same ethically relevant features, including contextual features, the same decision would again be absolutely right.[21]

[21] Martha Nussbaum, 'Non-Relative Virtues', in Martha Nussbaum and Amartya Sen (eds.), *The Quality of Life* (Oxford: Clarendon Press, 1993), 257.

Aquinas establishes this 'objectivity' based upon the dispositional properties which ground his concept of human nature.

It is over the content of an essence, which is necessary for moral theory, that the Aristotelian parts company with the existentialist. Referring to categories found in MacIntyre's analysis in *After Virtue*, the 'way of Nietzsche' is as irreconcilable with the 'way of Aristotle' — and the 'way of Aquinas' — as Enlightenment moral theory is with Aristotelian moral theory. None the less, Aquinas reiterates often the radical contingency of the moral decision process. This contingency suggests a theoretical restraint on the part of those natural law critics who imply that Aquinas's normative theory is both restrictive to one cultural situation and overly rule-dependent.

Recent Biological Work and Natural Kind Ontology

Recent work in biological science may have some interesting claims useful for the analysis of Aquinas's theory of natural law. This is especially true of the 'nature/nurture' discussions. Writing in the *New York Times* on the nature/nurture debate, T. Edward Reed expressed disappointment about the gulf which separates too many social scientists from his colleagues in the biological sciences. In this analysis, Reed writes:

Most biologists, but not most social scientists, are willing to consider the possibility that almost any behavioral trait may be importantly influenced by both nature and nurture. I believe this attitude follows from knowing the biology, present and past, of our species. This knowledge shows that, in addition to being social beings with a cultural evolution, we are also organisms molded by a biological evolution. This evolution, in fact, is a long interaction between nature (our genes and their consequences) and nurture (natural selection by the environment).[22]

Reed also argues that for the past twenty years, the behavioural genetic literature has been directed towards understanding behavioural traits and not towards human group differences.

In his thoughtful analysis of natural kind theory, Michael Ayers writes:

Nevertheless biology and chemistry are different from sociology. Living organisms and stuffs, in their different ways, do come packaged by reality,

---

[22] T. Edward Reed, 'Human Nature and Nurture', letter in response to a review of Carl Degler's *In Search of Human Nature*, *New York Times Book Review*, 21 Apr. 1991, 34.

if less neatly than Aristotle supposes. We *can* ask the question, 'How many species of living creatures are there?' . . . In biology we have been able to make do, in effect, with the primitive notion of a kind of 'tribe', a naturally bounded group of individuals, identifiable by their broad and more or less striking resemblance, but also distinguished from others by more or less variable peculiarities at the level of fundamental structure, by origin and by group behavior, in particular by their capacity (and tendency) to interbreed. The notion has been deepened, as an explanatory one, by genetic and evolutionary theory, but not significantly modified.[23]

Ayers reflects briefly on what Professor E. B. Ford, whom Ayers calls 'a distinguished modern biologist', suggests on the topic of natural species. Ayers notes that what Ford argues is that there are 'objectively natural' properties which ground the organization of a species. Ayers calls this the 'degree of cognateness for each type of kind'. Ayers argues that the evidence of modern biology suggests that a species, as a natural kind, 'is a far cry from the radical arbitrariness that Locke (and most empiricists) took to infect all classification'.[24]

What is interesting about Reed's suggestions and Ayers's argument is that they are similar structurally to the metaphysical biology which Aristotle and Aquinas proposed. The biological background and the social being characteristic of human nature all have a quite familiar Aristotelian ring to them. What this indicates is that there may be some scientific evidence which is congruent conceptually with the philosophical anthropology necessary to develop a coherent position of natural law meta-ethics. The chasm traditionally suspected between Aristotelian moral theory and its dependence on essential properties may not be so deep and unbridgeable as many modern critics have affirmed.

Carl Rogers and Self-Actualization Psychology

Thirdly, the research and writing of Carl Rogers indicate that a self-actualization theory of development may have some interesting empirical roots. In his article, 'The Valuing Process in the Mature Person', Rogers suggests four themes which are, on reflection, conceptually similar to the structure of Aristotle and Aquinas's account of moral theory. Rogers argues that mature persons organize their actions around a theory of 'self-actualization'. This concept is similar

---

[23] Michael R. Ayers, 'Locke Versus Aristotle on Natural Kinds', *Journal of Philosophy*, 78/5 (May 1981), 267.
[24] Ibid. 268.

to the *eudaimonia* common to Aristotle and Aquinas. Rogers writes that these four propositions are capable in some degree of being tested 'through the methods of psychological science'. These four propositions are:

1. There is an organismic base for the organized valuing process within the human individual. Rogers suggests that human beings share this characteristic with the rest of the animate world.

2. Choosing values in human beings is effective in achieving self-actualization only if the person is open to the experiences going on within the organism. The awareness of self-actualization is very important, and the awareness is related to the openness to experiences necessary for functioning well as a human being.

3. Persons who are becoming more open in their 'experiencing' share an organismic commonality of value directions. Rogers's research indicates that maturing humans exhibit what he calls 'a surprising commonality'. In addition, Rogers argues that this commonality is not due to the influences of any one particular culture. His empirical evidence suggests a cross-cultural basis for this commonality. Rogers writes that 'this commonality of value directions is due to the fact that we all belong to the same species'.

4. The common value directions enhance the development of the individual, of others in the community, and 'make for the survival and evolution of [his/her] species'. This proposition is similar to Hart's natural necessity of survival. In addition, Rogers appears to suggest that the social dimension of human activity is as important and central as Aristotle and Aquinas considered it to be. Human persons as social beings have a natural capacity towards community. The 'no man is an island' theme appears once again!

In Roger's account, the naturalist basis for value theory is strongly affirmed. He argues that a viable naturalism is grounded in the experience of the human organism. There exists a strong conceptual similarity between Rogers's account of the mature, self-actualized person and the functional concept of *eudaimonia* articulated by Aristotle and Aquinas. The 'organismic commonality' which Rogers proposes suggests that human beings function essentially the same way. In many ways, this concept points towards a renewed version of Aristotelian 'human nature' with a set of 'basic needs' or 'natural necessities'. Like Aristotle and Aquinas, Rogers rejects any set of values which are not derived from an organismic base in the human person. Rogers refers to non-organismic values as 'introjected values'. These introjected values hinder the process of self-actualization. An introjected value is forced upon the human organism rather than developed from within. The naturalism found in Aristotelian ethics also resists what Rogers calls introjected values.

The goal of the value theory proposed by Rogers's analysis is 'the fully functioning person'. Once again, the similarity with Aristotelian *eudaimonia* is striking. As self-actualization and functioning well are necessary in determining a value theory in Rogers's analysis, so too is *eudaimonia* central to the moral philosophy enunciated by Aristotle and Aquinas. In some remarkable ways, the psychological theory Rogers develops is similar conceptually and structurally to the meta-ethical naturalism central to natural law theory.[25]

Another interesting insight regarding the role of human nature in the studies of social scientists comes from Philip Selznick. In discussing the problems usually associated with the concept of a theory of human nature, Selznick once wrote that contemporary philosophers should not overlook the 'psychic unity' of humankind and the existence of cross-cultural universals.[26] Selznick suggests that there is sociological evidence affirming these propositions.

This concludes the analysis of problems which limit the nature of the inquiry into Aquinas's meta-ethical theory. This chapter is heavily dependent upon contemporary work in several academic disciplines, thus indicating the cross-disciplinary dimension of natural law studies. There is a conceptual difference between laying out the conditions necessary to justify the possibility of natural law meta-ethics and understanding the biological and anthropological work needed to provide an empirical foothold for the metaphysical theory. To provide the empirical evidence is, of course, another issue. Here it has been indicated that some recent biological and psychological work has ventured into areas structurally similar to the propositions central to natural law theory.

[25] Carl R. Rogers, 'The Valuing Process in the Mature Person', *Journal of Abnormal and Social Psychology*, 68/2 (1964), 160–7. The similarity between Rogers's theory and Aristotelian *eudaimonia* was suggested earlier by the author in his book, *Philosophy Matters* (1977), 446–56.

[26] Philip Selznick, 'Sociology and Natural Law', *Natural Law Forum*, 6 (1961), 84–104.

In addition, this chapter indicates the role natural kind metaphysics and a theory of nomic universals can play in providing a coherent, contemporary *explicatio textus* for Aquinas's account of essence necessary to natural law. Themes in contemporary metaphysics also have a familiar ring to the ontological demands for natural law theory as found in the writings of Thomas Aquinas.

9

Human Rights and Natural Law

IN the twentieth century, the issue of the nature, structure, and foundation of human rights has been the centre of much discussion, both in the scholarly and the popular arena. The American Civil Rights Movement initiated a renewed interest in both the existence and the nature of human rights. Since the 1960s, rights-talk has been a central part of much political discussion in the United States. Various national and international bodies, the United Nations in particular with its Declaration on Human Rights, have also contributed to the pressing necessity of these discussions. In addition, human rights organizations such as Amnesty International call attention to what are judged to be violations of human rights across the globe. Beyond the sphere of rights ascribed to human persons, advocates of differing political positions argue for 'welfare rights', 'reproductive rights', 'animal rights', 'rights' for other living organisms, and at times 'rights' are heard ascribed even to the entire planet. Advocacy journals routinely consider the questions of rights as these might affect the organizations under discussion. In addition, committees oversee the impact of certain activities, judicial and otherwise, on the rights of their members. The influence of 'rights-matters' is not to be dismissed. It is a central aspect of our social and political fabric.

Recently political scientists and philosophers from several different perspectives have exerted a fair amount of energy discussing the nature and limits of rights theory. The bewildering nature of certain aspects of the political climate involving these discussions and activities undertaken in the name of rights theory has caused one philosopher to bemoan that 'the rhetoric of rights is out of control'.[1] When mat-

---

[1] L. W. Sumner, 'Rights Denaturalized', in R. G. Frey (ed.), *Utility and Rights* (Oxford: Basil Blackwell, 1986), 20.

ters as serious to the human condition as rights theory are claimed to be 'out of control', it behoves political philosophers and philosophers of law to undertake serious investigations into these troubled waters.

CONTEMPORARY DISCUSSION OF RIGHTS THEORY

Historians of rights theory usually write that in the early nineteenth century, Jeremy Bentham set the stage for the contemporary discussions articulating and delimiting the nature and scope of human rights theory. Contemporary work often notes the opposition between the utilitarian rights theory and the absolutist rights theory. H. J. McCloskey once remarked that 'Jeremy Bentham saw clearly enough that utilitarians can have no truck with theories of natural human rights'.[2] Readers familiar with rights literature know that both Bentham and Edmund Burke ferociously attacked the theories of absolute human rights. In spite of Bentham's clear and distinct warning, none the less, contemporary utilitarians have attempted some rights theory justification. This attempt concentrates on the principle of utility as a principle of justification.

On the one hand, what if a utilitarian analysis fails? If human rights, then, are based on a non-utilitarian method, one must articulate clearly this non-consequentialist foundation. Natural law philosophers such as Maritain, Finnis, and Veatch provide one instance of this kind of foundational analysis. However, natural law discussions have not been in the forefront of contemporary rights theory analysis. If utilitarianism is insufficient for an adequate justification, then how are rights justified? If natural law theory is ruled out, then where does one go for a theory justifying human rights? A Kantian formalist theory based on the autonomy of reason itself is one response. Another response claims that basic rights are 'intuitively obvious'. If neither of these approaches works, then where does the philosopher of law and political philosopher turn? These are the questions to which a reconstructed version of natural law theory provides a general proposal for a resolution. This chapter offers a general discussion, albeit a brief and sketchy account, suggesting how a theory of human rights might be derived from Aquinas's account of natural law theory.

One view of the development of rights theory in modern Western

---

[2] H. J. McCloskey, 'Respect for Human Moral Rights versus Maximizing Good', in Frey (ed.), *Utility Rights*, 121.

thought goes something like this. Historically, two general theories of rights developed. The first general discussion took place in the seventeenth century and culminated in the work of John Locke. The second major development in the philosophy of rights theory, closer to our own era, fostered the discussions on rights theory following the Second World War. The beginning of the United Nations contributed to the relevance of these discussions.

Philosophers in the natural law tradition, however, have not been considered central to either of these discussions. While a certain amount of natural law writing has emerged on rights issues, these efforts did not have general influence on most contemporary philosophy discussions of rights theory. For example, in R. G. Frey's contemporary collection of rights theory essays, *Utility and Rights*, the recent work of John Finnis on natural rights receives but two brief footnotes. One of these footnotes suggests almost disparagingly that natural rights talk is 'too uninformative to be very useful'.[3] The general thrust of this chapter, on the contrary, indicates how useful indeed natural law can be in articulating a provisional yet foundational theory of human rights.

Philosophers who reject both a natural law foundation for human rights and the principle of utility often resort to forms of intuitionism and the appeal to self-evident principles in order to ground rights. McCloskey suggests, for example, that a plausible approach to the justification of human rights 'is that the basic fundamental moral rights are self-evidently so'.[4] In contemporary political theory, a rights-based theory such as McCloskey suggests has become important if utilitarianism cannot provide the theoretical justification for basic human rights. Such theories have come to the forefront of philosophical discussion principally as attacks on the theoretical weaknesses inherent in utilitarian justifications. For instance, in his *A Theory of Justice*, Rawls noted that because 'utilitarianism does not take seriously the distinctions between persons', a serious difficulty arises in any utilitarian attempt to justify human rights. Finnis too argues against the theoretical possibility of any form of consequentialist moral and legal theory. Ronald Dworkin, like Rawls and Finnis, argues for individual rights as 'political trumps' to be asserted as claims against intrusion on a moral agent either by others or by a govern-

---

[3] Sumner, 'Rights Denaturalized', 40 n. 4.
[4] McCloskey, 'Respect for Human Moral Rights', 126.

mental agency. Simply put, individual rights protect against actions directed against an individual when the purported justification for such actions is based on the principle of utility applied to the general welfare alone. Rawls develops a theory of rights around the theoretical constraints concerning what rational persons would agree to in the 'veil of ignorance'. He brings to our attention the role 'rational choice' plays in the development of human rights theory. Rawls's analysis is, as the discussions in Chapter 3 suggested, an example of the good-reasons approach to moral decision-making. Furthermore, the theories of individual rights put forward by Rawls, Nozick, and Dworkin are usually called forms of a 'contractarian theory of rights'.

A principal tension in contemporary discussions on the nature of rights focuses attention on the meta-ethical choice between utilitarianism as an attempt to justify rights on the one hand and rights-based theories absolutely considered on the other. As John Mackie once wrote in commenting upon Hare's utilitarianism, 'the real dispute, then, concerns the choice between utility and rights as the central concepts in higher level, critical, moral thinking'.[5]

In considering contemporary discussions on the nature of rights, in addition to the shadow of Bentham, the writings of Rawls, Dworkin, and Nozick are always in the background. Dworkin's *Taking Rights Seriously* and 'A Model of Rules' have together served as an important impetus to much recent thinking on rights matters, especially Dworkin's account of a right as a 'political trump'. That there is little agreement on the precise nature of the development of rights is obvious from but a cursory reading of Rawls, Dworkin, and Nozick. None of these three, furthermore, would accept any purported natural law justification for individual human rights.

Concerning the theoretical difficulties one faces in developing a coherent theory of rights, Henry Veatch once wrote: 'we are brought face to face with one of those singularly lamentable lacunae in nearly the whole of contemporary moral and political philosophy: there just does not seem to be any reasoned accounting for why and on what grounds we human beings can properly be said to have rights or duties either one.'[6]

---

[5] J. L. Mackie, 'Rights, Utility and Universalization', in Frey (ed.), *Utility and Rights*, 103.

[6] Henry B. Veatch, 'A Poor Benighted Philosopher Looks at the Issue of Judicial Activism', in *Swimming Against the Current in Contemporary Philosophy* (Washington: Catholic University of America Press, 1990), 322

If Rawls is correct, then utilitarianism will not generate the kind of rights theory needed to solve philosophical and political problems. Whether a more formalist account of human rights — based obviously on Kantian themes — will generate substantial rights in their entirety, however, is a question natural law philosophers must raise. This issue will become central to the discussions which follow.

NEO-SCHOLASTICISM AND RIGHTS
THE MARITAIN PROPOSAL

Probably the foremost commentator on Aquinas regarding the development of rights theory in the twentieth century is Jacques Maritain. In works such as *The Rights of Man and Natural Law* (1944), *The Person and the Common Good* (1946), and *Man and the State* (1951), Maritain developed a theory of rights within the general context of Thomism as he understood Aquinas's philosophy. Maritain argued forcefully for the compatibility of the concept of democracy with his development of scholastic rights theory. In *Scholasticism and Politics*, he suggests that 'the rights of the human person ... must be recognized and guaranteed in such a way that an organic democracy should be by essence the city of the rights of the person'.[7] D'Entrèves once remarked that Maritain's position is 'a codified system of human rights based on the Christian view of the supreme value of the individual soul, the goal of Redemption'.[8] At times, Maritain appears to rest his theory of human rights on a religious foundation. While Maritain might argue that this foundation is the result of inquiries into natural or philosophical theology, the exact role theological claims play in his rights theory is ambiguous at best.

None the less, Maritain attempted to develop a theory of the state with a corresponding theory of human rights within the context of scholasticism but cognizant of Enlightenment rights theory. Like most, if not all, scholastic philosophers treating rights, Maritain attributes rights only to rational beings. Within this context, Maritain writes perceptively on rights theory, ascribing rights to individuals as individuals, individuals as citizens, and individuals as members of the working class. Throughout all his writings, Maritain considered

---

[7] Jacques Maritain, *Scholasticism and Politics*, trans. and ed. Mortimer Adler, 3rd edn. (London: Geoffrey Bles, 1954), 88.
[8] A. P. D'Entrèves, *Natural Law* (London: Hutchinson University Library, 1970), 48.

his theory of rights to be part of a larger project restoring a genuine humanism to twentieth-century Western political thought. In the appendix to *The Rights of Man and Natural Law*, Maritain includes an account of the 'International Declaration of the Rights of Man'. This declaration was adopted by the Institute of International Law in 1929. Maritain considers his theory of rights to be congruent with the Institute's proclamation of the nature and scope of human rights. In his *Man and the State*, Maritain discusses the 1948 International Declaration of Human Rights. In fact, Maritain was a member of the French delegation to UNESCO which drafted the universal declaration.

In his development of a theory of rights using scholastic philosophy as a foundation, Maritain appeals to a somewhat blurred notion of 'connatural knowledge'. This is a form of non-cognitive awareness through which a human agent becomes aware of those human aspirations directly related to morality. This theory of connatural knowledge is, it would seem, only marginally comprehensive. How one is aware of these inclinations is not clearly spelled out in Maritain's analysis of natural law theory. McInerny also is concerned about this aspect of connaturality in Maritain's proposal for natural rights. None the less, the content of natural law theory based on Aquinas's analysis is possible without accepting Maritain's idiosyncratic account of non-cognitive, connatural knowledge.

Outside scholasticism, Maritain's theory appears to have had little influence. For example, Frey's *Utility and Rights* contains but one brief mention to Maritain, which is a footnote referring to his work in Thomist theory. Analytic rights theory, in particular, has considered Maritain's work with indifference at best and hostility at worst.

AQUINAS ON NATURAL AND POSITIVE RIGHTS

It is fair to say that Aquinas does not consider the concept of 'right' as such. He does use the term *jus* often, and one might translate this Latin term as 'right'. However, the concept of right in the modern political sense was not part of Aquinas's philosophical lexicon.

In the *Summa Theologiae*, I-II q. 57, Aquinas discusses his understanding of the concept of *jus*. *Jus* is analyzed just prior to the general treatment of justice, which is *justitia*, in the Latin text. Not surprisingly, *jus* is considered as pertaining more to the nature of justice than it is to the modern role of right. This is an important context necessary for understanding Aquinas's account of right.

The historian of Roman law, Michel Villey, once noted that in order to understand what Aquinas meant by the concept of *jus*, one had to understand the corresponding concept as used in Roman law. John Finnis suggests, however, that the interpretation of the Roman texts on law are controversial at best. None the less, the nature and structure of Roman law are more helpful, so it seems, in attempting to come to terms with Aquinas's account of rights theory than any similarities with modern and contemporary accounts of human rights. Commenting on this discussion, Ralph McInerny has suggested that what fundamentally distinguishes Aquinas's concept of *jus* from the modern concept of right centres on the objective/subjective distinction. Aquinas's account of *jus* entailed that a matter of fact was determined to hold; from that factual situation, moreover, a certain relation in terms of justice comes about. *Jus* means, so Aquinas suggests, 'that which is right', which in turn, means 'that which is just'. Thus, *jus* refers to an objective state of affairs.

The modern concept of right, on the other hand, refers to a subjective 'claim' which a person might assert regarding something due to the person. The person asserting the claim has some property or quality which justifies the claim asserted. It should be noted, however, that this subjective status is not found in Aquinas's account of *jus*.

The texts of Aquinas in the *Summa Theologiae* considering *jus* indicate this objective character and the relation with the virtue of justice.

Therefore, it is the case that what is correct (*quod est rectum*) in the actions of all the other virtues (i.e. except justice), to which the intention of the virtue tends as to its proper object, is never accepted except in direct reference to the agent.

But, on the other hand, that which is correct in the works of justice, in addition to the direct reference to the agent, is constituted by a reference to the other person. It is the case, therefore, that in our works, what responds according to a certain equality [*aequalitatem* — fairness] to the other is what is called right (*justum*). An example of this would be the payment of money to the person owed for a service given or rendered. (*Summa Theologiae*, II-II q. 57 a. 1)

In the text of Aquinas from the *Summa Theologiae*, the right or *jus* is a relation or proportion among persons or things which in some way equalizes them. According to Aquinas, following Aristotle, it is the function of the virtue of justice to establish this relation of fairness or equality. McInerny notes that Aristotle, when discussing justice, distinguishes the just — *to dikaion* — which is the just thing or the just state of affairs, from the agent — *dikaios* — and from the action.[9] The *jus* is the 'right proportion between things' or the proper adjustment among persons and things. Finnis suggests that the primary meaning of *jus* in Aquinas is 'the just thing itself', or anything which might serve as the subject matter for objective relationships of justice. Commenting on this use of *jus*, Finnis offers this helpful and perceptive analysis: 'One could say that for Aquinas '*jus*' primarily means 'the fair' or 'the what's fair'; indeed, if one could use the adverb 'aright' as a noun, one could say that his primary account is of 'arights' (rather than of rights)'.[10]

Aquinas, in the next article of the *Summa Theologiae*, I-II q. 57, a. 2, makes what might appear to be a very modern distinction common to discussions of rights theory. Aquinas provides an account of the differences between a natural right (*jus naturale*) and a positive right (*jus positivum*). Once again, one notices the differences between Aquinas's account of *jus* and modern and contemporary discussions of human rights, whether natural or positive.

What I mean by right (*jus*) — which is the same as the just (*justum*) — is a certain work which is proportionate to another according to some method or mode of equality. However, it should be noted that there are two ways in which something can be made proportionate to another person. Indeed, one way is such that it is from the very nature of the case (or from the very state of affairs). For example, when someone gives or puts forward a certain amount so that what is received is proportionate to the amount paid. This I suggest we call a natural right (*jus naturale*).

In another way, however, something is proportionate or commensurate to another either through an agreement or through a form of common consent. For example, when a person is satisfied and content when a certain amount is received. This form of agreement is twofold. One manner is set up through a private agreement. An example would be when parties come to terms through an agreement made in private (*inter privatas personas*). The

⁹ Ralph McInerny, 'Natural Law and Natural Rights', in his *Aquinas on Human Action* (Washington, DC: Catholic University of America Press, 1992), 213–4.

¹⁰ John Finnis, *Natural Law and Natural Rights* corr. edn. (Oxford: Clarendon Press, 1982), 206.

second manner comes about through a public agreement. For example, when an entire citizenry consents that some item is held to be proportionate and commensurate with another; another example would be when the person in authority who has care for the citizens and acts as its person, ordains that this should hold. And this I suggest we call positive right (*jus positivum*).

These passages on the various uses of *jus* indicate how different indeed he considered the matter of rights from that construed since the seventeenth century. As McInerny notes, 'in the classical sense, the right was an external relation to be established between persons on the basis of things'.[11] The *jus* becomes, in a strong sense, the object of justice. It is the state of affairs about which an external relation needs to be established. On the contrary, McInerny notes that 'in the modern sense, right has become subjective, it attaches to the individual taken singly as an instantiation of human nature and amounts to a claim that he can make on the state or on others'.[12]

The foundation of the more modern analysis of right is found, for one place, in the *De Legibus* of Francisco Suarez, the Spanish Jesuit philosopher who wrote in the early seventeenth century. Finnis suggests that by the time of the publication of the *De Legibus*, the 'watershed' on the account of rights theory had been crossed from the objective analysis of *jus* as found in Aquinas's *Summa Theologiae* to the more subjective account found in modern political and legal theory. Finnis notes the contrasting accounts of *jus* found in Aquinas's *Summa* and Suarez's *De Legibus*:

We find [in Suarez] another analysis of the meaning of '*jus*'. Here the 'true, strict and proper meaning' of '*jus*' is said to be: 'a kind of moral power (*facultas*) which every man has, either over his own property or with respect to that which is due to him' (*De Legibus*, I, ii, 5). The meaning which for Aquinas was primary is rather vaguely mentioned by Suarez and then drops out of sight; conversely, the meaning which for Suarez is primary does not appear in Aquinas's discussion at all. Somewhere between the two men we have crossed the watershed.[13]

As Finnis notes so perceptively, here the emphasis has gone from 'that which is *just in a given situation*' to 'something beneficial – a *power – which a person has*'. In his *De Jure Belli ac Pacis*, Grotius adopts what he calls the 'proper or strict' meaning of *jus*, which is a moral

---

[11] McInerny, 'Natural Law and Natural Rights', 217.
[12] Ibid.
[13] Finnis, *Natural Law and Natural Rights*, 206–7.

quality found in the person which enables the person to have or to undertake something justly. Like Suarez, Grotius argues that a right is essentially something — a quality or a power — which a person — an agent — has. This quality becomes a 'power' or a 'liberty' possessed by the agent. What Aquinas argues as the principal meaning of *jus*, so Finnis suggests, has been transformed in Suarez and Grotius 'by relating it exclusively to the beneficiary of the just relationship, above all to his doing and having'.[14]

Given this analysis of Suarez and Grotius, albeit a brief account, one realizes how the meaning of *jus* was transformed in the three hundred plus years from the writing of Aquinas's *Summa Theologiae* to the writing of Suarez's *De Legibus*. The result of the transformation produced what we might call the paradigm use of right in modern and contemporary political philosophy and jurisprudence. This transformation also helps clarify the suggestion put forward by McInerny concerning the 'objective' status of *jus* in classical and medieval philosophy and the 'subjective' status found in modern rights theory. This meaning of 'subjective' suggests, not a relativism, but rather a quality or power — what Grotius, and Hobbes later, call a 'liberty' — possessed by the agent.

One should note that Aquinas's discussion of *jus naturale* is separated both textually and conceptually from his discussion of natural law. The former, as noted above, is a prelude to the discussion of the virtue of justice, while the latter is connected centrally with the development of the theory of law. Furthermore, as Michel Villey has suggested and as the preceding analysis has indicated, not only is Aquinas's concept of natural right dependent on Roman law, but, more importantly, Aquinas's account differs fundamentally from later — and especially more modern — concepts of natural right. McInerny notes that both Villey and MacIntyre are sceptical and dubious about the foundation of modern rights theory.[15] Moreover, Aquinas's account differs radically from the contractarian schemes of human rights derivation familiar to the analyses offered by Rawls, Nozick, and Dworkin.

[14] Finnis, *Natural Law and Natural Rights*, 207.
[15] McInerny, 'Natural Law and Natural Rights', 212.

A DERIVATION OF HUMAN RIGHTS FROM
NATURAL LAW IN AQUINAS

It is possible to sketch in outline form a pattern for the development of a consistent theory of rights based upon Aquinas's writings on natural law. This development – or rather derivation – depends intrinsically on the analysis of Aquinas's system of natural law offered in Chapter 4. In one sense, the natural law which determines human obligations will also determine human rights. This is, of course, a form of natural rights theory.

Aquinas's account of rights based upon his theory of natural law occupies an intermediary place between the utilitarian view and the formalist rights-based theories considered above. While Aquinas is a kind of teleologist in his moral theory, as Chapter 4 indicated, none the less he is not a consequentialist in the utilitarian sense. Aquinas would not fit into the 'teleological' category of normative theories as discussed in meta-ethical writings in the twentieth century. Because more than the effects of the act or rule alone are important in determining the moral status of an action, Aquinas is not a 'teleologist' in the consequentialist mode, as this category is understood in contemporary meta-ethical theory, especially as elucidated by William Frankena. In Aquinas's theory, the concept of human nature determines in a specific way the content of right actions. Given this emphasis to the theory, Aquinas is more properly designated as a 'deontologist' rather than as a 'teleologist' in his normative ethical theory. None the less, to be a deontologist is neither identical to nor coextensive with any form of Kantian formalism.

A sketch of a position on rights derivation in Aquinas might go something like this. A human right for Aquinas is derived from or based upon the set of dispositions that make up the human essence. The dispositions determine the duties. An obligation, then, is derived from the rights. At the outset, this analysis assumes that in a general way rights and obligations are correlative concepts. Rights are derived from duties, a position to be discussed in the next section. Duties and obligations are neither identical nor coextensive.

Following a suggestion offered by Henry Veatch in *Human Rights: Fact or Fancy?*, and John Finnis in *Natural Law and Natural Rights*, the concept of a right is derived from the concept of a 'duty'. In the reconstructed analysis of Aquinas's theory of natural law given in Chapter 4, one can argue that duties are based upon the dispositions which define a human essence. The discussion of the dispositional analysis of human essence in Aquinas suggests that Schema 2 holds. A human essence is best defined in terms of a 'set of dispositional properties'. There are three generic sets of dispositions: living, sensitive, and rational.

Schema 2.

HUMAN ESSENCE AT SET OF DISPOSITIONAL PROPERTIES

1. Living dispositions
     to continue in existence
     nutrition and growth
2. Sensitive dispositions
     to have sensations and perceptions
     to care for offspring
3. Rational dispositions.
     to be curious rationally
     to live together in social units

It would be useful to consider again the foundational text in the *Summa Theologiae* in which Aquinas discusses the basic dispositions which determine the content of a human essence.

In so far as good has the intelligibility of end and evil the intelligibility of contrary to end, it follows that reason grasps naturally as goods (accordingly, as things to be pursued by work, and their opposites as evils and thus things to be avoided) all the objects which follow from the natural inclinations or dispositions central to the concept of human nature.

First, there is in human beings an inclination or disposition based upon the aspect of human nature which is shared with all living things: this is that everything according to its own nature tends to preserve its own being. In accord with this inclination or natural tendency, those things (actions, events, processes) by which human life is preserved and by which threats to human life are met fall under the natural law.

Second, there are in human beings inclinations or dispositions towards more restricted goods which are based upon the fact that human nature has common properties with other animals. In accord with this disposition, those things are said to be in agreement with the natural law (which nature teaches all animals) among which are the sexual union of male and female, the care of children, and so forth.

Third, there is in human beings an inclination or disposition to those goods based upon the rational properties of human nature. These goods are uniquely related to human beings. For example, human beings have a natural disposition to know the true propositions about God and concerning those necessities required for living in a human society. In accord with this disposition arise elements of the natural law. For example, human beings should avoid ignorance and should not offend those persons among whom they must live in social units, and so on.   (I-II q. 94 a. 2)

From this analysis of human essence or nature, one can derive a set of duties. These duties are the obligations one has towards oneself and others. These duties, in turn, determine the actions to be followed if 'flourishing' is to be attained. For instance, one has a duty to protect one's existence (this is derived from the disposition in the living segment, 'to continue in existence'). One also has a duty to protect the integrity of one's bodily composition (derived from the disposition in the sensitive segment, 'to have sensations and perceptions'). Continuing, one has the duty to search after true propositions (derived from the disposition in the rational segment, 'to be curious rationally'). Recall from the earlier discussion that an immoral action is, by definition, the hindering or frustration of the development of a dispositional property. This frustration results from the failure of the human person – via the essence – to 'flourish'. Earlier, 'to flourish' was suggested as a contemporary translation of Aristotle's *eudaimonia* and Aquinas's *beatitudo*. It follows that because 'flourishing' is the *telos* – the 'end' – of human activity, to prevent the attainment of this flourishing is to hinder the development of the human essence based upon its constitutive dispositional properties. Hence, one has a duty, in the Aristotelian and Aquinian schema, to attain the state of 'flourishing'. This is the obligatory teleology inherent in Aristotelian and Aquinian moral theory, which is the metaphysics of finality.

Using this analysis of a human person, a human right becomes a 'protection' of the duties based upon the development of the dispositions. It is a quality or power a person possesses because of the very constitution of the human essence. In one sense, the right is an 'acquired power' or 'acquired quality' derived from the human essence. Consider the following expansion of Schema 2 depicting Aquinas's account of the human essence:

Schema 2*a*. HUMAN ESSENCE A SET OF
DISPOSITIONAL PROPERTIES

	Dispositions	*Rights*
1. Life:	to continue in existence	to life
2. Sensitivity:	to perceive	to bodily integrity
3. Rationality:	to be curious intellectually	to knowledge of what is true
	to live together	to a just society

The individual human rights are acquired qualities or properties derived from the content of the set of dispositions. This theory provides a central core for natural rights based upon the natural necessities determined by the human essence. In this way, a natural right is based upon the reconstructed theory of natural law provided in Chapter 4.

A THICK THEORY OF HUMAN NATURE

What is one to make of this? The theoretical derivation of human rights is from the basic set of duties which in turn are derived from the set of dispositional properties which determine the content of a human essence. These rights as beneficiary qualities are what they are because the human nature is what it is. The set of 'natural necessities' determines the content of the human essence. If human nature had evolved or been created in some specifically different manner, then the set of dispositions would, of course, change. And with this change would come a change in the content of human rights. In discussing the natural necessities, H. L. A. Hart once suggested that human beings have a right to basic protection from harm and violence principally because violence renders the human person unable to function as a human being. In other words, if human beings had evolved or been created with a specific property developing hard, crustacean-like shells, then certain prohibitions against injuries would not be based upon human nature. This 'shell' would protect the human person from wanton injury. Hence, the disposition engendering the right to bodily integrity and protection from harm would not be derivable from human nature.

The point is that if human beings had been created or evolved differently, there would be a different set of dispositional properties making up the core of the human essence. Given the analysis of the derivation of rights proposed above, these dispositional properties would result in different duties and hence, different human rights. Of course, the point of all of this is that the human rights are what they are because ultimately the dispositions are what they are. A human right is not dependent upon the political demands of any government. Neither are rights based on the voluntary character of the will. Aquinas's theory of human rights, attained through the manner of derivation, does take rights seriously. But the serious nature of the rights depends ultimately on taking seriously the philosophical anthropology expressed in the concept of human nature or essence. The rights are based on a 'thick' theory of human nature and the concept of the human good, which is *eudaimonia*. This is a much richer and more developed theory of human nature and of the human good than the classic good-reasons political philosophers such as Rawls, Nozick, and Dworkin would accept as possible theoretically.

It will be useful to consider briefly the specific rights mentioned above. In the realm of the rational dispositions, Aquinas considers 'intellectual curiosity'. This is based on Aristotelian psychology, especially as articulated in the first line of Aristotle's *Metaphysics*: 'All humans, by nature, desire to know.' This intellectual desire — disposition — is best characterized as 'curiosity'. Aquinas suggests that if this is a disposition to 'know', then it will be hindered if it does not know that which is true. In other words, one has a right to the truth because false propositions will hinder the development of the rational disposition bent towards 'knowing'. This is what Aquinas has in mind in suggesting that false statements hinder the 'end purpose' of the rational disposition. This is a teleological analysis, but it is an analysis based on the development of the dispositional human nature. Not telling the truth leads to a situation hindering the fostering of *eudaimonia*.

In a similar manner, if human beings are, by nature, 'social and political animals', as both Aristotle and Aquinas suggest, then human persons have a disposition as part of their nature to live together. But to live together demands some account of just relations between the members of the social unit. Hence, while Aquinas's theory of natural law does not entail what the exact nature of society must be, none the less there must be some sense of justice — 'giving to each his or her due' — in the structure of the social unit.

This proposal offers an account, in a general way, of how Aquinas might derive the set of rights from the dispositions. This too indicates the 'teleology' inherent in Aquinas's moral system. It is a benign teleology in that it considers the 'end' of the natural human functions proper to a human person, who is a member of a natural kind possessing a dispositional essence. This teleology does not refer to a conscious purpose in the universe determining each and every function. While Aquinas did consider a provident God, none the less the account of teleology considered here is consistent theoretically with Aristotelian psychology, which is, of course, independent totally from the concept of a provident deity. That Aristotle's set of unmoved movers did not possess the later monotheist concept of 'providence' is well established in the history of philosophy.

Finnis argues for what he calls 'absolute human rights'. Finnis articulates his justification of these human rights by means of his account of what he calls the requirements of practical reasonableness. This entails, so Finnis argues, 'that it is always unreasonable to choose directly against any basic value, whether in oneself or in one's fellow human beings'. Finnis, steeped in the Aristotelian tradition, albeit his own reconstruction of Aristotle and Aquinas, argues that the fundamental human values are not reducible to mere abstractions. They are rooted in human beings and are 'aspects of the real well-being of flesh-and-blood individuals'.[16]

Finnis provides the following examples of what he takes to be human rights. One can see immediately the similarity with the structure and development of human rights based on the human dispositions as discussed above. Finnis writes as follows:

The right not to have one's life taken directly as a means to a further end; the right not to be positively lied to in any situation (e.g., teaching, preaching, research publication, news broadcasting) is reasonably expected; and the related right not to be condemned on knowingly false charges; and the right not to be deprived, or required to deprive oneself, of one's procreative capacity; and the right to be taken into respectful consideration in any assessment of what the common good requires.[17]

[16] Finnis, *Natural Law and Natural Rights*, 225.
[17] Ibid.

Finnis bases his account of human rights on the concept of individual well-being, which is a necessary condition in determining the content of human rights.

Of course, it is important to note at the outset that this reconstruction of Aquinas, at best, provides a very general construct for the development of rights. From his theory of natural law, rights can be generated from the structures that he has developed based on human nature. But this theory, derived from Aquinas's account of natural law, does not develop a complete set of specific, individual rights. Finnis also discusses this issue when he notes that the concept of 'casuistry' is a necessary condition in determining a list of human rights. Finnis also suggests how complicated and difficult casuistry is in the matter of determining individual rights and duties. This omission in natural law rights theory – i.e., the difficulty in an exact determination of a precise list of individual rights – probably would not wear well with some contemporary rights advocates.

In the end, this account of human rights in Aquinas may provide a way for Aquinas's theory to pass over what Finnis has called 'the watershed' into modern rights theory. The human right derived from the dispositional property is an acquired quality or power on which individual rights claims might be made. There is an objective foundation for the right, which is, of course, the natural law theory itself. But there is also a subjective aspect directly related to the agent. This account of the derivation of human rights provides both the objective and the subjective elements in a theory of natural rights based upon a theory of natural law.

In his account of human rights in *Natural Law and Natural Rights*, Finnis has argued that when one considers the contemporary manifestos of human rights, from the 1948 Universal Declaration, to the 1952 European Convention for the Protection of Human Rights, to the 1966 United Nations Covenants through the statement of rights promulgated by the Second Vatican Council, one central theme comes to the centre stage: 'we realize what the modern 'manifesto' conception of human rights amounts to. It is simply a way of sketching the *outlines of the common good*, the various aspects of individual well-being in community.'[18] Finnis further argues that the reference to rights is fundamentally an elucidation of what is contained within the concept of the 'common good'. Finnis suggests that this analysis

[18] Ibid. 214.

entails the following concerning the protection of individual rights in the context of consequentialism or utilitarianism: '*Each* and everyone's well-being, in each of its basic aspects, must be considered and favoured at *all* times by those responsible for co-ordinating the common life.'[19]

In arguing against any form of consequentialism and utilitarianism, Finnis further suggests that all the manifestos proclaiming human rights leave 'no room' for any appeal against the exercise of these individual human rights to the general welfare or the utilitarian 'greatest happiness' principle. In this argument, Finnis is remarkably similar to Ronald Dworkin's analysis of human rights as 'political trumps'. Dworkin argues that an individual right, as a trump, asserts a claim protecting an individual against an action or event perpetrated against the agent for the apparent greater good of the general welfare.

Yet Finnis does differ radically from Dworkin in so far as a justification for the human rights is offered. Finnis justifies his concept of individual human right within the concept of the individual wellbeing. This demands a so-called 'thick' theory of human nature, which Finnis no doubt holds. Dworkin — aligned with Rawls and Nozick — denies the possibility of developing such a thick theory of human nature which could be useful for either rights theory or moral theory. With his 'thick' theory of human nature, Finnis has the foundation, in principle at least, to develop his theory of rights based on the concept of human well-being, or what he refers to as 'human flourishing'. Of course, Chapter 6 questioned the arguments establishing this foundation. The basic thrust of this book has been, in a structurally similar sense, to argue that individual well being — *eudaimonia* — is based upon the development of the dispositional properties which constitute the concept of human nature. Given the insights of Finnis's analysis, it seems possible to develop a set of human rights from the foundation of human well-being based on an Aristotelian and Aquinian analysis. That this is merely a sketch is obvious. But it is, I suggest, an important sketch which might portend more important developments constructing a theory of human rights justified through the concept of the human person.

One needs to distinguish here between political or legal rights and natural rights. Political or legal rights are those rights created

[19] Finnis, *Natural Law and Natural Rights*, 214.

by a legislative body and conferred upon the citizens of a society. Natural rights are those rights that are founded upon the moral duties that in turn are developed from the basic set of dispositional properties that make up the concept of human nature.

The thrust of natural law theory on the formation of political rights is that a political right may not itself hinder or destroy a natural right. A natural right is the ontological possibility for a political right. It is not the political right. A political right is a piece of legislation. Hence, given the natural law dimension of human rights, a political right is limited by the same theoretical constraints under which a positive law is placed. A natural right is, in theory, the criterion which presents the possibility for the development of a political right. In turn, the natural right is a protection of the duty which is derivable from the concept of the human essence.

An important issue concerns when justifiably to create a political right. Can political rights be both 'positive' and 'negative' rights? How far can one extrapolate from the basic concept of a human nature to the creation of human rights? The next section briefly considers this issue as discussed in the writings of Henry Veatch. The contemporary thicket in jurisprudence surrounding the issues of judicial activism has determined the broad scope of the consideration of positive and negative rights.

VEATCH ON RIGHTS AND DUTIES

In *Human Rights: Fact or Fancy?* and *Swimming Against the Current in Contemporary Philosophy*, Henry Veatch has developed a theory of human rights based on the general insights of Aristotelian and Aquinian moral theory. Given the analysis in Chapter 7 of Veatch's interpretation of Aristotle and Aquinas, it is not difficult to develop his theory of rights and duties. Veatch derives his theory of rights from what he calls the obligatory duties, which in turn are derived from the actualization of the human person.

What Veatch does, however, is to articulate a position which entails only a consistent derivation of negative rights. He is worried about the theoretical and practical problems encountered in attempting to develop a justified account of positive rights. In *Human Rights: Fact or Fancy?*, Veatch appears to have the shadow of libertarianism hovering over some of his rights theory analysis. He denies that he is a libertarian, but the shadow is heavy indeed.

Veatch begins by suggesting that the classic rights of the United States Constitution articulated in the Fifth and Fourteenth Amendments — life, liberty, and property — are the rights which are derivable from the concept of individual duty, which in turn is based upon the concept of human essence. As Chapter 7 noted, Veatch's analysis depends upon a dispositional account of human essence, which is structurally similar to the account developed in Chapter 4.

What Veatch denies, however, is the theoretical justification for what might be called 'positive rights'. This is, to be sure, a controversial position. Veatch spells out his account of positive and negative rights in the following way:

> Thus, as for 'negative rights', why not say that these amount to such rights as we human beings might be said to have, simply not to be interfered with in, say, our lives, our liberties and our properties? Moreover, such an entitlement to noninterference is clearly to be construed as a noninterference by others, be these others either private persons or the public authorities. Hence, the term 'negative' rights.
>
> In contrast, when it comes to positive rights, these may be construed as being rights, not merely not to be deprived of what is already ours (like our lives, our liberties, and our property), but rather as being rights actually to have certain things bestowed upon us, such things as we presumably neither now have nor are likely ever to come to have, unless perchance or by good luck they should come to be bestowed upon us by others . . . For example, such goods and services as might be the objects of positive rights could clearly be any of the so-called welfare rights — such things as old-age benefits, health care, facilities for education, a living wage, etc., etc.[20]

Veatch argues that the negative rights — our right not to be interfered with in matters pertaining to our lives, our freedoms, and our properties — can be derived consistently from an Aristotelian/Aquinian account of natural law. However, what he refers to as a positive right cannot be so derived. A positive right indicates that a particular act, thing, or event is due to a human person. Veatch is concerned that the development of a theory of positive rights is incoherent theoretically and subject to abuse practically.[21]

Since Veatch bases his account on the metaphysical and moral insights of Aristotle and Aquinas, one question comes immediately

---

[20] Veatch, 'A Poor Benighted Philosopher', 315.

[21] Recently in private conversations, Professor Veatch has expressed some reservation about his earlier position denying the theoretical and practical viability of positive human rights.

to mind: is this Aristotelian/Aquinian interpretation articulated by Veatch justifying only negative rights compatible structurally with Aquinas's texts on natural law? The discussion above noted that Aquinas had neither the term nor the modern concept of 'right' in his philosophical lexicon. None the less, this chapter has sketched an account in which a theory of rights based on Aquinas's moral theory can be derived from the texts on natural law in his *Summa Theologiae*.

In response to Veatch's limitations of rights, one might argue that some positive rights can flow consistently and coherently from Aquinas's account of human essence. Some limited positive rights, such as the right to health care, the right to education, right to integrity of personhood, etc., would be based on the dispositional properties. For example, if the rational disposition can be developed only through the acquisition of sets of true propositions, and if this acquisition ordinarily depends on education, one might argue that access to some level of education is a fundamental human positive right.

The complete development of this theory would demand a fuller account of what might be called the 'natural necessities' central to Aquinas's analysis of human essence. The attainment of *eudaimonia* or *beatitudo* — the self-actualization of Aquinas's meta-ethical naturalism — should be able to support the derivation of some limited positive rights. This is a very general approach to the issue. None the less, it does sketch a mode indicating how the concept of positive right is possible in Aquinian natural law

At issue here is a theme which often divides rights-theorists who are liberal from their conservative counterparts. Is the function of a right to 'protect' some quality or trait? Or is a right a guarantee for some action to be undertaken on behalf of a person? While this suggestion is admittedly quite general in nature and scope, none the less rights as 'protection' appears to be a conservative position. On the other hand, rights as 'guarantee' appears to be a liberal position. If one can develop a satisfactory account of the human person philosophically, then the articulation of a 'protection' view of rights is not that difficult. Veatch's reconstruction of Aristotelian moral theory has led the way in this area of rights development and justification. However, it is more difficult to construct a coherent and consistent theory of positive rights which guarantee some particular activity for a person or a group of persons.

Commenting on her analysis of Aristotle's political theory, Martha Nussbaum has written:

I think there are a lot of good things here, and among the good things is an account of the proper function of government or politics as the provision to each citizen of all the necessary conditions for the living of a rich and good human life ... this view seems to me well worth examining today, as an alternative to views that see the job of government in connection with the maximization of utility.[22]

In 'Non-Relative Virtues', Nussbaum argues for much the same position:

I discuss an Aristotelian conception of the proper function of government, according to which its task is to make available to each and every member of the community the basic necessary conditions of the capability to choose and live a fully good human life, with respect to each of the major human functions included in that fully good life. I examine sympathetically Aristotle's argument that, for this reason, the task of government cannot be well performed, or its aims well understood, without an understanding of these functionings ... It shows how this understanding of the human being and the political task can yield a conception of social democracy that is a plausible alternative to liberal conceptions.[23]

Nussbaum's analysis would seem to be approaching an analysis suggesting a role for some form of minimal positive rights. The development of that argument, however, still needs to be made. None the less, Veatch's argument admitting only negative rights in Aquinas's system appears to be too limited and restricted a claim.

THE IMPACT OF JUDICIAL ACTIVISM

Veatch worries about this issue of negative rights for several reasons, both theoretical and practical. Influenced by the writings of the late Iredell Jenkins, Veatch believes that certain forms of judicial activism have determined rights which are to be observed in a society. Both Jenkins and Veatch have argued that, if positive rights are to become political entities, then they are to be defined and determined through the legislative or executive process. Jenkins wrote extensively on the

---

[22] Martha Nussbaum, 'Dialogue with Martha Nussbaum on Aristotle', in Bryan Magee, *The Great Philosophers* (Oxford: Oxford University Press, 1988), 53.

[23] Nussbaum, 'Non-Relative Virtues', in Martha Nussbaum and Amartya Sen (eds.), *The Quality of Life* (Oxford: Clarendon Press, 1993), 265.

case of *Wyatt v. Stickney*. This case, heard in a United States Federal Court, resulted in a judgment affirming positive rights for patients confined to mental hospitals located in the state of Alabama. The judicial resolution of this case forced huge expenditures and administrative changes, all of which Jenkins argued were matters belonging to the executive and/or legislative branches of government. These were not matters which pertained to the judicial branch, so Jenkins argued. This judicial activism, as Jenkins calls it, brought forward a set of positive or political rights not adopted by the legislature or by anyone in the executive branch. Jenkins was concerned that rights proliferation was taking place without due regard to the normal avenues for the development of these political rights, namely, the legislative and executive areas of the government. This forced Jenkins to defend only a theory of negative rights as applicable in judicial decisions, not positive rights. Jenkins, it appears, wanted to put some brakes on what he observed to be flagrant judicial activism.

The shadow of Ronald Dworkin hovers over much of this discussion on judicial activism. In his rights theory Dworkin suggests that judges must refer decisions to the major moral principles of the society. These principles in turn guarantee fundamental rights for individuals in the society. Jenkins wishes to put limits on the range of rights over which a judge might articulate a particular opinion in what Dworkin would call a 'hard case'.

In effect, Jenkins's argument entails that Dworkin's analysis of positive rights contained within the structure of the constitution has definite limits. Moreover, these are limits that Dworkin would not accept. More creative work needs to be undertaken in this area of rights theory. The development and articulation of a positive theory of rights is part of the fabric of modern American society. Both Jenkins and Dworkin appear to have brought to the discussion of rights theory an important set of concepts, one limiting while the other is more progressive. More serious thinking and analysis are required to forge ahead towards a resolution of this difficult bit of rights theory.

Given the analysis suggested in this book about the nature of Aquinas's theory of law, it does seem possible to derive a limited, broad set of positive rights from a dispositional account of human nature. Rights are based on the duties grounded in the developmental features of human essence. This is the Aquinian thrust into modern rights theory. Admittedly, this is but a mere sketch of the development. None the less, in rather broad strokes, one can derive an impression of how Aquinas's theory of natural law can be the source of a derivation of both natural and political rights, and with political rights, both positive and negative rights.

10

Concluding Comments: Prospects and Pitfalls for Natural Law Theory

A FEW items remain as this conceptual analysis of Thomas Aquinas's theory natural law forges ahead to its conclusion. Based on Aristotelian ethical theory, the argument advanced in this book suggests that Aquinas builds a natural law ethic by adopting the eudaimonistic meta-ethic of the *Nicomachean Ethics*. Within this Aristotelian framework, he develops his uniquely substantive natural law theory. In addition, the previous chapters offered suggestions about how Aquinas might respond to standard objections to ethical naturalism, especially those formulated in the mode, so common in analytic philosophy, of G. E. Moore's naturalistic fallacy. The importance of a thoroughly dispositional account of human nature has been discussed often in the preceding pages. This dispositional ontology is a necessary condition in elucidating an Aristotelian response both to analytic philosophers nurtured on Moore, the emotivists, and other non-cognitivists, and to existentialists groomed on Sartre and Camus. It also uses as a foil certain postmodernist claims suggesting the impossibility of ontological knowledge.

NATURAL LAW IN JURISPRUDENCE

Chapter 2 referred to several passages from jurisprudence scholars indicating their judgements that natural law theory was once again prominent in the philosophy of law. Martin Golding offered this observation in several places and Jeffrie Murphy and Jules Coleman asserted the same claim in both editions of their book, *The Philosophy of Law*. Chapter 2, however, also noted that often a claim of natural law indicates merely that the philosopher under discussion has used

moral principles in some form or other as a source or standard
against which the laws of a society are compared. Ronald Dworkin
wrote in this manner when considering natural law. The *explicatio
textus* of Aquinas's *Summa Theologiae* rendered above argues that the
adoption of moral principles alone is not a sufficient condition for
developing a natural law meta-ethical theory.

What is interesting about much contemporary work in jurisprudence is that frequently the use of moral principles is proposed as a
necessary condition for correct lawmaking. Ronald Dworkin's theory
of rights, for instance, depends heavily on a concept of moral principle. Chapter 2 indicated that Dworkin proposed the consideration
of moral principles as a necessary condition for a judge rendering a
decision in a so-called 'hard case'. Dworkin connects his theory of
rights with the moral principles rooted in the foundational claims
of the origin of a society, in particular, the United States Constitution. He argues that these moral principles as found in the constitution are the fundamental sources for individual human rights. This
political theory is often called liberal constitutionalism. In a manner
similar to that of natural law, Dworkin considers human rights as
based on moral principles, which are necessary in determining the
correctness of a legal decision. Of course, there are fundamental
differences between Dworkin and Aquinas. None the less, Dworkin's
serious work in the development of a consistent theory of rights –
and its acceptance by so many philosophers in the analytic tradition
of jurisprudence – has contributed significantly to a renewed interest
in naturalism. As a result, natural law theory can be proposed as an
alternative theory which might justify human rights. This is the
course taken by Henry Veatch in *Human Rights: Fact or Fancy?* and
John Finnis in *Natural Law and Natural Rights*. Dworkin's work,
arguing against the inherent weakness of any form of legal positivism, it would seem, has rendered natural law theory interesting
theoretically for jurisprudence. Of course, Dworkin rejects any form
of a thick theory of human nature which is a necessary condition for
Aquinas's account of natural law. Chapter 2 considered Dworkin's
unique analysis of the concept of 'naturalism'. Given the elucidation
of Aquinas's account of ethical naturalism in Chapter 4, it follows
that Dworkin's concept of naturalism is neither isomorphic with nor
coextensive with Aquinas's conditions for natural law explications.
In his *Defence of Natural Law*, Charles Covell notes the following
about the five philosophers of law considered in detail in his book

(Lon Fuller, F. A. Hayek, Michael Oakeshott, Ronald Dworkin, and John Finnis): 'with the exception of Finnis, none of the theorists looked back to the great Aristotelian-Thomist tradition in natural law philosophy'.[1]

In addition to Dworkin's work on rights theory, probably the two most significant influences in the renewed interest in natural law — both among philosophers and those primarily interested in jurisprudence — are the writings of Henry Veatch and John Finnis. The importance of their writings on contemporary natural law theory justifies their work being considered in separate chapters above. During the past decade, several conferences and sessions of regional and national philosophy meetings and a plethora of articles in philosophy journals have centred around the work of these two philosophers.

The work of Alasdair MacIntyre in Aristotelian meta-ethics certainly deserves a significant place in the structural chronology suggesting the re-emergence of natural law theory in contemporary philosophy. The insights and contributions of MacIntyre have been considered frequently in the preceding pages of this book. While saying rather little directly to issues in jurisprudence, MacIntyre's work has contributed immensely towards the development of Aristotelian ethical studies in the English-speaking world. His *After Virtue* marks a pivotal turning-point in the way a new generation of philosophers undertakes its work in meta-ethics. The term 'virtue ethics' is now almost a household word in philosophical circles, whereas before the 1981 publication of *After Virtue*, few philosophers took Aristotle's ethics seriously beyond a consideration of its historical role in Western thought.

In addition, the work of Martha Craven Nussbaum has contributed much towards a revitalization of studies in Aristotelian moral theory. Nussbaum's *Love's Knowledge* is a particularly informative account and articulate justification of Aristotelian practical reason. Using literary examples from the writings of Henry James, Nussbaum suggests that Aristotle's ethical analysis regarding what Aquinas calls 'contingent situations' is particularly useful for contemporary ethical studies.

The combined influences of Dworkin's jurisprudence, the reworking of natural law theory by Finnis and Veatch, MacIntyre's virtue

---

[1] Charles Covell, *The Defence of Natural Law* (New York: St Martin's Press, 1992), p. x.

ethics, and Nussbaum's work in practical reason and the literary connections with Aristotelian ethics, have all contributed towards establishing a renewed interest in Aristotelian and Aquinian meta-ethics. Given that Aquinas's adaption of Aristotle resulted in his natural law theory, the interest in various forms of Aquinian natural law has come along on the coat-tails of the work in Aristotle.

One result of this renewed interest in Aristotle's ethical naturalism and virtue ethics is that so much of the work objecting to natural law — especially as found in Aquinas — written since the middle part of this century now seems obsolete philosophically. That a paradigm shift has occurred in the way meta-ethics is undertaken is readily apparent. Hence, there is room now for much creative work to be undertaken in natural law theory, in normative ethics, in meta-ethics, and in jurisprudence. There is a need for philosophers to consider how best to elucidate the many issues central to contemporary natural law theory. Today Dworkin's worry expressed in his 1982 paper, 'Natural Law Revisited', that few philosophers of law want to be considered as adopting any form of natural law theory seems strangely out of date.

A SUBSTANTIVE THEORY

The re-emergence of natural law both in meta-ethics and in jurisprudence discussed in this book suggests that not only should more work be undertaken in these areas, but quite probably greater effort needs to be directed towards working out a substantive theory of natural law.

Yet there are pitfalls, especially historical ones, towards completing such an undertaking. As John Austin noted so long ago, one must be careful lest too close an association of law with morality lead to a repressive system of both law and morality. This concern has prompted the contractarians such as Rawls, Dworkin, and Nozick to defend at best a minimalist or 'thin' theory of human nature. This is in opposition theoretically to the so-called 'thick' theories of human nature necessary to analyse the natural law theory found in the writings of Aquinas. That Aquinas adopted a thick theory is a central theme determining the discussions of his theory of human nature begun in Chapter 4 and continued throughout this book. The contractarians reject any thick theory of human nature as being both incomprehensible theoretically and destructive practically of Enlightenment theory justifying freedom and liberty.

Given this concern, philosophically creative work in natural law theory needs to be undertaken with the following caveats:

1. A too close connection with theological requirements must be avoided.

Too often in the past, natural law theory — especially as developed from the writings of Aquinas — has been associated with conservative theological work, particularly in Roman Catholicism. The dependence of the arguments in the Roman Church's pronouncements against birth control — even quoting Aquinas as supporting evidence — is all too familiar. In the specific case of contraception, it can be argued, as Columba Ryan does, that Aquinas's theory does not offer support for a theological proscription in regard to a theoretical position on contraception.[2]

What is necessary in contemporary revisions of natural law is to read Aquinas's texts on moral theory as they appear in the *Summa Theologiae* and in the *Commentary on the Nicomachean Ethics*. Chapter 4 above attempts to articulate this argument conceptually and to offer an analytic *explicatio textus* of Aquinas's discussion. In natural law reconstructions, Aquinas's texts must be read philosophically and critically, and not theologically. In other words, theological positions should not be forced on to natural law theory as a means seeking a theoretical justification of a theological proposition. Historically, critics of natural law theory have often made this charge. While God certainly played an important role in the consistent explication of Aquinas's philosophical system, as Chapter 5 suggested, none the less the philosophical independence of his natural law theory can remain intact consistently and structurally. That this is a reconstruction of Aquinas is not to be denied; that this reconstruction is both possible and consistent is affirmed emphatically. This philosophical separation as developed in the reconstruction articulated in this book needs to be brought continually to the attention of readers generally unfamiliar with the Aquinian texts.

2. Contemporary natural kind ontology may be useful in articulating the metaphysical requirements for Aquinas's natural law moral theory. If the Kripke/Putnam model for natural kinds fails, however,

---

[2] Columba Ryan, 'The Traditional Concept of Natural Law', in Illtud Evans (ed.), *Light on the Natural Law* (Baltimore: Helicon Press, 1965), 22–3.

the Aristotelian/Aquinian account of essence as natural kind can still stand or fall on its own ontological grounds.

Chapter 4 suggested that a revived natural law jurisprudence and meta-ethics required a modified form of essence theory, one based upon a schema of dispositional properties. Chapter 8 suggested that recent metaphysical arguments explicating natural kind ontology may be used to assist the analysis of a metaphysics necessary for a natural law theory. As Yves Simon argued so well, without a concept of essence, natural law theory based on Aquinas's writings is inconsistent theoretically. Nominalism entails the demise of natural law moral theory. Given this demand, recent work in natural kind ontology appears to offer an avenue assisting in the development of natural law.

However, one needs to take account of some recent research indicating that possibly the structure of the argument for natural kinds in recent metaphysics such as that of Kripke and the earlier Putnam offers an analysis of essence not readily transformable to Aristotle and Aquinas. Earlier in this book, reference was made several times to Michael Ayers's article suggesting that the work of Kripke and Putnam is not that different conceptually and theoretically from that proposed by Aristotle. Chapter 8 noted the arguments of David Charles and Chenyang Li against this position. Charles's position, which is similar to Li's, is that contemporary natural kind ontology is not isomorphic with Aristotelian essence theory.

While it may be too early to come to terms definitively with the differences between contemporary natural kind ontology and Aristotelian and Aquinian essence theory, none the less some of the apparent similarities should not be too quickly dismissed. More work in the structural history of philosophy needs to be undertaken in this area of inquiry. For now, it is useful to offer a contemporary metaphysical analysis of natural kind ontology as a theoretical support for the defence of a theory of essence required for natural law theory. Natural kind essence theory in Aquinas, however, is not connected analytically with the Kripke/Putnam view of the 'rigid designation' of natural kinds. None the less, the analysis suggested by Christopher Martin on the similarities between Aquinas and recent metaphysics should not be overlooked. It is quite likely that recent work in metaphysics is more closely akin to Aquinas's ontology than some critics are wont to admit. Yet that argument needs to be articulated in more detail than has been undertaken in this book.

It is important to realize, however, that Aristotle and Aquinas are not discussing individual essences as such. In other words, Aquinas parts company with those contemporary philosophers who consider the concept of essence to refer only to an individual essence. While 'Peter', for instance, does have an essence, it is the essence as a set of constitutive properties which is shared with all members of the natural kind of human persons. The essence — the set of synthetic necessary properties — which makes an individual a member of a natural kind is what is important in Aristotelian and Aquinian philosophy. 'Matter' serves as the 'principle of individuation' for Aristotle and Aquinas, not an 'individuating essence'. That the individuating concept of *materia signata quantitate* cries out for analysis is not to be denied. None the less, that analysis too is beyond the scope of this discussion.

3. In rendering moral decisions, natural law moral theory always admits the radical contingency of the particular situation.

Natural law theory as established in Aristotle's *Nicomachean Ethics* and in Aquinas's *Summa Theologiae* has built-in limitations regarding its theoretical and practical consequences. It is very important that natural law theorists do not attempt to draw too much from the naturalist foundation for moral theory based on Aristotle and Aquinas. *Phronesis* and *prudentia* are moral concepts promoting non-rule-bound contingent situations for moral theory. Natural law theory as developed in this book is not an excessively rigid normative theory. There is a radical particularity in Aristotle and Aquinas involving moral situations that is opposed theoretically to the rule-bound directives of most post-Enlightenment moral theory. This is especially true of most rule deontological normative systems. Considering the particular action to be undertaken in a specific situation — what Aquinas often refers to as a 'contingent situation' — both Aristotle and Aquinas sound like existentialists lamenting against the strict constructionalism of rule-based theory. This radical contingency of Aristotelian and Aquinian moral theory should not be forgotten in the process of developing a consistent theory of natural law. What one has in this reconstructed account of Aquinas's natural law theory is a balanced account of existentialist subjectivity within the context of a dispositional theory of human nature.

In commenting upon Aquinas's *Summa Theologiae* text at I-II q. 94 a. 4, Columba Ryan suggests that one must call to mind two important claims:

1. To affirm a moral realism through natural law theory does not entail that every moral prescription must be clearly recognized by every human agent.
2. The general principles, while knowable and cognitive in nature, do not possess a rigidly universal application.[3]

Furthermore, Ryan suggests that 'human nature, upon which the whole fabric of the natural law is based, may change and develop ...' Given this, it follows, so Ryan suggests, that human agents, in confronting new situations (even those of human invention), may have 'new conclusions to draw from the general principles of natural law ... ' In addition, Ryan writes that '... conclusions earlier drawn may, in the changed circumstances, have no further application, or only a modified application'.[4]

Ryan emphasizes the contingent nature of moral decision-making within the context of natural law. Aquinas's moral theory expressed through his theory of natural law is far removed theoretically from the rule deontology put forward by Kantians, either traditional or modern.

It is useful to recall the passage Thomas Gilby offered from Aquinas's *Commentary on the Nicomachean Ethics* concerning the non-universalized character of natural law moral theory:

Disquisitions on general morality are not entirely trustworthy, and the ground becomes more uncertain when one wishes to descend to individual cases in detail. The factors are infinitely variable, and cannot be settled whether by art or precedent. Judgment should be left to the people concerned. Each must set himself to act according to the immediate situation and the circumstances involved. The decision may be unerring in the concrete, despite the uneasy debate in the abstract. Nevertheless, the moralist can provide some help and direction in such cases. (II lec. 2)

The radical particularity insisted upon by Aquinas for moral decision-making indicates once again the centrality of practical reason which he adopts from Aristotle's moral theory. Aquinas's theory of natural law is much more congruent with Aristotle's position on the contingency of moral judgements than many historians of philosophy are wont to admit. Aquinas is neither a theological definist nor an excessive rule deontologist in his analysis. Practical

[3] Ryan, 'The Traditional Concept', 30.
[4] Ibid. 32.

reason exercised through *prudentia* is always dependent upon the circumstances of the individual situation.

Often this book suggested the theoretical differences between Aristotelian and Aquinian moral theory on the one hand and Enlightenment and post-Enlightenment moral theory, especially in the Kantian tradition, on the other. MacIntyre has argued this point forcefully in *After Virtue*, especially in his discussion of the function view attributed to Aristotle and Aquinas. In many ways, as both Veatch and McInerny have indicated, contemporary meta-ethics must rid itself of its Cartesian slumbers and its dependence on the transcendental turn before it can consider anew Aristotelian moral theory. Nussbaum also is very critical of what she takes to be the limits endemic to Enlightenment moral theory. In his *The Tradition of Natural Law*, Simon argues in much the same way. Chapter 7 indicated briefly Gilson's worries about the radical opposition between Cartesian and Kantian metaphilosophy on the one hand, and Aristotelian and Aquinian metaphilosophy on the other. Aquinian metaphilosophy, what Gilson referred to as *le méthode thomiste*, is realist, non-Kantian, non-empiricist in the Humean sense, and separated conceptually from postmodernism.

The arguments expressed in this book have been in general agreement with the position suggesting the break with Enlightenment moral theory. Both what McInerny calls 'modernity' based on Cartesian metaphilosophy and what Veatch calls 'the transcendental turn' based on Kantian method, render natural law meta-ethics theoretically impossible.

One must not forget one crucial issue, however. Enlightenment philosophy has given Western liberal constitutional democracies its fundamental theory of individual rights. Rights theory is an important part of the development of Western thought. The proper elucidation of a theory of individual and social rights within the context of Aquinian moral theory is an indispensable project. On this matter, Covell notes: 'The mentalities of Fuller, Oakeshott, Hayek, Dworkin, and Finnis were shaped by the great intellectual conflict between the philosophy of liberal constitutionalism of the West and the various ideologies of totalitarianism which cast their shadow over the political culture of the modern world throughout most of the twentieth century.'[5]

While committed to the founding principles of Western liberal democracy, Dworkin and Finnis — and Fuller, Hayek, and Oakeshott too — argue that the moral foundations of liberal constitutional democracy are never reducible to a jurisprudence of legal positivism alone.

MacIntyre suggests that rights theory, as part of Enlightenment moral theory, can be dispensed with. He argues that a modified Aristotelianism congruent with the standards of rigour espoused by contemporary moral philosophy can handle the issues normally treated — and protected — through a theory of human rights. Earlier in this century, many Marxist philosophers argued against the possibility of developing a theory of rights. Dworkin, in particular, has offered rebuttals to the Marxists. Recently, some feminist philosophers of law and postmodern deconstructionists have rejected rights theory. Often these arguments are against the Enlightenment project justifying rights.

Veatch also argued, as indicated in Chapter 9, that Aristotelian moral theory can justify only a modest system of negative rights. The positive rights common to liberal democracies, according to Veatch and Iredell Jenkins, appear to lack justification. While justification of rights theory is important — few would accept McCloskey's position that the only justification for individual rights is through intuition and 'self-justification' — it is necessary that natural law theorists develop an adequate account of rights sufficient to be compatible with liberal democracy. The natural law theory is not based on the themes of Enlightenment philosophy, especially as developed by Kant. Hence, an interesting dialectic needs to take place between the natural law philosophers and those philosophers adopting differing strands of the postmodernist enterprise.

Chapter 9 attempted a brief analysis of this issue. That development is a beginning at best. The fundamental problem is to elucidate a consistent theory of both positive and negative rights based upon the concept of a human person. This theoretical development cannot be God-centred — as too often appears in Aquinian philosophers like Maritain. In addition, only a modest metaphysical theory should be developed upon which to base and justify human rights. This book

[5] Covell, *Defence of Natural Law*, p. xvii.

proposed that the theory needed, as elaborated in Chapters 4 and 5, would be a modest dispositional metaphysics of natural kinds.

The development of such a theory of rights would have the advantage of possessing an important content dimension. Moral and legal theory would not be reducible to either formalism or proceduralism. This would move beyond the prevalent objections brought against Dworkin and Rawls suggesting that unwanted conclusions are derivable from their respective theories. In a similar case found in his *Freedom and Reason*, Hare could not refute theoretically the 'moral fanatic'. This kind of problem is all too prevalent with the good-reasons approaches to moral and legal theory. In principle, a natural law theory rooted in the analysis of human nature provides a theoretical opportunity to propose and to justify a rejoinder to something like Hare's 'moral fanatic'.

What must be developed, therefore, is a substantive theory of human rights which goes beyond the limits of Dworkin and Rawls yet does not force the authoritarian repression of individuals in the name of — or under the guise of — ontological theories of the good. The modifications to Aquinas's analysis of natural law moral theory elucidated in Chapter 9 suggest that natural law theory may offer a 'window of opportunity' towards resolving this kind of objection. Some recent suggestions put forward by Martha Nussbaum on reconsidering Aristotelian political theory point in this direction.

PROSPECTS FOR NATURAL LAW THEORY

One fascinating aspect of current work in natural law theory is the blending of insights and analysis from various fields: history of philosophy, contemporary metaphysics, jurisprudence, existential psychology, philosophical anthropology, and political philosophy. All contribute to the development of a coherent meta-ethics of natural law. This interdisciplinary work, while fragmented at times, offers insights into the development of natural law theory. The philosophical thrust of this book is to move this interdisciplinary project forward.

The role of what Anscombe referred to as moral psychology becomes increasingly important as one develops natural law moral theory. Based upon a modest faculty psychology, natural law theory has the concept of 'functioning well' — Aristotle's *eudaimonia* — as the end process of human development. The concept of 'self-actualization' common to recent psychological theory, especially in the writings of Carl Rogers, provides interesting structural connections with Aristotelian moral theory. The exact role of the connections between psychologists like Rogers and Aristotelian moral theory demands more scholarly attention. This work should provide insights towards fulfilling the gaps in contemporary moral theory which Anscombe pointed out thirty years ago.

Natural law theory as reconstructed in the analysis put forward in this book provides a modest degree of substantive content for moral theory. Earlier chapters have suggested the problems with lack of content which most contemporary moral theories in the analytic tradition have faced, from intuitionism through emotivism to the good-reasons approaches. Natural law theory based on the self-development role of human nature offers a modest means to provide content for meta-ethical theory. In Chapter 3, Warnock's criticism of the good-reasons moral theories was discussed. Natural Law meta-ethics suggests a resolution to the problem Warnock raised. Cruelty is wrong, according to the natural law moral theory, because cruel actions strike at the human dispositional properties on the sensitive level and on the living level. Cruelty is not wrong only because we 'decide' to be against it. Cruelty violates a natural right to self-protection which is grounded in duty, itself founded upon the dispositional properties determining the content of human nature. This example indicates clearly why a theory of the human person rooted in a dispositional ontology of essence is an important foil against which to bring the weaknesses of a good-reasons theory.

Chapter 9 suggested a modest theoretical account developing a rights theory for natural law theory. This issue demands attention by natural law philosophers. Both Finnis and Veatch attempt to work through this issue. However, the work requires more attention by philosophers in the natural law tradition, especially given the fundamental metaphilosophical differences between Finnis and Veatch. In particular, the development of a consistent theory of positive rights in accord with Aquinas's natural law theory is fundamentally important.

This book closes with suggestions of the work still needing attention in the revival of natural law theory. The renewal of naturalism in moral theory in the late twentieth century has brought much enthusiastic discussion to the philosophical and legal communities.

Philosophers of meta-ethics and of law can expect the theoretical excitement to remain lively as the issues suggested by virtue ethics continue to be addressed.

APPENDIX I

The Texts of Aquinas on Law

Questions 90 to 97 in the *Summa Theologiae*, I-II, have often been referred to as the classical canon for natural law philosophical thinking. This present translation is based upon the Leonine edition (Thomas Gilby (ed.), Blackfriars, 28). The translation contained here, while it has been specifically rendered and edited for this book, none the less is dependent upon the insights of Father Gilby's translation and also the earlier translation by the English Dominicans under the general editorship of Father Shapcote. The author also consulted the generally excellent translation by Paul Sigmund in his *St. Thomas on Politics and Ethics* and the thoughtful rendition of the *Summa Theologiae* recently undertaken by Timothy McDermott. Whatever inaccuracies remain are due entirely to the author.

The following edited translation contains only the body of each article and omits the objections and responses as found in the original. This is primarily on account of space limitations. The translation is rather literal and, for the most part, depends heavily on an exact rendering of the Latin text. Hence, the fluidity of the Gilby translation is not present here. None the less, it is an attempt to be as literal as possible while rendering the Latin into meaningful contemporary English prose suitable for a philosophical text.

Translation of the *Summa Theologiae*, I-II, qq. 90–7

CONSIDERATIONS ON LAW

First of all, it is necessary to consider the general nature of law. Secondly, one must consider the various parts of law.

In considering the general nature of law, three things must be discussed: (1) the essence of law; (2) the different kinds of law; (3) the effects of law.

Question 90: On the Essence of Law

There are four issues to be considered here: (1) law and its relation to reason; (2) the end of law; (3) the cause of law; (4) the promulgation of law.

Article 1: Is law something pertaining to reason?

I suggest that the purpose of law is to prescribe and to prohibit. However, to command is something pertaining to reason, as was stated above (q. 17 a. 1). Therefore, law is something connected with reason.

The Statement of the Position: It has been argued that law itself is a certain rule and measure of human acts, according to which a human person chooses to act or is restrained from acting. It should be noted that law itself is derived from the Latin term, *ligare*, which means 'to bind'; hence, law itself obliges one to undertake certain actions. Now it is the case that the rule and measure of human actions is reason, which is the first principle of human actions, as we argued above (q. 1 a. 1 ad. 3). It should be remembered that the function of reason is to order or direct to an end; this is the first principle in undertaking actions according to the philosophy of Aristotle. It is the case that whatever is the first principle of any genus whatsoever is also the measure and rule of that genus. For example, unity in the genus of numbers and first movement in the genus of motion. From this it follows that law itself is something which pertains to reason.

Article 2: Is law something which is always directed to the common good?

I suggest that one should consider the following passage from Isidore, who once argued that 'law is never for the private profit, but is always commanded for the sake of the common good of the citizens' (*Etymologiae*, 5. 21).

The Statement of the Position: In the previous question, I argued that law is something that pertains to the principle of human acts. Because of its very nature, law is a rule and a measure. In so far as reason is the principle of human acts, so also is reason itself something which is the principle with respect to all other matters pertaining to human acts. Hence, to this principle it follows that everything else which pertains principally and especially to law must follow. Now it is the case that the first principle in undertaking activities – which we call practical reason – is the ultimate end. Now the ultimate end in human life, as we argued above (q. 2 a. 7; q. 3 a. 1) is *happiness* or *well-being* (*felicitas vel beatitudo*). It follows necessarily, therefore, that law in a special way must consider the order of actions towards happiness or well-being.

Moreover, since each part is ordained to the whole as the imperfect is ordered to the perfect, and since each human person is a part of the perfect community, it follows that law properly considered must consider the order to the common well-being of the community. It is the case that Aristotle, in considering the definition of legal matters, mentions both human well-being and the well-being of the political entity or *polis*. Aristotle writes in the *Ethics*, 5, that 'we call those legal matters just which have been made and are conserved in order to take care of the well-being both of individuals themselves and also of the political community or *polis*'. Recall that Aristotle argues that the *polis* (*civitas*) is a perfect community, as he writes in the *Politics*, 1.

In any genus whatsoever, that which belongs to it in a special or first way is the principle of all the others. Other matters in this genus are dependent upon the first principle in some way or other. In physics, for example, it is argued that fire, which is principally hot, is the cause of hotness in composite bodies; composite bodies are said to be hot in so far as they have fire. Therefore, since law of itself is said to be chiefly that which regards the order to the common good, any action or undertaking which is directed towards a specific or particular work lacks the definition of law unless it is ordered to the common good.

Therefore, I argue that each law of its very nature is ordered to the common good.

Article 3: Can any person whatsoever go about the process of making laws?

I suggest that we recall what Isidore once wrote: 'A law is an ordinance of the people according to which those in power (through birth) ordain something in conjunction with the citizens' (*Etymologiae*, 5. 10). Therefore, it is not the case that just any person whatsoever can go about the process of making a law.

The Statement of the Position: Law itself properly and principally is directed towards the common good. It must be argued, therefore, that to order something for the common good belongs either to the province of the whole body politic or to some person (the 'vicegerent') for the collected body of the people. Therefore, it follows that the making of a law pertains either to the entire multitude of the people or to a public person who in some way or other has care for the community. This is the case because, as in all other things, to be ordered to an end is proper to the person who has a direct concern for that end.

Article 4: Is it necessary that a law be promulgated?

I suggest that, as we find written in the *Decretum* [a work of canon law published in Bologna in 1141 by Master Gratian, a Camaldolese monk], 'a law is established only when it has been promulgated'.

The Statement of the Position: I intend to argue, as I suggested above (a. 1), that a law is imposed on others through the mode of rule and measure. However, a rule and measure is imposed through the process of being applied to those things which are to be ruled or measured. Hence, in order for a law to have binding force, which indeed is proper to a law, it is necessary that law be applied to all human persons who ought to be ruled by it. However, such an application comes about only through the people being notified about the law, which is the purpose of promulgation. Therefore it follows that promulgation itself is a necessary condition in order that a law have binding force.

From what I have put forward in the four preceding articles, I propose the following definition of law. Law of its very nature is an ordinance of reason for the common good which is made by the person who has care of the community, and this rule is promulgated.

Question 91: The Different Kinds of Law.

It is now time to consider the different kinds of law. There are six issues to be addressed: (1) eternal law; (2) natural law; (3) human or positive law; (4) divine law; (5) is divine law one or many?; and (6) the law of sin.

Article 1: Eternal law

I suggest that we recall Augustine, who once wrote that 'law is the supreme reason and must be named as that which is understood to be unchangeable and eternal' (*De Libero Arbitrio*, 1. 6).

The Statement of the Position: I suggested earlier that law indeed is a dictate of practical reason coming from the person who has charge of a perfect community (*polis*). It is obvious, however, if we suppose that the world is ruled by divine providence (as I argued in the first part of the *Summa Theologiae*) then the whole of the universe is governed by divine reason. Thus I suggest that the very idea of the governing of all things in God as the origin of the universe belongs to the principle of existing under law. Furthermore, because divine reason is never conceived under the concept of time, but falls under the concept of eternity (as the Proverbs argue), it is necessary, therefore, that we call this kind of law 'eternal'.

Article 2: Natural law

I suggest that we consider the specific gloss on the Epistle to the Romans which goes like this: 'When the Gentiles, who do not have the law, by nature do those kinds of things which are of the law, it follows that although they do not have a written law, none the less, they have a natural law, by which they understand those things and are conscious of them which are said to be good and evil.'

The Statement of the Position: As I suggested earlier, a law, which is a rule and a measure, can be found in a person in two ways. The first way would be in the person who is doing the ruling and the measuring, and the second way would be in the person or thing which is ruled or measured, in so far as the person shares in that which is the rule or the measure or the ruled and the measured. Thus all things which are subordinated to divine providence and are ruled by the eternal law are ruled and measured, as I suggested in the preceding article. It is obvious that everything participates in some way or another in the eternal law. This is so because everything participates in the eternal law in so far as it has certain inclinations or dispositions which come from the idea of the eternal law. This concerns the proper acts and ends of each particular being. Uniquely among all things in creation, however, a rational creature – a human person – participates in a more excellent way in so far as a person participates in divine providence because a person provides both for himself and for others. Thus, in its very nature, a human person participates in the eternal reason through which each person has a natural inclination towards deriving its proper act and end; this participation of the eternal law in a rational creature or a human being is called the 'natural law'.

We find that the author of the Psalms, after saying (P. 4: 6) that one should 'offer the sacrifice of justice', as if someone would ask, 'What are the works of justice?' wrote 'Many say, who will show us what are the good things to be done?' To this question the Psalmist responds 'the light of your will, O Lord, is signed upon on us'. This suggests that the light of natural reason by which we discern that which is good and that which is evil is that which pertains to the natural law, and this is nothing other than the impression of the divine light in us as human beings.

Hence it is obvious that the natural law is nothing other than the participation of the eternal law in the rational creature or human being.

Article 3: Human law

I suggest that in Augustine one discovers two kinds of law posited: eternal law and temporal law, and he referred to temporal law as human law.

The Statement of the Position: I suggest, as I indicated above, that law is a certain dictate of practical reason. Furthermore, I suggest that a similar process or procedure is to be found in both practical reason and speculative reason. Both proceed from certain principles and go towards arriving at certain conclusions, as I suggested earlier. Accordingly, it follows that in the speculative reason, from indemonstrable (self-evident) first principles naturally known are derived the conclusions of the specific sciences – whose knowledge is not known to us naturally but must be discovered by the disciplined inquiry of our reason; in a similar manner, from the precepts of natural law, as from certain common and indemonstrable principles, it is necessary that the human reason proceed towards making certain things more specific and determined.

These particular determinations put forward by the human reason are called 'human laws'. None the less, they must observe the conditions which pertain to the very idea of law itself, as I suggested above (q. 90 aa. 2–4). Hence we find that Tully says in his *Rhetoric* that 'the beginning point of justice is found in nature. Hence certain things come into being because of their utility. Afterwards these things which came forward from nature were sanctioned as law because of fear and a certain reverence.'

Article 4: The necessity of divine law

I suggest that we recall that David expected a law from God and prayed to Him saying in the Psalm: 'Do give me a law, O Lord, that I might see the way of your justification' (P. 118: 33).

The Statement of the Position: I suggest that in addition to the natural law and the human law, it is necessary that we have a divine law for the direction of human life. And I make this suggestion on account of four reasons. The first reason follows from the fact that through law, a human person is ordered through specific actions to the ultimate end. And if indeed a human person is ordered to such an end which does not go beyond the natural proportion of the human faculty, it is not necessary that a human being have any directive on the part of reason beyond what is postulated and derived from human and natural law. However, because a human person is ordained to the ultimate well-being of eternal life, which indeed does exceed the natural proportion of human reason, as I suggested above, it is therefore necessary that, in addition to the natural law and the human law, a human person should be directed towards her proper end as given by divine law.

Secondly, because there is always an unclarity and lack of certitude in human judgements, especially on contingent and particular matters, it follows that different human beings will make different judgements about different kinds of actions; it sometimes happens that not only diverse but sometimes contrary laws come about. Therefore, so that a human person might be free from all doubt about that which must be done and that which must be avoided, it is necessary that in the matter of right actions, a human being should be directed by being given a divine law, from which law one is not able to go astray.

Thirdly, it is the case that a human being is able to make a law only about those things concerning which she is able to judge. However, human judgement is never able to consider the realm of interior acts or intentions, which are hidden, but only to consider those exterior actions which are apparent and obvious to the senses. However, in order to reach the perfection of virtue which is required, it is necessary that a human person have rectitude in both kinds of actions — that is, interior and exterior. Therefore, human law is not able to curb or restrict and direct sufficiently the interior acts or intentions. Hence, it is necessary that, in order to cover these types of matters, a divine law be instituted.

Fourthly, Augustine once wrote that human law is not able to prohibit or punish every evil that might come about. This is the case because while doing away with certain evil events, it would follow also that many good things would be done away with, and this would directly impede the common good which is necessary for human discussion and well-being. Thus, so that no evil might go unprohibited or unpunished, it is necessary that a divine law come about so that everything which is sinful might be prohibited.

[Article 5 discusses what Aquinas considered to be the old law and the new law, and article 6 is a discussion of the *fomes pecati*. The latter is a discussion about the effects of original sin. Both articles are omitted in this translation.]

Question 92: The Effects of Law

It is now time to consider the effects of law, about which two points need to be discussed: (1) whether the effect of law is to help make human beings good; (2) whether the effect of law is to command, to forbid, to permit, and to punish, as Justinian wrote in the *Digest*.

Article 1: Whether the effect of law is to make human beings good

I suggest that, as Aristotle writes in his *Ethics* (2. 1): 'The will of any legislator is to make human beings good.'

The Statement of the Position: I have written above (q. 90 aa. 3–4) that law is nothing other than a dictate of reason in the person governing through which those subject to the ruling are to be governed. Now the strength of any person who is subject to the law is that the person is well subjected to the law by which the person is governed. For example, virtue, when applied to the irascible and the concupiscible appetites, occurs when these appetites are well ordered and obedient to reason. And in this manner, as Aristotle writes in his *Politics*, 'the virtue of any subject consists in the subject being well ruled by the person who is in charge of governing'.

Every law is such that it is ordained so that it might be obeyed by those who are subject to it. Whence it is obvious that the proper role of law is to lead those subjected to it to their proper virtue. Therefore, because virtue of its very nature is what makes human agents acquire good, it follows that a proper effect of law is to make those good for whom it is given, either in itself or accidentally (*vel simpliciter vel secundum quid*).

Therefore, if the intention of the person making the law is directed towards attaining the human good, which is the common good according to the regulation of divine justice, it follows that human beings can be made good *simpliciter* through law. If the true intention of the legislator is to bring about that which is not good in and of itself (*simpliciter*), but rather what is useful or pleasurable to the legislator, or which is repugnant to the scope of divine justice, then the law does not make human beings good *simpliciter*, but accidentally (*secundum quid*), namely in the order of this particular government. However, a good is found even in something which is evil in and of itself — for example, a person might be called a 'good' robber, because the act of robbing itself is directed towards some end or other. [NB: The robber is called 'good' because the robber has acquired a certain skill to accomplish something with ease; this, of course, is not the 'moral' sense of good, but rather working towards an end.]

Article 2: Whether the acts of law are suitably determined (that is, are there four acts of law?)

I suggest that we recall what Isidore has written: 'Every law either permits something, as for example a brave person may claim his reward; or the law forbids something, for example a woman consecrated to God may not legitimately be sought in marriage; or the law punishes something, for example a person who commits murder may be subject to capital punishment' (*Etymologias*, 5. 19).

The Statement of the Position: I suggest that, just as a proposition is a statement of reason for the purpose of enunciating or describing, so also a law comes about through the mode of commanding. However, it is proper to reason to command from one thing to the other. Just as in the demonstrative sciences, reason leads through certain principles in order that the conclusion might be assented to, so also the reason leads in order that the command of the law towards something might also be assented to.

However, the precepts of law are directed towards human actions in which the law directs, as I discussed above (q. 90, 91). Now there are three different kinds of human actions, as I suggested above (q. 18 a. 8). Some acts are good of their very nature, for example acts of virtue. In respect of these kinds of actions, the act of the law is to prescribe or command; for every law prescribes virtuous actions, as Aristotle suggested in the *Ethics*, 5, 1. On the other hand, some acts are of themselves evil, being considered an act of vice. The law must forbid these kinds of actions. Also, certain kinds of actions of their very nature are indifferent, and the law permits these kinds of actions. All those actions are called indifferent which are either of a little good or of a little evil.

The fear of punishment is what law uses to induce obedience; and thus to render punishment is an effect of the law.

LAW CONSIDERED IN MORE DETAIL

We must now examine each kind of law in and of itself: first of all, the eternal law (q. 93); secondly, the natural law (q. 94); thirdly, the human law (q. 95–7); fourthly, the old law (q. 98–105); fifthly, the new law (q. 106–8), which is the law of the Gospel; sixthly, concerning the law of concupiscence. I discussed this topic adequately when writing about original sin.

Question 93: The Eternal Law

Concerning the eternal law, there are six articles which need to be considered: (1) What is the eternal law? (2) Whether it is known by everybody; (3) Whether every law is derived from the eternal law; (4) Whether necessary matters are subject to the eternal law; (5) Whether natural contingent matters are subjected to the eternal law; and (6) Whether all human affairs are subjected to the eternal law?.

Article 1: Whether the eternal law should be considered as a supreme exemplar or divine idea existing in God

I suggest that we pay attention to what Augustine said when he wrote that 'the eternal law is the highest exemplar (*summa ratio*), to which one must always conform' (*De Libero Arbitrio*, 1. 6).

The Statement of the Position: I suggest that we consider how in any case of an art, there pre-exists a certain exemplar or pattern of that which is to be constructed through the art; so also in every person who is governing, it is necessary that there pre-exists some exemplar or structure of order of those things which are to be undertaken by the persons who are subject to the governor. Thus, for example, just as the structure or pattern of the things to be made through an art is called an art — or an exemplar of the things to be made — so also the pattern of governing the acts of those subjected to the governor holds for the *ratio* (structure) of law, provided the other conditions are present, which we discussed above about the nature of law (q. 90).

Now God, through His wisdom, is the creator of all things. In the first part of this treatise (I q. 14 a. 8) I have written that in the matter of those things created, God should be considered as having the relationship of artist to object of art. For God is the governor, as it were, of all actions and motions which are found in every creature, as I have written in an earlier part of this *Summa* (I q. 103 a. 5). Whence also the structure of divine wisdom, in so far as through it all created things have indeed been created, has the *ratio*, (or an 'exemplar' or an 'idea') of an art, so also the *ratio* of divine wisdom moving and ordering all things to their appropriate end brings about the structure or *ratio* of a law. Therefore I suggest that in this analysis, eternal law is nothing other than the *ratio* of divine wisdom, through which is directed every action and motion.

Article 2: Whether the eternal law is known by everybody?

I suggest that once again we refer to Augustine who has written that 'an awareness of the eternal law has been imprinted on us' (*De Libero Arbitrio*, 1. 6).

The Statement of the Position: I suggest that any matter might be considered in two ways: the first way is the thing in itself; the second way is through its effect in which are found some similarities from it. For example, any one of us might not see the sun in its own essence, but we could know it through its rays of light. In a like manner, therefore, I suggest that no one is able to understand the eternal law according to what it is in itself, but only God himself and the blessed who now see God through His essence. On the contrary, every rational creature is able to know about the eternal law through its reflection, either a large reflection or a smaller reflection.

I suggest the above because every knowledge of truth is in some way a reflection or participation of the eternal law, which is unchangeable truth, as Augustine has written. Now I suggest that every human person in some way or other knows the truth, at least in so far as it relates to the common principles of natural law. In other matters, truly they participate more or less in a knowledge of the truth; and because of this, they know more or less about the eternal law.

Article 3: Whether every law is derived from the eternal law?

I suggest that we recall what the Book of Proverbs says about divine wisdom: 'Through me the kings rule, and the makers of the laws determine the just matters' (Prov. 8: 15). I wrote above that the *ratio* of divine wisdom is the eternal law. Therefore each law proceeds from the eternal law.

The Statement of the Position: I wrote above (q. 90, aa. 1–2) that a law entails a certain *ratio* in some way directing human actions towards an end. In ordaining every action, it is necessary that the strength of the secondary movers be derived in some way from the strength of the first mover; this is so because the secondary mover cannot move at all except in so far as it is moved by the first. I suggest that we see the same occurrence in all matters pertaining to government, because the *ratio* of governing is derived from the first person in charge to the subordinates. For example, the reason for which things are done in a city state is derived through the command from the king in those administrative matters of a lesser degree; likewise in matters of art, the *ratio* of the thing to be made through the art is derived from the chief artist or architect to the subordinate craft people who work with their hands.

Since, therefore, the eternal law is the *ratio* of governing by the supreme governor, it is necessary that every pattern of governing which is found in the governing of the subordinates is derived from the eternal law. The patterns of the subordinate governors, however, are such that their laws are not identifiable with the eternal law. Hence, each law in so far as it participates in right reason is thus derived from the eternal law. On this matter, Augustine wrote as follows: 'In temporal law, nothing is just nor legitimate which human beings do not derive from the eternal law.' (*De Libero Arbitrio*, 1. 6).

Article 4: Whether necessary and eternal matters are subjected to the eternal law

I suggest that in considering those things which are necessary, it is impossible for them to be otherwise, and hence necessary matters do not need to be restrained. On the contrary, however, a law is imposed upon human beings in order that it may restrain humans from evil, as I suggested above. Therefore, those matters which are necessary are not found under the rubric of law.

The Statement of the Position: I argued above (a. 1) that the eternal law is the *ratio* of the divine rule of matters. Therefore, it follows that any matter which is subjected to the divine governance is also subjected to the eternal law. Also, anything which is not subjected to the divine governance is accordingly not subjected to eternal law.

How this distinction is applied can be seen from those things which are found around us. For those matters are subjected to human governance which are able to be undertaken by human beings. What truly pertains to the nature of human beings, however, is not subjected to human governance; for example, that a human being ought to have a soul, or hands, or feet. Therefore, it follows that everything which has been created by God in the created world is subjected to the eternal law, either those matters which are contingent or those matters which are necessary. Truly, however, those things which pertain to the divine nature or the divine essence are not subjected to the eternal law, but rather are indeed the eternal law itself.

Article 5: Whether natural contingent matters are subsumed under the eternal law

I suggest that one should refer to the Book of Proverbs where it is found: 'When he set up his limits for the sea, and placed his law on the water, lest they pass their ends' (Prov. 8: 29).

The Statement of the Position: I argue that it is one thing to consider human law and another thing to consider the eternal law, which is the law of God. For I suggest that a human law only extends to rational creatures, which are subjected in some way to the person making the law. The reason for this is that law is a directive for human actions which is appropriate only to those who are subjects of the person giving the action. Whence, it follows that no one, strictly speaking, can impose a law on his own actions. However, whenever something is done concerning irrational matters which are subjected to a human being, they are done through the act of the human person himself moving those things. For it is the case that an irrational thing in and of itself is not able to act for itself but only acts from another, as I suggested above (q. 1 a. 2). Thus it follows that a human being is not able to impose a law on irrational things, even though they might be subjected to the human person in some way or another. However, a human person is able to impose a law on rational beings in some way subject to the agent in so far as by his command or declaration, of any kind, he imprints on their minds a certain rule which is a principle of actions to be undertaken. However, just as a human agent through the process of commanding imprints a certain principle of action on a person subject to him, so also God imprints on the whole of nature the principles of its proper action. Therefore, in this way, God is said to command the whole of nature, as we find written in the Book of Psalms, 'He has given a command and this command will not pass away' (Ps. 148: 6). And therefore through this reason, every action and motion of the whole of nature is subjected to the eternal law. Hence, in the same manner, irrational creatures are subjected to the eternal law in so far as they are moved by divine providence. Irrational creatures, however, do not act from an understanding of the divine precepts, which is the province of rational creatures.

Article 6: Whether all human matters are subject to the eternal law

I suggest that we remember what Augustine wrote in the *City of God*: 'In no way does anything avoid the laws and ordinations of the highest creature, from which the peace of the entire universe is constructed' (19. 12).

The Statement of the Position: I argued above that the manner through which something is subjected to eternal law should be considered in a twofold way. The first way is in so far as something participates in eternal law through the mode of knowledge. The second way is the mode or manner of action and passion, in so far as something participates through the manner of an internal principle of motion. Irrational creatures are subjected to the eternal law in this second way, as I argued above (a. 5). However, because a rational nature has something in common with all other creatures, but also has something which is proper to itself in so far as it is rational, it follows that a rational creature is subject to the eternal law according to both modes. This is so because each rational creature has some knowledge of the eternal law in some way or another, as I argued above (a. 2); furthermore, it pertains to every rational creature to have a natural inclination to that which is consonant with the eternal law. Aristotle writes in the *Ethics* (2 1) that 'We have an innate disposition towards acquiring the virtues.'

However, I suggest that both modes or manners are in a certain way imperfect and somewhat corrupt in persons habitually undertaking evil actions. In evil persons, the natural inclination towards virtue is destroyed through the habitual undertaking of vicious actions, and likewise the natural knowledge itself to the good is darkened in them through their passions and habits towards undertaking that which is sinful or evil. In good persons, however, both modes or manners are found in a more perfect state because, beyond the natural knowledge of the good, there is found in a supervenient way a knowledge of that which is good coming from faith and wisdom. And beyond the natural inclination towards the good, there supervenes the interior motive for them given by grace and virtue. It follows, therefore, that good persons are perfectly subjected to the eternal law, in so far as they are always acting in accord with it. Bad persons, on the other hand, are subjected in a certain way to the eternal law, but in an imperfect way regarding their actions, in so far as they know the good imperfectly and are imperfectly inclined to the good. However, this defect on the part of undertaking actions comes from the passions, namely in so far as they suffer what the eternal law tells them to do because what they undertake is deficient regarding what the eternal law prescribes. Hence, Augustine wrote in his book on free will: 'I believe that the just undertake actions under the prescript of the eternal law. . . . ' (*De Libero Arbitrio*, 1. 15).

Question 94: The Natural Law

We must now consider the nature and scope of natural law, about which one might ask six questions: (1) Whether there is a natural law; (2) Whether there are precepts for the natural law; (3) Whether every act of virtue belongs to the natural law; (4) Whether the natural law is one for all human beings; (5) Whether the natural law is changeable; and (6) Whether the natural law can be deleted from the human mind.

Article 1: Is natural law a habit

I suggest that we recall what Augustine wrote in his treatise, *De Bono Conjugali*: 'A habit is that by which something is done when necessary.' However, the natural law is not of this kind for it is even in small children and those who are damned, who are not able to act through it. Therefore the natural law is not a habit.

The Statement of the Position: I suggest that something can be called a habit in two ways. In the first way, which is proper and essential; and in this way a natural law is not a habit. As I said above (q. 90 a. 1 ad. 2), natural law is something constructed through reason just as a proposition is in some way a work of reason. However it must be noted that that which somebody undertakes and that by which someone undertakes an action are not the same things. For instance, a person acts through the habit of grammar and makes a grammatically correct speech. Therefore, because a habit is that by which somebody acts, it is not the case that law is a habit properly and essentially.

In a second way, however, it might be said that something is a habit when it is held in such a way that is similar to a habit; for example, when we say that faith is that which is held by the faith. In like manner, the precepts of natural law sometimes are consciously in an act from reason, while other times they are in reason in a habitual way; in this second way, it can be said that natural law might be a habit. In a similar way, the indemonstrable principles found in a speculative science are not the very habit itself of the principles, but they are the principles of those things which indeed are the habit.

Article 2: Does the natural law contain several precepts or only one

We should recall that the precepts of natural law in human persons are directly related to practical matters. In like manner, first principles are related to matters of demonstration. Since there are several first indemonstrable principles, so too must there be several precepts of natural law.

The Statement of the Position: I suggest that the precepts of natural law are related to practical reason in the same manner that the fundamental principles of demonstrations are related to speculative (theoretical) reason. Both are sets of self-evident principles.

A principle is called 'self-evident' in two senses. In one way, objectively, and in another way as relative to us as knowers. A proposition is 'objectively self-evident' if its predicate is contained within the concept of the subject. However, if someone does not know the concept (intelligibility) of the subject, such a proposition will not be self-evident. For example, the proposition, 'Humans are rational,' when taken in itself is self-evident, because to say 'human' is to say 'rational'. None the less, if a person does not know the conceptual significance of 'human', this proposition would not be self-evident to that person. Therefore, as Boethius argues in his *De Hebdomadibus*, there are certain axioms or propositions which are generally self-evident to everyone. In this category are propositions whose terms every person understands. For example, 'Every whole is greater than its parts,' and 'Two things equal to a third are equal to one another.' However, there are some propositions which are self-evident only to those who are educated and who thus understand the meaning of the terms of such propositions. For example, if one understands that angels are incorporeal, then it is self-evident that angels do not occupy a place by filling it up. However, this is not evident to those who are uneducated and thus who do not understand this point.

Among those propositions which fall within the possibility of everyone's grasp, there is a certain order of precedence. What fundamentally falls within one's mental grasp is 'being'. The understanding of being is included in everything that a person grasps intellectually. Therefore, the first and fundamental indemonstrable principle is the principle of contradiction: 'To affirm and simultaneously to deny is excluded.' This first principle is founded upon the intelligibility of being and non-being. And as Aristotle argues in the *Metaphysics*, all other principles are based upon this first fundamental principle.

Now, just as 'being' is the first thing to fall within the intellectual grasp of the mind, so 'good' is the first thing to fall within the grasp of the practical reason. Practical reason is reason directed towards a work. Every active principle acts on account of an end, and the end includes in its concept the intelligibility of good.

It follows, therefore, that the first principle of practical reason is founded upon the intelligibility of good; that is, 'Good is what each thing tends towards.' The first principle of practical reason — the primary precept of the law — can be formulated in the following manner: 'Good is to be done and pursued and evil is to be avoided.' All the rest of the precepts of the natural law are based upon this principle. Hence, under precepts of the natural law come all those actions which are to be done and those actions which are to be avoided, which actions practical reason grasps naturally as uniquely human goods or their opposites.

In so far as good has the intelligibility of end and evil has the intelligibility of contrary to end, it follows that reason grasps naturally as goods (accordingly, as things to be pursued by work, and their opposites as evils and thus things to be avoided) all the objects which follow from the natural inclinations central to the concept of human nature.

First, there is in human beings an inclination based upon the aspect of human nature which is shared with all living things; this is that everything according to its own nature tends to preserve its own being. In accord with this inclination or natural tendency, those things (actions, events, processes) by which human life is preserved and by which threats to human life are met fall under the natural law. Second, there are in human beings inclinations towards more restricted goods which are based upon the fact that human nature has common properties with other animals. In accord with this inclination, those things are said to be in agreement with the natural law (which nature teaches all animals) among which are the sexual union of male and female, the care of children, and so forth. Third, there is in human beings an inclination to those goods based upon the rational properties of human nature. These goods are uniquely related to human beings. For example, human beings have a natural inclination to know the true propositions about God and concerning those necessities required for living in a human society. In accord with this inclination arise elements of the natural law. For example, human beings should avoid ignorance and should not offend those persons among whom they must live in social units, and so on.

Article 3: Whether every act of virtue belongs to the natural law

I suggest that we recall what John Damascene once wrote: 'The virtues are natural' (*De Fide Orthodoxa*, 2. 14). It follows, then, that virtuous actions are subjected to the natural law.

The Statement of the Position: I suggest that we consider that when we speak about virtuous actions, we can speak in a twofold way: (1) one mode in so far as the actions are indeed virtuous; and (2) another mode in so far as the actions are virtuous because they are considered in their appropriate species.

Therefore, if we speak about virtuous actions in so far as they are virtuous themselves, it follows that every act of virtue pertains to the natural law. I already suggested above (a. 2) that everything pertains to the natural law to which a human person is inclined according to one's very nature. However, it is the case that everything is inclined naturally to an operation which is appropriate to its very form. For example, a fire is proper to heating. Whence, therefore, because the rational disposition (soul) is the proper form of the human person, a natural inclination is found in every human person to act towards that which is appropriate to reason. And this is what we mean by undertaking actions according to virtue. Considered in this way, every act of virtue is directly related to the natural law, for it is the case that each person's proper reason dictates to himself how one might act virtuously.

However if we speak about virtuous actions in themselves, that is, considered according to their proper species, it is not the case that every virtuous action belongs to the natural law. It is the case that many actions become virtues, to which human nature is not inclined at the fundamental level. However, by means of a rational investigation, human beings come to the conclusion that some things are virtuous in so far as they are useful towards the process of attaining human well-being.

Article 4: Whether natural law is the same for all people

I suggest that we consider what Isidore once wrote: 'Natural law (*jus naturale*) is common to all nations' (*Etymologiae*, 5. 4).

The Statement of the Position: From what I said above (aa. 2–3), it follows that those things pertain to natural law to which a human person is naturally inclined. Among those things which are proper to human beings are the matters to which a human being is inclined, one of which is to undertake actions in accord with reason. However, the rational process proceeds from the more common and general to the more specific and singular, as Aristotle argues in the *Physics*, 1. However, it should be noted that concerning these matters, the speculative reason is related differently from the practical reason. I have argued that speculative reason concerns itself in a special way with necessary matters, about which it is impossible to have any other relation without there being found some defect; the truth in the proper conclusions is the same as found in the common principles. On the other hand, practical reason is concerned with contingent matters, in which are found human actions. Therefore, even though it is the case that there is a necessity found in the common principles, when one proceeds to proper and specific actions, so too is it more easy to discover mistakes.

I argue, therefore, that in speculative matters, the truth is the same for every human being both in principles and conclusions; however the truth is not always known by all human persons regarding conclusions but only in the principles which are said to be 'common principles'. In the matters of undertaking actions, however, truth and practical rectitude are not the same among everyone regarding specific human actions, but only regarding common principles. Furthermore, among those actions where the same rectitude is found in specific matters, there is not found an equal amount of knowledge in all people.

Therefore, it follows that in so far as we are considering the common principles of reason, either speculative or practical, the same truth or rectitude is found among all human beings, and all human beings equally know them. However, in so far as we are considering the proper conclusions of speculative reason, the same truth is found to be possible among all human beings, but certainly what is true is not equally known by all peoples. For example, among all peoples it is true that a triangle has three angles which are equal to two right angles; however, it is not the case that this mathematical truth is known by all peoples. But regarding the proper and specific conclusions of practical reason, neither is the same truth or rectitude the same among all peoples, nor is it equally well known even among those people who do hold the same truth.

Among all peoples, none the less, that which is right and true should be undertaken in so far as it is according to reason. From this, however, I suggest that it follows that the principle leads to a certain proper conclusion; for example, the rule that 'something which is deposited with another person ought to be given back to the rightful owner', and this indeed holds and is true in the majority of cases. But it is possible that it might happen in some case or other that what is contingent might cause damage and as a consequence be irrational; if, for example, what has been deposited is returned, and if the agent wants the materials returned in order to undertake a seditious revolution against his home country. Furthermore, I suggest that this principle will be found to fail more in so far as we descend more into particular cases; for example, if we were to say that those things deposited with us should be returned only with such and such a caution or in a particular circumstance. For it is the case that the more conditions that are placed on particular situations, so the more easily they will fail. Thus it might follow that it would be the case that it would neither be right to give back what has been deposited or not to give back what has been deposited.

Therefore, it is my argument that what pertains to natural law regarding the first common principles is the same among all peoples both according to rectitude and according to knowledge. However, what belongs to the proper and specific conclusions, which are 'quasi' conclusions of the common principles, is the same among all of us in many cases, and both according to rectitude and according to knowledge. But as in a minority of cases, the principle is able to fail both regarding rectitude, according to certain particular impediments – as for example when those things which can be generated and are corruptible fail in a minority of cases on account of some physical obstacle – and also according to knowledge. This happens because some people have a reason which has been depraved because of passion, either from a bad custom or from bad habits against the natural law. For example, among the Germanic tribes, as Julius Caesar writes in the *De Bello Gallico*, theft was not considered to be wrong, although certainly it is expressly against the natural law.

Article 5: Whether the natural law is able to be changed

One finds the following written in the *Decretum* (1, 5): 'The natural law began with the very moment of the creation of rational beings; it does not change over time but remains unchangeable.'

The Statement of the Position: In order to consider whether natural law is able to be changed, I suggest that one consider the concept of change in a twofold way. In one way, change occurs when something is added to it, and in this way nothing prohibited by the natural law is able to be changed. For many things have been added to the natural law which are useful for human life either through the divine law or even through human laws. In another way, one is able to understand change of the natural law through the mode of subtraction. In this way, something desists from being part of the natural law which was there in the beginning according to the natural law. In this regard, considering the first principles of natural law, the natural law itself is completely immutable. However, considering the secondary precepts, we must remember, as we have said (a. 4), that they are really particular and specific conclusions following from the first principles. Thus, the natural law is not changed regarding what happens in the majority of cases which might be right always in accord with the natural law. None the less, natural law is able to be changed both in some particular cases and in the minority of cases on account of certain impediments in the special cases which hinder the observance of these precepts, as I argued above (a. 4).

Article 6: Whether it is possible for the natural law to be completely obliterated from the human heart

I suggest that we consider what Augustine wrote in his *Confessions*: 'Your law is written in the hearts of human beings and it is not possible that evil actions obliterate it completely' (2). But the law written in the human hearts is the natural law. The natural law, therefore, is not able to be completely obliterated.

The Statement of the Position: Considering this matter one must remember what I wrote above (a. 4–5) about what pertains to the natural law; first, indeed regarding the common precepts which are known to all people; and secondly, the secondary precepts which are more proper and which are 'quasi' conclusions and proper principles.

Regarding those common principles, therefore, the natural law in no way is able to be obliterated completely from the hearts of human beings. None the less, in particular actions to be taken, it might be obliterated in so far as the reason is impeded in its attempt to apply common principles to a particular action to be undertaken, either on account of concupiscence or some other passion, as I argued above (q. 77 a. 2).

However, regarding the secondary precepts, the natural law is able to be obliterated from the hearts of human beings either on account of bad habits — for example, in a similar way in speculative matters, errors can come about from necessary conclusions — or also on account of bad customs or corrupt habits; for example, among those people for whom the sin of theft is not condemned, or even certain vices against nature, as the apostle Paul writes in his Epistle to the Romans.

INTRODUCTION TO HUMAN LAW

The next issues to be considered concern human law. Regarding this, there are three issues: (1) first, indeed concerning this very human law in itself; (2) concerning its power; and (3) concerning its changeability.

Question 95: Concerning Human Law In and Of Itself.

Concerning human law, one needs to treat four questions: (1) the usefulness of human law; (2) its origin; (3) the nature of its quality (or characteristics); and (4) its division.

Article 1: Whether it is useful that some laws indeed be made by human beings

I suggest that in considering this matter, we remember what Isidore once wrote: 'Human laws have been made so that human audacity might be held in check by their threat, and also so that the innocent might be protected from those exerting evil; and among those capable of doing evil, the dread of punishment might prevent them from undertaking harm.' It should be noted, however, that these matters are most important and necessary for human beings. Therefore it is necessary that human laws should be made.

The Statement of the Position: In discussing this matter, as I wrote above (q. 93 a. 1; q. 94 a. 3), human beings have a natural disposition towards virtue. However, the cultivation and attainment of virtue requires that human agents undertake a certain discipline or training. For example, we observe that regarding certain necessary things, a human being is helped towards attaining these things through a degree of industry; for example, in the matters of food and clothing. In this matter, certain beginnings come from nature; for example, reason and the use of one's hands. However, a human person does not have the full complement of these functions as other animals do to whom nature has provided sufficiently in the matters of clothing and food. In this matter of training and discipline, it is not easy to see how a human person would be able to suffice by himself, because the perfection of virtue consists especially in having a human being abstain from wanton pleasures to which all human beings are especially prone, and especially young people, about whom such training is more efficacious. It is necessary, therefore, for any human being to receive this discipline through which one attains virtue by being taught by others.

Indeed, to those young persons who are prone to acts of virtue from a good natural disposition or from habit, or more from a divine gift, paternal discipline suffices which is usually given through admonition and support. However, because some young folks are indeed found to be depraved and prone to vice – who are not able to be moved easily by words alone – it was necessary that they be hindered from undertaking evil actions through force or fear, in order that at least they might desist from undertaking evil actions and thus leave others in a certain peaceful state of existence. Furthermore, through this way even they themselves, through this forced custom, might be led to undertake voluntarily what earlier they did not do through fear, and thus embark upon a life of virtue. This discipline and training, therefore, which compels through the fear of punishment, is the discipline of human law.

It is necessary, therefore, that in order to obtain peace among human beings and the advancement of virtue, laws should be made, because, as Aristotle writes in his *Politics*, 1: 'For it is the case that as a human person, if one is perfect in virtue, is the best of all animals, so too if the person is separated from law and from justice, this person is the worst of all animals.' This is so because a human being has the armaments of reason in order to expel concupiscible desires and brutal desires, which the other animals do not possess.

Article 2: Whether each human positive law is derived from the natural law

I suggest that we remember what Cicero said in his *Rhetoric*: 'Things which come forth from nature and are established by custom are given sanction by fear of the law and through religion.'

The Statement of the Position: In considering this issue, I recommend that we follow what Augustine wrote in his *De Libero Arbitrio* (1. 5): 'It is the case that a law, which is not just, is not a law at all.' Whence it follows that in so far as a law comes from justice so also does it have the force or sanction of law. In human matters, however, it is said that something is just from the very fact that it is right according to the rule of reason. However, the first rule of reason is the law of nature as I suggested above (q. 91 a. 2 ad. 2).

Whence every human law which is made has as much of the justification of law in so far as it is derived from the natural law. If, therefore, in some matter it is in disagreement with the natural law, so also it will not be a law, but a corruption of law.

It must be noted, however, that something is able to be derived from the natural law in a twofold fashion: the first way, according to the conclusion from principles; the second way, as particular determinations of the common principles. Indeed, the first way is similar to that used in the sciences, which produce demonstrative conclusions from the first principles. The second way is similar to that which is undertaken in the arts, in which common forms are determined to be something specific and particular. For example, the architect must determine the general 'form' of a house to the particular structure of this or that specific house.

Therefore, certain precepts are derived from the common principles of natural law through the mode of conclusions. For example, the precept that 'One ought not to kill' is a conclusion which is able to be derived from the fact that 'No one should do evil to another.' On the other hand, certain laws are made by the method of determination, just as the law of nature has determined that the person who does evil should be punished. But which person should be punished, or punished in such and such a way, this is a determination of the law of nature. Therefore, I argue that both ways (or modes) of derivation are found in the making of human law. However, those things which are of the first mode are found in human law; not that they are posited alone in human law, but they have something of their force from natural law. However, those things which are of the secondary mode have their force only from human law itself.

Article 3: Whether Isidore has described adequately the qualities or characteristics of positive law

[This article begins with a long quotation from Isidore's *Etymologiae* in which the qualities (or characteristics) of positive law are discussed.] Isidore writes as follows: 'Law will be honest, just, possible, according to nature, according to the customs of the country, agreeable with both time and place, necessary, useful, expressed clearly, lest something through its obscurity lead to a misunderstanding, established for no private gain, but for the common usefulness of the *polis*.'

[Aquinas notes that earlier in the *Etymologiae*, Isidore had expressed the quality of law in three conditions when he wrote the following.] 'Law is something which is founded on reason; provided that it be consistent with religion, it should be helpful to discipline; and it should bring about the well-being of society.'

I suggest that the authority of Isidore stands by itself. [Aquinas refers to the two passages above.]

The Statement of the Position: I argue that everything which is according to its end must be determined by the form according to the proportion to the end. For example, the form of a saw is such that it performs its proper function by cutting, as is obvious in Aristotle's *Physics* (2. 9). Likewise, anything which is right and measured must have a form proportionate to its rule and measure. Human law, however, has both: because it is something ordered to an end and is a form of rule or measure ruling and measuring something by a higher measure. This higher measure is twofold, namely divine law and natural law, as I wrote earlier (a. 2; q. 93 a. 3).

Now it is the case that the end of human law is useful for human beings, as even Justinian has written (*Digest*, 1. 3. 25). Therefore, it is the case that Isidore postulates as a condition for law in the beginning at least three things: namely, that it be helpful to religion in so far as it is proportionate to the divine law; that it be agreeable with discipline or training, in so far as it is proportionate to the natural law; and that it helps bring about the commonweal of the *polis*, in so far as it is proportionate to those things useful for human beings.

All other conditions which he mentioned later are reducible to these three conditions spoken above. For when he said that law is honest, he was referring to its agreeableness with religion. And when he says that law should be 'just, possible, according to nature, according to the customs of a country, agreeable with the time and place', this is reduced to what he said when he suggested that law is 'helpful to the cultivation of discipline'. This is the case because human discipline in the first place attends towards an order of reason, to which he gives importance when he says in this matter that law is 'just'.

Secondly, in so far as it depends on the ability of the agent. For it is the case that discipline and training ought to be agreeable to any particular person based upon his or her potentialities, having observed his or her natural abilities – for indeed the same things should not be placed upon children which are placed upon grown persons; moreover, according to the human condition, for indeed a human person is not able to live in a solitary way in society, that is, by paying no attention to the custom of others.

Thirdly, regarding the due circumstances, Isidore writes 'agreeable with the time and place'. The words which remain, namely 'necessary, useful, etc.' refer to the fact that law ought to make expedient the common good of society. In this case, necessity refers to the removal of evil things, utility to the cultivation of good matters, clearness of expression to the need of preventing harm which might come about from the law itself. And as I have argued above (q. 90 a. 2), law is ordered to the common good; this very fact is plainly expressed in the last part of the discussion.

Article 4: Whether Isidore provides an appropriate division of human laws

Once again I suggest the authority of Isidore suffices on this matter.

The Statement of the Position: I suggest that in this manner anything is able to be divided according to that which is contained in its very essence. For example, in the definition of an animal, the concept of soul is contained, which is rational or irrational. Therefore, I suggest that animal (as a genus) properly and *per se* considered, is divided according to rationality and irrationality, not however according to white and black, which are completely beyond its essence. However, many things belong to the nature of human law, according to which any human law might properly and *per se* be divided.

In the first place, concerning the essence of human law, I suggest that it is derived from natural law, as I explained above (a. 2). In this regard, human law is divided into *jus gentium* (law of nations) and *jus civile* (civil law). Something is derived from a law of nature according to both of these two modes, as was suggested above. For to *jus gentium* pertains those things which are derived from the law of nature as conclusions from principles. An example would be the just buying and selling and other things in this regard, without which human beings would not be able to live together. These things belong to the law of nature because human beings are by nature social animals, as Aristotle established in the *Politics*, 1. Therefore, those things derived from the law of nature through the manner of a particular determination pertain to *jus civile* in so far as any *polis* (*civitas*) determines those things which are appropriate for it.

Secondly, it belongs to the definition of human law to consider those things which are ordained to the common good of the *polis* – the commonweal. And according to this, human law is able to be divided according to the diversity of those things which provide work for the common good and the commonweal. For example, priests praying to God on behalf of the people, princes governing the people, and soldiers fighting in order to protect the well-being of the people. Therefore, I suggest that to these people certain special things pertain through the law.

Thirdly, it belongs to the definition of human law in order that it be instituted by the person who has charge of the community in the *polis*, as I argued above (q. 90 a. 3). On account of this, I suggest that human laws are distinguished according to the diverse kinds of city states. Aristotle considers such uses in the *Politics*, 3. One example is a monarchy; namely, when the *polis* is governed by one person, and in this case one has ordinations of the prince or king. Another type of government is an aristocracy; that is, those who rule are the best, or the politically best; and according to this are found the prudent responses and the counsel of those in the senate. Another form of government is the oligarchy, which is when the persons in charge are a few rich and powerful persons; and according to this, we have 'praetorian law' which is also called 'honorary law'. Another form of government is of the people, which is called a democracy. And according to this are found the rules of a plebiscite.

Another form, however, is a tyranny, which is a complete corruption; hence from this it is not possible to have any law whatsoever. There is also a type of government which is a kind of mixture of all of those mentioned, which indeed is the best form of government; and from this we have a law, which Isidore discusses as one which is 'sanctioned both by those of high birth and those found in the common ranks' (*Etymologiae*, 5. 10).

Fourthly, I suggest that the essence of human law is that which is directive of human actions. According to this, diverse matters determine the ways in which laws are distinguished. Sometimes these laws are named after their authors; for example, the *Lex Julia* is a discussion about adultery. The *Lex Cornelia* is about assassins; and so on about other kinds of things which are not distinguished on account of their authors but on account of the things which they consider.

Question 96: Concerning the Power of Human Law

We ought to consider the following issues about the power of human law. On this topic, one might ask six questions: (1) whether human law ought to be established with regard to common matters? (2) whether human law ought to forbid every vice? (3) whether human law ought to prescribe the following of all acts of virtue? (4) whether human law binds human beings in the matters of conscience? (5) whether all human beings are subjected to human law? and (6) whether those who are bound by law might on occasion act beyond the letter of the law?

Article 1: Whether a human law should be established for the common good rather than for particular goods

I suggest that on this matter we need to consider what Justinian has written: 'Laws ought to be made about those matters which happen in the majority of cases; laws are not made for those things which may happen to occur by chance every now and then.'

The Statement of the Position: In discussing this matter, I propose that we consider that whatever acts for a proper end should be considered as pro-portionate to that end. However, the end of law is the common good, because, as Isidore has written, 'the law ought to be written in such a way that it is never undertaken for a private good but rather for the common good and well being of the community'. Hence it is necessary that human laws be proportioned directly to the common good.

The common good, however, comes about from many things. It is neces-sary, therefore, that the law take into consideration many things according to persons, according to matters, and according to times. For the community of citizens is constituted from a multitude of persons, and hence its good is procured through a multitude of actions. Neither is it the case that law is instituted for a short time, but rather it should persevere for some time through a succession of citizens, as Augustine writes in the *City of God* (2. 21).

Article 2: Whether it pertains to human law to prohibit all vices

I suggest that we consider what Augustine wrote in *De Libero Arbitrio*: 'It seems to me that the law by which are written those things which govern a people rightly permit certain things which are punished by divine law.' But divine law punishes nothing but vices. Therefore human law correctly established permits some vices by not forbidding them.

The Statement of the Position: As I wrote earlier (q. 90 a. 1, 2) law is established as a certain rule or measure of human actions. However, a measure, as Aristotle writes in the *Metaphysics*, 9, 'ought to be of the same kind as the thing it measures'. It is the case that different things are measured by different measures. Hence it follows that laws are placed upon human beings according to their particular conditions, because, as Isidore has written, 'a law ought to be possible, both according to nature and according to the customs of the country' (*Etymologiae*, 2).

However, I argue that the power or faculty of undertaking actions proceeds from an interior habit or disposition. For the same thing is not possible for someone who does not have the habit of virtue as is possible for the virtuous person. Likewise, the same things are not possible for a small child and for a fully developed person. And according to this, the same kind of law is not held to be binding for little children which is binding for adults; for many things are permitted children which are punished in adults by the law, or which at least are found to be blameworthy. In a like manner, many things are permitted to human persons not well developed in virtue which would not be tolerated in virtuous human beings.

I argue that a human law is established for the multitude of human beings, in which the greater part of human beings are not perfect in virtue. I suggest, therefore, that human law does not prohibit all vices from which virtuous persons abstain, but only the more grievous things from which it is possible for the greater part of the multitude of human persons to abstain. This is especially true of those actions which are able to hurt other people, without the prohibition of which a human society would not be able to be conserved. Hence by human law are prohibited such actions as homicide, theft, and other activities of a similar kind.

Article 3: Whether human law prescribes every act of virtue

I suggest that as Aristotle writes in the *Ethics*, 'the law prescribes the perform-ance of the acts of a brave person, and the acts of a temperate person, and the acts of a meek person; and in like manner regarding the other virtues and vices, indeed prescribing the former and forbidding the latter.' (5. 1)

The Statement of the Position: In considering this matter, I suggest that the species of virtues be distinguished according to their objects, as I have written above (q. 54 a. 2, and other places). However every object of a virtue is able to be referred either to the private good of some person or to the common good of the multitude. For example, those things which pertain to fortitude (courage) can be executed either on account of the conservation of the city or towards the conservation of the rights of one's friend. Like situations hold for other cases.

The law, however, as I argued earlier (q. 90 a. 2), is ordained for the common good. Therefore, it follows that there is no virtue which is of its very action not able to prescribe a law. None the less, human law does not prescribe every action of every virtue, but only those virtues which are ordainable for the common good; this occurs either immediately, as when some law is made strictly for the common good, or mediately, as when some law is ordained by a legislature which pertains to the good order of the society, through which the citizens are informed so that they might conserve the common good of justice and peace.

Article 4: Whether human law binds a human person necessarily through conscience

I suggest that in discussing this issue we consider what Peter wrote in his Epistle (1 Peter 2:19): 'This is worthy of commendation, if a person suffering injustice on account of conscience bears the sadness.'

The Statement of the Position: In considering this issue, I suggest that laws established by human beings are either just or unjust. If indeed they are just, they have the force of obliging in the matter of conscience through the eternal law from which they are derived. This is found in the Book of Proverbs where it is written: 'It is through me that kings rule and that the givers of law establish just laws' (Proverbs 8: 15). I argue, however, that just laws are indeed just, from their very end, when they are ordained to the common good. Also a just law must come from the author, when, for example, the law as given does not exceed the power of the person giving the law, and from the form when indeed according to the equality of pro-portion the law binds through penalty in order to foster the common good. For it is the case that each human person is part of the multitude of human beings. Thus a human person in and of himself or herself, who the person is and what the person has, belongs to this multitude as indeed a part is that which is found in the whole. Whence nature brings about some infliction on the part in order to save the whole. And according to this account, laws such as these which impose proportionate burdens are just and are binding in conscience, and are legal laws.

On the other hand, I suggest that laws are unjust in two ways. In the first way, a law is unjust when it is contrary to the human good and contrary to the things we have discussed above: either from the end as when a person presiding imposes a law with undue burdens or prescribes a law which does not pertain to the commonweal of the society but rather to his own proper desires and glories. Or even on the part of the author, as when someone makes a law beyond the power commissioned to him. Or also from the very form, for example, as when burdens are dispensed unequally upon members of the community, even if they are ordained to the common good. Cases like this are more like acts of violence than laws, because, as Augustine writes, 'a law that is not seen as just is no law at all'. Whence such laws do not oblige in the matter of conscience except perhaps in order to avoid scandal or a disturbance. On this account, a person may be asked to yield his right, as Matthew has written, 'whoever forces you to walk a mile, go with him for two miles, and whoever will take away your coat, give him your cloak as well' (Matthew 6: 40).

In the second case, laws are able to be unjust according to their going against the divine good. An example would be the laws of tyrants forcing one to undertake acts of idolatry or anything else which is contrary to the divine law. Such laws as these in no way whatsoever ought to be observed because, as is stated in the Acts of the Apostles (5: 29), 'It is necessary to obey God rather than human beings.'

Article 5: Whether everyone is subject to the law

I suggest that on this matter we consider what the Apostle Paul said in his Epistle to the Romans (13: 1): 'It should be the case that every soul is indeed subject to the higher powers.' However, it doesn't seem to be the case that one is subject to powers who is not subjected to the law that power has made. Therefore, all human beings ought to be bound to the law.

The Statement of the Position: As I argued above, it is the case that law of its very nature has two components: Indeed first of all, it is a rule of human actions. Secondly it has an obligatory, coercive power. In this double way, therefore, each person is bound to be subject to the law. In the first way, as the person regulated is subject to the regulator, and in this way all those who are subject to the power are subject to the law which the power has made.

It is the case, however, that someone might not be subjected to the power in two ways. First of all, because the person considered is absolutely free of this subjection. Hence, those citizens who live in one city or kingdom are not subject to the laws made by the princes of another city or kingdom because they are not part of the dominion of that other place. In another way, in so far as the person ruled is subject to a higher law. For example, if someone is the subject of a 'proconsul', this person should be ruled by the proconsul's command; not, however, in those matters which might dispense someone from the command of an emperor. For example, one is not bound by the command of a lower authority when this person has been directed by the command of a higher authority. Whence according to this, one who is subject to the law simply (*simpliciter*) should not be bound to some law when what is ruled comes from a higher law.

In another way, or secondly, a person is said to be subject to the law as the person coerced is subject to the person giving the coercion. In this way I suggest that virtuous and just human persons are not subjected to the law, but only those evil persons. For what is coerced and violent is contrary to the will. However, the will of the good person is in agreement with the law, whereas the will of the evil person is not in harmony with the law. Therefore, I suggest in this sense the good persons are not subject to the law, but only the evil persons.

Article 6: Whether a person who is subject to the law is able to act beyond the letter of the law

I suggest we consider what Hilary wrote in the fourth book of the *De Trinitate*: 'Therefore it is more important to attend to the cause which motivates a legislator than to the very words of the law.'

The Statement of the Position: It should be noted as I said above (a. 4) that every law is ordained to the common good of human beings, and in this way it obtains its force and reason. In so far as it is deficient, it does not have the power of obliging persons. Hence, Justinian writes as follows: 'There is no reason in law or benign aspect of equity which permits that which would allow us to introduce harsh rules for the well being of human persons; nor should we take those things to a severity whose interpretation would help human beings.' However, it happens that something which is observed to be useful and salutory in many cases for the common good, none the less, in some other cases produces much hurt.

Therefore, because the legislator is not able to know in advance each singular case, the legislator makes a law according to those things which happened in the majority of cases, and by directing his attention to the common good. Whence if a case comes about in which a strict observance of such a law might be very harmful to the common good, the law ought not to be followed. For example, consider the case of a city under siege which has a law that the gates of the city are to remain closed; this is useful for the common welfare in the majority of cases. If it happens, however, that the enemy are in pursuit of certain citizens, who have been defending the city, it would be a severe loss to the city if the gates were not to be opened for them. In such a case, therefore, the gates should be opened, which goes against the strict words of the law, in order that the common good, which the legislator intended, might be followed.

None the less, I think it should be noted that if the observance of the law according to the letter does not involve any sudden risk which must be immediately cured, it does not pertain to just anyone to interpret what might be useful for the city and what might be not useful to the city. This pertains only to the person in charge, and who, in accord with similar cases, has the authority to dispense from the rigours of the law. If, however, the danger is so sudden and does not admit of any possible delay which might bring about a discussion with the person in authority, the very necessity has with it a dispensation, because necessity itself is never subject to the law.

Question 97: Concerning the Possibility of Changing the Law.

It is now time to consider the possibility of change in the law. Concerning this issue, four questions might be asked: (1) whether human law itself is changeable? (2) whether a law always ought to be changed when something better occurs? (3) whether law ought to be abolished because of custom and whether custom itself ever takes on the force of law? and (4) whether the use of human law ought to be changed through the process of the dispensation of the governing authorities?

Article 1: Whether human law ought to be changed in any way whatsoever

I suggest that on this matter we ought to consider what Augustine wrote: 'A temporal law, even if it is just, is able to be changed, nevertheless, through the passage of time' (*De Libero Arbitrio*, 1. 6).

The Statement of the Position: As I said above (q. 91 a. 3), human law is a dictate of reason by means of which human actions are directed. According to this account, there are two ways in which a human law might be changed. The first way is on the part of reason itself. The second way is on the part of the human beings whose actions are regulated by the law.

From the part of human reason, it seems to be natural to human reason that one strive towards perfection gradually from the imperfect to the perfect. Hence, we see this in the speculative sciences which, from the very first, philosophers held certain positions which were imperfect; afterwards these positions were made more perfect by those who succeeded them. So also in matters undertaking actions. For those who first intended to discover something about the common good for human beings, not being able to consider everything from themselves, instituted certain things which were imperfect and deficient in a number of ways; these were changed later by those who followed, instituting certain things which in fewer ways might be deficient from the common good.

On the part of human beings, however, whose actions are regulated by the law, a correct law is able to be changed on account of the changing conditions of human persons to whom, accordingly, different conditions are expedient at different times. On this matter, Augustine puts forward an example in the *De Libro Arbitrio*, 1, when he writes: 'If a people possess a sense of moderation and seriousness, and are very diligent about the common good, it is a good law for such a people to be able to choose their own magistrates through which a republic will be governed. However, if, as time goes by, the same people become depraved so that they might sell their votes, and give their government to scoundrels and criminals, then they rightly have given up their power of electing to office, and at this time the choice goes to a few good persons.'

Article 2: Whether human law ought to always be changed whenever something better is found

I suggest that we consider what has been stated in the *Decretum*: 'It is ridiculous and quite abominable that traditions which we have received from long ago from our patriarchs ought to be changed.' (12. 5)

The Statement of the Position: As I stated above (a. 1) in matters such as this, human law is to be considered as rightly changed in so far as it provides for a change in the common good. However, it is the case that the very change of law itself, in so far as it is a change, is detrimental in a certain way to the common good. This happens because the observance of the law by the majority ought to be as a custom. I hold this because those things which go against common custom are seen in such a way that, even if the matters might be slight, they are judged to be grave. Whence, however, when a law is changed, the binding power of the law itself is diminished, because the custom itself is abolished. Therefore, I suggest that no one ought to change a human law except for the very reason that the common good is compensated regarding the extent to which harm might be done in this specific instance.

Indeed such compensation might arise either from this, that a very great and most evident utility comes about by means of the new statute, or that there is a great necessity, or that the existing law is either obviously unjust or its observance is the cause of much harm. On this matter, the jurist, Ulpian, has said the following: 'In the manner of establishing new laws, one ought to consider the usefulness of the law in order that it might be seen that the law which one is taking away will be as equally good' (*Digest*, 1.4. 2).

Article 3: Whether custom is able to have the force of law

I suggest that in considering this matter, we read what Augustine said in his *Letter to Casulanum*: 'The customs of the people of God and the institutions put forward by our ancestors should be considered as law. Therefore, for example, those who throw contempt at the divine laws also ought to be coerced as those who are contemptuous of ecclesiastical customs' (36).

The Statement of the Position: I argue that every law proceeds from the reason and the will of the legislator. Indeed divine law and natural law come from the rational will of God. However, human law comes from the will of a regulated human reason. For example, however, in matters of things to be done, reason and will are made evident by both words and deeds. For thus it is the case that any person is seen to choose that which is good in order that he might carry out a work. It is obvious, however, that through human speech, a law is able to be changed and also to be expounded in so far as it brings forward the interior motive and concept of human reason. Also, however, it is the case that through actions, especially those actions that can be repeated, and thus bring about a custom, a law is able to be changed and expounded; and also something is able to be brought about which has the force of law in so far as through the repetition of many exterior actions, the interior motion of the will and the reason might be more efficaciously declared. For when something is done again and again, it is seen to come forward from a deliberate judgement of the reason. Accordingly, it is the case that a custom has the force of law and abolishes law and also can be an interpreter of laws.

Article 4: Whether the rulers of the people are able to dispense from human laws

I suggest that in considering this issue, we refer to what the apostle Paul said in his Letter to the Corinthians (9:17): 'A dispensation has been given to me.'

The Statement of the Position: It should be understood that a dispensation properly considered denotes a measuring out to someone concerning common matters about a particular case. For example, the head of a household might be called a 'dispenser', because the head gives to each person in the family, with due weight and measure, the works and necessities for life. It follows, therefore, that in any group of people, it is said that there is someone who is able to dispense because this person orders how some general principle might be applied to a particular person.

It sometimes happens, however, that a precept which is for the common good of the multitude is not working appropriately for a particular person. Either in this case because it impedes something which is better or it leads towards something evil, as I said above (q. 96 a. 6). It should be noted, however, that it would be dangerous if this judgement were left with just anybody whomsoever, except perhaps on account of an evident and sudden danger, as I mentioned above (ibid.). It follows, therefore, that the person who has ruling control over a multitude of people has the power to dispense from the human law which rests upon his own authority, so that namely when the law fails either regarding persons or regarding particular cases, the person in authority may allow the force of the law not to be applied.

If one gives this permission without any reason other than one's own will, however, the person in authority will be an imprudent and unfaithful person in the matter of dispensations. The person indeed is unfaithful because the intention to promote the common good is absent. Likewise, the person is imprudent because the very reason for the dispensation itself is ignored. On this matter, I remind you that our Lord said the following, as is recorded in the Gospel of Luke (12: 42): 'Who, do you think, is the faithful and prudent servant (*dispensator*), the person whom the master will set up as the person in charge of his own household?'

[This concludes the texts in the *Summa Theologiae* in which Aquinas discusses the nature and conditions of law. Appendix II considers the role Aquinas's account of natural law plays in the tradition of Western jurisprudence.]

APPENDIX II

The Place of Aquinas in the Development
of Legal Philosophy

This short postscript is a sketch indicating the place Aquinas holds in the development of Western jurisprudence. It also provides a glimpse of the nature and scope of legal philosophy as found in the writings of Aquinas.

LIFE AND WORK

Born in 1224 of Italian noble parents, Thomas at an early age wished to join the then newly formed mendicant friars, the Dominicans. He embarked upon this religious life voyage against his parents's desires – for they had seen their son as becoming the reigning abbot of the wealthy monastery of Monte Casino near the ancestral home of Aquino. Young Thomas persevered in his decision to join the Dominicans. Sent first to Cologne to study under Albert the Great, Aquinas soon gave great promise of adding substantially to the intellectual life of the Dominicans.

The Dominicans saw themselves as preachers and teachers above all else. Moving away from the pastoral conditions of the country, which had been traditional with Western religious orders, the Dominicans set up priories in the large European cities, usually associated with nearby universities. It was in this new style of religious order that Thomas of Aquino invested his life and his tremendous intellectual gifts.

Thomas's intellectual star shone brightly under the tutelage of Albert the Great. In fact, Albert predicted that Aquinas would go on to great intellectual matters. Of course, he did just that. On two distinct occasions he taught at the University of Paris, then, in the thirteenth century, the leading centre of academic and intellectual work. Aquinas was also assigned to Rome and to Naples at various times during his much too short but extremely productive life.

Aquinas's principal contribution to Western thought was his establishment of the reconciliation of Aristotelian science and philosophy with the tenets of Western Christianity. Aquinas wrote several commentaries on Aristotle's texts, one of the more famous being his *Commentary on the Nicoma-*

chean Ethics, a work considered often in this book. Yet his greatest achievement undoubtedly is the composition, organization, and writing of his monumental *Summa Theologiae*. It is in this work that one finds his treatise on law. Questions 90–97 of the *Summa Theologiae*, I-II, have come down as the classical canon in Western jurisprudence theory of natural law. Beginning in 1266, Thomas wrote the *Summa Theologiae* during the last years of his productive life. It remained incomplete at his untimely death. Thomas died at the age of 49, probably a victim of a what medical science now would call a stroke. Simon Tugwell suggests that today we would probably call Thomas a 'workaholic'.

LEGAL WRITINGS

The following account of Thomas's legal writing and study is heavily dependent upon a thoughtful article, 'St Thomas Aquinas and Law', by Vincent McNabb, an English Dominican, which appeared in the journal *Blackfriars*, in 1929.[1] McNabb traces many of the influences on Aquinas's work in legal matters and also suggests the influence they in turn had on the development of Western jurisprudence.

McNabb notes that what distinguishes Aquinas's mode of doing philosophy is nothing other than searching out the order of the objects of investigation. McNabb writes that Aquinas's search for order and regularity determined his way of proceeding: 'In seeking for order, even amongst a mass of seemingly disorderly facts or theories, it is often amazing how he finds a hidden law. It would almost seem as if unity, order, law was the first quality his mind sought in all its life-long searching' (p. 1048).

While absorbed in Aristotelian studies, McNabb notes that Aquinas rethought the ethical system of Aristotle. McNabb suggests, in a more optimistic view than contemporary scholars would affirm, that even the *Nicomachean Ethics* 'is so enriched in form and matter by Aquinas that it might be well disputed who is the real founder of Ethics as a Science' (ibid.) Aquinas's studies on law were deep and continuous. His early *Commentary on the Sentences of Peter Lombard* suggests that the 'Law of the Decalogue' was foremost in his mind. Aquinas refers often to Aristotle's *Ethics* and *Metaphysics* in this early commentary. These insights are developed a bit more in his *Summa contra*

---

[1] Vincent McNabb, 'St. Thomas Aquinas and Law', *Blackfriars* (May 1929), 1047–67. This priceless article was discovered while the author was rooting through old copies of *Blackfriars* in the remote storage stacks of the Xavier University Library in Cincinnati, Ohio. This underlies the importance to scholars that published materials be kept in libraries, even though the journals may be more than 50 years old. Had not the library staff at Xavier University decided to keep the dated copies of *Blackfriars*, this article by the late Father McNabb would not have been discovered as easily and therefore would probably not have provided assistance to the research efforts of this study of Aquinas on natural law.

Gentiles, written five years after the Lombard commentary. Yet the final work on law, *De Lege*, is part of the *Summa Theologiae*, I-II. McNabb suggests that this treatise on law was written during the final years of his life while he was living in Bologna, whose university was famous in medieval times as the home of Legal Science. While this brief account certainly does not pretend to be a serious study of the complicated dating of Aquinas's work and his journeys, none the less, I can find no reference in recent Aquinian biographical work indicating that Aquinas had lived in Bologna at this time.[2]

Aquinas fully developed his thoughts on law in the *Summa Theologiae*. His list of references looks like a listing of the 'Great Books' of ancient and medieval philosophy – Plato, Aristotle, Cicero, Ulpian, John Chrysostom, Hilary, Jerome, the Pseudo-Dionysius, Augustine, Boethius, Isidore, Moses Maimonides, among others. Aristotle is the Greek and Augustine the Christian philosopher quoted most often. Moses Maimonides too is referred to frequently. Yet it is the metaphysics of Aristotle which hovers over Aquinas's treatise on law. McNabb writes as follows:

It would be difficult to narrow even into a lecture, and still more difficult to compress into a paragraph all that St. Thomas's treatise on Law owes to the thought of Aristotle. No little of that debt to the one he calls 'the Philosopher' is the hellenic austerity of style, which is as perfect an expression of intellectual truth as the Parthenon is of intellectual beauty. But although the *Metaphysics* of Aristotle is only rarely quoted, the ideas of unity and causality are too closely woven into the treatise for us to be able to estimate the debt to Aristotle by mere quotations. Again, it would be impossible to appraise the influence of Aristotle's Ethics and Psychology. These two sciences are of such importance to any true knowledge of the function of Law that the legal profession, like any other liberal profession – medical, sacerdotal – if shorn of them becomes mere craftsmanship instead of culture. [ibid. 1053]

McNabb also suggests that Augustine's *City of God* and Maimonides' *Guide for the Perplexed* served as special influences on Aquinas's thinking about the nature and scope of law. McNabb emphasizes this suggestion by writing that 'had Moses Maimonides not written his famous book, *Guide for the Perplexed*, there would never have been written a still more famous book, St. Thomas's treatise on Law' (ibid. 1055). Moreover, as Michel Villey and Ralph McInerny have noted, Aquinas's account of right (*jus*) is more understandable within the context of Roman law than it is in the context

[2] Cf. Simon Tugwell, 'The Life and Works of Thomas Aquinas', *Albert and Thomas* (New York: Paulist Press, 1988). Brian Davies's study on Aquinas, *The Thought of Thomas Aquinas*, also has no mention of a stay at Bologna. Mandonnet does write that Thomas visited Bologna on Whit Sunday, 1267. Yet there is no evidence that he worked there. Cf. 'Chronology of the Life of St. Thomas Aquinas', found in the Dominican translation of the *Summa Theologiae*, 3rd edn. (London: Burns, Oates & Washbourne Ltd., 1920), p. xl.

of modern rights theory. Roman law, and its expression found in canon law, exerted an influence on Aquinas's treatment of legal matters.

It is difficult to elucidate clearly and evenly the exact contributions Aquinas's theory of law — especially his account of natural law — have made in the development of Western jurisprudence. That Aquinas's theory of law had a profound effect on the later development of a theory of international law is generally accepted as historically correct. The sixteenth-century Dominican friar Franciscus de Victoria is often regarded as one of the pioneer thinkers responsible for a theory of international law. His work, *De Indis Relectio Prior*, a series of lectures first given at Salamanca in 1532, serves as the harbinger of later discussions on international law. Grotius refers to de Victoria in the *Prolegomena* to his *De Jure Belli ac Pacis* and in his *Mare Liberum*. McNabb suggests that de Victoria certainly was well trained in classical Thomism then common in Spanish universities. As noted in Chapter 9, Francisco Suarez's contributions to the analysis of what eventually became the modern concept of individual human right is dependent on the earlier, though opposite, account of *jus* in the *Summa Theologiae*, II.

The general influence of Aquinas's theory of natural law on the development of the United States Constitution, especially the first ten amendments known as the 'Bill of Rights', is often suggested but difficult to establish. In his *Ancient Law*, the American jurist Henry Sumner Maine suggests that Thomas Jefferson was influenced by the French philosophers, who in turn had written about human rights in the context of natural law. Maine further suggests that the especially French concept that 'all men are born equal' was coupled with the more familiar English concept that 'all men are born free' in the very first lines of the Declaration of Independence. In his *The Philosophy of the American Revolution*, Morton White writes that Locke, in considering the nature of self-evident principles necessary for his account of natural law, was 'indebted — directly or indirectly — to Aquinas for some of the views to be found in the English philosopher's *Essays on the Law of Nature*.'[3]

Aquinas also spent considerable time and effort offering an extended analysis of what he termed the 'Old Law'. This, of course, refers to the Torah of the Jewish people. Aquinas considers the Torah thus: 'We must, therefore, distinguish three kinds of precepts in the Old Law: (1) Moral Precepts, which are dictated by the natural law; (2) ceremonial precepts, which are determinations of the divine worship; and (3) judicial precepts, which are determinations of the justice to be maintained among human persons' (*Summa Theologiae*, I-II q. 99 a. 4).

This concludes our analysis, of the general influences which affected Aquinas's theory of law and in turn the influence his theory has had on the

---

[3] Morton White, *The Philosophy of the American Revolution* (New York: Oxford University Press, 1978), 23.

APPENDIX III

An Outline of Aquinas's Theory of Law

In his excellent analysis of Thomas Aquinas's theory of law, 'St. Thomas Aquinas and Law',[1] Vincent McNabb provides the following outline of Aquinas's treatment of law in the *Summa Theologiae*.

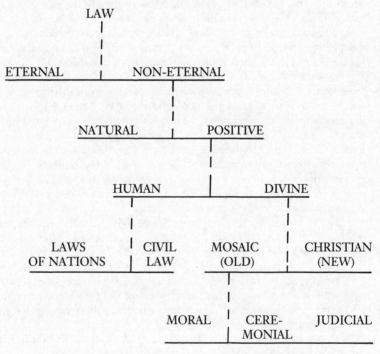

[1] Vincent McNabb, 'St. Thomas Aquinas and Law', *Blackfriars*, (May 1929), 1058.

SELECT BIBLIOGRAPHY

I PRINCIPAL AQUINAS TEXTS

AQUINAS, THOMAS, *Summa Theologiae*, Blackfriars edn. (ed.), Thomas Gilby (New York and London, 1963–1975).

— — *Commentary on the Nicomachean Ethics*, trans. C. I. Litzinger, 2 vols. (Chicago, 1964).

— — *Summa Theologiae: A Concise Translation*, ed. Timothy McDermott, (Westminster, Md., 1989).

— — *Selected Philosophical Writings*, trans. and ed. Timothy McDermott, (Oxford, 1993).

— — *The Treatise on Law: Summa Theologiae, II q 9, 90–97*, ed. R. J. Henle (Notre Dame, 1993).

— — *Treatise on Law*, ed. Stanley Parry (Chicago, 1963).

— — *Philosophical Texts*, trans. and ed. Thomas Gilby (New York, 1960).

— — *Aristotle's De Anima with the Commentary of St. Thomas Aquinas*, trans. Kenelm Foster and Sylvester Humphries (New Haven, Conn., 1965).

— — *Commentary on the Posterior Analytics of Aristotle*, trans. F. R. Larcher (Albany, NY, 1970).

— — *On Law, Morality, and Politics*, eds. William P. Baumgarth and Richard J. Regan (Indianapolis, 1988).

2 SECONDARY SOURCES

ADLER, MORTIMER, 'A Sound Moral Philosophy', *Reforming Education* (New York, 1990), 254–62.

— —'Mortimer Adler and Bill Moyers: A Dialogue on the Nature of Goodness', Paul Sigmund (ed.),   *St. Thomas Aquinas on Politics and Ethics* (New York, 1988), 193–204.

ALTMAN, ANDREW, 'Legal Realism, Critical Legal Studies, and Dworkin', *Philosophy and Public Affairs*, 15/3 (1986), 205–35.

ANSCOMBE, G. E. M., 'Modern Moral Philosophy', *Philosophy*, 33/124 (Jan. 1958), 1–19.

ANSCOMBE, G. E.M., AND GEATCH, P. T., *Three Philosophers* (Ithaca, NY, 1973).

AYERS, MICHAEL R., 'Locke Versus Aristotle on Natural Kinds', *Journal of Philosophy*, 78/5 (May 1981), 247–72.

BARNES, W. H. F., 'A Suggestion about Value', *Analysis*, 1 (1934), 45–6.

BAYLES, MICHAEL, 'What is Jurisprudence About? Theories, Definitions,

Concepts, or Conceptions of Law?', *Philosophical Topics: Philosophy of Law*, 18/1 (Spring, 1990), 23–40.

BELLOW, SAUL, *More Die of Heartbreak* (New York, 1987).

BERGMANN, GUSTAV, 'Inclusion, Exemplification and Inference in G. E. Moore', E. D. Klemke (ed.), *Studies In the Philosophy of G. E. Moore* (Chicago, 1969), 81–94.

BORRADORI, GIOVANNA, *The American Philosopher*, trans. Rosanna Crocitto (Chicago, 1994).

BOURKE, VERNON J., 'The *Nichomachean Ethics* and Thomas Aquinas', *St. Thomas Aquinas, 1274–1974: Commemorative Studies*, 1 (Toronto, 1974), 239–59.

BROAD, C. D., *Scientific Thought* (London, 1927).

CHARLES, DAVID, 'Aristotle and Natural Kinds', a paper delivered at the American Philosophical Association (Central Division), 3 May 1986.

COOKE, VINCENT M., 'Moral Obligation and Metaphysics', *Thought*, 66/260 (Mar. 1991), 65–74.

COPLESTON, FREDERICK C., *Aquinas* (London, 1955).

— —*Medieval Philosophy* (New York, 1961).

COVELL, CHARLES, *The Defence of Natural Law* (New York, 1992).

D'ENTRÈVES, A. P., *Natural Law*, 2nd rev. edn. (London, 1970).

DAVIES, BRIAN, *An Introduction to the Philosophy of Religion* (Oxford, 1982; new edn., 1993).

— —*Thinking About God* (London, 1985).

— —*The Thought of Thomas Aquinas* (Oxford, 1992).

DIETL, PAUL J., 'On Miracles', *American Philosophical Quarterly*, 5 (1968), 130–4.

DONAGAN, ALAN, 'The Scholastic Theory of Moral Law in the Modern World', *Proceedings of the American Catholic Philosophical Association* (1966), 29–40.

— —*Human Ends and Human Actions: An Exploration in St. Thomas's Treatment* (Milwaukee, 1985).

DURBIN, PAUL, 'Human Intelligence', *Summa Theologiae*, Blackfriars edn., 12 (New York, 1967), 170–2.

DWORKIN, RONALD, Interview, in Bryan Magee, *Men of Ideas* (New York, 1978), 242–60.

— —'Natural' Law Revisited', *University of Florida Law Review*, 34/2 (Winter, 1982), 165–88.

— —'Liberalism,' *A Matter of Principle* (Cambridge, Mass., 1985), 181–204.

FINNIS, JOHN, *Natural Law and Natural Rights*, corr. edn. (Oxford, 1982).

— —*Fundamentals of Ethics* (Oxford, 1983).

— —'Practical Reasoning, Human Goods and the End of Man', *Proceedings of the American Catholic Philosophical Association*, 58 (1984), 23–36.

— —and GRISEZ, GERMAIN, 'The Basic Principles of Natural Law: A

Reply to Ralph McInerny', *American Journal of Jurisprudence*, 26 (1981), 21–31.

— —GRISEZ, GERMAIN, AND BOYLE, JOSEPH, 'Practical Principles, Moral Truths, and Ultimate Ends', *American Journal of Jurisprudence*, 32 (1987), 99–151.

FLEISCHACKER, SAMUEL, 'On the Enforcement of Morality: Aquinas and Narcotics Prohibition', *Public Affairs Quarterly*, 4/2 (Apr. 1990), 139–58.

FREY, R. G. (ed.), *Utility and Rights* (Oxford, 1985).

FULLER, LON, 'Positivism and Fidelity to Law', *Harvard Law Review*, 71 (1958), 630–72.

— —*The Morality of Law* (New Haven, Conn., 1964).

GEACH, PETER, *Mental Acts* (New York, 1953)

GEORGE, ROBERT P., 'Natural Law and Human Nature', Robert P. George (ed.), *Natural Law Theory: Contemporary Essays* (Oxford, 1992), 31–41.

GEWIRTH, ALAN, 'Natural Law, Human Action, and Morality', Rocco Porreco (ed.), *The Georgetown Symposium on Ethics: Essays in Honor of Henry Babcock Veatch* (1984), 67–90.

GILSON, ÉTIENNE, *The Unity of Philosophical Experience* (New York, 1937).

— —*The Christian Philosophy of Thomas Aquinas* (London, 1957).

GOLDING, MARTIN, 'Philosophy of Law, History of', *Encyclopedia of Philosophy*, 6 (New York, 1967), 254–64.

— —*Philosophy of Law* (Englewood Cliffs, NJ, 1975).

— —'Aquinas and Some Contemporary Natural Law Theories', *Proceedings of the American Catholic Philosophical Association*, 48 (1974), 238–47.

GOTTHELF, ALAN, 'Aristotle's Conception of Final Causality', *Review of Metaphysics*, 30/2 (Dec. 1976), 226–54.

GRISEZ, GERMAIN, 'The First Principle of Practical Reason', *Natural Law Forum*, 10 (1965), 168–96.

HARRE, R., AND MADDEN, E. H., *Causal Powers* (Totowa, NJ, 1975).

HART, H. L. A., 'Positivism and the Separation of Law and Morals', *Harvard Law Review*, 71 (1958), 593–629.

— —*The Concept of Law* (Oxford, 1961).

HIBBS, THOMAS, 'MacIntyre's Postmodern Thomism: Reflections on *Three Rival Versions of Moral Enquiry*', *Thomist*, 57/2 (Apr. 1993), 277–97.

HITTINGER, RUSSELL, *A Critique of the New Natural Law Theory* (Notre Dame, Ind., 1987).

— —'After MacIntyre: Natural Law Theory, Virtue Ethics and Eudaimonia', *International Philosophical Quarterly*, 29/4 (Dec. 1989), 449–61.

— —'Natural Law and Virtue: Theories at Cross Purposes', Robert P. George (ed.), *Natural Law Theory: Contemporary Essays* (Oxford, 1992), 42–70.

HOCHBERG, HERBERT, 'Albert Camus and the Ethic of Absurdity', *Ethics*, 75/2 (Jan. 1965), 87–102.

KENNY, ANTHONY, 'Intellect and Imagination in Aquinas', Anthony Kenny (ed.), *Aquinas: A Collection of Critical Essays* (Garden City, NY, 1969), 273–96.

——*Aquinas* (Oxford, 1980).

KRETZMANN, NORMAN, AND STUMP, ELEONORE (eds.), *The Cambridge Companion to Aquinas* (Cambridge, 1993).

——KENNY, ANTHONY, AND PINBORG, JAN (eds.), *The Cambridge History of Later Medieval Philosophy* (Cambridge, 1982).

KRIPKE, SAUL, 'Identity and Necessity', Milton K. Munitz (ed.), *Identity and Individuation* (New York, 1971), 135–64.

LI, CHENYANG, 'Natural Kinds: Direct Reference, Realism, and the Impossibility of Necessary *A Posteriori* Truth' *Review of Metaphysics*, 47/2 (Dec. 1993), 261–76.

LISSKA, ANTHONY J., 'Deely and Geach on Abstractionism in Thomistic Epistemology', *Thomist*, 37/3 (July, 1973), 548–68.

——*Philosophy Matters* (Columbus, Ohio, 1977).

——'Finnis and Veatch on Natural Law in Aristotle and Aquinas', *American Journal of Jurisprudence*, 36 (1991), 55–71.

MCCLOSKEY, H. J., 'Respect for Human Moral Rights', R. G. Frey (ed.), *Utility and Rights* (Oxford, 1985), 121–136.

MACDONALD, SCOTT, 'Theory of Knowledge', Norman Kretzmann and Eleonore Stump (eds.), *The Cambridge Companion to Aquinas* (Cambridge, 1993), 160–96.

MCINERNY, RALPH, *Ethica Thomistica: The Moral Philosophy of Thomas Aquinas* (Washington, DC, 1982).

——*St. Thomas Aquinas* (Notre Dame, Ind., 1982).

——*A First Glance at St. Thomas Aquinas* (Notre Dame, Ind., 1990).

——*Aquinas on Human Action* (Washington, DC, 1992).

——'Aristotle and Aquinas: Pére Gauthier', *Aquinas on Human Action* (Washington, DC, 1992), 161–77.

——'Natural Law and Natural Rights', *Aquinas on Human Action* (Washington, DC, 1992), 207–19.

MCNABB, VINCENT, 'St. Thomas Aquinas and Law', *Blackfriars* (May 1929), 1047–1067.

MACINTYRE, ALASDAIR, *A Short History of Ethics* (New York, 1966).

——*After Virtue*, 2nd edn. (Notre Dame, Ind., 1984).

——*Whose Justice? Which Rationality?* (Notre Dame, Ind., 1988).

——*Three Rival Versions of Moral Enquiry* (Notre Dame, Ind., 1990).

MACKIE, J. L., 'Rights, Utility and Universalization', R. G. Frey (ed.), *Utility and Rights* (Oxford, 1985), 86–105.

MARITAIN, JACQUES, *Man and the State* (Chicago, 1951).

——*Scholasticism and Politics*, trans. and ed. Mortimer Adler, 3rd edn. (London, 1954).

MARTIN, CHRISTOPHER, *The Philosophy of Thomas Aquinas* (London, 1988).

MARTIN, MICHAEL, *The Legal Philosophy of H. L. A. Hart: A Critical Appraisal* (Philadelphia, 1987).

MOODY, ERNEST A., *Studies in Medieval Philosophy, Science and Logic* (Berkeley, Calif., 1975).

MOORE, G. E., *Principia Ethica* (Cambridge, 1965).

MURPHY, JEFFRIE, AND COLEMAN JULES, *Philosophy of Law*, Rev. edn. (Boulder, Cal., 1990).

NELSON, EVERETT J., 'The Metaphysical Presuppositions of Induction', presidential address, American Philosophical Association (Western Division), *Proceedings and Addresses of the American Philosophical Association*, 1966–8 (Yellow Springs, Ohio, 1967), 19–33.

NOZICK, ROBERT, *Anarchy, State and Utopia* (New York, 1974).

NUSSBAUM, MARTHA, *Aristotle's De Motu Animalium* (Princeton, NJ, 1978).

— — *The Fragility of Goodness* (Cambridge, 1986).

— — 'Dialogue with Martha Nussbaum on Aristotle', Bryan Magee, *The Great Philosophers* (Oxford, 1988), 34–54.

— — 'Non-Relative Virtues', Martha Nussbaum and Amartya Sen (eds.), *The Quality of Life* (Oxford, 1993), 242–69.

— — *Love's Knowledge: Essays on Philosophy and Literature* (Oxford, 1990).

O'CONNOR, D. J., *Aquinas and Natural Law* (London, 1967).

REED, T. EDWARD, 'Human Nature and Nurture', *New York Times Book Review* (21 Apr. 1991), 34.

ROGERS, CARL R., 'The Valuing Process in the Mature Person', *Journal of Abnormal and Social Psychology*, 68/2 (1964), 160–7.

ROMMEN, HEINRICH A., *The Natural Law*, trans. Thomas R. Hanley, (St Louis, Mo., 1947).

ROSS, ALF, 'On Law and Justice', Martin Golding (ed.), *The Nature of Law* (New York, 1966), 134–43.

RYAN, ALAN, 'Utility and Ownership', R. G. Frey (ed.), *Utility and Rights* (Oxford, 1985), 175–95.

RYAN, COLUMBA, 'The Traditional Concept of Natural Law', Illtud Evans (ed.), *Light on the Natural Law* (Baltimore, 1965), 13–37.

SELZNICK, PHILIP, 'Natural Law and Sociology', Robert M. Hutchins (ed.), *Natural Law and Modern Society*, (Cleveland, Ohio, 1966), 154–93.

SHOOK, LAURENCE K., *Etienne Gilson* (Toronto, 1984).

SIGMUND, PAUL E., 'Thomistic Natural Law and Social Theory', Anthony Parel (ed.), *Calgary Aquinas Studies* (Toronto, 1978), 67–76.

— — *St. Thomas Aquinas on Politics and Ethics* (New York, 1988).

— — 'Law and Politics', Norman Kretzmann and Eleonore Stump (eds.), *The Cambridge Companion to Aquinas* (New York, 1993), 217–31.

SIMON, YVES, *The Tradition of Natural Law*, Vukan Kuic (ed.), (New York, 1965).

SUMMERS, ROBERT S., *Lon L. Fuller* (London, 1984).

SUMNER, L. W., 'Rights Denaturalized', R. G. Frey (ed.), *Utility and Rights* (Oxford, 1986), 20–41.

TOULMIN, STEPHEN, *The Place of Reason in Ethics* (Cambridge, 1970).

TUGWELL, SIMON, 'The Life and Works of Thomas Aquinas', *Albert and Thomas* (New York, 1988), 201–351.

URMSON, J. O., *Aristotle's Ethics* (Oxford, 1988).

VEATCH, HENRY B., *Rational Man: A Modern Interpretation of Aristotelian Ethics* (Bloomington, Ind., 1962).

— —*For an Ontology of Morals* (Evanston, IL, 1971).

— —'Telos and Teleology in Aristotelian Ethics', Dominic J. O'Meara (ed.), *Studies In Aristotle* (Washington, DC, 1981), 279–96.

— —Review of *Natural Law and Natural Rights*, *American Journal of Jurisprudence*, 26 (1981), 247–59.

— —*Human Rights: Fact or Fancy?* (Baton Rouge, La., 1985).

— —*Swimming Against the Current in Contemporary Philosophy* (Washington, DC, 1990).

— —and RAUTENBERG, JOSEPH, 'Does the Grisez–Finnis–Boyle Moral Philosophy Rest on a Mistake?', *Review of Metaphysics*, 44 (June 1991), 807–30.

WALLACE, WILLIAM A., *Causality and Scientific Explanation*, 2 vols. (Ann Arbor, Mich., 1974).

WARNOCK, G. J., *Contemporary Moral Philosophy* (New York, 1967).

WEINREB, LLOYD, *Natural Law and Justice* (Cambridge, Mass., 1987).

WEISHEIPL, JAMES A., *Friar Thomas D'Aquino* (Garden City, NY, 1974).

WEST, ROBIN, 'Jurisprudence and Gender', *University of Chicago Law Review*, 55/1 (Winter, 1988), 1–72.

WESTBERG, DANIEL, *Right Practical Reason: Aristotle, Action and Prudence in Aquinas* (Oxford, 1994).

WHITE, MORTON, *The Philosophy of the American Revolution* (New York, 1978).

WHITE, JOHN AND PATRICIA, 'Education, Liberalism and Human Good,' David E. Cooper (ed.), *Education, Values and Mind: Essays for R. S. Peters* (London, 1986), 149–71.

GLOSSARY

A Brief Lexicon of Philosophical Terms Used in this Book

The following list comprises a lexicon of philosophical terminology central to understanding Aquinas's analysis of natural law theory. This lexicon is based on the work of analytic philosophers prominent in the twentieth century. This list is not exhaustive; rather, it pertains to the study of natural law theory undertaken in this book.

accidental universal: A proposition which will not support a contrary-to-fact conditional. This indicates that an accidental property and not an essential property is referred to.

analytic philosophy: A way of doing philosophy undertaken and developed in English- and Scandinavian-speaking countries during the twentieth century. Close attention is paid to the analysis of concepts and languages and the criticism of presuppositions and beliefs.

disposition (dispositional property): A property which has a fundamental 'tending towards' built into its very nature. A disposition is in itself an incomplete property. It tends towards its 'completion' (in Aristotelian philosophy, its 'actualization').

essence: A foundational category which places a group of individuals into a specific kind. An essence determines the specific differences of a group; the group is what it is as a group because of the properties which make up its essence.

explicato textus: The use of the techniques of analytic philosophy to clarify and elucidate the major concepts in a philosophical argument, usually from the history of philosophy.

meta-ethics: An inquiry into the nature of ethical language and the formation of arguments in ethics. Meta-ethics presupposes that normative theories have been developed. Meta-ethics asks important questions about the language used and the arguments developed in normative ethics.

metaphilosophy: An inquiry into the nature of the activity of philosophy itself. Metaphilosophy considers how different philosophers approach the craft of doing philosophy. In a large measure, metaphilosophy considers the differing presuppositions from which philosophers embark on the activity of philosophy.

metaphysics: An inquiry into the nature and structure of the fundamental questions about the nature of reality. Metaphysics as a discipline discusses those concepts and categories that apply to all aspects of reality. Metaphysics is not limited to a transcendental inquiry into trans-temporal entities. Metaphysics, as used in this book, is certainly not connected with the books found in the 'New Age' sections of major bookstores.

natural kind: A basic category of reality which places individuals into groups based on natural functions. Following Plato's suggestion that the Forms 'show reality divided at its joints', a natural kind is a foundational category determining specific differences among individuals grouped together. A natural kind metaphysics argues that the fundamental dividing characteristics among groups are rooted in their natures.

nomic universal: A proposition which will support a contrary-to-fact conditional. Used by Everett J. Nelson, this method of using contrary-to-fact conditional statements indicates the existence of a synthetic a priori connection; this concept elucidates the need for an essential as opposed to an accidental property.

normative ethics: An inquiry into and the development of a system of moral norms and values about which human agents make moral decisions. Normative ethics is interested in the development of a consistent system of morally justified norms. The judgements in normative ethics assist human agents in leading morally praise-worthy lives.

philosophical realism: A theory arguing for the real existence of individuals independent of the mind. These individuals are all members of real categories called natural kinds.

structural history of philosophy: A way of critically analysing issues in the history of Western philosophy developed and articulated by Gustav Bergmann. The emphasis is on an analysis of the issues discussed by the major figures in the history of philosophy rather than on a mere rendition of what the historical texts report.

Synthetic a priori property: A necessary property found in an essence of a natural object. This is equivalent to a synthetic necessary property; it refers to a necessary property in things. As used in this context, this concept is not reducible to a Kantian mental category. Rather, it refers to a necessary connection in the external world. Everett J. Nelson, among others, has used this concept in this manner.

INDEX